FORMAL SPECIFICATION

and

SOFTWARE DEVELOPMENT

Prentice-Hall International
Series in Computer Science

C.A. R. Hoare, Series Editor

Published

BACKHOUSE, R.C., *Syntax of Programming Languages: Theory and Practice*
de BAKKER, J.W., *Mathematical Theory of Program Correctness*
BJØRNER, D. and JONES, C.B., *Formal Specification and Software Development*
DROMEY, R.G., *How to Solve it by Computer*
DUNCAN, F., *Microprocessor Programming and Software Development*
GOLDSCHLAGER, L and LISTER, A., *Computer Science: A Modern Introduction*
HENDERSON, P., *Functional Programming: Application and Implementation*
JONES C.B., *Software Development: A Rigorous Approach*
REYNOLDS, J.C., *The Craft of Programming*
TENNENT, R.D., *Principles of Programming Languages*
WELSH, J. and ELDER, J., *Introduction to Pascal,* 2nd Edition
WELSH, J. and McKEAG, M., *Structured System Programming*

FORMAL SPECIFICATION and SOFTWARE DEVELOPMENT

DINES BJØRNER
Technical University of Denmark
and Danish Datamatics Centre

and

CLIFF B. JONES
The University, Manchester, England

in collaboration with:

Derek Andrews
Elizabeth Fielding
Wolfgang Henhapl
Peter Lucas
Hans Henrik Lövengreen
and
Joseph E. Stoy

Prentice/Hall International

ENGLEWOOD CLIFFS, NEW JERSEY LONDON NEW DELHI
SINGAPORE SYDNEY TOKYO TORONTO WELLINGTON

Library of Congress Cataloging in Publication Data
Bjørner, D. (Dines, 1937—
Formal specification and software development.
Bibliography: p.
Includes index.
1. Electronic digital computers—Programming.
2. Programming languages (Electronic computers) I. Jones,
C. B. (Cliff B.), 1944— II. Title.
QA76.6.B575 1982 001.64'2 82-7656
ISBN 0-13-329003-4 AACR2

British Library Cataloguing in Publication Data

Bjørner, D.
Formal specification and software development.
1. Computer programs 2. Software compatibility
I. Title II. Jones, C.
001.64'25 QA76.6

ISBN 0-13-329003-4

ISBN 0-13-329003-4

PRENTICE-HALL INTERNATIONAL, INC., *London*
PRENTICE-HALL OF AUSTRALIA PTY. LTD., *Sydney*
PRENTICE-HALL CANADA, INC., *Toronto*
PRENTICE-HALL OF INDIA PRIVATE LIMITED, *New Delhi*
PRENTICE-HALL OF JAPAN, INC., *Tokyo*
PRENTICE-HALL OF SOUTEAST ASIA PTE., LTD., *Singapore*
PRENTICE-HALL, INC., *Englewood Cliffs, New Jersey*
WHITEHALL BOOKS LIMITED, *Wellington, New Zealand*

1 0 9 8 7 6 5 4 3 2 1

Printed in the United States of America

To

TONY HOARE

on the occasion of his being elected

a Fellow of the Royal Society

CONTENTS

PREFACE

People today use an enormous number of 'systems' ranging in complexity from washing machines to international airline reservation systems. Computers are used in nearly all such systems: accuracy and security are becoming increasingly essential. The design of such computer systems should employ development methods as systematic as those used in other engineering disciplines. A systematic development method must provide a way of writing specifications which is both precise and concise; it must also include a way of relating design to specification.

A concise specification can be achieved by restricting attention to what a system is to do: all consideration of implementation details is postponed. With computer systems this is done by: a) building an abstract model of the system — operations being specified by pre- and post-conditions; b) defining languages by mapping program texts onto some collection of objects whose meaning is understood; c) defining complex data objects in terms of abstractions known from mathematics. Ths last topic, the use of abstract data types, pervades all work on specifications and is necessary in order to apply the ideas to systems of significant complexity. The use of mathematically based notation is the best way to achieve precision.

A design generates a number of sub-components and a way of combining them. These sub-components must be specified. Ultimately sub-components satisfying these separate specifications will be combined to form a system which should satisfy the overall specification. If all the specifications are precise enough, it is possible to prove that a design step is correct: that is, it fulfils the original specification. This is done before the sub-components have been implemented. Such proofs of correctness are of particular importance in the early stages of a design because any mistakes made then are likely to be particularly expensive to detect and correct later.

The early stages of design frequently involve choosing machine representations for abstract data objects. For this reason, special emphasis is given to proofs of data refinement (also called object transformation).

The lowest level of design for computer systems is often called 'coding', this is distinguished from the earlier design stages only by the fact that the sub-components required are all available in the language or support software being used, and techniques are available to prove that the code meets the module specifications. This description is somewhat oversimplified: design is by no means a strictly 'top-down' activity, but in order to be understandable, the eventual documentation must be presented in a top-down structure.

The work on specifications of large systems was at the outset prompted by the need for formal definitions of programming languages. John McCarthy argued for the provision of such definitions (a more complete historical background, with references, is given in chapter 1 of this book). The size of the PL/I language prompted the attempt to apply to it some of the ideas on formal language definition, and in the mid 1960's a definition of the PL/I language was developed in the IBM Laboratory at Vienna. This definition used 'operational semantics' and the overall approach became known as the 'Vienna Definition Language (VDL).

Christopher Strachey's group in Oxford University developed the concept of 'denotational' or 'mathematical semantics'. In the early 1970's, prompted by Hans Bekic, this new approach was adopted by the Vienna group: the more recent work of the group is thus based on the denotational approach. Some confusion has, perhaps, been caused by the decision to refer to the new work as the '*Vienna Development Method*' (whose initials, *VDM*, are too like those of the other work). The meta-language used in VDM was known internally as '*META-IV*': it is denotational in approach. VDM is, however, more than just a formal definition language: as the name implies it is a complete systematic development method. The other part of the background to the VDM work is provided by the work on program development methods of people such as Bob Floyd, Peter Naur, Tony Hoare, Robin Milner, Niklaus Wirth and Edsger Dijkstra. In particular the idea of 'data refinement' (or object transformation) is a key component of VDM.

There is emerging an increasing acceptance of the need for formal specification and design techniques. VDM is a systematic development method which has a wide variety of applications; it has been, and is being used in major companies and courses on it have been given throughout Europe. Even within the confines of this book, actual programming languages and database systems are discussed.

The aim of this book is to provide a source document for both industrial application of, and for post-graduate courses on, VDM. The only knowledge assumed of the reader is that of set and logic notation. The book is divided into three major parts. General ideas, and in particular the meta-language, are covered in the three chapters of part I. Part II is concerned with use of the VDM on programming languages; other applications are considered in part III. (Recent work on parallelism is mentioned only via references in this book.)

The parts and chapters are connected by 'link material' which provides the context for the individual contributions, gives further reference and provides hints on alternative ways to read the book.

We should like to acknowledge help from the following people. Gordon Plotkin reviewed two versions of the whole book; Tony Addyman, Stephen Bear, Ian Cotton, Chris Kirkham and Ann Welsh each reviewed various chapters. The typists, Annie Rasmussen and Birte Skovlund did a superb job in entering extremely difficult manuscripts. Finn Hansen prepared the artwork. The Danish Datamatics Centre provided the word processing system. Jørgen Fischer Nilsson, Bo Stig Hansen, Jan Storbank Pedersen, and Lennart Schultz worked on early versions of chapters 12 and 13. We should also like to thank the contributors without whom this volume would have been impossible. Finally Ron Decent and many others at Prentice-Hall International were most helpful in the final stages of the preparation of this book.

D.B.

C.B.J.

PART I

FORMAL SPECIFICATION META-LANGUAGE

This part of the book discusses general aspects of the systematic development method known as the "Vienna Development Method" (VDM). such a systematic development method provides, at the minimum, a notation for writing specifications and a way of relating designs to specifications. In [Jones 81c] it is argued that emphasis must be put on the early stages of system development (that is specification and high level design). In order to correct errors made in these stages enormous amounts of work may have to be discarded. The meta-language to be used in writing specifications is the cornerstone of the method: chapters 2 and 3 are concerned with the meta-language of VDM. Chapter 1 provides some historical background to the work on formal definition. Those aspects of VDM concerned with relating designs to their specifications are covered in Parts II and III below. Some notation is used in examples prior to its definition: the Glossary of Notation (towards the end of the book) should be consulted for any unfamiliar symbols.

CHAPTER 1

MAIN APPROACHES TO FORMAL SPECIFICATIONS

The work on the formal definition of programming languages spans some twenty years. This chapter sets the historical context of the VDM work. It does not, however, purport to be a complete history of the subject (more detail of the Vienna work in particular can be found in [Lucas 81a]). The three main approaches to the definition of programming languages are described. (The so-called "Vienna Definition Language" (VDL) is probably the first to be used in the definition of large languages: it is based on the "operational approach") Although coming later in time, "mathematical" or "denotational semantics" has become the most widely accepted approach to formal definition. Because of its position as a reference point mathematical semantics is here described before the other two approaches. In order to prove that programs in a language satisfy some specification, it is normal to use rules of deduction about the language. It is possible to regard such rules as axioms and to treat them as a definition of the language: such "axiomatic semantics" is also described. In addition the concept of, and the reasons for the use of, "abstract syntax" are explained. A final section considers some of the open research problems relating to formal specifications.

(This chapter is a revised version of [Lucas 78a])

CONTENTS

1.1 THE NEED FOR FORMAL SPECIFICATIONS

Computer systems can be viewed as machines capable of interpreting languages; they accept and understand declarative sentences, obey imperative sentences and answer questions, all within the framework of those languages for which the systems were built. A computer system accomplishes its tasks on the basis of a prescription of these tasks, that is on the basis of a program expressed in some programming language.

There is no inherent disparity between human languages (including natural language and the artificial languages of science) and languages used to talk to computers. Thus there is no need to apologize for "anthropomorphisms" in the above point of view; in fact, our only way to talk scientifically about the relation of humans to their natural languages is in terms of computer notions (or so it seems to me).

By viewing computers as language interpreting machines it becomes quite apparent that the analysis of programming (and human) languages is bound to be a central theme of somputer science.

Part of the fascination of the subject is of course related to its intimate connection to human language, that is the mechanisms we study mirror in some way at least part of our own internal mechanisms.

Although there is no inherent disparity between human language and computer language, there is at present a huge gap between what we can achieve by human conversation and our communication with machines. A little further analysis will indicate the nature of the gap.

First we consider the structural aspect of language, that is how phrases are composed of words and sentences are built from phrases, commonly called "syntax". There are efficient and precise methods to define the syntax of a language and algorithms to compose and decompose sentences according to such definitions. The problem is more or less solved. Yet, computer languages usually have a simpler and more regular syntax than natural languages (and even some scientific notations) and there are technical problems yet to be solved. Moreover, it seems to me, there is not much of a gap.

Second, there is the aspect of meaning, or "semantics" as it is usually called. Now we get into more subtle problems. Let me restrict the discussion, for the time being, to the objects we can talk about in the various languages (rather than considering what we can say about them). Programming languages in the strict sense talk invariably about rather abstract objects such as numbers, truth-values, character strings and the like. Certainly, the major programming languages in use do not let us talk about tables, chairs or people, nor even about physical dimensions of numbers such as: hours, pounds, or feet. The commercial languages do not know about the distinction of dollars and francs, and scientific languages do not know about time and space. There have been some attempts to include those notions or a device that makes it possible to define these notions within a language (e.g. the class concept in SIMULA and PASCAL and the investigations around abstract data types). If we extend the notion of programming language to include query languages and database languages, we may observe a tendency in the indicated direction. Yet, there is a gap. Artificial Intelligence has experimented for some time with languages that can be used to talk about objects other than numbers and we should probably try to learn from these experiments.

Definition methods concerning semantic, and even more so, mechanical ways to use semantic definitions are much less understood than in the case of the syntactic aspect.

Thirdly, there is the aspect of language understanding; I hesitate to call this "pragmatics" since the latter term has been used for too many things.

Suppose I ride on a train with a friend. The friend observes: "The windows are wet" (*). The statement is presumably structured according to the English grammar and has a certain meaning. However, I would probably not just analyze the sentence and determine its meaning. Most likely I would react by looking at a window, observe that there are drops, conclude that it is raining, prepare my umbrella so that I don't get wet when I get off the train.

(*) It would not make any difference to the following argument if my friend had used *META-IV* and passed a note saying: *"wet(windows)"*. That is to say, I do not discuss the distinction between natural language and standard (formal) notation, but the distinction of the human and computer use of the statement irrespective of the form.

To draw all these conclusions and act accordingly I need to use a lot of knowledge about the physical world in general and about my specific environment. It is in this area of language understanding, where I see the bigger gap between our interaction with the computer as opposed to humans. What is lacking in the machine are models of the external world and general mechanisms to draw conclusions and trigger actions. Again artificial intelligence and natural languages research have been concerned with the problem. But, this has not as yet had any practical influence on for example commercial applications. With the increase in computer power it might very well be worth seeking such influence.

With the preceding paragraphs I wanted to put the present subject into a much larger context than is usual. Thank God, there is more to programming languages than procedures, assignment and goto's (or no goto's). The rest of this chapter is a lot less ambitious and remains more or less within the traditional concepts of programming languages. It presents my subjective perceptions of the various origins of the methods of semantic definitions.

1.2 HISTORICAL BACKGROUND

The theory of programming languages and the related formal definition techniques, have roots in, and are related to, several other disciplines such as linguistics, formal logic, and certain mathematical disciplines. In fact, the terms "syntax" and "semantics" and the distinction between the respective aspects of language, have been introduced by the American philosopher Charles Morris [Morris 38a, Zemanek 66a]. He developed a science of signs which he called semiotics. Semiotics, according to Morris, is subdivided into three distinct fields: syntax, semantics, and pragmatics. In his book [Morris 55a] Morris defines:

Pragmatics deals with the origin, uses and effects of signs within the behavior in which they occur;

Semantics deals with the signification of signs in all modes of signifying;

Syntax deals with the combination of signs without regard for their specific significations or their relation to the behavior in which they occur.

The clear distinction between syntax and semantics was first applied to a programming language in the ALGOL 60 report [Naur 63a]. The resulting insight has turned out to be tremendously useful. There have been several not so successful attempts to carry the notion of pragmatics into the theory of programming languages (see e.g. San Dimas Conference [ACM 66a]). We may start the history of formal definition methods for programming languages with the year 1959 when J. Backus proposed a scheme for the syntactic definition of ALGOL 60 [Backus 60a]. This scheme (a generative grammar) was then actually used in the ALGOL 60 report; the related notation is known as BNF (for Backus Normal Form or Backus Naur Form). BNF, or variations thereof, have been used in many instances; it has stimulated theoretical research as well as practical schemes for compiler production (both automatic and non-automatic). Roughly speaking, BNF grammars coincide with the class of context free grammars in [Chomsky 59a]; it is worth mentioning that Chomsky defined his grammatical formalisms in an attempt to obtain a basis for the syntax of the English language. Much research has been devoted to the study of subtypes and extended types of BNF grammars. The latter in support of the desire to capture more syntactic properties of the language to be defined; the former, that is the study of subtypes is usually motivated by the wish to find properties which permit fast syntax recognition and analysis algorithms. The subject of formal syntax definition, and the related computational problems and methods, have found their way into textbooks and computer science curricula; in fact, the larger part of compiler writing courses is usually spent on syntax problems.

After the ALGOL 60 report, the lack of rigorous definition methods for the semantics of programming languages has become widely recognized. Furthermore, the success of formal syntax definitions invited similar attempts for the semantic aspects of programming languages. The problem turned out to be of an obstinate nature. To date, there is no solution that enjoys the consensus of the whole computing community.

The instructions of machine languages are defined by the behaviour of the respective machine upon execution of these instructions. The associated manuals usually describe first what constitutes the state of the specific machine (e.g. content of main storage, content of registers, etc.) and then for each instruction and any given state the successor state after execution of the instruction to be defined. Hence, for a programmer, the most direct way to define a programming language is in terms of an interpreting machine; however, for higher level languages, we must abstract from particularities of hardware machines and implementation details and use a suitable hypothetical machine instead. E.W.Dijkstra formulated the situation in 1962 [Dijkstra 62b] as follows: "A machine defines (by its very structure) a language, viz. its input language; conversely, the semantic definition of a language specifies a machine that understands it" (*).

The classic paper that has led to much research is by McCarthy [McCarthy 62a]. The paper outlines a basis for a theory of computation; more important for our subject, it establishes the main goals and motivation: methods to achieve correctness of programs in general and of compilers in particular; rigorous language definitions constitute an intermediate problem. The schema for language definitions proposed by McCarthy contains a number of novel subjects. Firstly, a complete separation of notational issues, that is the representation of phrases by linear character strings, from the definition of the essential syntactic structure of a language. The latter definition is called "Abstract Syntax". It is, at least for complicated languages, much more concise than the concrete syntax. Thus, a semantic definition on the basis of an abstract syntax becomes independent of notational details and is also more concise. Secondly, state vectors are introduced as the basis of the semantic definitions proper, that is the meaning of an instruction or statement is defined as a state transition. The paper shows in principle the task of proving compilers correct. The basic scheme of language definitions has been elaborated in many instances during the past decade, e.g. by the earlier work of the Vienna Laboratory on PL/I [Lucas 69a] and the ECMA-ANSI standard [ANSI 76a].

Another successful direction of research was initiated by P. Landin [Landin 64a, 65a], using the lambda-calculus [Church 41a] as the fundamental basis. He revealed that certain concepts of ALGOL 60 (and similar languages) can be viewed as syntactic variations (syntactic "sugar") of the lambda-calculus. The inherently imperative concepts, assignment and transfer of control, were captured by introducing new primitives into the lambda-calculus; the extended base is defined by the so-called

---

(*) It would be unfair to include this quotation and not say that E.W. Dijkstra would probably no longer defend this position, and rather tend to be a proponent of the direction described under "Axiomatic Approach" in this chapter.

SECD machine, a hypothetical machine whose state consists of four components: Storage, Environment, Control and Dump. The machine state has more structure than the state vectors of McCarthy, because the machine had to reflect more complicated concepts (blocks, local names) than McCarthy's original simple example was intended to.

In 1964 C.Strachey [Strachey 66a] argued that, with the introduction of a few basic concepts, it was possible to describe even the imperative parts of a programming language in terms of the lambda-calculus. C. Strachey initiated a development that led to an explication of programming languages known as "mathematical" or "denotational semantics". The fundamental mathematical basis for this development was contributed by D.Scott in 1970 [Scott 70a]. The joint paper, by D.Scott & C.Strachey [Scott 71a] offers a description method and its application to essential language concepts based upon the indicated research.

Research on axiom systems and proof theory suitable as a base for correctness proofs of programs was initiated by R.Floyd [Floyd 67a], with a simple flow-diagram language. C.A.R.Hoare [Hoare 69a,71a], extended and refined the results to apply to constructs of higher level languages. Less formalized, but similar thoughts were expressed in [Naur 66b]. The area has been the most actively pursued, including experiments in automatic program verification.

There are several pioneering research efforts, which do not so evidently fall into the categories introduced above. Among the very early results published on semantics is A. van Wijngaarden's *"Generalized ALGOL"* [van Wijngaarden 62]. J. de Bakker [de Bakker 69a] discovered that the schema proposed by A.van Wijngaarden can be viewed as a generalized Markov Algorithm. A.Carraciolo [Forino 66a] also used Markov Algorithms as the starting point for the formalization of programming language semantics.

For anyone familiar with syntax directed compilers it is tempting to apply similar ideas to the definition of semantics. A definition method on this basis is due to D. Knuth [Knuth 68a]. In some way or another, a formal definition of the semantics of a language invariably specifies a relation between any phrase of the language and some mathematical object called the denotation of the phrase. D. Knuth provides a convenient schema that permits the specification of functions over the phrases of a language (assuming that the phrase structure of the language is given by a production system). Most research so far has been devoted to the definition and analysis of existing languages (or concepts found in existing languages). Yet, formal semantics could be a most valuable intellectual tool for the design of novel programming concepts (or new programming language constructs). There are rare instances of such applications of formal semantics are found in [Dijkstra 74a, Dijkstra 75a, Dennis 75a, Henderson 75a]).

1.3 BASIC METHODOLOGICAL APPROACHES

1.3.1 Abstract Syntax

The notion of abstract syntax is of considerable value for practical definitions of notationally complex languages. There exist several methodological variations, which all achieve the same objective: to abstract from semantically irrelevant notational details and reduce the syntax to define the essence of the linguistic forms only.

For illustration consider the following examples. Let v be the category of variables and e be the category of expressions. Several notational variants are in use to denote assignment statements e.g.:

$$v = e \quad \text{or} \quad v := e \quad \text{or} \quad e \to v$$

The semantically essential structure common to these notations is that there is a syntactic category called assignment statement, and that an assignment statement has two components, a variable and an expression.

An abstract syntax may define an expression to be either an elementary expression (variable, constant, etc.) or a binary operation consisting of an operator, a first operand, and a second operand (the definition of expressions may have several other alternatives); operands are also expressions. As a concrete syntax, meant to define character strings, such a definition would be hopelessly insufficient and ambiguous, for example we would not know whether to parse $x+y\times z$ into:

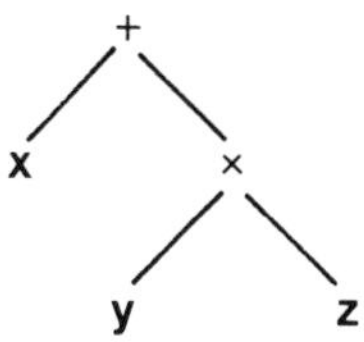

or:

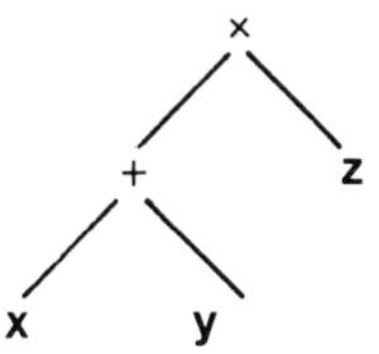

Thus the concrete syntax has to introduce punctuation marks such as parentheses, and, in the example of expressions, precedence rules of operators to avoid ambiguities. However, the definition of expressions given above is perfectly usable as an abstract syntax definition. It can be regarded as a definition of parsing trees, hence the ambiguity problem is completely avoided. Thus there are advantages gained even in the case where only one language is considered: representational details are suppressed and each phrase is given a kind of normal form.

For practical cases, such as *PL/I*, the number of rules necessary to define an abstract syntax is much smaller than for the corresponding concrete syntax; hence we have obtained a more concise basis for the semantic definition. The price we pay is an additional part for the formalization of a language, which establishes the relation between the concrete and the abstract syntax.

1.3.2 Mathematical Semantics

The semantics of a given language is formalized by associating a suitable mathematical object (set, function, etc.) with each phrase of the language; the phrase is said to denote the associated object; the object is called the denotation of the phrase. Furthermore, to gain a "referentially transparent" view of the language to be defined, denotations of composite phrases are defined solely in terms of the denotations of subphrases. The major problem in establishing the mathematical semantics for a given language is to find suitable mathematical objects, that can serve as the denotations. We will write *M[p]* for the denotation of a phrase *p* (*). To indicate the various phrases to be discussed, we will use an ALGOL-like notation, for example *M[x:=x-1]* is the denotation of the assignment statement *x:=x-1*. Further elaboration of the subject considers a series of programming language concepts in increasing order of complexity. Take first a simple language with a fixed set of variables (*id*), expressions (*e*) without side effects, assignments (*id:=e*) and compound statements (*s1;s2*). If we were to construct a definitional interpreter, we would certainly introduce a state vector (à la McCarthy).

(*) For small languages it is possible to use concrete syntax and basic function notation. In order to be clear, definitions of larger languages must use abstract syntax and combinators.

Although we do not wish to specify particular ways to compute the effect of executing programs and their parts, we still have to characterize the overall effect of this execution. Therefore we introduce state vectors σ, which are (usually) partial functions from variable names *ID* into the set of values, *VAL*, that is:

$$\sigma: ID \underset{m}{\rightarrow} VAL.$$

Let Σ be the set of all possible states. The kinds of denotations that occur in the example language can now be chosen as follows:

$$M[e] : \Sigma \overset{\sim}{\rightarrow} VAL$$
$$M[st]: \Sigma \overset{\sim}{\rightarrow} \Sigma$$

that is the denotations of expressions are functions from states into values and the denotations of statements are functions from states to states.

Assuming that $M[e]$ has been defined elsewhere, the definition of assignment and compound statements according to the philosophy of mathematical semantics read:

$$M[id{:=}e](\sigma) = assign(\sigma, id, M[e](\sigma))$$
$$\text{where: } assign(\sigma, id, val) = \sigma', \ \sigma'(x) = \begin{cases} val & \text{for } x = id \\ \sigma(x) & \text{for } x \neq id \end{cases}$$

$$M[s1;s2] = M[s2]^{\circ}M[s1] \qquad \text{where } {}^{\circ} \text{ denotes functional composition}$$

Note that denotations of composite phrases are given in terms of denotations of immediate subphrases and that we have avoided introducing a statement counter. For each additional language feature we may have to revise the definition of states, introduce new ways to compose denotations or even define new kinds of mathematical objects.

As a first complication we introduce a loop statement of the form: <u>*while*</u> *e* <u>*do*</u> *s*. We assume that *e* returns a truth value and intuitively expect that the denotation of the loop statement can be defined as:

$$M[\underline{while}\ e\ \underline{do}\ s](\sigma) = \begin{cases} M[\underline{while}\ e\ \underline{do}\ s](M[s](\sigma)) & \text{if } M[e](\sigma) \\ \sigma & \text{if } \neg M[e](\sigma) \end{cases}$$

The definition is of the form $f=F(f)$, with f = M[while e do s] that is: f is defined as a fixed point of F. Before this definition can be accepted as meaningful, one has to ask whether such a fixed point always exists and whether it is unique. The existence can be asserted under appropriate mathematical restrictions (introducing concepts of monotonicity and continuity); there will in general be more than one fixed point satisfying the equation. Thus an additional rule has to be introduced which makes the defined object unique (the "smallest" fixed point under a suitably defined ordering relation). This is not the place to elaborate the issue at length. Chapter 3 discusses this issue in depth.

However, it should by now be evident that we are led into deep mathematical issues, and this at a stage where, from a programming language point of view, we have only introduced the most primitive language constructs. At this point, it seems that we have to consider the potential uses of a semantic definition. One should distinguish between the foundation of the subject matter and more practical problems like the description of real-life programming languages for compiler writers. Like the foundations of mathematics on the one hand and applied mathematics on the other, these two fields are not unrelated but are distinct. If we accept the program of mathematical semantics, the steps we have tried to indicate follow, and the difficulties observed above are inevitable. However, it seems unrealistic and in fact unnecessary to require that each compiler writer be fluent in modern algebra. Rather, one would expect that the foundations are used to justify, once and for all, useful practical methods which in turn can be applied directly by the practitioner.

A further important concept in most programming languages is that of local names, that is names which are declared for a specific textual scope of a program. The syntactic category is called block and takes the form:

<u>*begin*</u> <u>*dcl*</u> *id*; *st* <u>*end*</u>.

Since the same name may now be used in different blocks for different purposes we have to introduce some device in the definition which enables us to distinguish the different uses of a name. One usually introduces an auxiliary object called environment, *env*, which is a function from names (variable names in the present example) to so called locations; the state then maps location into values. Thus a state σ is now a function of type $LOC \xrightarrow{m} VAL$, where LOC is a set of primitive objects called locations; the auxiliary object *env* is of type $ID \xrightarrow{m} LOC$.

In order to interpret a given phrase we always have to have an environment which associates the names occurring in the phrase with locations. The mathematical types of the denotations have to be revised so that *M[st]* when applied to an environment, yields a function which transforms a state. The types of denotations of the other constructs are designed similarly.

The last features to be discussed in this section are procedure declarations and parameter passing. What should the denotation of a procedure (in the sense of *ALGOL* or *PL/I*) be? According to the philosophy of mathematical semantics this must be an object which yields a state transformation ($\Sigma \rightarrow \Sigma$) when applied to the denotations of the arguments to the procedure. It is important that the procedure denotation is built in the environment where the procedure is declared. In some higher level programming languages, procedures can be passed as arguments. In particular, a procedure might be passed as an argument to itself. This concept presents certain mathematical problems and the establishment of a suitable domain of denotations is a major achievement [Scott 70a] - cf. chapter 3.

There are some language constructs whose treatment is not yet so widely accepted in the framework of mathematical semantics. In particular, parallel and quasi-parallel execution give rise to the use of rather complicated mathematical objects (see [Plotkin 76a, Smyth 76a] on "power domains").

Condition handling in *PL/I*; labels and goto's have been formulated, but, the models do not closely correspond to the intuitive concept of the construct, cf. chapter 5.

There are sizable language definitions in the denotational style (e.g. a definition of *ALGOL 60* [Mosses 74a], and a definition of a subset of *PL/1* [Bekić 74a]). There is an excellent introductory book on the subject by J.Stoy [Stoy 77a].

1.3.3 Operational Semantics

The semantics of a programming language can be defined via a hypothetical machine which interprets the programs of that language; such methods have been called "operational", or "constructive". The latter term is, however, misleading, because the specification of hypothetical machines may contain non-constructive elements, such as quantifiers, implicit definitions and infinite objects. The term "definitional interpreter" is sometimes used instead of "hypothetical machine".

By machine we understand a structure consisting of a set of states, two subsets thereof: the initial states and the end states, a state transition function and a function which maps programs and their input data into initial states; also usually not given explicitly, there should be a function which takes end states as arguments and yields:

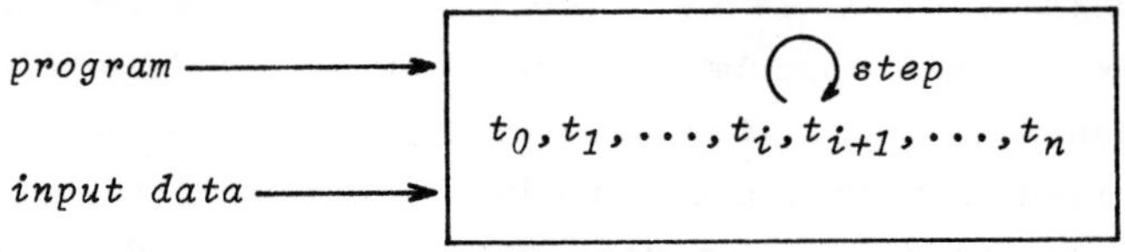

t_0 ... initial state t_n ... end state
step ... state transition function $t_0, \ldots, t_n$ ... computation

an end state which is the result of the program. Since most higher level languages are such that the program remains constant, that is is not modified, during its interpretation, one could also keep the program separate and only include a statement counter to the currently executed statement within the state itself. The definition of the step function, if properly done, will reflect the syntactic structure of the language, such that we cannot only relate an entire program to a computation, but also sub-phrases of the program to sections of the computation, that is we may ask what a specific subphrase in a given context means. In languages, like *PL/I*, where the order of operations is not entirely fixed, the defining hypothetical machine is non-deterministic, that is the *step* function will, in general, yield a set of possible successor states and a program will thus be related to a set of computations.

For simple languages, mathematical and operational definitions of languages are very similar. In fact, if the latter are carefully constructed, there is a direct correspondence between such definitions. The strength and danger of the operational approach comes from its machine-like behaviour. For example, the VDL definitions showed that a language could be non-deterministic by building a control tree of possible next actions. The early operational definitions tended, however, to put rather too much in the state. For example, it is tempting to put the environment which was discussed above in the state: since environments change and have to be restored, one ends up with a stack of environments. This, the "grand state" approach causes considerable difficulties in deducing properties about language definitions. It is possible to construct "small state" operational definitions (e.g. [Allen 72a, Plotkin 81a]) which offer many of the advantages of mathematical semantics but which avoid deep mathematical issues.

In the literature there exist various examples relating language definition to implementations (e.g. [McCarthy 67a]). A comprehensive elaboration of this subject would complement the existing material on the subject of syntax definition and parsing. The step from the syntax definition to the respective parser can be automatic. There are current efforts to master the semantics part of the problem, e.g. [Mosses 76a]. The subject is further elaborated in chapters 8 and 9.

The method has been applied to several large languages; in fact the proposed *ECMA-ANSI PL/I* standard [ANSI 76a] has been formulated using an operational definition. The method is the only one presently known which is capable of covering the currently existing language constructs. There is an introduction to the subject by A.Ollongren [Ollongren 75a], and several summaries, e.g. [Lucas 69a] on VDL and an in depth evaluation by J.Reynolds [Reynolds 72a].

1.3.4 Axiomatic Approach

Each of the two approaches so far described provide models for the languages to be defined. In contrast, the axiomatic approach implicitly defines the semantics of a programming language by a collection of axioms and rules of inference, which permit the proof of properties of programs, in particular that a given program is correct, that is realizes a specified input/output relation. Of course, one can prove assertions about programs using either a mathematical or operational definition and ordinary mathematical reasoning. In fact, the axioms and rules of inference can be regarded as theorems within the framework of mathematical semantics.

However, the objective of the axiomatic method is a formal system which permits the establishment of proofs using only the uninterpreted program text (that is without referring to denotations of the program or program parts). Whenever we talk about denotations in this section, this is for explanatory purposes and is not part of the axiomatic system.

The problem of correctness proofs of programs is usually split into two subproblems; the first is conditional correctness (that is correctness under the assumption that the execution of the program terminates); the second is the proof that the program terminates. Until further notice this section deals with conditional correctness.

To illustrate the approach we will refer to the simplest language level of section 1.3.2 above, that is a fixed set of variables, assignment and compound statements. The notation and particular axioms of the example are due to C.A.R. Hoare [Hoare 69a]. The basic new piece of notation are propositions of the form:

$p1\{st\}p2$

where *p1* and *p2* are propositions referring to variables of the program, and *st* is a statement. The intuitive meaning of the form is: if *p1* is true before the execution of *st* and the execution of *st* terminates, then *p2* is true after the execution of *st*. *p1* is called pre-condition, *p2* is the so-called post-condition or consequence.

The axiom (more precisely the axiom schema) for the assignment statement reads:

$p^x_e\{x:=e\}p$ $\quad$ p^x_e means: replace all free occurrences of x in p by e

In fact, p^x_e is the weakest possible precondition given p. Conversely, given p^x_e as the precondition, p is the strongest possible consequence. That is the schema captures all there is to know about the assignment statement. A specific instance of the schema would be:

$0<x+1 \ \{x:=x+1\} \ 0<x$

Note that in order to use the schema it is not necessary to refer to the denotation of $x:=x+1$.

The definition of the compound statement takes the form of a rule of inference and reads:

$$\frac{\underline{IF}\ p1\{st_1\}p2\ \underline{AND}\ p2\{st_2\}p3}{\underline{THEN}\ p1\{st_1;st_2\}p3}$$

For a full language definition there will usually be an axiom per primitive statement and a rule of inference per composite statement; in addition, there are some general rules which have not been exemplified in this section.

The structure of the proofs reflects the syntactic structure of the program text, as one would hope.

There is a simple relation between the discussed axiomatic approach and a corresponding definition using mathematical semantics. As already mentioned the axioms and rules of inference can be interpreted as theorems within mathematical semantics. In particular we interpret the new propositional form $p1\{st\}p2$ as follows. Assume for the moment that $p1$ and $p2$ are expressions that are also valid expressions in the programming language, denoting truth values.

$$p1\{st\}p2 \;=\; M[p1](\sigma) \supset M[p2](M[st](\sigma))$$

for all σ for which $M[st]$ is defined, that is st terminates.

The various axioms and rules of inference may now be rewritten according to the above interpretation and proven with respect to the definitions of mathematical semantics (see [Manna 72a]).

Neither the generation of the proof nor solving the termination problem can be completely mechanical, since both are in general undecidable. However, there is hope that, for frequently occurring program structures, the problems can be solved effectively by algorithms. Proposals to solve the termination problem frequently rely on an indirect proof (in particular on finding a quantity which decreases as the computation proceeds, but cannot decrease indefinitely).

The subject of axiomatic definitions and program verification has stimulated widespread research activities due to the intellectually pleasing content and its potential economic value. The belief in the value is based on the vision that program testing can ultimately be replaced by systematic program design and verification and possibly to some extent automated.

There are many examples of correctness proofs of specific programs (see [London 70a]) and several automated verification aids (e.g. [King 75a,

Boyer 79a, Good 78a, SVG 79a, Lee 81a]). The existing examples are mostly small programs for complicated mathematical problems. Some of the algorithms published in the respective section of the *CACM* are certified by proofs. An attempt to axiomatize a full language, *Pascal*, has been undertaken by Hoare and Wirth [Hoare 73d] resulting in the definition of a large subset (see also [London 78a] on *Euclid*).

Intimately connected to axiom systems for programming languages is the issue of programming style and development methodology. The essence of structured programming is the recommendation to use only language constructs which have simple axioms (this excludes, for example, the general form of goto statements, although restricted forms may well lead to simple correctness arguments). As it turns out, the process of developing a program is intimately connected to the generation of the corresponding correctness proof. Thus we obtain guidance on how to develop programs rather than merely learn how to prove ready made programs correct.

There is, at present, an enormous gap between, on the one hand, current programming practice and the complexity of the software being produced and, on the other hand, the vision and capabilities of the systematic techniques described. The proper discussion of the dilemma needs a larger context than has been given in this section and will therefore be deferred to the next section.

1.4 CHALLENGES

The scope of this section excludes topics considered to belong to the theory of computation. With this restriction in mind we may certainly say that the definition of programming language semantics is not an end in itself; consequently, the discussion of research challenges cannot be isolated from the intended applications of semantic definitions (that is precise definition of real life languages, compiler development, program development and language design).

There are two topics that should be clearly separated to avoid confusion: firstly, the semantic analysis and formal definition of existing programming languages; secondly, the design of novel, useful language constructs.

Current programming languages are a compromise between the desire to pro-

provide the most comfortable and elegant language for the human user and the aim to construct efficient implementations on given systems with known compiler technology. Furthermore, the more intensely used languages undergo an evolution over the years to support new system functions. It is now important to design languages with the aim to make formal correctness proofs easy or to fit into the framework of mathematical semantics. However, it would be a mistake to conclude that existing languages are no longer worth the attention of computer science. In view of the heavy investment by users as well as manufacturers it is not likely that the current programming languages will change radically in the near future. Thus the carriers of new programming style will be, at least for some time, current languages. The initial motivation of formal semantics, precise definition to achieve portability, is still valid; there is a need for semantic analysis of *COBOL* (the most widely used programming language). A comparative language study on the semantics level would be quite valuable [Strachey 73a]. Finally, there should be a comprehensive representation of the existing implementation techniques related to formalized semantic concepts.

Whereas *BNF*, or variations thereof, are widely accepted as a means to define a concrete syntax, there is no such widespread consensus for any of the semantic description schemes. Finding such an agreed semantic meta-language should be treated as an urgent problem.

Next I wish to offer a top down argument to justify the major long range goals of the present subject. Firstly, we can observe that over the past two decades the speed and storage capacity of computers have been increased roughly at a rate of about 40 percent a year. This trend has been balanced by a similar decrease of cost per operation and per storage unit. Similarly the size of system-code (operating system, compilers, etc.) has increased exponentially as well. However, in this case no balancing trend of decreasing cost per line-of-code can be observed. Furthermore, we will not only have to master greater quantity but larger complexity as well. We conclude that software production is or soon will be the bottleneck for the use of computers unless some progress is made on three general research directions promising to improve the situation:

1. Advance Automatic Programming
2. Remove Testing in Favor of Correctness Proofs
3. Advance Modular Programming

By the first research area we mean to extrapolate the development of "very high level languages" by introducing more abstract data-types (e.g. sets) and their associated operations; relax restrictions in current languages and introduce more powerful control structures. The intent is, of course, to automate part of the production process: in short, to follow the trends suggested under the term "very high level language". Topics one and two are intimately connected. As J.Schwartz [Schwartz 75a] observes, it is much easier to prove the correctness on an abstract level rather than on the level of detailed representations. If the abstract program can be compiled, the task of the programmer is completed, provided the compiler has been proven as well. Thus the step from the abstract algorithm to its ultimate representation in machine form is proven once and for all by a compiler proof. The author believes that research in correctness proofs must therefore be investigated hand in hand with the development of very high level languages. Even under the assumption that the level of programming languages can be raised, correctness proofs will remain sufficiently complicated to warrant machine assistance in the form of proof generators and checkers. Although study of the latter subject has advanced over the last decade, it has not yet reached the stage of applicability in practical programming.

Various subgoals may be envisaged, e.g. conversational systems like *EFFIGY* [King 75a] which offer a combination of generalized testing by symbolic execution and some assistance for generating proofs. A notorious problem in designing large pieces of software is modularity. It is rarely the case that existing modules can be used to build new systems without major trimming. As J. Dennis [Dennis 75a] observes, the success of modular modular programming not only depends on how modules are written, but also on the characteristics of the linguistic level at which these modules are expressed. Dennis supports this observation by a detailed analysis of some high level languages. Modules are usually expressed by procedures, subroutines or programs (depending on the specific languages used). In short, we have to look for constructs other than procedures and the related traditional ways to compose procedures into larger units, in order to achieve the desired modularity.

In conclusion we ask what is the relevance of formal semantics to these issues? Firstly, axiomatic semantics provides the proof theory for program correctness proofs, and thus is also the basis for the mechanical aids in this area. It is difficult to propose useful axioms and rules of inference without having an interpreted system (such as provided by a mathematical or operational system).

In search for new language constructs (such as a useful notion of module), formal semantics ought to provide the framework for formulating the problem and for stating and justifying solutions [Strachey 73a]. So far, most research in formal semantics has been concerned with constructs as found in traditional languages. ("Here is a piece of language, what does it mean?") In order to tackle new applications we should start from the other end: construct novel denotations and associate a name after we are satisfied with their properties.

CHAPTER 2

THE META-LANGUAGE

Chapters 2 and 3 are both concerned with the meta-language ("META-IV") in general; chapter 4 provides more motivation by showing how features of the meta-language are used in the denotational definition of programming languages. Readers who are new to semantic definitions are advised to read this chapter rather quickly and then use it as a reference after studying chapter 4. Those readers who are familiar with the Oxford work on denotational semantics will be struck by the large number of combinators used in "META-IV". The need for the extra "syntactic sugar" results from the definition of large systems.

The only knowledge assumed is of elementary set and logic notation -- thus, chapters 1-4, 14, and 15 of [Lipschutz 64a] would serve as adeqaute preparation. Lambda notation is introduced as a way of defining functions in general and combinators in particular. The notation for describing and manipulating objects is also described. The mathematical foundations of these concepts are reviewed in the next chapter.

A programmer's view of the meta-language is given in [Bjørner 78c]. (This chapter is a replacement for [Jones 78a].) Other related work includes that of the "Z" group [Abrial 80*], CLEAR [Burstall 77a, Burstall 80a], and several projects at SRI (Stanford Research Institute, Menlo Park, Ca., USA).

CONTENTS

2.1 DENOTATIONAL SEMANTICS

Chapter 1 introduces the fundamental ideas of denotational semantics: in order to define the semantics of some set of objects (*L*), a meaning function (*M*) is written which maps elements of *L* to some understood set of denotations *(DEN)*; the structure of the elements of *L* is exploited in the rule that *M* should derive the denotation of structured elements of *L* (only) from the denotations of their components. Thus the meaning function is of type:

M: L → DEN

and is defined by cases over the structure of *L*.

An example can be made of the definition of binary numerals (some notation is used in the examples which is defined only later in the chapter - it should, however, be clear enough to communicate the general idea). The binary digits are simply symbols and this fact can be emphasized by using rather clumsy names:

Bindigit = <u>*0SYM*</u> | <u>*1SYM*</u>

A binary numeral can either be a composite object or simply a digit:

Binnumeral = Bincomposite | Bindigit

A composite object is made up of two parts the first of which is a numeral and the second a digit:

Bincomposite :: Binnumeral Bindigit

The natural numbers can be used as denotations:

Nat0 = {*0,1,2,...*}

Thus the meaning of binary numerals is to be defined by a function of type:

M: Binnumeral → Nat0

This function can be defined by cases. For composite objects:

M[mk-Bincomposite(n,d)] $\triangleq$ *M[n]*2 + M[d]*

Notice that this function builds the denotation (i.e. value) of the composite from the denotations of its components as required by the denotational method. The denotations of digits are given as follows:

M[<u>0SYM</u>] = 0
M[<u>1SYM</u>] = 1

Most definitions require a more complicated set of "understood Denotations". In particular, systems or languages normally require denotations which are functions over states. Thus, for a simple language:

M: Lang → TR
TR $\dot{=}$ *STATE* $\tilde{\rightarrow}$ *STATE*

(The distinction between total and partial functions is marked by superimposing a tilde on the arrow of the latter). It is, then, necessary to use notation for the creation and manipulation of functions: this is the topic of the next section.

2.2 FUNCTIONS

An example of the familiar style of function definition is:

f(x) $\triangleq$ *x * x + 2*

When the argument and result sets are not obvious from context, a type clause can be written:

f: Nat0 → Nat0

The use of conditional expressions in function definitions is familiar from many programming languages. For example, a function which yields the maximum of two integers is:

max: Nat0 × Nat0 → Nat0
max(x,y) $\triangleq$ <u>*if*</u> *x≤y* <u>*then*</u> *y* <u>*else*</u> *x*

The "application" of a function (*D → R*) to an element of its argument set

(D) yields an element of the result set (R), thus:

$$f(3) = 11$$
$$max(2,4) = 4$$

For various reasons, functions will frequently need to be recursive. A simple example of a function definition for square shows that the familiar style of presenting function definitions can be used:

$$square: Nat0 \to Nat0$$
$$square(n) \underline{\underline{\Delta}}\ \underline{if}\ n=0\ \underline{then}\ 0\ \underline{else}\ square(n-1) + 2*n - 1$$

(Although the use of *square* within its own definition is familiar to programmers, it is necessary to consider below exactly what such a "definition" means).

But, when writing a denotational semantics definition, there will also be two further needs. Because of the need to create and manipulate functions as objects, a notation for unnamed functions is required. The "Lambda calculus" [Church 41a] is such a notation. The function named f above can be defined:

$$\lambda x.x*x + 2$$

This is an expression for the function. If it is required to name the function, it is possible to write:

$$f = \lambda x.\ x*x + 2$$

But the expression can be used without providing a name. For example, just as f can be applied to arguments, the unnamed function can be applied to values:

$$(\lambda x.x*x+2)(3) = 11$$
$$(\lambda x.x*x+2)(1+3) = 18$$

The form of such a "lambda expression" is:

$$\lambda x.E$$

in which x should be a name and E an expression (normally involving x).

The whole expression denotes the function which maps any argument to the value obtained by evaluating E when x equals the argument value.

Lambda expressions can be written which fulfil the need to create functions. Thus:

$$\lambda y.(\lambda x.x*x+y)$$

denotes a function which, for example, can be used to create the function considered above.

$$(\lambda y.(\lambda x.x*x+y))(2) = \lambda x.x*x+2$$

Functions of more than one argument (e.g. *max* above) can be reduced, by a process known as "Currying", to the simpler form:

$$\lambda x,y.E(x,y) = \lambda x.\lambda y.E(x,y)$$

Thus *max* can be defined:

$$max = \lambda x,y.\ \underline{if}\ x\leq y\ \underline{then}\ y\ \underline{else}\ x$$

In addition to defining functions whose values may be functions, lambda expressions can be written which take functions as arguments. For example:

$$twice = \lambda f.\lambda x.f(f(x))$$
$$twice(square) = \lambda x.square(square(x))$$
$$(twice(square))(1) = 1$$
$$(twice(square))(2) = 16$$

The ability to define functions which take functions as arguments (known as "functionals") opens up a new way of understanding recursive "definitions". The definition of *square* given above can be viewed as an equation with *square* as an unknown (just as the quadratic:

$$2*x^{**}2 = 14 - 3*x$$

is an equation with x as an unknown). If a new function is defined:

$$H = \lambda f.\lambda n.\underline{if}\ n=0\ \underline{then}\ 0\ \underline{else}\ f(n-1) + 2*n - 1$$

then *square* must be a solution to the equation:

$$square \quad = H(square)$$

The fact that such solutions exist (and the choice of the "least fixed point" solution) is discussed in chapter 3. Also in need of mathematical foundations are the types of functionals. Chapter 3 explains why the familiar view of the set of all functions must be restricted when considering functions which take themselves as arguments.

In this chapter, the lambda notation is used on the assumption that it is sound (i.e. that the foundations are given). This section closes with some examples of the use of the rather general functions in the definition of programming languages.

(The first of these examples illustrates a use of recursion where proper "domains" -- see chapter 3 -- are required as denotations. In the *Binnumeral* example above, recursion was controlling a macro-expansion-like definition and the denotations could be ordinary sets.)

If a "while" statement is built according to the following syntax:

While :: *Expression Statement*
Statement = *Assign* |...| *While*

then a meaning function might be defined of type:

$$M\colon Statement \to STATE \xrightarrow{\sim} STATE$$

For this simple example it is assumed that expression evaluation causes no side-effects and that:

$$MX\colon Expression \to STATE \xrightarrow{\sim} Bool$$

where the defined elements of *Bool* are:

$$\{\underline{true}, \underline{false}\}$$

A recursive function can then be used to define the while case for *M*:

```
M[mk-While(b,s)](state) ≜
    let wh = λσ.(let bv = MX[b](σ) in
                 if bv then wh(M[s](σ)) else σ) in
    wh(state)
```

The inner *let* introduces an abbreviation which is used *in* the following expression. The outer *let* introduces a name for a value which is defined recursively: some authors emphasize this by writing *letrec*. The possibility that the loop fails to terminate for some states is reflected by showing (with a tilde: ~) that the function is partial.

An example of the need for functions which take functions as arguments is found in languages which permit procedures to take procedures as arguments. The denotation of a procedure might be:

$$Procden = Argument^{*} \rightarrow STATE \stackrel{\sim}{\rightarrow} STATE$$

Arguments corresponding to "by value" arithmetic parameters might be numbers; those corresponding to "by reference" parameters might be locations; but the arguments corresponding to procedure parameters must be elements of *Procden*. Both of the issues raised here are considered further in chapter 3.

2.3 COMBINATORS

It would be possible to write out complete language definitions using the lambda notation. Meaning would be defined by a translation into a large lambda expression. For small languages, this is sometimes done. For larger languages, a much more readable definition can be given by using some "combinators" which correspond to commonly used ways of combining function values. For example, given functions:

$$f\colon D1 \rightarrow D2$$
$$g\colon D2 \rightarrow D3$$

then their "composition" is:

$$g \circ f = \lambda x . g(f(x))$$

Notice that f is applied first. Thus:

$g \circ f:\ D1 \to D3$

Since this is defined in terms of the Lambda calculus, no new foundation problems are introduced: the combinators simply provide a more perspicuous notation for writing a lambda expression.

One of the differences between definitions written by the "Oxford" and "Vienna schools", in the greater use of combinators by the latter. This difference has, at least in part, resulted from the fact that the Vienna group faced the task of defining rather large languages and systems. Just as in programming, the larger the final text the greater the justification for defining concepts of general use. Because the combinators can be (and are in this section) defined in terms of Lambda calculus, this difference between the two schools can be seen to be superficial.

The order of composition is the reverse of that which is frequently natural in a semantic definition. It is therefore convenient to define a combinator in which the first operand is applied before the second. This "semicolon" combinator is such that:

$f:\ D1 \to D2$
$g:\ D2 \to D3$
$f;g = g \circ f$

Thus:

$f;g:\ D1 \to D3$

In particular, where both operands are of type $STATE \to STATE$, so is their combination. This can be used, for example, within the definition of the meaning of a while construct given above to write:

$\underline{if}\ bv\ \underline{then}\ (M[s];wh)\ \underline{else}\ I_{STATE}$

where I_{STATE} is the identity function on states.

A small extension to the same example shows the desirability of another combinator. Suppose expression evaluation is allowed to create side-effects, then the type of the expression meaning function would be:

$MX:\ Expression \to STATE \xrightarrow{\sim} STATE \times VAL$

The use of the semicolon above has removed the need to write the σ for part of the definition: how can this be extended to the whole definition with the above type for *MX*? A "define" combinator can be given:

$$f \quad : D1 \to D2 \times D3$$
$$e(x) \quad : D2 \to D4, \qquad x \in D3$$
$$(\underline{def}\ x\colon f; e(x)) : D1 \to D4$$
$$(\underline{def}\ x\colon f; e(x)) = f; (\lambda\sigma, x . e(x)(\sigma))$$

In particular:

$$(\underline{def} x\colon \_ ; \_)\colon (STATE \xrightarrow{\sim} STATE \times VAL) \times (VAL \to STATE \xrightarrow{\sim} STATE) \to (STATE \xrightarrow{\sim} STATE)$$

The association rules for $\to$ and $\times$ are that $\times$ binds more strongly than $\to$ and is associative, and that $\to$ is right associative. Thus:

$A \times B \to C \to D \times E$ is the same as: $(A \times B) \to (C \to (D \times E))$

The complete definition of the meaning of the while construct can now be given:

$$M[mk\text{-}While(b,s)] \ \underline{\Delta}$$
$$\underline{let}\ wh = (\underline{def}\ bv\colon MX[b];$$
$$\underline{if}\ bv\ \underline{then}\ M[s]; wh\ \underline{else}\ I_{STATE})\ \underline{in}\ wh$$

The elimination of parameters (i.e. *state*, σ) corresponding to states in this example has made the definition clearer. The difference is even more significant on larger examples.

Some cases of such a transformation may determine a value without changing the state. The *return* combinator can be used to promote a simple value to a transformation. Thus for $v \in VAL$:

$$\underline{return}\ v\colon STATE \xrightarrow{\sim} STATE \times VAL$$

The conditional used in the definition of the while statement is also a simple combinator. It should be noticed that this use is "dynamic" in the sense that the result is determined by a value which is created by one of the transformations. There are other uses of conditionals which depend only on the "static" text whose denotation is being defined. Another useful static combinator is *for*. Thus in defining the meaning of a list of statements in a *compound* statement:

```
Statement =  Assign | Compound | ... | While
Compound  :: Statement*
```

it is possible to write:

```
M[mk-Compound(sl)] ≜ for i=1 to lensl do M[sl[i]]
```

Rather than using recursion, as in:

```
M[mk-Compound(sl)] ≜
   if lensl=0 then I_STATE
   else M[hdsl];M[mk-Compound(tlsl)]
```

A similar static expansion can be used for *def*:

```
def vl: <M[al[i]] | 1≤i≤lenal>; ... vl ...
```

is the same as:

```
def vl1: M[al[1]];
def vl2: M[al[2]];
:
:
def vln: M[al[lenal]];
let vl = <vl1,vl2,...,vln> in ... vl ...
```

A language or system without any exception type constructs could be defined using only the above combinators. The handling of exception constructs presents problems for the denotational method precisely because the effect of an exception cuts across the structure over which the denotations are supposed to be constructed. The archetypal construct in this area is the goto statement. The difficulty, is to provide a denotation for simple statements which can be used to derive the denotation for sequences of statements. The definition of goto statements provides, in chapter 4, the motivation for the *exit* approach used in VDM. Chapter 5 contrasts and connects this approach with the "continuations" used by the Oxford school. Here, the combinators relating to the *exit* approach are defined for reference. Readers should probably skip the remainder of this section at first reading.

The basic idea is to use denotations which are capable of reflecting the exception. The result of applying the denotation to a particular state is a state plus an exception indication: a *nil* value indicates the lack of an exception whereas information about the exception is given in non-*nil* values. Combinators are defined which simplify the move from transformations of type:

$T = STATE \xrightarrow{\sim} STATE$

to ones which can reflect any abnormal result:

$TR = STATE \xrightarrow{\sim} STATE \times [ABNORMAL]$

The set *ABNORMAL* is chosen to fit the system being defined; here only the distinction between *nil* and non *nil* is of importance. The basic *exit* combinator causes a non *nil* value to be returned with an unchanged state. Thus:

$v \in ABNORMAL$
$\underline{exit}\ v\colon TR$
$\underline{exit}\ v = \lambda\sigma.(\sigma, v)$

The handling of non *nil* abnormal values is defined by a *tixe* combinator. For:

$m\colon ABNORMAL \underset{m}{\to} TR$
$f\colon TR$

then:

$(\underline{tixe}\ m\ \underline{in}\ f)\colon TR$
$(\underline{tixe}\ m\ \underline{in}\ f) = (\underline{let}\ r = (\lambda\sigma, a.\underline{if}\ a \in \underline{dom} m\ \underline{then}\ r(m(a)(\sigma))$
$\qquad \underline{else}\ (\sigma, a))\ \underline{in}\ r \circ f)$

The semicolon combinator is redefined to reflect the need to propagate abnormal returned values. With:

$f\colon TR$
$g\colon TR$

then:

f;g: TR
(f;g) = (λσ,a.__if__ a=__nil__ __then__ g(σ) __else__ (σ,a))∘f

Similar changes are made to the *def* combinator. Where a simple transformation (*T*) occurs in a context of an exit transformation, it is automatically interpreted as returning a *nil* abnormal component. Thus:

f: STATE ⥲ STATE

is interpreted, in appropriate contexts as:

λσ.(f(σ),__nil__)

One other combinator relating to *exit* transformations takes:

f: STATE ⥲ STATE
g: TR

to give:

(__always__ f __in__ g) : TR
(__always__ f __in__ g) = (λσ,a.(f(σ),a))∘g

The combinators given in this section are not a fixed set for the meta-language. Others may be defined in the same way if there is a need. This collection suffices however for the language definitions given in this book. Certain others are used in the "systems definitions" in part III - they are defined in the "Glossary of Notation".

2.4 LOGIC NOTATION

The symbols to be used for the propositional operators are ¬ (not), ∧ (and), ∨ (or), ⊃ (implies), ≡ (equivalence). The operators have been given in decreasing order of priority.

The truth values are:

Bool = {__true__,__false__}

The quantifier symbols are ∀ (universal) and ∃ (existential). Quantified expressions will normally be bounded. For example:

$(\forall x \in Nat)(is\text{-}even(2*x))$

$(\exists x \in \{11,12,13\})(is\text{-}prime(x))$

The careful use of bounds can avoid using operators on values for which they are not defined. Thus we write:

$(\forall x \in Int-\{0\})(p(1/x))$

rather than:

$(\forall x)(x \neq 0 \supset p(1/x))$

Where bounded quantifiers are insufficient, conditional expression can be used. For example:

$\underline{if}\ x=0\ \underline{then}\ q(y)\ \underline{else}\ p(1/x)$

rather than:

$x=0 \wedge q(y) \vee x \neq 0 \wedge p(1/x)$

2.5 OBJECTS

Thus far in the discussion of semantics the structure of the states has not been considered. Given the careful foundations which are provided for general functions, it would be possible to view most semantic objects as functions. For example, store can be viewed as a function from locations to values - even a subset of some given set can be viewed as a function from the given set to the set of Boolean values. Such a view would, however, limit the operations which can be applied. The domain of a function is, for example, undecidable in general and it would not be obvious that it was sound to write an expression involving the domain of store. For this reason, authors of VDM specifications carefully distinguish "sets", "maps", and "lists" from more general functions. Objects to be used in definitions are restricted as follows: "sets" are finite and contain only distinguishable elements (not functions for example); "maps" are finite functions which are constructed in ways which ensure that their domains are apparent; "lists" are also finite.

The class of all finite subsets of some given set *X* is written:

X-set

Notice that if *X* is infinite, this is a proper subset of the power set since only finite sets belong to the class *X-set*.

The operators involving sets are shown in the "ADJ" diagram in figure 1. These diagrams (cf. [Goguen75a]) show the types in ovals and fix the type of each operator by the arcs. (The subset operator, e.g. is between two operands each of type set and yields a Boolean result.)

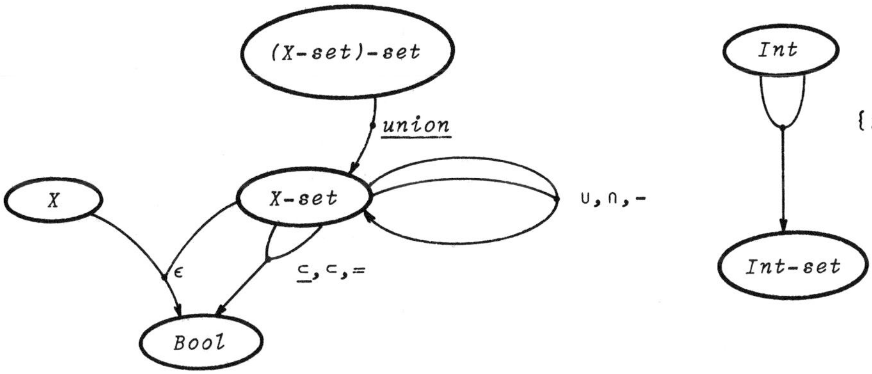

Fig. 1: Set operators

Notice that the distributed union operator is written:

$\underline{union}\ SS = \{e \mid (\exists S \in SS)(e \in S)\}$

The shorthand for a set of integers is:

$\{i:j\} = \{k \in Int \mid i \leq k \leq j\}$

The basic sets used in this book are:

$\{\}$ = empty set
Bool = $\{\underline{true}, \underline{false}\}$
Nat = $\{1, 2, \ldots\}$
Nat0 = $\{0, 1, 2, \ldots\}$
Int = $\{\ldots, -1, 0, 1, \ldots\}$

The class of functions which satisfy the constraints of maps are defined:

$$D \underset{m}{\rightarrow} R$$

with obvious extensions for domains which are Cartesian products. One-one maps are marked:

$$D \underset{m}{\leftrightarrow} R$$

The operators involving maps are shown in figure 2.

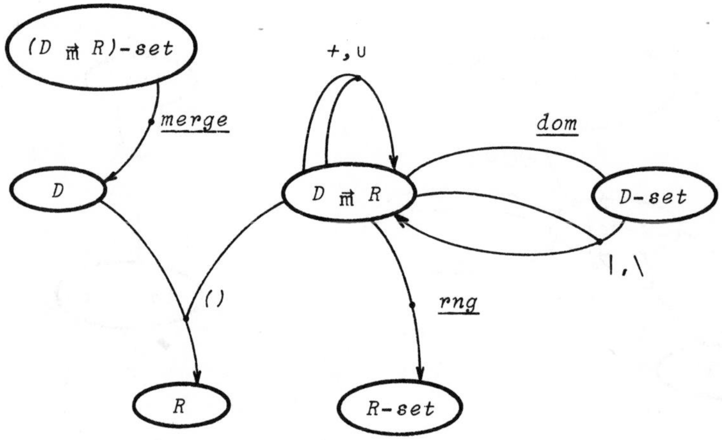

Fig. 2: Map operators

The empty map is written:

$$[\,]$$

Other maps can either be written explicitly:

$$[a \mapsto b,\ b \mapsto c,\ c \mapsto a]$$

or implicitly:

$$[x \mapsto x! \mid x \in \{1:4\}] = [1 \mapsto 1,\ 2 \mapsto 2,\ 3 \mapsto 6,\ 4 \mapsto 24]$$

Application is written exactly as for functions.

Assuming domain and application (over the domain) are understood, the remaining operators can be defined. The range of a map is:

$$\underline{rng}M = \{M(d) \mid d \in \underline{dom}M\}$$

The map "overwrite" operator is defined:

$$M1 + M2 = [d \mapsto (\underline{if}\ d \in \underline{dom}M2\ \underline{then}\ M2(d)\ \underline{else}\ M1(d)) \mid d \in (\underline{dom}M1 \cup \underline{dom}M2)]$$

Map "union" is only defined if the domains of the maps are disjoint. Its definition is otherwise the same as for overwrite. The advantage of using a separate operator for this special case is that it is commutative. A map can be "restricted":

$$M \mid S = [d \mapsto M(d) \mid d \in (\underline{dom}M \cap S)]$$

or a set of domain elements can be removed:

$$M \setminus S = [d \mapsto M(d) \mid d \in (\underline{dom}M - S)]$$

The $\underline{merge}$ operator provides a distributed form of map union. Assuming:

$$(\forall m_1, m_2 \in ms)(m_1 = m_2 \lor \underline{dom}m_1 \cap \underline{dom}m_2 = \{\})$$

then $\underline{merge}ms$ gives the map whose domain is the union of the domains of the individual maps and whose results match that from the appropriate individual map.

Lists (or Tuples) could be viewed as maps from a set of natural numbers. Reasoning about lists can, however, be aided by providing operators which are intuitively obvious. The list operators are shown in figure 3, next page. The class of all finite lists is defined by X^* and all non-empty lists by X^+.

Here again taking two operators ($\underline{len}$ and application) as basic makes it possible to define the others. The set of indices of a list is:

$$\underline{inds}L = \{1 : \underline{len}L\}$$

The set of elements in a list is:

$$\underline{elems}L = \{L[i] \mid i \in \underline{inds}L\}$$

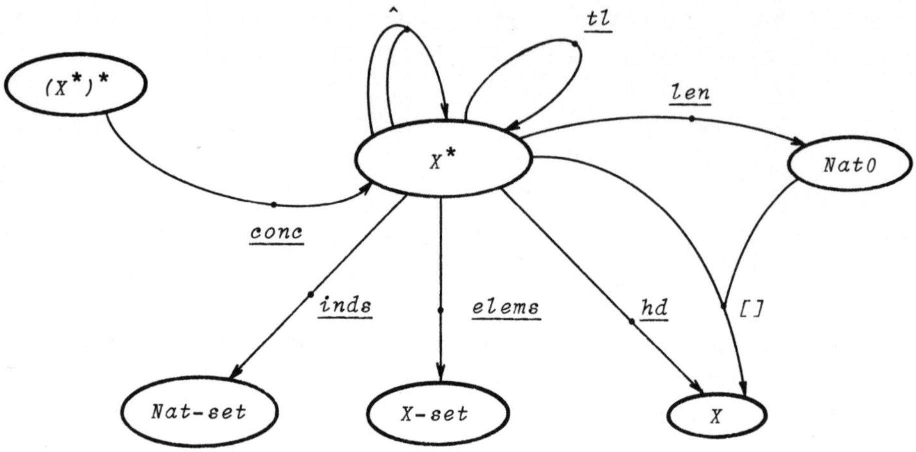

Fig. 3: List operators

The first element in a list is given by:

$$\underline{hd}L = L[1]$$

The list remaining when the head has been removed is given by:

$$L' = \underline{tl}L \supset \underline{len}L' = \underline{len}L-1 \wedge (\forall i \in \underline{inds}L')(L'[i] = L[i+1])$$

Notice that neither the head nor the tail operators are defined on the empty list. Concatenation of two lists is defined:

$$\begin{aligned} &L = L1 \,\hat{}\, L2 \supset \\ &\quad \underline{len}L = \underline{len}L1 + \underline{len}L2 \wedge \\ &\quad (\forall i \in \underline{inds}L1)(L[i] = L1[i]) \wedge \\ &\quad (\forall i \in \underline{inds}L2)(L[i+\underline{len}L1] = L2[i]) \end{aligned}$$

Distributed concatenation is defined:

$$\underline{conc}LL = \underline{if}\ LL=\langle\rangle\ \underline{then}\ \langle\rangle\ \underline{else}\ \underline{hd}LL \,\hat{}\, \underline{conc}(\underline{tl}LL)$$

2.6 DEFINING OBJECTS

In writing a specification, both elementary and structured objects are required. Most of the ways of structuring objects (classes of maps, etc.) are given above. Thus if:

$M = Int \underset{m}{\rightarrow} Bool$

then:

$\{[\,], [\, 1 \mapsto \underline{true}\,], [\, 2 \mapsto \underline{false},\ 7 \mapsto \underline{true}\,]\} \subset M$

An "abstract syntax" notation is given below. "Elementary objects" are those whose structure is of no interest for a particular specification. These can be elements of *Token* or *Quot*. *Token* is an infinite set of objects whose representation is not exposed: the identifiers in a programming language would normally be treated as tokens. Where there is a need to enumerate specific elementary objects, quotations are written as sequences of underlined (usually upper-case) letters (e.g. A, ABC, LABEL).

The most extensive object definitions to be written are for "abstract syntax". It is therefore suggestive to make the rules look similar to concrete syntax (e.g. BNF notation). Thus:

$Stmt = Assn \mid Goto$

(Notice that this is a simple, nondiscriminated, union.) Similarly, the convention of using square brackets for an optional element is adopted. Thus:

$[X] = X \cup \{\underline{nil}\}$

The *nil* object showing absence of the optional *X*.

Because of the use in abstract syntax, there is a need to build "record" type composite obejcts which have inhomogenous fields. For example:

$Assign :: Varref \;\; Expr$

defines that any element of the set of objects named *Assign* has two components, the first of which is an element of the set named *Varref* and the second an element of the set named *Expr*. The set of elements of a class defined by a "constructor" rule is, for the above example:

$Assign = \{mk\text{-}Assign(vr,e) \mid vr \in Varref \wedge e \in Expr\}$

The constructor function:

$mk\text{-}Assign\colon Varref \times Expr \to Assign$

can be thought of as installing a hidden flag which ensures that sets defined by different (constructor) rules are disjoint. Formally, it is sufficient to know this uniqueness property without showing how the elements are flagged. (The use of such constructor rules obviates the need to have a disjoint union operator.)

Given constructed objects, it is frequently necessary to decompose them. One way of doing this is by writing the constructor in a "left-hand-side" position (i.e. on the left of a definition or as a parameter). Thus:

$\underline{let}\ mk\text{-}Assign(vr,e) = s\ \underline{in}\ \ldots e \ldots vr \ldots$

defines *vr* and *e* to have the values of the appropriate components of the (previously defined) value *s*.

As an additional convenience the components of a constructed object can be named. For example:

$Assign :: s\text{-}lhs{:}Varref \quad s\text{-}rhs{:}Expr$

These "selector" names can be used as functions to obtain the components of a constructed object. Thus:

$s\text{-}lhs\colon Assign \to Varref$
$s\text{-}rhs\colon Assign \to Expr$

$s\text{-}lhs(mk\text{-}Assign(vr,e)) = vr$
$s\text{-}rhs(mk\text{-}Assign(vr,e)) = e$

The constructor rules and definitions which use *X-set* etc. can be used recursively: in any such use the valid objects are all finite instances satisfying the (syntactic) equations.

Where a state is itself a constructed object, it is permissible to use the selector names like variables in an assignment combinator. Thus:

$(\mathrm{F1} := e(\underline{c}\ \mathrm{F1}))\colon\ STATE \to STATE$
$(\mathrm{F1} := e(\underline{c}\ \mathrm{F1})) = \lambda\sigma.(mk\text{-}STATE(e(F1(\sigma)),F2(\sigma),\ldots))$

Notice that the use of the reference on the right hand side of the assignment is marked with a contents (*c*) operator. This is more explicit than in programming languages where the use of a name has a different meaning depending on context.

2.7 ON NON-DETERMINISM

Non-determinism is something which need be considered in many specifications. For example, in most programming languages (including ALGOL 60) the order of access to variables within expressions is not defined. Thus in:

$$a + (b + c)$$

the variables can be accessed in any one of six orders. Notice that order of access is separate issue from the order in which the operators are applied. The problem is that if some sub-expressions include references to functions which cause side-effects, the value of the variables might differ depending on the order of access. Why should the designers of a language leave such an odd non-determinism unresolved? It is reasonable to assume that this was done to permit optimization like common sub-expression elimination. There is a warning that users of ALGOL should not write programs which depend on a particular order. But then there are also many languages which contain features which deliberately introduce nondeterminism (cf. "guarded commands" in [Dijkstra 75a]). One approach to the semantics of non-determinism is to use relations on states as the denotations (cf. [Park 80a], [Jones 81a]). This approach cannot, unfortunately, be extended to cover procedures which can take themselves as arguments. An alternative approach is to use "power domains" (cf. [Plotkin 76a], [Smyth 76a]). The topic of specifying non-deterministic systems is not covered in this book.

There is, however, some non-determinism used in the specifications given below. In certain places it can aid the proof of correctness of an implementation to show that the result is not affected by a particular choice. For example, the choice of a free store location should not be fixed by the specification. Even to hypothesize a choice function requires fixing what influences the choice. Showing the possible results makes it easier to show that an implementation is correct. Strictly, however, each such non-deterministic choice should be accompanied by a proof that the non-determinism has no effect on the overall outcome. This is necessary to justify the use of functional (rather than relational or power) domains.

CHAPTER 3

MATHEMATICAL FOUNDATIONS

The need to be sure that the semantics of a language are precisely understood applies to the meta-language. Indeed, if the meta-language is not adequately defined, all attempts to employ it may be wasted. Chapter 2 uses some extremely powerful concepts. In particular, recursive functions defined in Lambda notation and the self-application of functions need detailed mathematical foundations. These foundations were, in fact, lacking when Christopher Strachey and Peter Landin first used Lambda notation to define programming languages. The mathematical problems were first solved by Dana Scott. Scott has gone on to offer several mathematical models: the treatment here gives an outline of the recent "neighborhood" approach. A pedagogic treatment of the general problem can be found in [Stoy 77a].

Readers who are less interested in mathematics than their use in defining semantics, might choose to omit reading this chapter. If they are concerned with defining systems where there is no recursion, this could be done quite safely. Readers involved in the definition of programming languages should, however, be aware of the problems involved and are recommended to read at least the first two sections.

CONTENTS

3.1 INTRODUCTION

The VDM meta-language, presented in this book, is intended to be used as a vehicle for rigorous mathematical reasoning about systems specified with it. In this chapter we aim to examine some of the problems that seem to arise when we use it for this purpose, and to indicate how they may be resolved.

It might be hoped that this kind of study would play a subsidiary part in a course of training in the use of VDM. After all, a knowledge of the formal construction of the real numbers by Dedekind cuts is hardly essential before undertaking everyday arithmetical calculations. For this hope to be fulfilled we must provide some kind of guarantee that every grammatical construct in the notation means something sensible in the mathematical framework on which the notation is based -- or, at the very least, some simple rules of thumb about what to avoid (such as division by zero in the real number example). For the most part we shall in fact be able to give the appropriate guarantees, so that someone who writes a specification in this language can be assured that he is indeed specifying something -though not necessarily what he intended, of course.

The foundational work on which the apparatus of denotational semantics rests was principally done by Dana Scott. The present chapter will be largely devoted to an introduction to his theory: for a fuller account readers must be referred to [Scott 81a].

3.2 BASIC PROBLEMS

3.2.1 Circular Definitions

The first problem we must face concerns circular definitions. These arise not only in the semantics of recursive procedures (or data structures) but also for any constructs which involve looping. For example, we may wish to define the *while*-loop in such a way that

$$\text{"}\underline{\textit{while}}\ B\ \underline{\textit{do}}\ S\text{"} \ \underline{=}\ \text{"}\underline{\textit{if}}\ B\ \underline{\textit{then}}\ (\ S;\ \underline{\textit{while}}\ B\ \underline{\textit{do}}\ S\ )\text{"} \qquad (1)$$

In the VDM language this same idea might be expressed (as in section 2 of chapter 2) as follows

$M[mk\text{-}While(b,s)](state) \triangleq$ (2)

$(\underline{let}\ wh = \lambda\sigma.(\underline{let}\ bv{=}MX[b](\sigma)\ \underline{in}\ \underline{if}\ bv\ \underline{then}\ (M[s](\sigma))\ \underline{else}\ \sigma)\ \underline{in}$
$wh(state)$

(Notice that (2) uses Church's λ-notation [Church 41a], which was also described in chapter 2.)

Example (1), since it is circular, is not *a priori* a definition at all. It is in effect an <u>equation</u> which we must try to solve for the value of

"<u>*while*</u> *B* <u>*do*</u> *S*"

and similarly in (2) the circular "definition" of the function $wh(\sigma)$ is an equation which we must try to solve for wh. However, the mere fact that we can write an equation does not guarantee that it has a solution: for example, in arithmetic the equation

$$x = x + 1$$

has none. Nor need any solution be unique; consider

$$x = x$$

Or, to take another example, consider the following recursively defined function.

$$f(x) = \underline{if}\ x{=}0\ \underline{then}\ 1\ \underline{else}\ \underline{if}\ x{=}1\ \underline{then}\ f(3)\ \underline{else}\ f(x-2) \qquad (3)$$

We have to solve this for f. The solution which would naturally occur to most computer scientists is

$$f(x) = \begin{cases} 1 \text{ if } x \text{ is even and } x \geq 0 \\ \\ \text{undefined otherwise} \end{cases} \qquad (4)$$

But another solution is

$$f(x) = 1 \text{ (for all } x \text{)} \qquad (5)$$

and so is

$$f(x) = \begin{cases} 1 \text{ if } x \text{ is even and } x \geq 0 \\ a \text{ if } x \text{ is odd and } x > 0 \\ b \text{ otherwise} \end{cases} \qquad (6)$$

for any values of a and b. Thus part of the job of our theory is to guarantee the existence of solutions to any such circular equational definitions we need to write, and to tell us which solution is to be understood as the meaning of the "definition" when the solution is not unique.

3.2.2 Fixed Points

Using λ-notation we may rewrite our equations in the form

$$f = H(f)$$

where H is a λ-expression. For example, (3) might now become

$$f = H(f) \qquad (7)$$

where

$$H = \lambda g.\lambda x.\underline{if}\ x{=}0\ \underline{then}\ 1\ \underline{else}\ \underline{if}\ x{=}1\ \underline{then}\ g(3)\ \underline{else}\ g(x-2)$$

Now our search for a solution of the equation becomes a search for a <u>fixed point</u> of H; i.e., a value which is mapped by H to the same value. In most of our work these values will be functions themselves (notice that H above is a function of a function), but simpler functions may have fixed points too.

Examples of Fixed Points

Considering integers and functions on them:

- a fixed point of $\lambda x.x$ is x
- a fixed point of $\lambda x.8-x$ is 4
- a fixed point of $\lambda x.x$ is any integer
- a fixed point of $\lambda x.x+1$ does not exist.

Considering more general functions:

fixed points of $\lambda g.\lambda x.\underline{if}\ x{=}0\ \underline{then}\ 1$ $\underline{else}\ \underline{if}\ x{=}1\ \underline{then}\ g(3)\ \underline{else}\ g(x-2)$

are the functions defined in (4), (5) and (6).

Fig. 1 Examples of Fixed Points

3.2.3 Self-Application and the Existence of Domains

The other main problem which we wish our theory to settle for us concerns the existence of the various value spaces we might define. Some of these seem unlikely. For example, consider the function (introduced in chapter 2)

$$twice(f) \triangleq \lambda x.f(f(x))$$

The argument of *twice* is itself a function; thus, for example *(twice square)3 = square(square(3)) = 81*. So far so good. But what are we to make of

((twice twice)square)3?

Obviously (at one level) this works out to be

$$((\lambda x.(twice(twice\ x)))square)3$$
$$= (twice(twice\ square))3$$
$$= (twice\ square)((twice\ square)3)$$
$$= 81^{**4} = 43046721$$

But notice that in this calculation the function *twice* was applied to itself. Another example of such self-application is afforded by the following definition of the factorial function

$$a(b,x) \quad \triangleq \underline{if}\ x{=}0\ \underline{then}\ 1\ \underline{else}\ x \times b(b,x-1)$$
$$Factorial(y) \triangleq a(a,y)$$

Notice carefully that this involves no recursion: *a* is defined solely in terms of its parameters, and *Factorial* is defined solely in terms of its parameter *y* and the previously defined *a*; *a*, however, is required to take itself as an argument.

This kind of example is quite permissble in many programming languages. For example, chapter 2 mentions

$$PROCDEN = (VALUE \mid PROCDEN)^{*} \tilde{\to} STATE \tilde{\to} STATE$$

and remarks that the arguments in some particular *Argument-list* which corresponds to procedure parameters must be elements of *PROCDEN* itself.

Other languages might allow commands to be stored. A command is a value in the domain

$$STATE \rightarrow STATE$$

and

$$STATE = LOC \rightarrow VAL$$

where *VAL* is the domain of storable values, here including commands. So once again we have a circular domain definition.

Why should the circular definition of domains present any more of a problem than the circular definition of functions, already discussed? Let us consider a simpler case. Let *F* be a set of functions whose domain is *G*, another set of functions, and whose range is the set with the two elements *0* and *1*. So

$$F = G \rightarrow \{0,1\}$$

Now if *G* has *n* elements it is easy to see that *F* will have 2^n elements: that is to say, the number of elements in *F* will always be greater than the number in *G*, and this remains so even when *G* contains *infinitely* many elements (this is Cantor's theorem). So even in this simple case there is no space of functions *F* such that

$$F = F \rightarrow \{0,1\}.$$

If the right hand side of this equation denotes all the functions from *F* to $\{0,1\}$ it will necessarily have too many elements.

Until we can resolve these difficulties we have no right to use any circular definitions, of functions or of domains, in our discussions. This would very much restrict our treatment of programming languages, but it would be necessary, in order to avoid the risk that we were talking nonsence by referring to things that could not possibly exist. Fortunately, however, these difficulties can be resolved, and in the remainder of this chapter we shall outline how this may be done.

Strictly speaking, perhaps, our investigation should proceed in two phases. First we should work out what is the minimal set of properties our system should have in order for the things we wish to do with it to be possible. Then secondly we should see if we could construct a system (a "model") satisfying all these properties. That would avoid the danger of ending up with a system which had unnecessary constraints. Here, however, we shall begin inventing a model at once - taking care, though, that all the assumptions we make are reasonable requirements for a theory of computations.

3.3 INFINITARY OBJECTS

Functions provide one example of a class of infinitary objects, objects which can contain an infinite amount of information -- in this case the mapping for every element of an infinite domain. Infinitary objects cannot be handled explicitly within a finite machine. Instead we have to be satisfied, on each occasion, with a finite approximation to the object which will nevertheless be adequate for that particular occasion. The same situation arises with other infinitary objects, such as real numbers. We cannot write down π completely, because it would go on for ever; but we can always choose a finite approximation (25 decimal places, say) good enough for some particular occasion. All we can actually do with a function (that is, a mapping) is apply it to various arguments; and in a finite time we shall only be able to apply it to finitely many arguments. So in any particular execution of a program our knowledge of a function will be confined to the results it has given for just one particular finite set of arguments - that one particular finite approximation to the function is all that is relevant to that particular occasion. (We do not know in advance, of course, which particular subset we shall require for any particular execution -- that is why we represent the function by an algorithm, a procedure capable of generating any subset, though only ever a subset, as required.)

This is the general idea that we shall exploit: a theory about computing with infinitary objects must handle them as the limits of sets of finite approximations, so that in any particular computation one of these approximations will be adequate in itself. We now embark on the construction of such a system of elements.

3.3.1 Neighborhood Systems

We shall regard an approximation to an object as specifying the attributes that the object might actually possess. So let Δ be a set of such attributes, which we shall call *tokens*. We shall not have to worry too much about what atom of information a single token represents: we shall only be concerned with collections of such tokens, subsets of Δ.

A <u>neighborhood system</u> over Δ is the family of those subsets of Δ which might possibly represent approximations to our objects. A particular member of this family, a <u>neighborhood</u> can be thought of as containing just those attributes which are not yet ruled out, and which <u>might</u> still apply to the object -- it might perhaps be thought of as a region of "possibility space".

There are two constraints on this family. In the first place, before any any computation has taken place <u>no</u> tokens will have been ruled out, so the whole set Δ is itself a neighborhood. Secondly, consider a pair of neighborhoods X and Y. These might, of course, be approximations of two quite different objects, with nothing in common; alternatively it might be possible to regard them as two approximations of the <u>same</u> object. This will certainly be possible if there is a third neighborhood, Z, in the system such that $Z \subseteq X$ and $Z \subseteq Y$. In this case, then, we insist that there be a neighborhood corresponding precisely to the information contained in just X and Y taken together, since X and Y together rule out all tokens which are not in their intersection. So we formally state

<u>Definition 1</u>: A family D of subsets of a given set Δ is called a <u>neighborhood system</u> over Δ if

1. $\Delta \in D$;
2. whenever $X, Y, Z \in D$ and $Z \subseteq X \cap Y$, then $X \cap Y \in D$

Notice that a smaller neighborhood represents a better approximation.

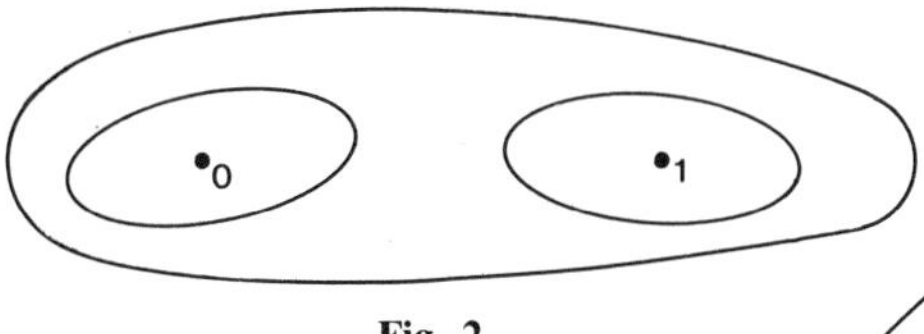

Fig. 2

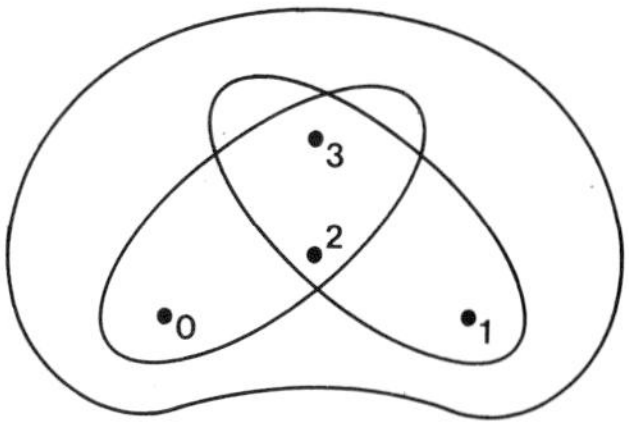

Fig. 3

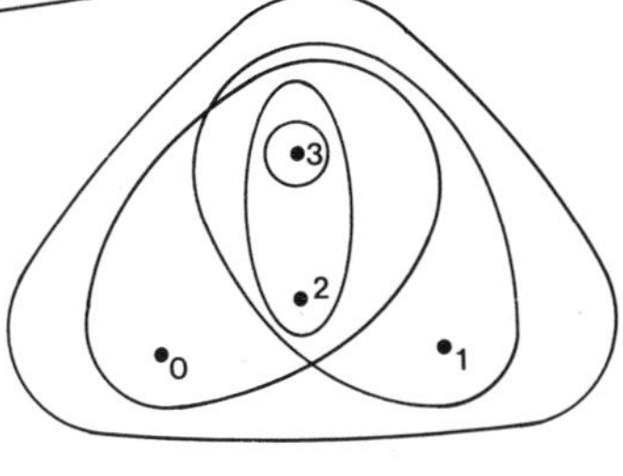

Fig. 4

Let us look at two simple examples. In the first (Fig. 2) there are two tokens and three neighborhoods. Either we have no information, or one of the tokens has been ruled out. In the next (Fig. 3) we have added two more tokens; notice that this does not require us to add any more neighborhoods -- the new system has precisely the same configuration of neighborhoods (under the set inclusion relation) as the previous one. However, if we choose to add neighborhood {3} to the system, the rules force use to add {2,3} too, and we have the system shown in Fig.4.

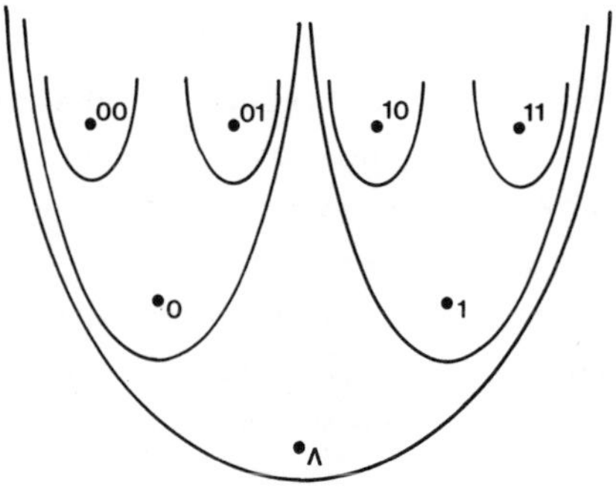

Fig. 5

In the other example (Fig. 5), the completely determined objects correspond to sequences of length two made up of zeroes and ones. The neighborhood labelled A, for example, encapsulates the approximation that the sequence begins with a zero.

3.3.2 Elements

We stated earlier that an element was to be regarded as the limit of a set of approximations. We now formally identify an element with the sub-family consisting of all those neighborhoods which could correspond to its approximations. That is to say, we are never going to be concerned about which particular sequence, of better and better approximations, is chosen from this sub-family. More precisely we have

Definition 2: The elements of a neighborhood system D are those sub-families $x \subseteq D$ where

1. $\Delta \in x$;
2. $X \in x$ and $Y \in x$ implies $X \cap Y \in x$,
3. whenever $X \in x$ and $X \subseteq Y \in D$, then $Y \in x$.

The third of these conditions, for example, says that whenever any particular neighborhood is a member any neighborhood corresponding to a worse approximation will also be a member. The collection of all the elements of D is written as $|D|$ and is known as a domain.

In the first of our examples (Fig. 2) there are three elements, as follows

$\{\{0,1\}\}$, $\{\{0,1\},\{1\}\}$, $\{\{0,1\},\{0\}\}$.

The first modification of this (Fig.3) similarly has just three elements:

$\{\{0,1,2,3\}\}$, $\{\{0,1,2,3\},\{0,2,3\}\}$, $\{\{0,1,2,3\},\{1,2,3\}\}$;

the other version, however, with its extra neighborhoods (Fig.4), has extra elements as follows:

$\{\{0,1,2,3\}\}$, $\{\{0,1,2,3\},\{0,2,3\}\}$, $\{\{0,1,2,3\},\{1,2,3\}\}$
$\{\{0,1,2,3\},\{0,2,3\},\{1,2,3\},\{2,3\}\}$,
$\{\{0,1,2,3\},\{0,2,3\},\{1,2,3\},\{2,3\},\{3\}\}$

In the other example there is an element corresponding to each of the tokens; it consists of all the neighborhoods containing that token.

3.3.3 Finite Elements

Each neighborhood of any neighborhood system determines a partial element, containing that neighborhood and all those corresponding to worse approximations. More precisely

Definition 3: For $X \in D$ the element *upto* X is defined by

$$\underline{upto}\ X = \{\ Y \mid Y \in D \wedge X \subseteq Y\ \}$$

These elements are called the finite elements of the domain $|D|$. The remaining elements, the infinitary ones, do not themselves correspond to particular neighborhoods, but must be regarded as the limits of infinite sets of neighborhoods.

Notice that the finite elements are dense in $|D|$, in the sense that for each x in $|D|$

x = union { upto X | $X \in x$ }.

So every element of $|D|$ is uniquely determined by its finite approximations.

Notice also that if $X \subseteq Y$ then upto $X \supseteq$ upto Y. If $x \subseteq y$, x is less defined than y. In this case we say that x approximates y and often writes this relation as

x sub y.

Notice that every domain has a least defined element ({Δ}), which we call ⊥ (pronounced "bottom"). If a domain also has elements maximal with respect to the approximation relation they are called total elements. In our first example, for instance, there are two such maximal elements (and the only other element is ⊥). This domain, in fact, with two fully defined elements, is the one usually taken to model the truth values; in VDM we would call it *Bool*, with elements

{⊥, *true*, *false*}

Moreover, this example easily extends to a larger one, equally useful. Instead of just two tokens, 0 and 1, take all the natural numbers, and let the neighborhoods be the complete set of tokens (of course) and all the singleton subsets. The domain thus produced has, together with ⊥, a countably infinite number of completely defined (maximal) elements; this domain will be what VDM calls *Nat*. If we rename the elements appropriately, the same domain -- or, if the reader prefers, an isomorphic copy -- will do duty for *Nat0* and *Int* too. (More precisely speaking, a domain comes with some associated primitive operations to give it some extra structure, and it is these which will distinguich *Nat*, *Nat0*, and *Int* -- even though these three domains are isomorphic as neighborhood systems.)

3.3.4 Changing the Token Sets

In our previous two examples the tokens corresponded respectively to the total elements and to all the elements. This is by no means a necessary feature. For example, suppose we are constructing a domain whose elements are intended to correspond to integer sets, and where the approximation ordering is to be the same as the set inclusion ordering. We could take the integers themselves as the tokens and, informally, understand the presence of token n in a neighborhood to convey the property that the integer n is not a member of the set we are approximating. Thus the finite element corresponding to the neighborhood in Fig. 6 would be {1}. Fig. 7 gives slightly more of the structure of this neighborhood system. It will be seen that although the tokens are countable, there are uncountably many partial elements; but there is only one total element, the complete set of integers.

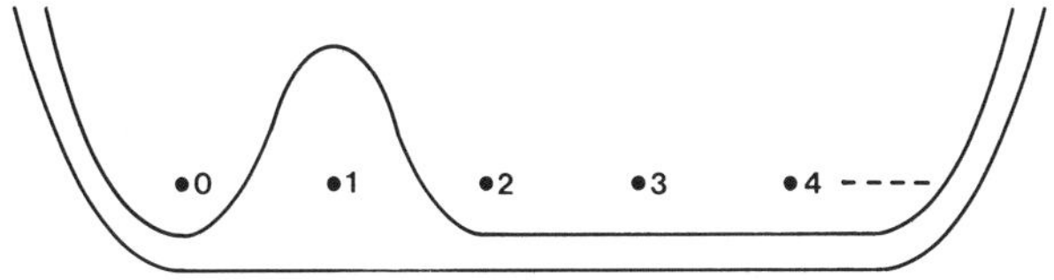

Fig. 6

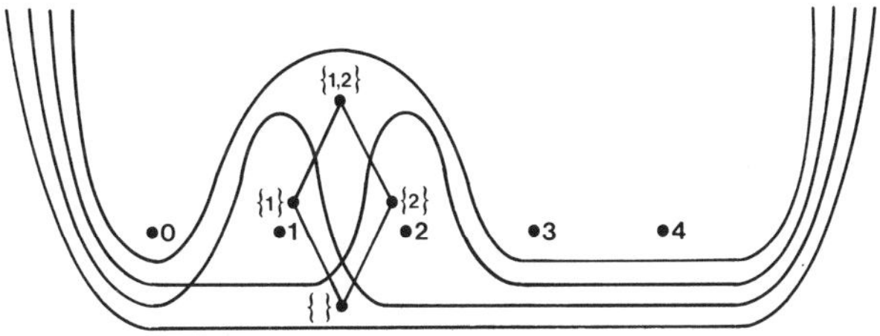

Fig. 7

We remarked earlier that the exact nature of tokens in a neighborhood system was not crucial: the important thing was the neighborhoods themselves. We illustrate this by showing how, given any neighborhood system, we can construct an isomorphic system (that is one with an isomorphic domain of elements structured by the approximation relation and, indeed, an isomorphic system of neighborhoods structured by set inclusion) with different tokens. For example, if D is a neighborhood system, for any $X \in D$ we define

$$[X] = \{ x \mid X \in x \in |D| \}$$

It can be shown that the family of sets like $[X]$ itself forms a neighborhood system and, moreover, that the domain determined by this new system is isomorphic to that of the old one. It will be seen that the tokens of the new system are the elements of the old one, and so are isomorphic with the elements of the new system too.

Alternatively, define

$$\underline{downto}\ X = \{\ Y \mid Y \in D \wedge Y \subseteq X\ \}$$

It can be shown that this family of sets, too, forms a neighborhood system determining a domain isomorphic to the old one. In this case the tokens of the new system are the neighborhoods of the old one, and thus correspond to the finite elements of either domain.

3.3.5 Permissible Functions

We must next consider how to treat functions between domains of elements. Remember that an actual computation about infinitary objects must be conducted solely in terms of their finite approximations. Thus at any stage in the computation of the application of a function to an infinitary argument (another function, perhaps), the argument will be represented only by an approximation, a neighborhood, and we shall require the function to specify similar approximations for the result. That is to say, for neighborhood systems D_0 and D_1 we shall regard a function f between the corresponding domains as a binary relation between the two families of neighborhoods.

It is reasonable to require this relation to satisfy certain properties. In the first place, before the computation starts we have no information about either the argument or the result, which moves us to demand

$$\Delta_0 f \Delta_1$$

Moreover the relation must be consistent, in the sense that

$$XfY \ \underline{\text{and}}\ XfY' \ \underline{\text{imply}}\ Xf(Y \cap Y')$$

Finally, the relation should exhibit a property called monotonicity. That is to say, an improvement in the approximation to an argument may not cancel any definite information we already have about the result. Moreover, whenever any particular neighborhood is specified by the relation as an approximation to the result then any worse approximation must also be speficied. More formally this means that

$$\underline{\text{if}}\ X' \subseteq X,\ XfY\ \underline{\text{and}}\ Y \subseteq Y'\ \underline{\text{then}}\ X'fY'$$

Definition 4: A relation satisfying all these properties is called an approximable mapping.

It can easily be seen that any approximable mapping between neighborhood systems determines a function between the corresponding domains of elements. For all $x \in |D_0|$ we define

$$f(x) = \{ Y \mid Y \in D \wedge (\exists X \in x)(XfY) \}$$

Conversely, each function on elements determines the original relation on neighborhoods, which is given by

$$XfY \Longleftrightarrow Y \in f(\underline{upto}\ X)$$

This two-way correspondence justifies us in using the same letter for the function and the relation. Notice that the function is also monotonic

$x \sqsubseteq y$ always implies $f(x) \sqsubseteq f(y)$

As an example, Fig. 8 tabulates all the approximable maps from *Bool* to *Bool*, listing them both as relations on neighborhoods and as functions on elements.

Tokens: $\Delta = \{0,1\}$
Neighborhoods: Δ, $A = \{0\}$, $B = \{1\}$
Elements: $\bot = \{\Delta\}$, $\underline{true} = \{\Delta, A\}$, $\underline{false} = \{\Delta, B\}$

1.	$\Delta f \Delta$ $Af\Delta$ $Bf\Delta$							$\bot$	$\bot$	$\bot$
2.	$\Delta f \Delta$ $Af\Delta$ $Bf\Delta$	AfA						$\bot$	true	$\bot$
3.	$\Delta f \Delta$ $Af\Delta$ $Bf\Delta$		AfB					$\bot$	false	$\bot$
4.	$\Delta f \Delta$ $Af\Delta$ $Bf\Delta$			BfA				$\bot$	$\bot$	true
5.	$\Delta f \Delta$ $Af\Delta$ $Bf\Delta$				BfB			$\bot$	$\bot$	false
6.	$\Delta f \Delta$ $Af\Delta$ $Bf\Delta$	AfA		BfA				$\bot$	true	true
7.	$\Delta f \Delta$ $Af\Delta$ $Bf\Delta$	AfA			BfB			$\bot$	true	false
8.	$\Delta f \Delta$ $Af\Delta$ $Bf\Delta$		AfB	BfA				$\bot$	false	true
9.	$\Delta f \Delta$ $Af\Delta$ $Bf\Delta$		AfB		BfB			$\bot$	false	false
10.	$\Delta f \Delta$ $Af\Delta$ $Bf\Delta$	AfA		BfA		ΔfA		true	true	true
11.	$\Delta f \Delta$ $Af\Delta$ $Bf\Delta$		AfB		BfB		ΔfB	false	false	false

Fig. 8 Approximable Maps from *Bool* to *Bool*

3.3.6 Continuity

Although we have been regarding neighborhoods as corresponding to finite approximations of elements, sometimes it is convenient to think of the elements themselves as approximating each other. We therefore need to be able to characterize those sets of elements which are in some sense tending to a limit. The appropriate concept is that of a directed set.

Definition 5: A non-empty set S, partially ordered by a relation $\leq$, is directed if, whenever $x, y \in S$, $x \leq z$ and $y \leq z$ for some $z \in S$.

Notice that z is not necessarily the least upper bound of x and y. A chain of elements

$$x_1, x_2, x_3, \ldots, x_n, \ldots$$

in which $x_n \leq x_{n+1}$ for all n, is a simple example of a directed set.

If S is a directed set of our particular kind of elements (ordered by the relation $\subseteq$), then it is easy to show that

$$\underline{union}\ \{\ x \mid x \in S\ \}$$

is itself an element. Using more technical jargon, we may say that domains are closed under directed unions.

Now, if $f: D \to D'$ is approximable and $S \subseteq |D|$ is a directed set of elements, we can also easily show that

$$f(\underline{union}\ \{\ x \mid x \in S\ \}) = \underline{union}\{\ f(x) \mid x \in S\ \}$$

That is to say, the functions determined by approximable mappings are continuous: they preserve directed unions. This is an important property, giving rise to important techniques for proving properties of our specifications. There is a one-one correspondence between continuous functions on elements and approximable maps between neighborhood systems.

3.3.7 Function Spaces as Domains

We make one further remark about approximable mappings. Suppose D_0 and D_1 are neighborhood systems. Let us construct a further system, in which the tokens are the approximable mappings between D_0 and D_1 and of which the neighborhoods are the finite non-empty intersections of sets given by

$$[X,Y] = \{ f \mid XfY \}$$

where $X \epsilon D_0$ and $Y \epsilon D_1$. It can be shown that this system is a neighborhood system, and its elements correspond uniquely with the approximable mappings between D_0 and D_1 (it is this that moved us to call the mappings approximable in the first place).

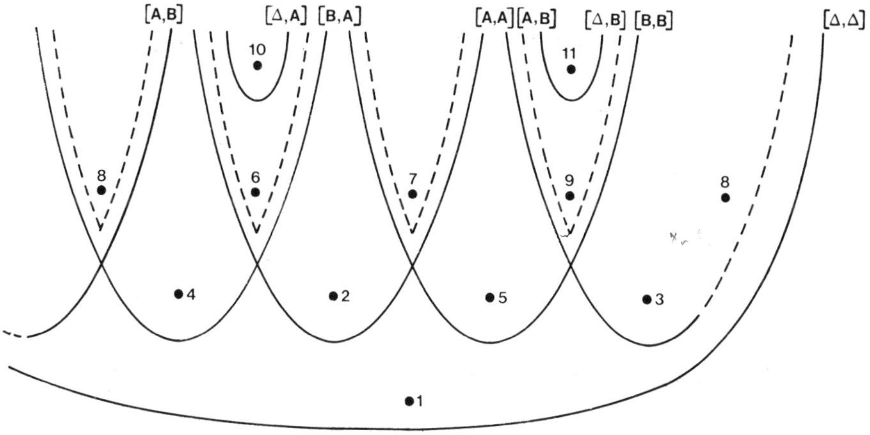

Fig. 9

Fig. 9 shows an example of this construction, for the system corresponding to the approximable mappings from *Bool* to *Bool*: the mappings are denoted by their numbers in the list given in Fig. 8; notice that the neighborhood $[A,B]$ "wraps round, and appears at both edges of the figure. The neighborhoods shown by dashed lines correspond to the "finite intersections" mentioned in the construction.

As a further example, consider the mappings from *Nat* to *Nat*. In this system, assuming that the tokens and elements of *Nat* are given corresponding enumerations, the neighborhood $[\{1\},\{3\}]$ (for example) contains all the functions which map 1 to 3. The neighborhood

$$[\{1\},\{3\}] \cap [\{2\},\{4\}]$$

contains all the functions which map 1 to 3 and 2 to 4. Thus the complete family of neighborhoods in this system has members for all finite maps from *Nat* to *Nat* - that is, those which map only a finite number of integers to anything other than $\perp$. The remaining functions correspond to infinitary elements of the function space. Similarly, if we carry out the construction for

$$(Nat \to Nat) \to (Nat \to Nat),$$

the neighborhoods correspond to finite maps of finite maps: that is to say, in all cases the neighborhoods themselves correspond exactly to what may actually be computed in finite time.

All this indicates that (provided that we confine ourselves to approximable mappings, which we shall henceforth do) function spaces between domains can be considered domains in their own right. We may therefore now begin to consider functions of functions within our framework.

3.4 LEAST FIXED POINTS

In an earlier example of a recursive function definition (3) we noticed that when there was a choice of solutions of the fixed point equations it was the least defined solution (4) we required. We now show that such a least fixed point always exists. That it to say, if $f\colon D \to D$ is approximable, there is a least x such that $f(x)=x$.

Let us consider how such an x might be approximated. Δ is always a neighborhood of any x, and if X is one neighborhood and XfY, then Y will be another neighborhood. This suggests that

$$x = \{\ X \mid X \in D \wedge \Delta f^n X,\ \underline{\text{for}}\ \underline{\text{some}}\ n \in Nat\ \}$$

might be a candidate for our required x. We now show that this guess is correct.

According to our suggestion, $X \in x$ if for some n there exists a sequence

$$X_0, X_1, \ldots, X_n$$

where $X_0=\Delta$ and $X_n=X$, such that $X_i f X_{i+1}$. We must prove first that the x

formed in this way is an element of $|D|$. Now $\Delta \in x$ (consider sequences of length 1); and since f is approximable, $X \in x$ and $X \subseteq Y$ together imply that $Y \in x$. It remains to prove that if $X \in x$ and $Y \in x$ then $(X \cap Y) \in x$. First we note, since $\Delta f \Delta$, the two sequences of neighborhoods relating Δ to X and to Y can be made of equal length by prefixing enough Δs to the shorter one. We also note that if UfV and $U'fV'$ are consistent, then $(U \cap U')f(V \cap V')$. Thus taking intersections element by element of our two sequences we see that $(X \cap Y) \in x$.

Having shown that x is a valid element, we must show that it is the least fixed point of f. We notice that if $X \in x$ and XfY then $Y \in x$, so $f(x) \subseteq x$. Indeed, x is the least such element (since any other must contain Δ and hence all of x too). But, since f is monotonic, $f(f(x)) \subseteq f(x)$; so $f(X)$ is itself another such element, and hence $x \subseteq f(x)$. Combining these two results we have $x = f(x)$ as desired, and we have already seen that x is the least element with this property.

We have thus shown that if we confine ourselves to neighborhood systems, and to functions determined by continuous mappings, then we can assume that recursive function definitions always specify the least solution of the corresponding fixed point equation, secure in the knowledge that such a least solution exists and is unique. So there is a function

$$fix: (\ |D| \to |D|\ ) \to |D|$$

which maps any function $f: |D| \to |D|$ to its least fixed point. *fix* may be defined by

$$fix(F) = \underline{union}\{\ F^n(\bot)\ \mid\ n \in N\ \}$$

and *fix* can itself can be shown to be an approximable mapping.

We have thus sketched out how the first of our two problems may be solved. We now turn to the other.

3.5 NEW SYSTEMS FROM OLD

We have already seen one way in which a neighborhood system may be constructed from two others - the space of approximable mappings from one system to another is a neighborhood system in its own right. We now mention one or two other methods for constructing new neighborhood systems from old.

3.5.1 Product Spaces

Suppose D_0 and D_1 are neighborhood systems over Δ_0 and Δ_1, and suppose Δ_0 and Δ_1 are disjoint (if they were not we could, of course, tag all the tokens in some way to make them so). Then we define

$$D_0 \times D_1 = \{ X \cup Y \mid X \in D_0 \wedge Y \in D_1 \}$$

This can easily be seen to be a neighborhood system itself, over $\Delta_0 \cup \Delta_1$; each neighborhood has a contribution from one neighborhood of D_0 and from one of D_1. It has elements which may be written $\langle x,y \rangle$, where $x \in |D_0|$, and $y \in |D_1|$, defined by

$$\langle x,y \rangle = \{ X \cup Y \mid X \in x \wedge Y \in y \}$$

Thus the elements of this system correspond to pairs of elements drawn from the given systems. The ordering of these elements behaves as expected

$$\langle x,y \rangle \sqsubseteq \langle x',y' \rangle \quad = \quad x \sqsubseteq x' \wedge y \sqsubseteq y' \tag{8}$$

The selector functions may be easily defined too: if $z = \langle x,y \rangle$, then

$$x = \{ X \in |D_0| \mid X \cup \Delta_1 \in z \} = \{ Z \cap \Delta_0 \mid Z \in z \}$$
$$y = \{ Y \in |D_1| \mid Y \cup \Delta_0 \in z \} = \{ Z \cap \Delta_1 \mid Z \in z \}$$

All this indicates that the cartesian product of two domains is a domain too.

3.5.2 Sum Spaces

Once again, let D_0 and D_1 be neighborhood systems over the disjoint sets Δ_0 and Δ_1. Define

$$D_0 + D_1 = D_0 \cup D_1 \cup \{\Delta_0 \cup \Delta_1\}$$

This, too, is a neighborhood system again over $\Delta_0 \cup \Delta_1$; each of its elements, apart from the new minimal one $\{\Delta_0 \cup \Delta_1\}$, corresponds to an element of either $|D_0|$ or $|D_1|$. This correspondence is given by the functions

$$in_i: \ |D_i| \rightarrow |D_0 + D_1|$$
$$out_i: \ |D_0 + D_1| \rightarrow |D_i|$$

where $i \in \{0,1\}$, defined by

$$in_i(x_i) = x_i \cup \{\Delta_0 \cup \Delta_1\}$$
$$out_i(x) = \{X \in x \mid X \in |D_i|\} \cup \{\Delta_i\} \qquad (9)$$

This system, then, corresponds to the disjoint union of the two given domains: the partial ordering is inherited from the two components.

3.5.3 The "Strict" Versions

We can give the following alternative versions of the preceding two constructions.

$$|D_0|\otimes|D_1| = \{\Delta_0 \cup \Delta_1\} \cup \{\ X \cup Y \mid X \in D_0 - \{\Delta_0\} \wedge Y \in D_1 - \{\Delta_1\}\}$$
$$|D_0|\oplus|D_1| = \{\Delta_0 \cup \Delta_1\} \cup \{\ X \mid X \in D_0 - \{\Delta_0\}\} \cup \{\ Y \mid Y \in D_1 - \{\Delta_1\}\}$$

The effect of these variations is to reduce the number of elements in the constructed domains. In the first case, $|D_0 \otimes D_1|$ contains no elements $\langle x,y \rangle$ for which x or y (but not both) is the minimal (least defined) element of the respective component domain: the pairing function defined in (8) takes all such elements to the minimal element of the new domain ($\perp$, which is also $\langle \perp, \perp \rangle$). In the second case, $|D_0 \oplus D_1|$ contains no separate elements corresponding to the minimal elements of the component domains: in_i (for each i) maps each to the minimal element of the sum domain. This disjoint construction, with the minimal elements identified in this way, is sometimes known as the coalesced sum, as distinct from the the separated sum given earlier. Which version of the sum or product domain construction is required depends on the particular circumstances (though VDM does not provide separate notation for both). We shall have more to say about this when we come to apply this work to the VDM notation more specifically.

3.6 RECURSIVE DOMAIN EQUATIONS

We have now discussed the three principal ways of combining given domains into bigger structures - by forming product, sum or function spaces. (There are, of course, other constructions, but they are not too relevant to VDM.) So we now know how to interpret an equation such as

$$Val = Bool + Int + (Int \times Int)$$

provided *Bool* and *Int* have been defined (they were discussed in examples above). We must now consider equations in which a domain is described circularly, as in the following example

$$Tree = Int \oplus (Tree \otimes Tree)$$

From this equation we may infer, for a start, that there is an element of *Tree* corresponding to each element of *Int*, and to every pair of elements of *Tree*. This structure (together with the actual $Int \rightarrow Tree$ and $(Tree \times Tree) \rightarrow Tree$ functions specifying the correspondence) would amount to an algebra of trees. But we shall require more. An algebra might associate (for example) two different pairs of trees ($\langle A,B \rangle$ and $\langle B,A \rangle$, say) with the same element of *Tree*. We shall forbid such "confusion". The fact that we have written a domain equation is meant to imply that the two sides are to be isomorphic: two elements of the domain are to be identified only if they arise from the same structure of components. Even this is not enough, however, to specify a unique solution of the equation. The domain *Tree* (for example) might include extra elements which, though their presence does not invalidate the domain equation, are not essential for a solution. We therefore forbid such "junk" elements, too. Elements are to exist in the domain only if their existence is required (not merely permitted) by the defining equation.

An example of unnecessary elements for our particular equation is afforded by infinite trees, such as

$$\langle 1, \langle 1, \langle 1, \ldots \rangle\rangle\rangle$$

The presence of such trees would not invalidate our equation, but they are not required by it; so they are not present in the particular solution we have in mind. Notice, though, that if we had used the alternative (uncircled) versions of the domain construction operators some infinite trees (those which are the limits of their finite approximations) would have been part of the solution too. For example, all the elements of the sequence

$\bot$, $<1,\bot>$, $<1,<1,\bot>>$, $<1,<1,<1,\bot>>>$, ...

will be present, and therefore (since, as we have seen in section 3.3.6, domains are closed under directed unions) their least upper bound will also be present, and this is the infinite tree we have mentioned - otherwise our solution would not be a domain at all. The use of the strict operators (in particular $\otimes$), however, will ensure that any attempt to produce a tree containing $\bot$ will in fact produce $\bot$ itself; thus no (non-trivial) finite approximations of infinite trees are in the domain *Tree*, and neither are the limitpoints. Another way to see the difference between the two versions of *Tree* may be to consider what is the least solution of the equation

$$x = <1,x>$$

in the two domains - it will be $\bot$ in the strict version, but the infinite tree in the other. (Notice that the version for which infinite trees are present by necessity may nevertheless have solutions which include other "junk" elements -- an example would be the domain which also included infinite trees of Boolean atoms.)

The particular kind of solution that interests us ("no confusion, no junk", in Burstall's phrase) corresponds to the initial algebra and is, in the sense which we have outlined, the unique minimal solution of the equation. We now have the obligation of showing that an initial solution exists for any such equation. One way of doing this is, firstly, to define the implicit partial ordering on domains.

Definition 6: D is subsystem of E, written "D *sub* E", (and the corresponding domains are in the subdomain relationship) if D and E are both neighborhood systems over the same set of tokens and

1. $D \subseteq E$;
2. whenever $X,Y \in D$ and $X \cap Y \in E$, then $X \cap Y \in D$

That is to say, D is a "smaller" family of neighborhoods, but neighborhoods in it are consistent whenever they are consistent in E.

Then we consider

$$T(X) = Int \oplus (X \otimes X)$$

as defining a "function", T, from the class of domains (into itself), and we define what it means for such a "function" to be monotonic and continuous. Then if we have a token set Δ such that

$$\{\Delta\}\ \underline{sub}\ T(\{\Delta\})$$

we can show that the required initial solution of

$$D = T(D)$$

is given by

$$D = \underline{union}\ T^n(\{\Delta\})$$

Notice that $\{\Delta\}$ is the minimal neighborhood system over Δ, and if it is a subsystem of $T(\{\Delta\})$ then the whole sequence of systems will be over the same set Δ. (Of course this is no more than the barest of possible outlines - strictly speaking, for example, T is not only a function on the class of domains but has to do the right thing to the approximable mappings on those domains too. The neatest way to say it properly is in the notation of category theory, making T a functor, and the interested reader will find it all in [Scott 81a].)

3.7 AN ALTERNATIVE APPROACH TO DOMAIN EQUATIONS

In a sense we have now dealt with all the problems outlined in section 3.2. We have shown that, under constraints which hold for the cases with which we are concerned, solutions exist for our circular definitions both of functions and of domains themselves, and we have discussed how it is always the minimal solution that interests us in particular. We choose, however, to approach the matter of domain equations from another direction. The point is that the methodology for which we are seeking to provide the foundations is to be used for specifying computer languages and systems; so, if possible, we should try to keep track of whether what we are specifying is computable. We must therefore extend our treatment to take computability into account, and we shall find that the alternative approach will allow us to do so more easily.

3.7.1 Computability of Domains and Mappings

We recall that the basis of this model is that the neighborhoods represent the finite approximations to our finitary or infinitary values: so it is with neighborhoods that we actually compute. In order that these computations with neighborhoods be possible, we require the neighborhood system to be effectively presented - that is to say, we require neighborhoods inside the machine (or on paper) in such a way that the necessary calculations can be carried out. This in turn means that there must be no more than countably many neighborhoods, so that we may think of them as indexed by the natural numbers (that is, we may think of a typical neighborhood as X_n for some natural number n); More than this is needed, however: for we must be able to tell which neighborhoods are which, and how they relate to each other, in an effective way. The formal requirements are spelled out in the following definition.

Definition 7: A neighborhood system D has an effective presentation (or "D is effectively presented") if

$$D = \{ X_n \mid n \in N \},$$

where the two propositions

$$(\exists k \in N)(X_k \subseteq X_n \wedge X_k \subseteq X_n), \text{ and } \qquad X_n \cap X_m = X_k$$

are recursively decidable (in m,n and k,m,n respectively).

Elements, and particularly infinitary elements, are thought of as the limits of their finite approximations. So all we have a right to expect, when computing a particular element, is that any particular approximation to that element will be produced sooner or later. That is to say

Definition 8: An element x of an effectively presented domain is said to be computable if the set

$$\{ n \in N \mid X_n \in x \}$$

is recursively enumerable.

In a similar way we define what it means for an approximable mapping to be computable.

Definition 9: An approximable mapping $f\colon X \to Y$, where X and Y are effectively presented, is computable if the relation

$$X_n f Y_m$$

is recursively enumerable in m and n.

The reader unfamiliar with recursive function theory need not be too concerned to study the details of these definitions. Suffice it to say that they express our requirements using the standard apparatus, and that when they overlap with the standard theory (for example, when they are applied to the domains of integers and integer functions) they are precisely compatible. We may now go back over our previous working, and check that we can find effective presentations for the domains we have introduced, such that any "primitive operations" specified for any particular domains - or any operations defined for families of domains - are computable in terms of that presentation. In this summary the only example we have explicitly mentioned is *fix* (this is, incidentally, the only fixed point operator which is in general computable). We should check that our domain constructors (×, + and so on) produce domains which are effectively presented whenever the constituents are (that is to say, we can work out algorithms for the necessary calculations with the new neighborhoods given those for the constituent domains). Note, too, that a function is computable, considered as an approximable mapping, just when it is computable considered as an element of the function space domain.

We now give a method for finding solutions to domain equations that better allows us to keep track of this notion of computability.

3.7.2 Retracts

Our new programme for finding solutions of domain equations involves exploiting the subdomain relation *sub*. Our plan is to find the solution of any domain equation as a subdomain of one particular "universal" domain which contains them all. One convenient way to characterise a particular subdomain of a given domain is as the range of some function; an even better plan is to confine our attention, if we can, to functions which are idempotent (that is to say, which are the identity function on their range, so that their ranges and fixed-point sets coincide). Such a function is called a retraction, and its range set a retract, of the given domain.

Definition 10: A retraction of a neighborhood system E is an approximable map $a: E \to E$ such that

$$a \circ a = a$$

Now to relate retractions and their retracts with subdomains, we note that if D *sub* E, then there exists a pair of approximable maps relating the two domains, namely $i: D \to E$ and $j: E \to D$ defined as follows

$$i(x) = \{ Y \mid Y \in E \wedge (\exists X \in x)(X \subseteq Y) \}$$
$$j(y) = y \cap D$$

These two maps are known as a projection pair; note that

$$j \circ i = I_D \text{ and } i \circ j \subseteq I_D$$

If we look more closely at this last-mentioned $i \circ j$, which may alternatively be defined as the approximable mapping a given by the relation

$$X \; a \; Z \iff (\exists Y \in D)(X \subseteq Y \subseteq Z),$$

we see that it is a retraction, since

$$a \circ a = i \circ j \circ i \circ j = i \circ j = a,$$

and, moreover, that $|D|$ is isomorphic to the fixed-point set of a. To show this last point, we note, on the one hand, that for any $x \in |D|$, $i(x)$ is an element of a's fixed-point set, since

$$a(i(x)) = i \circ j \circ i(x) = i(x);$$

and, on the other hand, that for any fixed point y of a there is an element of $|D|$, namely $j(y)$, such that

$$i(j(y)) = y$$

So i sets up a 1-1 correspondence between the fixed-point set of a and the domain $|D|$ which (since i and j are both monotonic) is an isomorphism under the $\subseteq$ ordering.

Notice that not every retraction corresponds to a subdomain of the given domain in this kind of way. We call a retraction a of E a projection if

$$a \subseteq I_E$$

and we call it a finitary projection if its fixed-point set is indeed isomorphic to a subdomain. The finitary projections of E are just the functions a which satisfy

$$a(x) = \{ Y \mid Y \in E \wedge (\exists X \in x)(X \; a \; X \wedge X \subseteq Y) \}$$

3.7.3 A Universal Domain

Our final step in this development is to produce a domain which is "universal" in the sense that any required domain may be found as one of its subdomains. There are many possible candidates - even if we confine ourselves to domains which are effectively given - a convenient one uses as its tokens the rational numbers in the half-open interval [0,1), where

$$[r,s) = \{q \in Q \mid r \leq q < s\}$$

We define the system U over [0,1) to have as neighborhoods all non-empty finite unions of intervals

$[r,s)$ where $0 \leq r < s \leq 1$

This can easily be seen to be effectively given. This system U is universal in that every countable neighborhood system D is a subsystem of U and, moreover, if D is effectively given the relevant projection pair (and hence the associated retraction) is computable.

Next we find isomorphic versions of our favourite primitive domains as subdomains of U. *Bool*, for example, may be found as the neighborhood system

{[0,1),[0,1/2),[1/2,1)}

giving rise to the domain

{{[0,1)},{[0,1),[0,1/2)},{[0,1),[1/2,1)}}

The reader might care to define a suitable retraction function for this domain (remember that when applied to any element of U it must produce an element corresponding to an element of *Bool*, and those particular elements must be mapped to themselves), and perhaps also for a suitable version of the domain of integers as a subdomain of U.

Finally we must cover the constructors for compound domains. First we note that (because they are effectively given) $U \times U$, $U + U$, $U \rightarrow U$ are themselves sub-domains of U, and so we can assume the existence of projection pair functions

$$i_\times : U \times U \rightarrow U \text{ and } j_\times : U \rightarrow U \times U$$

and similar functions for the other forms of construction. (When we came actually to design a suitable pair of functions $i_\times$ and $j_\times$ we would have to take care to make the tokens corresponding to the two subdomains disjoint -- perhaps by mapping them to [0,1/2) and [1/2,1) respectively). Now for any $a,b \in U \rightarrow U$, define

$$a \times b = i_\times \circ (\lambda x.\langle a(x[0]), b(x[1])\rangle) \circ j_\times$$

where $x[0]$ and $x[1]$ are the two components of x whenever x is a pair, and $\bot$ otherwise. Similarly, we may define

$$a \rightarrow b = i_\rightarrow \circ (\lambda f . b \circ f \circ a) \circ j_\rightarrow$$

and so on for the other constructions. If a and b are finitary projections then so are $a \times b$, $a \rightarrow b$ etc. and their fixed-point sets are isomorphic to the domains obtained by applying the corresponding domain constructor to the domains characterised by a and b. This programme may be continued: an important step is to show that if f is a function such that $f(a)$ is a finitary projection whenever a is, then $fix(f)$ is also a finitary projection.

Thus, instead of working with the domains themselves, we may work instead with their finitary projections. Since, if a and b are finitary projections of U

D_a <u>*sub*</u> D_b <u>just when</u> $a \sqsubseteq b$,

this new view is isomorphic with the old. So we may now think of a recursive domain equation as defining the domain given by the corresponding recursively defined finitary projection: both equations specify the minimal solution (just as we understood circular domain equations to do in the earlier approach), but now we know when the resulting domains are effectively given and accordingly appropriate vehicles for specifying a computation.

3.8 APPLICATION TO VDM

We must finally discuss how these notions map onto the VDM matalanguage that is the subject of this book. This is partly a notational change - our notation up to now has been very similar to Scott's. For example, VDM uses domain names such as *State*, unadorned with bars, to denote families of elements which we have denoted, up to now, by $|State|$.

3.8.1 Primitive Domains

The primitive domains of VDM correspond to systems we have already discussed. We should remember, however, that these systems are structures consisting of a neighborhood system and a number of primitive operations, in terms of which we could define all other operations involving elements of the domain. For example, the non-negative integers (the domain VDM calls *Nat0*) could be defined as the structure

$$\langle N, 0, pred, succ, zero \rangle$$

where N is the countably infinite system introduced in section 3.3.3. Other numeric domains (such as *Int* and *Nat*) would correspond to similar, but different structures. The truth-value domain, *Bool*, would have its own family of operators including, for any other domain D, the conditional combinator

$$Cond: Bool \times D \times D \rightarrow D.$$

The other primitive domains (domains of Quotations (Characters), or of explicitly enumerated elements - such as the domain {CLUBS,HEARTS,SPADES,DIAMONDS}, for example) have their own families of operators too: these often consist merely of an equality test, sometimes together with some ordering relation.

For all these structures we must check that we can first define suitable enumerations of their neighborhoods, and then define the primitive operators as computable functions in terms of these enumerations. This presents no problem for the domains we have discussed.

3.8.2 Compound Domains

Our job for the compound domains is very similar - we must provide enumerations for the neighborhoods (in terms of the enumerations for the component domains), and definitions for a sufficient set of primitive operators. We should also clarify what properties (if any) we need to assume about the component domains in our construction.

Many of the domain constructions require little discussion. The construction for product spaces, for example, has been sufficiently described, and the VDM notation is the same as used in this chapter.

3.8.3 Sum Domains

For sum spaces the VDM notation is $A \mid B$. In many cases this is best regarded as equivalent to our $A \oplus B$; for example, in the specifications of syntactic domains (where, of course, the sum domain notation is used to give alternatives for nodes in the parse tree) we do well to rule out the infinite parse trees that would be elements of our domain if we used the non-strict versions of the sum and product operators. Occasionally, though, the other version is appropriate. For example, consider a semantic value domain defined to be

$$Val = Int \mid Bool \mid Proc$$

Here *Proc* is supposed to be a domain of procedure values, presumably functions from parameter lists to some appropriate space; so its minimal element will be the function mapping all parameter lists to $\perp$. This is indeed the least-defined procedure, but it must not be confused with the minimal element of *Val* itself. $\perp_{Val}$ is such that any attempt to evaluate it will fail to terminate - in our terminology, no neighborhood will be produced in the enumeration of neighborhoods except for the trivial neighborhood (Δ) conveying no information beyond the fact that the value is an element of *Val*. The minimal procedure, however, is at least a procedure, and as such might be passed around as a parameter to other procedures or whatever; it is only when it is applied to a parameter list that a non-terminating computation might be expected to result.

(In fact this point does not arise in the language given in Chapter 4 - the only place where it might is in the definition of the domain *Den* by

$$Den = Loc \mid Labden \mid Procden$$

but in this case since $\perp_{Procden}$ is the only element that can ever arise there is no real need to distinguish it from any other.)

The best rule of thumb in deciding whether the strict or the non-strict constructions are required is probably to use the strict versions whenever the component domains are all flat (that is, they contain only maximal elements and $\perp$): this will result in a new domain which is also flat, thus avoiding extra complication which is almost always unnecessary. When a component domain has a richer structure, however, or alternatively when the construction is part of a circular definition of a domain that is to include infinitary elements, the non-strict versions are usually the appropriate ones to use. Note, however, that this is merely a rule of thumb, and often more careful analysis is required. Even in the example we discussed in section 3.6, the various different choices for the operators result in domains which are quite different, and would be appropriate for list systems with quite different semantic properties. Donahue and Cartwright (in [Donahue 82a]) discuss just this taxonomy for a comparison of various definitions of "lazy evaluation".

3.8.4 Abstract Syntax

We must now discuss the difference between the use of "=" and of "*::*" as the defining operator in a domain equation, since either may be used, particularly when a product domain is being defined. In fact there is nothing abnormal about the "=" operator; in particular, if two domains are defined using this operator with the same right hand sides the domains will be identical. The "*::*" operator, on the other hand, always defines a domain together with a family of named constructor and selector functions, and names for the test functions which are implicitly defined when the domain is used in sum domain constructions with others. Thus the difference between the two operators is basically one of associated naming conventions.

3.8.5 Functions

The VDM notation for function spaces corresponds closely to ours, though an additional distinction may be made, between a domain of total functions and one containing partial functions too. Since this is well known to be an uncomputable distinction, we regard it as making no difference to the domain, which will be the same in either case; it is merely a matter of more or less informal comment, indicating that those writers who use both symbols in their definitions are, when they use the "total" version, perhaps prepared to prove that the functions they are defining are total. (The vagueness of this remark is intentional, since in practice some authors tend to use the plain arrow for the unrestricted class.)

3.8.6 Sets

The notation provided for specifying set domains in VDM is so general that it is possible to define domains which are not effectively presented and for which some of the operators provided in VDM are uncomputable. For example, unless it is possible to tell effectively whether two elements of a set are equal it will not be possible to compute the set's cardinality. We therefore allow as elements of set domains only finite sets, of elements of some flat domain (but excluding $\perp$). Since the cardinality function *card* must, as usual, be monotonic, the domain of sets must be ordered in such a way that sets of different cardinalities are incomparable: the set domain, in fact, is a flat domain too. If the domain of members is countably infinite (no effectively given flat domain can be uncountable), the set domain will be yet another domain isomorphic to the domain of integers, as can be seen by considering the standard representation of sets as bit patterns, and regarding them as binary numbers. This representation technique immediately suggests a strategy for formulating the details of the neighborhood system and the primitive operations, and for defining a suitable projection pair, to allow such set domains to be viewed as subdomains of our universal domain U. When this is worked out, it will be seen that the construction makes use of more properties of the component domain than any previous one (it will, for example, rely on its flatness).

It should be remarked that other kinds of domains of sets are also sometimes used in denotational definitions (though not, as yet, in the VDM notation). One example is the domain of sets of possible results of non-deterministic computations. The theory of these "powerdomains" is quite different from that for the much simpler domains we are considering here - for example, such domains need not necessarily be effectively given (the computer, after all, produces only one of the set of possible results). For a discussion of the various forms of powerdomain see [Plotkin 76a] or [Smyth 76a]. or (for the kind which does fall inside the framework of neighborhood systems) [Scott 81a].

3.8.7 Lists

One possible way of constructing a domain of *A*-lists, where *A* is some domain, is as the initial solution to the equation

$$L = L \oplus (A \otimes L).$$

It is straightforward to define the appropriate set of primitive operators in terms of this domain.

3.8.8 Maps

Maps in VDM are finite functions on flat domains. Moreover, given a map, it is possible to compute the element of a set domain containing the elements for which the function is defined, implying that maps defined on sets of different cardinality are incomparable.

One possible way to provide a construction for map domains is to proceed by representing a map as a pair, consisting of the set on which it is defined together with an approximable mapping of the usual kind. All the VDM operators involving maps are then straightforward, except possibly for those involving the range. For example. if *m* is a map from *A* to *B*, *rng* *m* is allowable only if a domain may be defined for elements of *B* (see above); even then, *rng* *m* will be computable only if *m* happens to be a total map on its domain.

Maps in VDM, however, are most frequently (though certainly not always) used in definitins where the members of their range sets are known to be elements (excluding $\perp$) of some flat domain. Then the map domain is flat too, and none of the problems just described arises. Thus, for example, chapter 4 section 8 contains the definition

$$STORE = SCALARLOC \underset{m}{\rightarrow} [SCALARVALUE]$$

where

$$SCALARVALUE = Bool \mid Int$$

and *SCALARLOC* is also a flat domain. We see that *STORE*, too, is flat and, and, therefore, so is the domain of states in that definition (since *State* is a product of *Store* together with other flat domains).

o o o

The discussion of this section may seem to be calling for some fairly conventional programming, albeit in terms of neighborhoods. It should be remembered that the object of such exercises is to check that the domains being considered can be effectively presented, and that they can be provided with an adequate set of computable primitive operators. This does not in any way prejudice any decision about how an actuial implementation might represent the elements of any domain. It does, however, provide us with quarantees on the following points which would otherwise, if necessary, have to be proved explicitly.

1. The domains may be used in recursive definitions of other effectively given domains;

2. the domains may be used as the basis for the specification of functions which we may reasonably expect to implement on a computer.

PART II

VDM AND PROGRAMMING LANGUAGES

Programming Languages are the communication bridge between the programmer and the machine — if they are not precisely defined, they cannot be used with confidence. Compilers translate programs for execution — if they contain errors, they can frustrate the programmer's attempts to obtain a desired result. It is, therefore, not surprising that formal definition ideas were first applied to programming languages. Such definitions aim to provide a precise reference point for understanding and implementing a language. This part of the book describes the use of VDM on programming languages. Chapters 4 to 7 cover writing a definition in VDM; chapters 8 and 9 discuss how such a definition can be used as the basis of compiler design. The initial examples given are of small, contrived languages. But chapters 6 and 7 apply VDM to complete programming languages which are widely known.

CHAPTER 4

MODELLING CONCEPTS OF PROGRAMMING LANGUAGES

The design of the meta-language (known as "META-IV") used in VDM is motivated here by considering programming language concepts which are to be formally defined. In particular, the combinators which are introduced in chapter 2 are shown here to provide readable definitions of language concepts like block structure and goto statements. Although programming language definition was the first use of META-IV, part III shows that most of the meta-language applies to the specification of other systems. The individual language concepts are collected together to form a mini-language whose complete definition is given in section 4.10. Alternative ways of handling exception constructs are discussed in the next chapter.

This chapter is a rewritten version of [Jones 78c]. Similar motivations for denotational semantic definition techniques are given in [Tennent 80a] and [Gordon 79a].

CONTENTS

4.1 INTRODUCTION

This chapter introduces many of the basic concepts of programming languages and, for each such concept, shows how it can be defined using denotational semantics. The emphasis is on the underlying model required although the metalanguage used to present these models is that used throughout this book. The concepts have been selected so as to motivate features of the metalanguage. For this reason, it might appear that each new language feature requires some extension of the metalanguage. In the definition of a full language (e.g. chapter 6) the features of the metalanguage are used far more intensively.

4.2 EXPRESSIONS

The denotational method defines semantics by mapping the objects to be defined to some known objects. The objects which are the target of this mapping are referred to as "denotations" and are assumed to be already understood. The essence of this chapter is to show the different denotations used to define various concepts of programming languages. A language whose constructs are expressions requires only simple denotations and will provide a useful introduction to the denotational method.

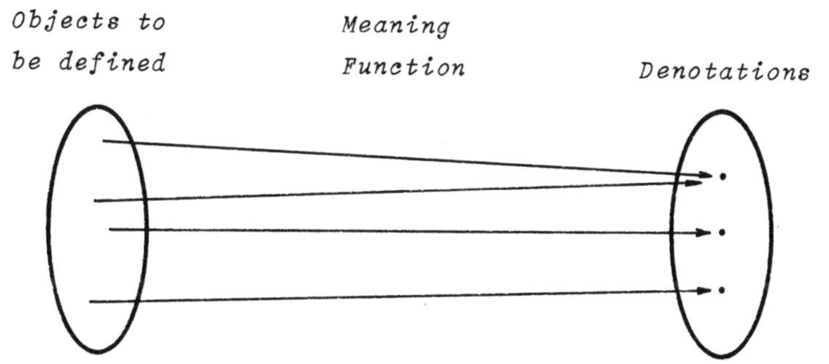

Fig. 1 The Denotational Method

Fig. 1 illustrates the denotational approach to defining semantics. The first task is to fix the class of objects whose semantics are to be defined. For a small finite language, it is possible to do this by enumeration.

Fig. 2 enumerates all of the Boolean expressions which can be constructed with an implication sign and the Boolean constants. The next part of the the general method requires choosing a set of objects to use as denotations. For the language of Fig. 2 this can be the Boolean values and the mapping of expressions to denotations is given in the same figure by enumeration.

Language	Denotation
false ⊃ *false*	*true*
false ⊃ *true*	*true*
true ⊃ *false*	*false*
true ⊃ *true*	*true*

Fig. 2 Semantics of Implication with Constants

For infinite, or even very large, languages it is not possible to define the class of objects of interest by enumeration. The strings of such a language are normally defined by syntax rules and the structure created by such a syntax is used in fixing the semantics. Fig. 3 gives an *abstract syntax* of an (infinite) language of logical expressions. The notation used is that for describing objects discussed in chapter 2. The valid expressions are any finite objects matching this recursive definition.

Boolexpr	=	*Boolinfixexpr* | *Negation* | *Boolconst*
Boolinfixexpr	::	*Boolexpr* *Boolop* *Boolexpr*
Negation	::	*Boolexpr*
Boolconst	=	*true* | *false*
Boolop	=	AND | OR | IMPL | EQUIV

Fig. 3 Abstract Syntax of Logical Expressions

What denotations are to be used for the logical expression language? The same set of Boolean values will suffice:

Bool = {*true*, *false*}

The mapping from the language to the denotations can be given by a function of type:

M: Boolexpr → Bool

There are different ways of presenting such functions. Because the language involved is small, it will be clearest to provide a definition for each case separately. Thus:

```
M[mk-Boolinfixexpr(e1,op,e2)] ≜
  let v1 = M[e1] in
  let v2 = M[e2] in
  cases op:
    AND   → if v1 then v2 else false,
    OR    → if v1 then true else v2,
    IMPL  → if v1 then v2 else true,
    EQUIV → if v1 then v2 else (if v2 then false else true)
```

M[mk-Negation(e)] ≜ let v = M[e] in if v then false else true

The mapping for the constants is the identity. This actually shows that the objects contained in the expressions of Fig.3 are, in part, semantic objects. This could easily be avoided by choosing some syntactic representation for the semantic objects.

Looking at the definition of *M* it is clear that the semantics are built up over the structure of the syntax. This corresponds to a rule of the denotational method that the semantics of a compound construct should be derived (only) from the semantics of its components. It is perhaps this rule more than anything else which distinguishes between denotational and operational semantics. The point could be further emphasized by redefining:

M[mk-Boolinfixexpr(e1,op,e2)] ≜ M[op](M[e1],M[e2])

M[AND] ≜ λv1,v2.(if v1 then v2 else false)

etc. Notice that, although *M* is defined recursively, there is no need to introduce domains (cf. chapter 3): since no fixed-points are taken; a set of defined values is adequate to define the denotations.

Fig.3 contains an *abstract syntax*. This term is used to distinguish it from the normal form of (concrete) syntax which is concerned with the strings of symbols of the language. The advantage of an abstract syntax is that it can provide a smaller class of objects which are more clearly structured as a basis for the semantic definition. Objects corresponding to an abstract syntax can often be represented in many ways by character strings. Although this becomes more apparent in languages with richer sets of abbreviations and defaults, the points can already be seen in the language of logical expressions. A Backus-Naur Form (BNF) definition would have to show the possibility of bracketing subexpressions as a way of defining priority of operators. The abstract syntax also makes it possible to avoid issues of representation; the BNF definition would have to choose a specific way of showing a negation. The correspondence between (concrete) strings and (abstract) trees is also part of the definition of the language. Although this book tends to focus on semantics, it is clear that both BNF and the concrete/abstract relationship are part of a full definition of a system.

Expressions in programs are not usually restricted to constants and operators. It is normal to have some form of reference to variables. Thus the definition of *Boolexpr* might be extended with:

Boolexpr = ... | *Varref*
Varref :: *Id*

It is clear that an expression of this extended language does not denote a simple Boolean value. What is denoted will depend, in general, on the values of the various variables. A first step in choosing the denotations is to recognize the concept of a store which associates identifiers with values. Using a mapping, this can be written as:

$STORE = Id \xrightarrow{m} Bool$

This leads naturally to the idea of a denotation which is a function from stores to values. Thus:

M: *Boolexpr* → (*STORE* → *Bool*)

M[*mk-Boolinfixexpr*(*e1*,*op*,*e2*)](σ) $\underline{\Delta}$
  <u>*let*</u> *v1* = *M*[*e1*](σ) <u>*in*</u>
  <u>*let*</u> *v2* = *M*[*e2*](σ) <u>*in*</u> *M*[*op*](*v1*,*v2*)

$M[mk\text{-}Negation(e)](\sigma) \triangleq \underline{let}\ v = M[e](\sigma)\ \underline{in}\ \underline{if}\ v\ \underline{then}\ \underline{false}\ \underline{else}\ \underline{true}$

$M[mk\text{-}Varref(id)](\sigma) \triangleq \sigma(id)$

(The problem of ensuring that the stores have values for all necessary variables is postponed until more realistic languages are considered.) Writing the store parameter everywhere can become tedious and it is necessary below to find a way of avoiding having to do so.

4.3 STORE CHANGES

The dependence of the value of an expression on the values of variables has been defined by using functions as denotations. The next step is to consider language constructs which change the store and here again functional denotations will be required. The assignment statement is the obvious way of changing the store. (In fact, the read/write nature of the von Neumann computer architecture has influenced much more than just programming languages. Operating systems and data management systems are built around the notion of a changeable store. Only the enthusiasts of a functional programming style resist this notion (e.g. [Burge 75a, Backus 78a, Henderson 80a]).)

The abstract syntax of assignment statements is defined by:

$Assign\ ::\ Id\ \ Expr$

The denotation of such statements is to be a store to store function:

$M\colon Assign \to (STORE \to STORE)$

$M[mk\text{-}Assign(id,e)](\sigma) \triangleq \underline{let}\ v = M[e](\sigma)\ \underline{in}\ \sigma + [id \mapsto v]$

It is interesting to notice how the different uses of identifiers are brought out by the definition. In the source language assignment:

```
x := x + 1
```

the occurrence of 'x' on the right hand side of the assignment denotes the value of the variable whereas the occurrence on the left denotes the "address" which has to be modified. This is seen by comparing the uses of the *id* in the semantic function for *Assign* and in that given above for *Varref*. The introduction of *locations* below will provide a mechanism for making the distinction between left and right values of variables more explicit.

The use of functional denotations is not only a natural result of the denotational method. It has the further advantage that the functions are familiar objects with known methods of manipulation. The task of defining the meaning of a sequence of assignments can be performed by using functional composition of the denotations of the individual assignments. Thus:

$$Ml: Assign^* \rightarrow (STORE \rightarrow STORE)$$

$$Ml[<>] \triangleq I_{STORE}$$
$$Ml[al] \triangleq Ml[\underline{tl}al] \circ M[\underline{hd}al]$$

Notice that the denotation of the empty list of statements is the identity function on stores. It would have been equivalent to write:

$Ml[<>](\sigma) = \sigma$ or: $Ml[<>] = \lambda\sigma.\sigma$

The denotation for a non-empty list is given by composition: composing two functions of type Store to Store gives a denotation of the correct type. Composition is a "combinator" which makes it possible to build up expressions without having to write all of the arguments. A tasteful choice of combinators will do much to aid the readability of definitions. Expanding the meaning of the functional composition used above, gives:

$$Ml[al](\sigma) = Ml[\underline{tl}al](M[\underline{hd}al](\sigma))$$

The need to do one thing followed by another is familiar from programming. If a (semicolon) combinator is defined:

$$f1;f2 = \lambda\sigma.(f2(f1(\sigma)))$$

then the definition can be restated as:

$$Ml[al] \triangleq M[\underline{hd}al];Ml[\underline{tl}al]$$

This is more natural for a programmer to read. There is no danger of circularity in the use of a combinator which might be the same as the (syntactic) symbol used in the language to be defined providing the combinators are themselves defined formally in terms of mathematical concepts.

It is also quite safe to define a *for* combinator which provides the obvious (static) expansion into a sequence of semicolon compositions. The definition of *Ml* can then be rewritten:

$$Ml[al] \triangleq \underline{for}\ i=1\ \underline{to}\ \underline{len}\,al\ \underline{do}\ M[al[i]]$$

Thus given:

$$M[x:=x+1] = \lambda\sigma.(\sigma + [x \mapsto \sigma(x)+1])$$
$$M[x:=x-2] = \lambda\sigma.(\sigma + [x \mapsto \sigma(x)-2])$$

then:

$$\begin{aligned}
&Ml[x:=x+1;x:=x-2;x:=x+1] \\
&\quad = M[x:=x+1];M[x:=x-2];M[x:=x+1] \\
&\quad = \lambda\sigma.(M[x:=x+1](\lambda\sigma'.M[x:=x-2](M[x:=x+1](\sigma')))(\sigma) \\
&\quad = \lambda\sigma.M[x:=x+1](M[x:=x-2](M[x:=x+1](\sigma))) \\
&\quad = \lambda\sigma.M[x:=x+1](M[x:=x-2](\sigma + [x \mapsto \sigma(x)+1])) \\
&\quad = \lambda\sigma.M[x:=x+1](\sigma + [x \mapsto \sigma(x)+1-2]) \\
&\quad = \lambda\sigma.\sigma + [x \mapsto \sigma(x)-1+1] \\
&\quad = \lambda\sigma.\sigma \\
&\quad = I_{STORE}
\end{aligned}$$

The need for another combinator becomes apparent if the expression language is entended to permit function invocation. It should be clear that the possibility of side effects in such a language complicates the denotations of expressions. In general the evaluation of an expression yields both a changed store and a value. Thus, for such a language:

$$M\colon Expr \to (STORE \to STORE \times Bool)$$

Without combinators, it would be necessary to write:

$$\begin{aligned}
&M[mk\text{-}Assign(id,e)](\sigma) \triangleq \\
&\quad \underline{let}\ (\sigma',v) = M[e](\sigma)\ \underline{in} \\
&\quad \sigma' + [id \mapsto v]
\end{aligned}$$

M[mk-Boolinfixexpr(e1,op,e2)](σ) $\triangleq$
    <u>*let*</u> *(σ',v1) = M[e1](σ)* <u>*in*</u>
    <u>*let*</u> *(σ",v2) = M[e2](σ')* <u>*in*</u> *(σ",M[op](v1,v2))*

A <u>*def*</u> combinator can, however, be defined:

(<u>*def*</u> *v: f1; f2(...v...)) = λσ.(*<u>*let*</u> *(σ',v) = f1(σ)* <u>*in*</u> *f2(...v...)(σ'))*

Using this combinator the definitions can be written:

M[mk-Assign(id,e)] $\triangleq$ <u>*def*</u> *v: M[e]; assign(id,v)*

assign(id,v)(σ) $\triangleq$ *σ + [id ↦ v]*

M[mk-Boolinfixexpr(e1,op,e2)] $\triangleq$
    <u>*def*</u> *v1: M[e1];*
    <u>*def*</u> *v2: M[e2];*
    <u>*return*</u>*(M[op](v1,v2))*

The *return* combinator elevates a pure value to an object of appropriate type:

<u>*return*</u>*(v) = λσ.(σ,v)*

It should be noted in passing that the definitions given for expressions define the order of evaluation of sub-expressions.

4.4 COMPOSITE STATEMENTS

The sequential composition discussed above is the simplest of the techniques provided in most programming languages for building composite statements. Only slightly more complicated is the conditional statement. The abstract syntax might be written:

If :: Expr Stmt Stmt

The semantics which are to be defined are firstly to evaluate the expression to a Boolean value and then to use the function corresponding to the denotation of the appropriate statement. Given a value *v∈BOOL* a combinator can be defined:

$$\underline{if}\ v\ \underline{then}\ f1\ \underline{else}\ f2 = \lambda\sigma.(\underline{if}\ v\ \underline{then}\ f1(\sigma)\ \underline{else}\ f2(\sigma))$$

This combinator combines two functions from stores to stores to yield a function of the same type. The semantics of the conditional construct in the language can then be defined:

$$M[mk\text{-}If(e,th,el)] \triangleq \underline{def}\ v\colon M[e];\ \underline{if}\ v\ \underline{then}\ M[th]\ \underline{else}\ M[el]$$

(The reader should try expanding the combinator definitions and check that the resulting semantics of the conditional is a function from stores to stores.) Once again a combinator ($\underline{if}$) has been used which is similar to a construct of the language to be defined. The use with a value rather than an expression was simpler than the feature being defined and the same combinator is now used to define a more involved construct.

One iterative construct found in programming languages is the "while statement". Its syntax is:

$$While :: Expr\ Stmt$$

Its semantics can be given by:

$$M[mk\text{-}While(e,s)] \triangleq$$
$$\underline{let}\ L = (\underline{def}\ v\colon M[e];\ \underline{if}\ v\ \underline{then}\ (M[s];L)\ \underline{else}\ I_{STORE})\ \underline{in}\ L$$

The definition of L is recursive. Assuming L to be of the appropriate type one might write:

$M[e]$:	$STORE \to STORE \times Bool$
$M[s]$:	$STORE \to STORE$
$(M[s];L)$:	$STORE \to STORE$
I_{STORE}	$STORE \to STORE$
$(\underline{def}\ v\colon M[e];$ $\underline{if}\ v\ \underline{then}\ (M[s];L)\ \underline{else}\ I_{STORE})$:	$STORE \to STORE$

The recursion in the definition of L is exactly the sort which has been explained in chapter 3: it is here that the denotations must be domains. The definition of L denotes the least fixed point of the recursive equation. There is, however, a factor to be considered which has not occurred above. Such functions will only be partial. To see this it is only necessary to ask what denotation to associate with a loop which (for some starting stores) fails to terminate. Thus the type of the semantic function for the iterative construct is:

M: While → *(STORE* $\xrightarrow{\sim}$ *STORE)*

The syntactic definitions given above permit arbitrary nesting of the composite statements. Thus the syntax rule for statement is:

Stmt = *If* | *While* | *Assign*

A consequence of this is that the partial nature of the denotations inherit, so that:

M: Stmt → *(STORE* $\xrightarrow{\sim}$ *STORE)*

4.5 SCOPE

Block-structured programming languages employ the notion of the scope of a variable. Many other systems have ways of binding different values to names at different times so the way of handling scope is of general interest. Furthermore, the need to restrict the class of objects to be defined, which is handled here by "context conditions", occurs in nearly all definitions.

Suppose that the programs of some language fit the following abstract syntax:

Program	::	*Stmt*
Stmt	=	*Block* | *Call* | *Assign*
Block	::	*s-vars:Id-set* *s-procm:(Id* $\xrightarrow{m}$ *Proc)* *s-body:Stmt**
Proc	::	*s-parml:Id** *s-body:Stmt*
Call	::	*s-proc:Id* *s-argl:Varref**
Assign	::	*Varref* *Boolexpr*
Varref	::	*Id*
Boolexpr	=	*Boolinfixexpr* | *Rhsref* | *Boolconst*
Rhsref	::	*Varref*

The language still has only one type of variable (say Boolean), but variables are now either declared in the *s-vars* part of a block or are names of parameters within procedures. The statements which comprise the bodies of blocks or procedures should use only identifiers which have been declared. It is well-known that context-free syntax rules cannot capture such constraints. The abstract syntax definition is essentially context-free and some way of defining which programs are valid is required. One possibility is to insert suitable tests into the definition of the semantic functions. Since this would lengthen that part of a definition which is anyway long, this proposal is rejected. Instead the class of objects of interest will be restricted as a separate task. Rather than adopt one of the exotic syntax schemes like two-level grammars (cf.[van Wijngaarden 75a]), the restriction is defined here by a predicate *(WF)*. Those objects which satisfy the "context conditions" are said to be "well-formed" or "valid".

The intent, then, is to define a predicate:

WF: Program → Bool

This is defined using a (recursive) sub-function:

WF: Stmt → Staticenv → Bool

The static environment is a mapping which contains information about declared names:

$$\begin{array}{lll} Staticenv & = & Id \underset{m}{\to} Attribute \\ Attribute & = & \underline{\mathrm{BOOL}} \mid Proctype \\ Proctype & :: & Nat0 \end{array}$$

With only one variable type, the context conditions are easy to define. In particular, the only information required about a procedure is the number of its arguments.

$$WF[mk\text{-}Program(s)] \ \underline{\underline{\Delta}}\ WF[s]([\,])$$

$$\begin{array}{l} WF[mk\text{-}Block(vars,procm,sl)](\rho)\ \underline{\underline{\Delta}} \\ \quad vars \cap \underline{dom}procm = \{\} \ \wedge \\ \quad (\forall p \in \underline{rng}procm)(WF[p](\rho)) \ \wedge \\ \quad (\underline{let}\ \rho' = \rho + (\ [id \mapsto \underline{\mathrm{BOOL}} \mid id \in vars] \ \cup \\ \qquad\qquad\qquad [id \mapsto ATTR[procm(id)] \mid id \in \underline{dom}procm]\ )\ \underline{in} \\ \quad (\forall s \in \underline{elems}sl)(WF[s](\rho'))) \end{array}$$

WF[mk-Proc(pl,b)](ρ) $\triangleq$
(∀i,j∈<u>inds</u>pl)(pl[i]=pl[j]⊃i=j)∧
(WF[b](ρ+[pl[i] ↦ <u>BOOL</u> | i∈<u>inds</u>pl]))

ATTR[mk-Proc(pl,b)] $\triangleq$ *mk-Proctype(<u>len</u>pl)*

WF[mk-Call(pid,al)](ρ) $\triangleq$
pid∈<u>dom</u>ρ ∧ ρ(pid)∈Proctype ∧
(<u>let</u> mk-Proctype(n) = ρ(pid) <u>in</u> <u>len</u>al=n)

(These context conditions prohibit recursion - this restriction is removed below.)

In practice, some of the rules can be mechanically generated and need not be written out. For example, there is no need to write that the wellformedness of the assignment statement depends (with the same environment) on that of the variable reference and expression. This leaves, then, only:

WF[mk-Varref(id)](ρ) $\triangleq$ *id∈<u>dom</u>ρ ∧ ρ(id)=<u>BOOL</u>*

It is now necessary to turn to the question of providing semantics for the well-formed programs of the language. So far the store has directly associated values with identifiers. But now it is possible to have programs like:

```
begin Boolean a,b,c;
      begin Boolean a; ... end;
      ...
      begin Boolean b; ... end
end
```

The scope rules ensure that not only do the two declarations of 'a' introduce different variables, but also that execution of the first inner block cannot affect the value of the outer variable named 'a'. In this case it would be possible to define the semantics in terms of the simple store by systematically changing identifiers in the program so as to avoid name clashes. This is, however, a patch and, as so often with patches, will not work in the general case. Consider the following program fragment in which parameters are assumed to be passed by reference (or location):

```
begin Boolean a;
      procedure p(x,y); x:=a+y;
         ... ;p(a,a); ...
end
```

Within the procedure 'p', all of the identifiers 'a', 'x', 'y' refer to the same entity. The necessary model introduces an abstraction of the machine address which the implementation would associate with the entity. This abstraction is called here a (scalar) location. The problem of having different uses of the same identifier can now be solved by associating different locations with the identifier at different times. Sharing can be defined by associating different identifiers with the same location as in fig. 4. The association between identifiers and locations is recorded in an environment and *STORE* now associates values with locations:

$$ENV = Id \xrightarrow{m} SCALARLOC$$
$$STORE = SCALARLOC \xrightarrow{m} Bool$$

It is now necessary to decide how the environment is to be handled in semantics. Placing it in the store causes a number of problems and it serves the purposes of the definition far better to treat the environment as a parameter used in determining the (store to store) denotation. Thus:

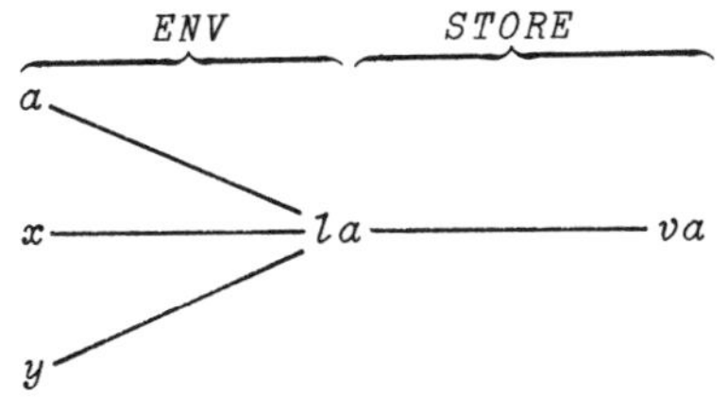

Fig. 4: The Use of Locations

$$M : Stmt \rightarrow ENV \rightarrow STORE \xrightarrow{\sim} STORE$$
$$ENV = Id \xrightarrow{m} DEN$$
$$DEN = SCALARLOC \mid \ldots$$
$$STORE = SCALARLOC \xrightarrow{m} [Bool]$$

The semantic functions can now distinguish clearly between the places where a left hand denotation (i.e. location) and a right hand denotation (i.e. value) are required.

$$M[mk\text{-}Assign(vr,e)](\rho) \triangleq \underline{def}\ l: Mloc[vr](\rho);$$
$$\underline{def}\ v: M[e](\rho);$$
$$assign(l,v))$$

$$Mloc: Varref \to ENV \to SCALARLOC$$
$$Mloc[mk\text{-}Varref(id)](\rho) \triangleq \rho(id)$$

$$assign(l,v) \triangleq \lambda\sigma.\sigma + [l \mapsto v]$$

The parts of the expression semantics all require the extra environment argument. The interesting case is:

$$M[mk\text{-}Rhsref(vr)](\rho) \triangleq \underline{def}\ l: Mloc[vr](\rho);\ contents(l)$$

$$contents(l) \triangleq \lambda\sigma.\sigma(l)$$

New locations must be associated with all declared identifiers in a block. Locations are considered to be new if they are not in the domain of the store. Given this technique it is necessary for the *newloc* function to reserve an identifier even before it is assigned a value. This is achieved by associating the identifier with the *nil* object. Subsequent development of an implementation (cf. chapter 8) has to show that some particular way of choosing locations satisfies the specification being constructed here. For this reason the constraints on, among other things, locations should be minimized. The set *SCALARLOC* is an arbitrary infinite set of objects. The function *newloc* chooses an arbitrary free location. In order to show that a stack implementation is possible (but not to prescribe it) all locations corresponding to local variables should be deleted from the store after the block semantics have been determined. Thus:

$$M[mk\text{-}Block(vars,procm,sl)](\rho) \triangleq$$
$$\underline{def}\ \rho' : \rho + (\ [id \mapsto newloc() \mid id \in vars] \cup$$
$$[id \mapsto \ldots \mid id \in \underline{dom}procm]\ );$$
$$\underline{for}\ i=1\ \underline{to}\ \underline{len}sl\ \underline{do}\ M[sl[i]](\rho');$$
$$epilogue(\underline{rng}(\rho' | vars))$$

$$newloc()(\sigma)=(\sigma',l) \supset \neg(l \in \underline{dom}\sigma) \wedge \sigma'=\sigma \cup [l \mapsto \underline{nil}]$$

$epilogue(ls) = \lambda\sigma.\sigma \backslash ls$

The environment is a map (i.e. a restricted function). Chapter 3 shows that passing such maps as arguments to semantic functions is quite safe. This provides the basis of the definition method. It may, however, be useful to give a less mathematical view of environments before turning to the subject of procedures. The *for* combinator can be viewed as a technique for defining a static or macro-expansion of the text. Essentially it provides a way of generating an expression with semicolon combinators which one would naturally associate with a program containing a sequence of statements. The environment can be viewed in a similar way. Consider the following expansion:

```
M[begin integer a,b; a:=a+b end]([])
  = def la: newloc();
    def lb: newloc();
    M[a:=a+b]([a ↦ la, b ↦lb]);
    epilogue({la,lb})

  = def la: ... ;          def lb: ... ;
    def va: contents(la); def vb: contents(lb);
    assign(la,(va+vb));
    epilogue ...
```

The environment argument has been completely eliminated in the expansion. The final expression is the one which one might write down for the program in giving an informal explanation. The role of the environment is to avoid the problem of naming the locations for an unknown number of new identifiers.

The ellipsis points relating to procedures in the semantics for *Blocks* should now be replaced. It is clear that, to agree with what has been done above, the meaning of a call statement must be:

$M: Call \to ENV \to STORE \xrightarrow{\sim} STORE$

A procedure denotation must be generated, and recorded in the environment, which makes the derivation of the call statement semantics possible. It would be a mistake to store the text of the procedure because of the choice of most programming languages to bind names to the textual (or static) environment. Thus in:

```
begin Boolean a;
     procedure p ... a ... ;
     ...
     begin integer a; ... p ...  end; ...
 end
```

the invocation of 'p' from the inner block must give rise to a reference to the Boolean variable 'a'. In order to bind the identifiers in the text of the procedure to the appropriate locations, the procedure denotation is made into a function as follows:

$$DEN = \ldots \mid PROCDEN$$
$$PROCDEN = SCALARLOC^{*} \to STORE \xrightarrow{\sim} STORE$$

The outer argument to this function is a list of locations. Thus it can be seen that parameter passing is to be by location (or reference). This gives rise to:

$$\begin{array}{l} M[mk\text{-}Call(pid,al)](\rho) \triangleq \\ \quad \underline{let}\ f = \rho(pid)\ \underline{in} \\ \quad \underline{let}\ locl = \langle Mloc[al[i]](\rho) \mid i \in \underline{inds}\,al \rangle\ \underline{in}\ f(locl) \end{array}$$

Procedure denotations are to be functional and their generation can be defined by:

$$\begin{array}{l} M[mk\text{-}Proc(pl,s)](\rho) \triangleq \\ \quad \underline{let}\ f(locl) = (\underline{let}\ \rho' = \rho + [pl[i] \mapsto locl[i] \mid i \in \underline{inds}\,pl]\ \underline{in} \\ \qquad\qquad M[s](\rho'))\ \underline{in} \\ \quad f \end{array}$$

This function is used in defining the denotation of a block:

$$\underline{def}\ \rho' : \rho + (\ \ldots \cup [id \mapsto M[procm(id)](\rho) \mid id \in \underline{dom}\,procm]\ )$$

It should, by now, be clear that the use of an abstract syntax is simplifying the definition by avoiding representation details of a language. When faced with a large language or system, there is considerable scope for choice in "how abstract" the syntax should be. Clearly, minor syntactic variants (e.g. abbreviations or default values) should be subsumed. It is also obvious that constructs with different semantics cannot have the same abstract representation. These extremes do not, however, provide a clear rule for deciding when to abstract (e.g. the problem of factored declarations in Pascal).

4.6 RECURSIVE PROCEDURES

The definition of recursive procedures requires no new features in the meta-language but it does warrant some words of explanation. The context condition given above for blocks explicitly prohibits the direct call by a procedure of itself. All that is necessary to permit such calls, or to admit mutual recursion among procedures, is to use the intended environment in checking the well-formedness of procedures. Thus:

```
WF[mk-Block(vars,procm,sl)](ρ) ≜
   vars ∩ domprocm = {}  ∧
   (let ρ' = ρ + ([id ↦ BOOL            | id∈vars]      ∪
                  [id ↦ ATTR(procm(id)) | id∈domprocm] ) in
      (∀p∈rngprocm)(WF[p](ρ')) ∧
      (∀s∈elemssl)(WF[s](ρ')))
```

A similar change will suffice to extend the semantic equations so that the recursive case is covered:

```
M[mk-Block(vars,procm,sl)](ρ) ≜
   def ρ' : ρ + ([id ↦ newloc())          | id∈vars]     ∪
                 [id ↦ M[procm(id)](ρ') | id∈domprocm] );
   ...
```

But this recursive use of the extended environment (in creating the extended environment) requires some comment. Mathematically, there is no difficulty: chapter 3 explains how the least fixed point of recursive equations can be found and the ordering on functions can be used to define one on environments. In programming terms, it is also easy to accept that the denotations will be available by the time they are called. It is, however, possible to provide another explanation using the macro-expansion view discussed above. Consider:

```
M[begin procedure p1;...p2...;
        procedure p2;...p1...p2...;
   ...p1... end]([])
```

```
= let ρ' = [p1 ↦ M[...p2...](ρ'),
            p2 ↦ M[...p1...p2...](ρ') ] in
  M[...p1...](ρ')
```

If names are introduced to stand in place of the procedure denotations this becomes:

```
let pden1 = ... pden2 ...              in
let pden2 = ... pden1 ... pden2 ...    in
... pden1 ...
```

The environment has been eliminated and has thus removed the recursion which was causing concern. There remains a recursion on the (names of) procedure denotations but this is the recursion on functions from stores to stores which has occurred elsewhere. The environment can therefore be viewed as a part of the process of expanding a program into an (expression for the) denotation of a program.

4.7 EXCEPTIONS

There are a number of concepts in systems which permit the definition of exceptional sequencing: the '<u>goto</u>' statement in languages, exception traps or error handlers in both languages and other systems and the definition of the effect of some errors. There is often heated controversy about the wisdom of such features. It is not the intention here to enter into such debates. Providing a definition method is capable of defining such features, it becomes a tool with which one can compare alternative approaches. The purpose here is to show how the denotational approach can define various forms of '<u>goto</u>' statements. Other chapters in this book apply the same model to other exception handling problems. It is possible to envisage '<u>goto</u>' statements of varying degrees of generality and the implications on the definition are studied here. The simplest form serves to introduce the general idea. A program might restrict its use of '<u>goto</u>' statements to defining the flow of control within a single phrase structure. Thus:

```
begin st1; lab1:st2; st3; goto lab2; st4; lab2:goto lab1 end
```

An abstract syntax which covers this case is:

Program :: *Namedstmt**
Namedstmt :: *s-lab*:[*Id*] *s-body*:*Stmt*
Stmt = ... | *Goto*
Goto :: *Id*

It is clear that some space of denotations is required for named statements, but what is this to be? The meaning of a simple named statement might be given by:

M: *Namedstmt* → ?

However, the denotational approach requires that the denotation of a list of such statements be derived (only) from their individual denotations. The problem is that it is precisely the fact that a "goto" statement appoints a successor (which is not a component) that has to be captured as its semantics. There are two ways of providing a denotational definition: *exit*s and continuations. These approaches are compared in the next chapter, here the *exit* approach is described. The basis of the *exit* approach is to extend the transformations, which are used as denotations, so that they can carry an indication of abnormal termination. Thus:

$$TR = STORE \xrightarrow{\sim} STORE \times [ABNORMAL]$$

The effect is to elevate the abnormal sequencing to something which is anticipated; the cost is that denotations become more difficult to compose but combinators are provided below which ameliorate this problem. The second component of the range of a transformation is *nil* in the case of normal return; but will contain some indication of what is to be done next in the abnormal case. The choice of the *ABNORMAL* values depends on the system being defined. For the current language it will be sufficient to use the labels themselves. Thus:

$$TR = STORE \xrightarrow{\sim} STORE \times [Id]$$

The meaning of a 'goto' statement can be given by:

$$M[mk\text{-}Goto(id)] \;\underline{\underline{\Delta}}\; \lambda\sigma.(\sigma, id)$$

The meaning of a 'goto' statement is to leave the store unchanged but to appoint an explicit successor. The meaning of, for example, an assignment statement is to change the store and to signal normal return:

$M[mk\text{-}Assign(vr,e)] \triangleq$
$\quad \lambda\sigma.(\underline{let}\ l = Mloc[vr]\sigma\ \underline{in}$
$\quad\quad \underline{let}\ v = M[e]\sigma\ \underline{in}$
$\quad\quad assign(l,v)(\sigma),\underline{nil})$

The next problem to be resolved is the combination of two transformations to yield another of the same type. If the first transformation yields a *nil* abnormal component, then the second transformation is to be composed with the store to store part of the first. Alternatively, if the first transformation yields an abnormal return, this must be propagated. Thus, formally:

$Ml\colon Namedstmt^{*} \rightarrow TR$
$Ml[\langle\rangle] \triangleq \lambda\sigma.(\sigma,\underline{nil})$
$Ml[nsl] \triangleq (\lambda\sigma,a.\mathit{if}\ a{=}\underline{nil}\ \underline{then}\ Ml[\underline{tl}nsl](\sigma)\ \underline{else}\ (\sigma,a))\circ$
$\quad\quad M[s\text{-}body(\underline{hd}nsl)]$

For the program shown above:

$M[\text{st4}] = \lambda\sigma.(f(\sigma),\underline{nil})$
$M[\text{lab2:}\underline{\text{goto}}\ \text{lab1}] = \lambda\sigma.(\sigma,\text{lab1})$
$Ml[\text{st4;lab2:}\underline{\text{goto}}\ \text{lab1}] = \lambda\sigma.(f(\sigma),\text{lab1})$

etc. The final problem is to show how the abnormal return values are handled. The meaning of any label is the transformation determined by beginning execution at that label. If such a transformation ends with an abnormal exit, the meaning of another label must be composed with that transformation. Since 'goto' statements can be used to define loops, it is convenient to make this trap (see *r* below) recursive. Thus:

$M[mk\text{-}Program(nsl)] \triangleq$
$\quad \underline{let}\ \rho = [id \mapsto Ml[sel(id,nsl)] \mid id{\in}dlabs(nsl)]\ \underline{in}$
$\quad \underline{let}\ r = \lambda\sigma,a.\underline{if}\ a{\in}\underline{dom}\rho\ \underline{then}\ r(\rho(a)(\sigma))\ \underline{else}\ (\sigma,a)\ \underline{in}$
$\quad r\circ Ml[nsl]$

Where:

$dlabs(nsl) \triangleq \{id \mid (\exists i{\in}\underline{inds}nsl)(s\text{-}lab(nsl[i]){=}id \wedge id{\neq}\underline{nil})\}$

sel(id,nsl) selects the subsequence of *nsl* whose first statement is labelled with *id*.

(It has been assumed here that context conditions have established that each label occurs as the name of at most one statement and that 'goto' statements refer only to valid labels.) It is interesting to note that the recursion in r can again be eliminated by macro expansion. The above definition is the one required but it is clouded by the explicit mention of stores etc. A group of combinators can be defined which greatly ease the task of understanding a definition. Thus:

$$\underline{exit}\ a = \lambda\sigma.(\sigma,a)$$

An object, say t, of type $STORE$ to $STORE$ is automatically interpreted as a transformation if required by context:

$$t = \lambda\sigma.(t(\sigma),\underline{nil})$$

The 'semicolon' combinator is redefined to give the semantics used above:

$$t1;t2 = (\lambda\sigma,a.\underline{if}\ a{=}\underline{nil}\ \underline{then}\ t2(\sigma)\ \underline{else}\ (\sigma,a))^\circ t1$$

The "trapping" effect is achieved by the $\underline{tixe}$ ($\underline{exit}$ backwards) combinator:

$$\begin{aligned}(\underline{tixe}\ m\ \underline{in}\ t) \ \underline{\Delta}\ & \underline{let}\ \rho = m\ \underline{in} \\ & \underline{let}\ r = (\lambda\sigma,a.\ \underline{if}\ a\in\underline{dom}\rho\ \underline{then}\ r(\rho(a)(\sigma)) \\ & \qquad\qquad\qquad\qquad \underline{else}\ (\sigma,a)) \quad \underline{in} \\ & r^\circ t\end{aligned}$$

The use of these combinators permits the earlier definition to be rewritten as:

$$\begin{aligned}& M[mk\text{-}Program(nsl)]\ \underline{\Delta} \\ & \quad \underline{tixe}\ [id \mapsto Ml[sel(id,nsl)]\ |\ id\in dlabs(nsl)]\ \underline{in}\ Ml[nsl]\end{aligned}$$

$$Ml[<>] \quad \underline{\Delta}\ I_{STORE}$$

$$Ml[nsl] \quad \underline{\Delta}\ M[s\text{-}body(\underline{hd}nsl)];Ml[\underline{tl}nsl]$$

$$M[mk\text{-}Goto(id)] \quad \underline{\Delta}\ \underline{exit}(id)$$

Thus, the semantics of the example given at the beginning of this section is:

```
tixe [lab1 ↦ Ml[<st2,st3,goto lab2,st4,goto lab1>],
     lab2 ↦ Ml[<goto lab1>]] in
Ml[<st1,st2,st3,goto lab2,st4,goto lab1>]
```

Little change is required to define a language in which 'goto' statements can leave (and thus close) static phrase structures. Thus with:

```
Block :: .... s-body:Namedstmt*
```

it is only necessary to ensure that the epilogue semantics are performed even on abnormal block termination. Thus for:

```
begin ...
   begin ... goto lab ... end;
   ... lab: ...; ...
end
```

```
M[mk-Block(vars,procm,nsl)](ρ) ≜
    def ρ' : ... ;
    (λσ,a.(epilogue(...)(σ),a))∘
        (tixe [id ↦ Ml[sel(id,nsl)](ρ') | id∈dlabs(nsl)] in
         Ml[nsl](ρ'))
```

Again a combinator can be defined:

```
always t1 in t2 = (λσ,a.(t1(σ),a))∘t2
```

The *always* combinator can then be used to give:

```
M[mk-Block(vars,procm,nsl)](ρ) ≜
    def ρ' : ... ;
    always epilogue(...)                                    in
    (tixe [id ↦ Ml[sel(id,nsl)](ρ') | id∈dlabs(nsl)]  in
     Ml[nsl](ρ'))
```

Some languages permit 'goto' statements to branch into a phrase structure. Thus, in ALGOL 60:

```
begin goto lab; ... ;if p then lab:st1 else st2; ... end
```

is valid. The CPL language [Barron 63a] even allowed 'goto' statements into loops and blocks. The definition of such a language can use the same transformations but must define *cue* functions which determine the appropriate starting point. *Cue* functions occur in the next chapter and their use in ALGOL 60 is shown in Chapter 6.

Languages in which "goto" statements can terminate dynamic objects like procedures present a further complication. Consider:

```
begin procedure p; ...  goto lab; ... ;
          ...
          lab:...; ...
          call p; ...
end
```

The dynamic invocation of 'p' can be closed by the 'goto' statement. There are two problems which are closely akin to those treated above with variables. Firstly there might be other instances of the same label occurring in the environment of the call of 'p' - ALGOL 60 requires the "goto" to ignore such labels in the dynamic environment and to locate that instance of 'lab' in the static (textual) environment of 'p'. This problem might be resolved by making static changes to identifiers to make them unique. This solution would, however, not work for a language in which procedures can be passed as parameters across recursive calls. In this case it is necessary to have a precise indication of the activation in question. In the case of variables, new locations are chosen with respect to the domain of the store. For labels, a new set of *Activation identifiers* is introduced and appended to label denotations. These *Label denotations* are stored in the environment. Thus the definition might be written:

Block	::	... *s-procm:(Id* $\underset{m}{\rightarrow}$ *Proc)* *s-body:Namedstmt**
TR	=	*STORE* $\overset{\sim}{\rightarrow}$ *STORE* × [*LABDEN*]
LABDEN	::	*AID Id*
AID		An infinite set
ENV	=	*Id* $\underset{m}{\rightarrow}$ *DEN*
DEN	=	... | *PROC* | *LABDEN*
PROCDEN	=	*SCALARLOC** × *AID-set* → *TR*

M: Block → *ENV* → *AID-set* → *TR*

```
M[mk-Block(...,procm,nsl)](ρ)(cas) ≜
   let aid∈(AID-cas)                                              in
   def ρ' : ρ + (...∪
              [id ↦ mk-LABDEN(aid,id) | id∈dlabs(nsl)] );
   always epilogue(...)                                           in
   (tixe ...                                                      in
    Ml[nsl](ρ')(cas ∪ {aid}))

M[mk-Goto(id)](ρ)(cas) ≜ exit(ρ(id))
```

The set *(cas)* of current activation identifiers must be passed along the dynamic calling sequence and a convenient way of doing this is shown below.

It is possible to prove useful results about such a definition. The most important such theorem shows that, for well-formed programs with '<u>goto</u>' statements referring only to statically known labels, there is no way that a (dynamic) jump can lead to an inactive or closed piece of text. This is true of ALGOL 60 even with procedures and labels being allowed as parameters. Even the '<u>switch</u>' declaration is so constrained as to preserve the property. This important property is, however, lost as soon as (unconstrained) label or procedure variables are allowed. ALGOL 68 [van Wijngaarden 75a] manages to keep the lid on this Pandora's box by syntactic rules. PL/I [ECMA 76a] is less inhibited. The need to define which such uses are in error, gives rise in [Bekić 74a] to a new entity which keeps track of the active activations.

As mentioned above, there are other aspects of systems which can be conveniently defined using *exit*s. The most prevalent class of such features is error handling. Three types of errors must be distinguished:

(i) for some system, it might be required that certain diagnostics are to be produced by any implementation, such error handling becomes part of the system definition like any other feature.

(ii) for many systems which are to be implemented more than once, there are some user errors for which it is thought unwise to constrain the implementation treatment (for example referencing uninitialized variables in a programming language).

(iii) any misuse of the meta-language which makes the definition meaningless (for example mismatch of arguments and parameters to semantic functions) must clearly be avoided.

It is the second category of error which remains to be discussed. The definition must show that certain use leads to an error but leaves open what action follows the error. Some implementations may check and produce a useful diagnostic; others may omit the necessary checking code and just run on after the error. The definition is essentially stating further constraints on the domain of valid inputs but, unlike context conditions, invalidity is in general only detectable dynamically. The error situations where further computation is undefined are indicated in the definition by writing:

error

The semantics being the same as:

exit(*error*)

with the additional rule that no *tixe* can trap such an exit value. Examples of the use of *error* occur below in the handling of input, reference to variables and evaluation of subscripts. It might be argued that the presence of features which result in undetected errors makes a system dangerous to use. Once again, no position is taken on this (pragmatic) issue here: the definition method provides a way of indicating and checking for such "features".

4.8 STORAGE MODEL

In the *STORE* above, only one type of variable has been considered; furthermore only scalar variables are allowed. Some modest extensions can now be considered. The syntax of a block can be extended to permit declarations of different types of variable:

Block :: *s-dclm*:(*Id* $\underset{m}{\to}$ *Scalartype*)...
Scalartype = INT | BOOL

Clearly the range of store must be extended to permit the storage of appropriate values. Thus:

STORE = *SCALARLOC* $\underset{m}{\to}$ [*SCALARVALUE*]
SCALARLOC = Infinite Set
SCALARVALUE = *Bool* | *Int*

The environment is also suitably extended. If variables of either type are to be passed (by location) as parameters, type checking must be included. Different languages vary as to whether this checking can be done statically or dynamically. A dangerous lacuna can result from passing procedures as parameters: ALGOL 60 loses type control; Pascal retains it but introduces a restriction; ALGOL 68 erects a whole structure of types in order to give a complete solution.

The other extension of the storage model to be considered here is the treatment of arrays. The syntactic extension is:

Block :: *s-dclm*:(*Id* $\underset{m}{\to}$ *Type*) ...
Type :: *Scalartype* [*Expr*$^+$]

A non-*nil* subscript list defines the dimensions of an array. A *nil* subscript list being used to indicate scalar variables. A check must be made on block entry to establish that all expressions evaluate to positive integers. What is to be done with *STORE*? This depends on other language features. If arrays are always handled as a unit, the structure of the array value can be made part of store:

STORE = *LOC* $\underset{m}{\to}$ *VALUE*
VALUE = *SCALARVALUE* | *ARRAYVALUE*
ARRAYVALUE = *Int*$^+$ $\underset{m}{\to}$ [*SCALARVALUE*]

Alternatively, if elements of arrays are to be passed (by location) as arguments to procedures, then locations themselves must become structured objects. Thus:

STORE = *SCALARLOC* $\underset{m}{\to}$ [*SCALARVALUE*]
ENV = *Id* $\underset{m}{\to}$ *DEN*
DEN = *ARRAYLOC* | *SCALARLOC*
ARRAYLOC = *Int*$^+$ $\underset{m}{\leftrightarrow}$ *SCALARLOC*

(Notice that members of *ARRAYLOC* are one-one mappings.) This is the combination of features defined below. Dynamic checking of array bounds is also indicated.

The treatment of records is similar to arrays (cf. chapter 7). Some languages require more basic extensions. In particular, some of the PL/I features need an implicit characterization of locations (see [Bekić 71b, 74a]).

4.9 STATES

The transformations considered above have been concerned only with *STORE*. The main criteria for choosing to place entities in the domain and range of transformations is that they can be both read and written. It is for this reason that the environment is treated separately. Certain language features prompt the need for further state components and these are handled by using structured objects (*STATE*) in the domain and range of transformations.

One language area requiring more state components is input/output statements. Suppose the language includes the notion of one input (read only) and one output (write only) "file". If the only values which can be handled by input/output are integers the state becomes:

$$\mathit{STATE} \;::\; \mathrm{STR}{:}\mathit{STORE} \quad \mathrm{IN}{:}\mathit{Int}^* \quad \mathrm{OUT}{:}\mathit{Int}^*$$
$$\mathit{TR} \;=\; \mathit{STATE} \xrightarrow{\sim} \mathit{STATE} \times [\mathit{LABDEN}]$$

Creation of an initial state and disposal of the final state is illustrated below. The final combinators to be given here provide clearer reference to components of the state. Thus:

$$\mathrm{IN} := e \;=\; \lambda\sigma.\mathit{mk\text{-}STATE}(\mathrm{STR}(\sigma), e, \mathrm{OUT}(\sigma))$$
$$\underline{c}\ \mathrm{IN} \;=\; \lambda\sigma.\mathrm{IN}(\sigma)$$

then (using the syntax of the next section):

```
M[mk-In(vr)](ρ)  ≜
   if c IN=<> then error
   else (def v:  hd c IN;
         def l:  Mloc[vr](ρ);
         STR := c STR + [l ↦ v];
         IN  := tl c IN)
```

4.10 A DEFINITION

The definition of a small language illustrating all of the points made in this chapter can now be given. The main static and dynamic semantic functions are split under the syntactic objects; auxiliary functions are collected at the end of the section.

Abbreviations

Names of sets are abbreviated as indicated in *italics:*

*Bool*ean	*op*erator
*Const*ant	*par*ameter
*decl*aration	*proc*edure
*den*otation	*ref*erence
*env*ironment	*r*ight *h*and *s*ide
*expr*ession	*st*atement
*id*entifier	*tr*ansformation
*int*eger	*var*iable
*loc*ation	

The following type clause abbreviations (~) are used:

$M: D =>$ ~ $M: D \rightarrow Tr$

$M: D => R$ ~ $M: D \rightarrow STATE \xrightarrow{\sim} (STATE \times [LABDEN] \times R)$

Static Environment

The validity of an abstract program with respect to context conditions is defined by the *WF* function. This function creates and uses a static environment which contains attribute information. This same *Staticenv* is used by the *TP* function which determines the types of expressions etc. (*Attr* is defined in the section on procedures below.)

$Staticenv = Id \underset{m}{\rightarrow} (Attr \mid \underline{LABEL} \mid Procattr)$

$Procattr :: Attr^*$

Certain obvious steps have been taken to shorten the *WF* functions given below. For example, if:

$Q :: Q_1\ Q_2\ \ldots\ Q_n$

then a rule (or part of a rule) of the form:

$$WF[mk\text{-}Q(Q_1, Q_2, \ldots, Q_n)](senv) \triangleq$$
$$WF[Q_1](senv) \wedge WF[Q_2](senv) \wedge \ldots \wedge WF[Q_n](senv)$$

is omitted.

Semantic Objects

The state for this simple language contains the values for the (scalar) locations, the set of activation identifiers in use and the input and output files:

```
STATE        :: STR:  STORE
                AIDS: AID-set
                IN:   Int*
                OUT:  Int*
STORE        =  SCALARLOC m→ [SCALARVALUE]
SCALARLOC       Infinite set
SCALARVALUE  =  Bool | Int
AID             Infinite set
```

The denotation of (local) identifiers are contained in an environment which is a parameter to the meaning function (M).

```
ENV       =  Id m→ DEN
DEN       =  LOC | LABDEN | PROCDEN
LOC       =  SCALARLOC | ARRAYLOC
ARRAYLOC  =  Nat+ m↔ SCALARLOC where al∈ARRAYLOC⊃(∃nl)(domal=rect(nl))
LABDEN    :: s-aid:AID  s-lab:Id
PROCDEN   =  LOC* → TR
```

Transformations reflect possible abnormal termination:

$$TR = STATE \xrightarrow{\sim} STATE \times [LABDEN]$$

Programs

Program :: Stmt

```
WF[mk-Program(s)] ≜ WF[s]([])
type: Program → Bool
```

comment the empty environment passed to the context condition for statements reflects the fact that there are no (global) variables.

```
M[mk-Program(s)](inl) ≜
    let state0 = mk-STATE([],{},inl,<>)  in
    OUT(M[s]([])(state0))
type: Program → Int* → Int*
```

comment the only result of executing a program is its output list of values - the state transition is purely local.

Statements

```
Stmt = Block | If | While | Call | Goto |
        Assign | In | Out | NULL
```

Within this section the following types are to be assumed unless otherwise stated.

```
WF: Stmt → Staticenv → Bool
M:  Stmt → ENV → TR

Block :: s-dclm:Id ⇀m Dcl s-procm:Id ⇀m Proc s-body:Namedstmt*

WF[mk-Block(dclm,procm,nsl)](senv) ≜
   let labl = contndll(nsl)  in
   is-uniquel(labl) ∧
   is-disjointl(<elemslabl,domprocm,domdclm>) ∧
   (let lenv = [id ↦ ATTR[dclm(id)]   | id∈domdclm] ∪
               [id ↦ ATTR[procm(id)]  | id∈domprocm] ∪
               [id ↦ LABEL            | id∈elemslabl] in
    let renv = senv \ domlenv                          in
    let nenv = senv + lenv                             in
    (∀dcl∈rngdclm)(WF[dcl](renv))      ∧
    (∀proc∈rngprocm)(WF[proc](nenv))  ∧
    (∀ns∈elemsnsl)(WF[ns](nenv)))
```

comment *renv* is used for declarations because local variables should not be used in defining array bounds - use of *nenv* for procedures shows that (mutual) recursion is permitted in the language.

```
M[mk-Block(dclm,procm,nsl)](env) ≜
    def cas: c s-aids;
    let aid ∈ (AID - cas)  in
    s-aids := c s-aids ∪ {aid};
    def nenv: env +
        ([id ↦ M[dclm(id)](env)      | id∈domdclm]              ∪
         [id ↦ M[procm(id)](nenv)    | id∈domprocm]             ∪
         [id ↦ mk-LABDEN(aid,id)     | id∈elemscontndll(nsl)]);
    always epilogue(domdclm,aid)
    in (tixe [mk-LABDEN(aid,id) ↦ M[sel(id,nsl)](nenv)
                                | id∈elemscontndll(nsl)] in
        M[nsl](nenv))
```

note: declarations, procedures and *epilogue* are defined after the remaining statements.

```
Namedstmt :: s-nm:[Id] s-body:Stmt
```

```
M[nsl](env) ≜
    for i = 1 to lennsl do M[s-body(nsl[i])](env)
type: Namedstmt* → ENV =>
```

```
If :: s-test:Expr  s-th:Stmt  s-el:Stmt
```

comment the branches of the conditional cannot be labelled.

```
WF[mk-If(e,th,el)](senv) ≜ TP[e](senv) = mk-Scalarattr(BOOL)
```

```
M[mk-If(e,th,el)](env) ≜
    def b: M[e](env);
    if b then M[th](env) else M[el](env)
```

```
While :: s-test:Expr  s-body:Stmt
```

```
WF[mk-While(e,s)](senv) ≜ TP[e](senv)=mk-Scalarattr(BOOL)
```

```
M[mk-While(e,s)](env) ≜
   let wh=(def v:M[e](env); if v then M[s](env);wh else I_STATE)
   in wh
```

comment *wh* is defined recursively.

```
Call :: s-pn:Id  s-app:Varref*
```

```
WF[mk-Call(pid,apl)](senv) ≜
    pid∈domsenv ∧ senv(pid)∈Procattr ∧
    (let mk-Procattr(fpl) = senv(pid) in
     lenapl=lenfpl ∧ (∀i∈indsfpl)(TP[apl[i]](senv)=fpl(i)))
```

comment the actual parameters must match the formal parameter type

```
M[mk-Call(pid,apl)](env) ≜
   def locl: <M[apl(i)](env) | 1≤i≤lenapl>;
   let f = env(pid)  in
   f(locl)
```

comment creation of procedure denotations is shown in the handling of *Procedure* below.

```
Goto :: s-lab:Id
```

```
WF[mk-Goto(lab)](senv) ≜ lab∈domsenv ∧ senv(lab)=LABEL
```

```
M[mk-Goto(lab)](env)  ≜ exit (env(lab))
```

```
Assign :: s-lhs:Varref  s-rhs:Expr
```

```
WF[mk-Assign(lhs,rhs)](senv) ≜ TP[rhs](senv)=TP[lhs](senv)
```

```
M[mk-Assign(lhs,rhs)](env)  ≜  def loc :  M[lhs](env);
                               def v   :  M[rhs](env);
                               STR     := c STR + [loc ↦ v]
```

```
In :: s-var:Varref

WF[mk-In(vr)](senv) ≜ TP[vr](senv)=mk-Scalarattr(INT)

M[mk-In(vr)](env)   ≜  def inl: c IN;
                        if inl = <> then error
                        else (def loc :  M[vr](env);
                              IN      := tlinl;
                              STR     := c STR + [loc ↦ hdinl])

Out :: s-val:Expr

WF[mk-Out(e)](senv) ≜ TP[e](senv)=mk-Scalarattr(INT)

M[mk-Out(e)](env)   ≜  def v  :  M[e](env);
                        OUT   := c OUT^<v>

M[NULL](env)          ≜ I_STATE
```

Declarations

```
Dcl          =  Scalardcl | Arraydcl
Scalardcl   ::  Scalartype
Arraydcl    ::  s-sctp:Scalartype   s-bdl:Expr+
Scalartype  =   INT | BOOL

ATTR: Dcl → Attr

ATTR[mk-Scalardcl(sctp)]       ≜ mk-Scalarattr(sctp)

ATTR[mk-Arraydcl(sctp,bdl)] ≜ mk-Arrayattr(sctp,lenbdl)

WF[mk-Arraydcl(sctp,bdl)](senv) ≜
     (∀bd∈elemsbdl)(TP[bd](senv)=mk-Scalarattr(INT))
type: Arraydcl → Staticenv → Bool

M[mk-Scalardcl(sctp)](env) ≜  def ulocs : dom c STR;
                               let l∈(SCALARLOC - ulocs) in
                               STR := c STR ∪ [l ↦ nil];
                               return(l)
```

```
epilogue(ids,aid)(env) ≜
    let sclocs = {env(id) | id∈ids ∧ env(id)∈SCALARLOC} ∪
        union {rng(env(id)) | id∈ids ∧ env(id)∈ARRAYLOC}  in
    STR  := c STR \ sclocs;
    AIDS := c AIDS - {aid}

type: Id-set × AID → ENV → TR

M[mk-Arraydcl(sctp,bdl)](env) ≜
    def bdvl : <M[bdl(i)](env) | 1≤i≤lenbdl>;
    if (∃i∈indsbdvl)(bdvl(i)<1) then error
    else (def ulocs : dom c STR;
          let al∈ARRAYLOC be s.t. is-disjointl(<ulocs,rngal>) ∧
                                  domal = rect(bdvl)          in
          STR := c STR ∪ [scl ↦ nil | scl∈rngal];
          return(al))
type: Dcl → ENV => LOC
```

Procedures

```
Proc        :: s-fpl:Parm*  s-body:Stmt
Parm        :: s-nm:Id  s-attr:Attr
Attr        =  Scalarattr | Arrayattr
Scalarattr  :: Scalartype
Arrayattr   :: s-sctp:Scalartype  s-bdinf:Nat
```

```
ATTR[mk-Proc(fpl,s)] ≜
   mk-Procattr(<s-attr(fpl(i)) | 1≤i≤lenfpl>)
type: Proc → Procattr

WF[mk-Proc(fpl,s)](senv) ≜
   is-uniquel(<s-nm(fpl[i]) | 1≤i≤lenfpl>) ∧
   (let nenv=senv + [s-nm(fpl[i]) ↦ s-attr(fpl[i]) | i∈indsfpl] in
    WF(s)(nenv))

M[mk-Proc(pl,s)](env) ≜
   let f(al)=(let nenv = env + [s-nm(pl[i]) ↦ al[i] | i∈indspl] in
              M[s](nenv))
   in f
type: Proc → ENV → PROCDEN
```

comment note that it is the environment of the declaring block (static) which is used as the basis for *nenv*

Expressions

Expr = *Infixexpr* | *Rhsref* | *Const*

In this section functions, unless otherwise stated, are of types:

WF: Expr → Staticenv → Bool
TP: Expr → Staticenv → Attr
M: Expr → ENV => SCALARVALUE

Infixexpr :: Expr Op Expr

Op = *Intop* | *Boolop* | *Comparisonop*

WF[mk-Infixexpr(e1,op,e2)](senv) ≜
  op∈Intop ∧ *TP[e1](senv)=TP[e2](senv)=mk-Scalarattr(*INT*)* ∨
  op∈Boolop ∧ *TP[e1](senv)=TP[e2](senv)=mk-Scalarattr(*BOOL*)* ∨
  op∈Comparisonop ∧ *TP[e1](senv)=TP(e2)(senv)=mk-Scalarattr(*INT*)*

TP[mk-Infixexpr(e1,op,e2)](senv) ≜
  *if op∈Intop then mk-Scalarattr(*INT*) else mk-Scalarattr(*BOOL*)*

M[mk-Infixexpr(e1,op,e2)](env) ≜ *def v1 : M[e1](env);*
  def v2 : M[e2](env);
  return M[op](v1,v2)

M for the various operators yields their meaning:

M: Op → (SCALARVALUE × SCALARVALUE → SCALARVALUE)

Rhsref :: Varref
Varref :: s-nm:Id s-bdp:[Expr⁺]

WF[mk-Rhsref(vr)](senv) ≜ *TP[vr](senv)∈Scalarattr*

TP[mk-Rhsref(vr)](senv) ≜ *TP[vr](senv)*

```
WF[mk-Varref(id,bdp)](senv) ≜
    id∈dom senv ∧ senv(id)∈Attr ∧
    (bdp=nil ∧ senv(id)∈Scalarattr) ∨
    (senv(id)∈Arrayattr ∧
         (let mk-Arrayattr(sctp,dim) = senv(id) in
          len bdp = dim ∧
          (∀bd∈elems bdp)(TP[bd](senv)=mk-Scalarattr(INT)))))
type: Varref → Staticenv → Bool

TP[mk-Varref(id,bdp)](senv) ≜
    if senv(id)∈Scalarattr then senv(id)
    else if bdp≠nil then (let mk-Arrayattr(sctp,bdi) = senv(id) in
                              mk-Scalarattr(sctp))
         else senv(id)
type: Varref → Staticenv → Attr

M[mk-Rhsref(vr)](env) ≜ def loc: M[vr](env);
                        def v: (c STR)(loc);
                        if v=nil then error else return(v)
```

comment note how the location is evaluated by access to store because the right hand side contexts require values.

```
M[mk-Varref(id,bdp)](env) ≜
    if bdp=nil then return(env(id))
    else (let aloc = env(id) in
          def esscl: <M[bdp(i)](env) | 1≤i≤len bdp>;
          if ¬(esscl∈dom aloc) then error else return(aloc(esscl)))
type: Varref → ENV => LOC

Const = Intconst | Boolconst

TP: Intconst  → Staticenv → {mk-Scalarattr(INT)}

TP: Boolconst → Staticenv → {mk-Scalarattr(BOOL)}
```

M function is an identity for constant.

Auxiliary Functions

*contndll: Namedstmt** $\rightarrow$ *Id**

yields the list of those identifiers used as *s-nm* part of the

elements of the given statement list

*is-uniquel: X** $\rightarrow$ *Bool*

indicates if a list contains unique elements (i.e. no duplicates)

*is-disjointl: (X-set)** $\rightarrow$ *Bool*

indicates whether the sets in the list are pairwise disjoint

*rect: Nat** $\rightarrow$ *(Nat*)-set*

generates the set of valid indices within the given bounds

sel: Id $\times$ *Namedstmt** $\rightarrow$ *Namedstmt**

pre-sel(id,nsl) $\underline{\Delta}$ *id*$\in$*elems contndll(nsl)*

returns the sublist whose first statement has *id* as a label providing that the arguments satisfy the pre-condition.

4.11 NON-DETERMINISM

It is observed above that this language definition fixes the order of evaluation of sub-expressions. This is in keeping with the decision to minimize the discussion of non-determinism in the current book. On the other hand, non-deterministic selection has been deliberately built into the selection of new locations and activation identifiers. The definition is showing that the particular choice made is irrelevant in the sense that it would not affect the overall outcome of the program. If, however, some particular choice were defined, it could make it more difficult to prove some implementations correct. Although admitting this non-determinism is useful for implementations, it would be unnecessarily confusing to employ relational or power domain denotations (cf. [Jones 81a], [Plotkin 76a]) to cope with this problem.

CHAPTER 5

MORE ON EXCEPTION MECHANISMS

This chapter concerns the specific concept of exception constructs such as goto statements. The material is of narrow interest (the main point is the statement of a number of equivalence theorems) and many readers might choose to omit reading this chapter.

There are two ways of defining exception-like constructs in the denotational style: the Oxford group use so-called 'continuations'; chapter 4 describes the 'exit' approach mostly used in VDM. This difference is perhaps the most substantive issue between the two groups. This chapter defines one language in the most extreme forms of the two styles and proves that the two definitions are equivalent. In fact the proof given here and the discussion in [Bjørner 80b] show that the distinction is not as absolute as might appear at first sight. It should also be mentioned that VDM is not restricted to the exit style.

This chapter is a rewritten version of [Jones 78b] and uses different proof steps. Other relevant papers are [Reynolds 72a] and [Salle 80a].

CONTENTS

5.1 INTRODUCTION

The difficulty of providing a denotational definition of the 'goto' statement is that its effect cuts across the phrase structure of the language. The denotational rule, however, requires that only the denotations of components are to be employed in determining the denotations of compound phrases. The resolution of this difficulty lies in choosing appropriately rich domains as denotations. The Oxford approach is to use functions of higher order than normal transformations. These functions between transformations ("continuations") are explained below. Nothing in the Vienna approach precludes the use of continuations. But, based on earlier work, the Vienna group have preferred to use the *exit* model (explained in chapter 4) where this is adequate. *exit*s are, in fact, weaker than continuations and one of the justifications of this choice is Strachey's own principle of "parsimony in definition tools".

This chapter is built around a small language fragment. The language has been chosen to illustrate the main points at issue while keeping the proof relatively straightforward. Definitions using both *exit*s and continuations are given and a proof that the two definitions are equivalent is outlined. The key to this proof is the intermediate definitions used. These are interesting in their own right since they show that there is not only one difference which distinguishes the *exit* and continuation models. The analysis of these subsidiary decisions shows different possibilities for definitions. Other variations are considered in [Bjørner 80b].

Either definition approach has been shown to be capable of defining the major high-level languages like ALGOL 60 and PL/I. The choice between the approaches must, therefore, be made on other, pragmatic, grounds. Several factors relevant to this choice are pointed out in the course of this chapter.

5.2 THE LANGUAGE

The problems of escape mechanisms in general can be well illustrated by the 'goto' statement. The language used for the comparison is a selection of the essential features of that of chapter 4. What is a 'block' in the full language is called here a 'compound' statement because the declaration of variables is not treated. 'Goto' statements which enter phrase structures are not allowed in the language but the definition tool required to define this is illustrated in the proof. The proof in [Jones 78b] does include '*cue* functions' in the language definition. Labels are assumed to be unique throughout the program. The abstract syntax is:

$$\begin{array}{lll} Program & :: & Stmt \\ Stmt & = & Compound \mid Goto \mid Assign \\ Compound & :: & Namedstmt^* \\ Namedstmt & :: & [Id]\ s\text{-}body{:}Stmt \\ Goto & :: & Id \\ Assign & :: & Varref\ Expr \end{array}$$

The context conditions are as in chapter 4 (mutatis mutandis) with the additional constraint that labels are unique throughout the program. Use is made of:

$$dlabs\colon Namedstmt^* \to Id\text{-}set$$

A new function to collect all (rather than just the direct) labels is defined:

$$\begin{array}{ll} labs\colon Stmt \to Id\text{-}set & \\ labs[mk\text{-}Goto(id)] & \triangleq \{id\} \\ labs[mk\text{-}Assign(vf,e)] & \triangleq \{\} \\ labs[mk\text{-}Compound(nsl)] & \triangleq \\ \quad contndll[nsl] \cup \underline{union}\{labs[s\text{-}body(nsl[i])] \mid i \in \underline{inds}\, nsl\} & \end{array}$$

The function from chapter 4 which selects a portion of a list based on an identifier is extended to cover labels which are not direct. The result is a sub-list of the argument where the given identifier is in the (indirect) labels of the head of the list:

$$\begin{array}{l} sel\colon Id \times Namedstmt^* \to Namedstmt^* \\ pre\text{-}sel[id,nsl] = id \in labs[nsl] \end{array}$$

The semantic definition given in this section follows that in chapter 4. The domain *STATE* can be taken as given and its detailed structure can be hidden behind a function:

$$assign\colon Varref \times Expr \to STATE \xrightarrow{\sim} STATE$$

The advantage of insisting that labels be globally unique is that no

Activation identifiers are required in the definition. Thus necessary transformations (called *Xtr* to link them to the exit definition) are:

$Xtr = STATE \xrightarrow{\sim} STATE \times [Id]$

The semantic functions are derived from those in chapter 4 in an obvious way. Once again, *X* is used to identify the definition approach. The definition given here uses the exit combinators. These are expanded and the types of all functions shown explicitly in the next-but-one section.

$X[mk\text{-}Program(s)] \quad \triangleq X[s]$

$X[mk\text{-}Compound(nsl)] \triangleq$
$\quad \underline{tixe}\ [id \mapsto Xl[sel[id,nsl]] \mid id \in dlabs[nsl]]\ \underline{in}\ Xl[nsl]$

$Xl[<>] \quad \triangleq I_{STATE}$

$Xl[nsl] \quad \triangleq X[s\text{-}body(\underline{hd}nsl)];Xl[\underline{tl}nsl]$

$X[mk\text{-}Goto(id)] \quad \triangleq \underline{exit}(id)$

$X[mk\text{-}Assign(vr,e)] \triangleq assign(vr,e)$

It is a property of this definition that the only "goto" exits which are not resolved by *X* are to non-local labels. Thus:

$(X[s](\sigma) = (\sigma',a)) \supset ((a=\underline{nil}) \vee \neg(a \in labs[s]))$

It follows from the context condition, which requires that all labels are defined, that:

$(X[mk\text{-}Program(s)](\sigma) = (\sigma',a)) \supset (a=\underline{nil}) \vee \neg(a \in labs[s])$

The fact that all labels are handled in this way could be formalized by writing:

$X[mk\text{-}Program(s)] \triangleq (\lambda\sigma,a.\sigma)\circ X[s]$

reducing the *Xtr* to an object in:

$STATE \xrightarrow{\sim} STATE$

One of the advantages of an *exit*-style definition is the way in which the effect of exits is automatically localized. It is clear that any compound, with only local branches, has one of the simpler transformations as its denotation.

A further effect of the use of *exit* combinators is that the impact of the 'goto' statement on the definition is limited. An early 'functional semantics' for ALGOL 60 ([Allen 72a]) shows how the use of the *exit* concept can permeate a complete definition without the use of combinators.

5.3 CONTINUATIONS

The alternative and more widely used approach to the definition of exception constructs is to use 'continuations'. These were invented independently by F.L.Morris [Morris 70a] and C.Wadsworth [Strachey 74a]. As with the *exit* approach, continuations resolve the problem of conforming to the denotational rule by complicating the domain of the denotations. Technically the idea is to move from simple transformations:

$$TR = STATE \xrightarrow{\sim} STATE$$

to the higher order:

$$TR \to TR$$

In order to clarify which definition method is being used at any time, this chapter uses:

$$CONT = STATE \xrightarrow{\sim} ANS$$
$$CTR \;= CONT \to CONT$$

The use of the answer domain (*ANS*) is explained in the proof - the reader can equate it to *STATE* in this section.

The idea behind these higher-order functions is that the "total transformation" is defined in the context of a "remaining transformation". Thus:

$$C\colon Stmt \to CTR$$
$$C[s]\{\theta\} \;\underline{\Delta}\; \theta'$$

(Parameters of continuation type are traditionally enclosed in braces rather than parentheses - this aid to readability is preserved here.) Both θ and θ' are members of:

$$STATE \xrightarrow{\sim} STATE$$

The meaning of *s*, where θ is to be done next, is θ'. '<u>Goto</u>' statements will actually be given a denotation which shows the passed continuation being ignored; they do, however, require denotations for labels to be stored in an environment:

$$ENV = Id \underset{m}{\rightarrow} CONT$$

Thus the actual semantic functions (with *C* for continuation) become:

$$C\text{: } Stmt \rightarrow ENV \rightarrow CTR$$

$$\begin{array}{l} C[mk\text{-}Program(s)] \triangleq \\ \quad \underline{let}\ \rho = [id \mapsto Crest[id,s](\rho)\{I_{STATE}\} \mid id \in labs(s)]\ \underline{in} \\ \quad C[s](\rho)\{I_{STATE}\} \end{array}$$

Which is of the type:

$$Program \rightarrow STATE \xrightarrow{\sim} STATE$$

Then:

$$\begin{array}{lll} C[mk\text{-}Compound(nsl)] & \triangleq & Cl[nsl] \\ Cl[<>](\rho)\{\theta\} & \triangleq & \theta \\ Cl[nsl](\rho)\{\theta\} & \triangleq & C[s\text{-}body(\underline{hd}nsl)](\rho)\{Cl[\underline{tl}nsl](\rho)\{\theta\}\} \end{array}$$

which is of type:

$$Named\text{-}stmt^{*} \rightarrow ENV \rightarrow CTR$$

$$\begin{array}{lll} C[mk\text{-}Goto(id)](\rho)\{\theta\} & \triangleq & \rho(id) \\ C[mk\text{-}Assign(vr,e)](\rho)\{\theta\} & \triangleq & \theta \circ assign(vr,e) \end{array}$$

The function which is used to derive the continuation for the "rest" of the execution from a particular label is only used for compound statements:

```
Crest[id,mk-Compound(nsl)](ρ){θ} ≜
   if id∈dlabs(nsl) then Cl[sel(id,nsl)](ρ){θ}
   else (let rl = sel(id,nsl) in
         Crest[id,s-body(hd rl)](ρ){Cl[tl rl](ρ){θ}})
```

Which is of type:

$Id \times Compound \to ENV \to CTR$

The reader who finds this whole definition back to front is to be sympathized with. The proponents of the continuation approach will offer reassurance that this way of thinking eventually becomes natural.

Once the initial difficulties of adjustment are overcome, there remain some concerns about continuation definitions.

The label denotations stored in the environment all represent the effect of starting execution at that label and continuing to the end of the whole program. The result of this is that the denotation of a block with no non-local 'goto' statements is still of type:

$ENV \to CTR$

Since the environment is computed at the program level, the denotation is not closed in the way it is with *exit*s (*nil* label returned). What appears to be lost in the definition is the fact that the continuation used to develop the denotations for the labels in a block is the same as the continuation for statements in the block.

There is another potential problem which does not manifest itself in this language.

The need for epilogue type action is discussed in chapter 4; it is clear how such transformations are composed with the denotation of a block using the exit approach; such transformations do not fit naturally with the continuation approach. The difficulty is that the denotation of a label (in so far as the number of blocks to be closed is concerned) has to vary from one block to another. Although somewhat messy, it is in fact possible to compose such actions onto label denotations even in a continuation definition (see [Bjørner 80b]).

5.4 PROOF PLAN

The preceding two sections each offer definitions which the remainder of this chapter shows to be 'equivalent'. Formally the result is that the *X* and the *M* semantics give the same transformation (as the denotation) for any (valid) program.

Careful analysis of the two definitions shows that the overall dissimilarity can be divided into three areas:

(i) In the continuation definition, the denotation which is associated with a label via the environment reflects the effect of starting execution at that label and continuing to the end of the entire program. The *exit* definition, however, provides denotations for labels which reflect only the transformation corresponding to the execution from the label to the end of its corresponding compound statement.

(ii) The mode of generating the denotations in the two approaches differs: continuations are built up from a remaining continuation composing "backwards"; in the exit definition the composition is "forwards" from the label.

(iii) The continuation definition passes the denotations of labels in the environment whereas the meaning of labels is used in the *exit* definition (by the *tixe* combinator) at the level of the compound statement.

The proof method to be used is to make these changes singly and to show that each of the definitions is equivalent in the required sense. The overall result obviously follows by transitivity. The first contribution to making the semantics appear more similar is to expand the combinator definitions used in the *exit* version. Thus what follows is simply a rewriting of the exit definition expanding the combinators of chapter 4.

$X[mk\text{-}Program(s)] \underline{\Delta} X[s]$

As indicated above, this can be shown to give a result of type:

$STATE \xrightarrow{\sim} STATE \times \{\underline{nil}\}$

The main semantic functions are of type:

$$X: Stmt \rightarrow Xtr$$

$$\begin{array}{l} X[mk\text{-}Compound(nsl)] \;\underline{\underline{\Delta}} \\ \quad \underline{let}\ \rho = [id \mapsto Xl[sel(id,nsl)] \mid id \in dlabs(nsl)] \quad \underline{in} \\ \quad \underline{let}\ r = \lambda\sigma,a.\underline{if}\ a \in \underline{dom}\rho\ \underline{then}\ r(\rho(a)(\sigma))\ \underline{else}\ (\sigma,a)\ \underline{in} \\ \quad r \circ Xl[nsl] \end{array}$$

$$Xl[\langle\rangle] \quad \underline{\underline{\Delta}}\ \lambda\sigma.(\sigma,\ \underline{nil})$$

$$\begin{array}{ll} Xl[nsl] & \underline{\underline{\Delta}}\ (\lambda\sigma,a.\underline{if}\ a=\underline{nil}\ \underline{then}\ Xl[\underline{tl}nsl](\sigma)\ \underline{else}\ (\sigma,a)) \circ \\ & \quad X[s\text{-}body(\underline{hd}nsl)] \end{array}$$

$$X[mk\text{-}Goto(id)] \quad \underline{\underline{\Delta}}\ \lambda\sigma.(\sigma,id)$$

$$X[mk\text{-}Assign(vr,e)]\ \underline{\underline{\Delta}}\ \lambda\sigma.(assign(vr,e)(\sigma),\underline{nil})$$

5.5 EXITS HANDLED GLOBALLY

One of the arguments used in favour of the *exit* style definition is the way in which the effect of 'goto' statements can be localized to the compound statement in which the label occurs. It is, however, possible to write a definition in which the handling of *exit*s is done globally. This is a first step towards the overall equivalence and also provides an opportunity to illustrate '*cue*-functions'. The name *cue* has been used because these functions are prompted to begin execution at a particular label. Here they are used to create a transition (of *Xtr*) from the label to the end of the whole program. In general, *cue*-functions can be used in defining languages which permit 'goto' statements to enter phrase structures.

The *E* semantic functions given here are of the same types as the corresponding *X* functions.

$$\begin{array}{l} E[mk\text{-}Program(s)]\ \underline{\underline{\Delta}} \\ \quad \underline{let}\ \rho = [id \mapsto Ecue[id,s] \mid id \in labs(s)] \quad \underline{in} \\ \quad \underline{let}\ r = \lambda\sigma,a.\underline{if}\ a \in \underline{dom}\rho\ \underline{then}\ r(\rho(a)(\sigma))\ \underline{else}\ (\sigma,a)\ \underline{in} \\ \quad r \circ (s) \end{array}$$

```
E[mk-Compound(nsl)] ≜ El[nsl]

El[<>]              ≜ λσ.(σ,nil)

El[nsl]             ≜ (λσ,a.if a=nil then El[tlnsl](σ)
                                  else (σ,a))∘E[s-body(hdnsl)]

E[mk-Goto(id)]      ≜ λσ.(σ,id)

E[mk-Assign(vr,e)]  ≜ λσ.(assign(vr,e)(σ),nil)

Ecue[id,mk-Compund(nsl)] ≜
  if id∈dlabs(nsl) then El[sel(id,nsl)]
  else (let rl = sel(id,nsl) in
       (λσ,a.(if a=nil then El[tlrl](σ)
              else (σ,a))∘
             Ecue[id,s-body(hdrl)]
```

This definition can be shown to be equivalent to the *X* semantics.

The first step is to relate the two definitions of *Compound* statement semantics by a lemma. The intention is to show that the *X* semantics are the same as the *E* semantics providing an extra *exit* trap is placed around the latter. This relies on a hypothesis about the ρ argument used in the trap:

```
(∀id∈labs(cpd))
   (ρ(id) = Ecue[id,cpd])  ⊃
    (let r = λσ,a.(if a∈domρ then r(ρ(a)(σ)) else (σ,a)) in
     r∘E[cpd])
     = X[cpd]
```

This lemma can be proved by induction on the depth of nesting of *Compound* statements. It is an immediate corollary of the lemma that for (valid) *Programs*:

```
E[mk-Program(s)]    ≜ X[mk-Program(s)]
```

This follows since the hypothesis of the lemma is discharged by the definition of ρ in *E*.

5.6 CONTINUATIONS WITHOUT AN ENVIRONMENT

The next step brings in a continuation-like treatment of '<u>goto</u>' statements. That is, the second difference listed in the section on "Proof Plan" is resolved in the direction of building up label denotations by composing from the back. In order to achieve this an extra (continuation) argument has to be passed to the *D* semantic functions. In this definition, however, label denotations are not passed in an environment. Furthermore, the objects which are passed and returned are not "normal" continuations: the freedom of defining the result of *CONT* to be *Ans* is used here to give:

D: Stmt → XTR → XTR

Thus:

```
D[mk-Program(s)] ≜
  let r=λσ,a.if a∈labs(s) then r(Dcue[id,s]){λσ.(σ,nil)}(σ)
             else (σ,a) in
  r∘D(s){λσ.(σ,nil)}

D[mk-Compound(nsl)]{θ}  ≜ Dl(nsl){θ}

Dl[<>]{θ}               ≜ θ

Dl[nsl]{θ}              ≜ D[s-body(hdnsl)]{Dl[tlnsl]{θ}}

D[mk-Goto(id)]{θ}       ≜ λσ.(σ,id)

D[mk-Assign(vr,e)]{θ}   ≜ λσ.θ(assign(vr,e)(σ))

Dcue[id,mk-Compound(nsl)]{θ} ≜
    if id∈dlabs(nsl) then Dl[sel(id,nsl)]{θ}
    else (let rl = sel(id,nsl) in
          Dcue[id,s-body(hdrl)]{Dl[tlrl]{θ}})
```

This definition can now be shown to be equivalent to the *E* semantics of the last section. As with the proof in that section, it is convenient to separate a lemma. This lemma states that the *Dl* semantics with an (continuation) argument θ is equivalent to *El* with θ used after it in the case of normal <u>*exit*</u>:

$(\lambda\sigma,a.\ \underline{if}\ a=\underline{nil}\ \underline{then}\ \Theta(\sigma)\ \underline{else}\ (\sigma,a))\circ El[nsl] = Dl[nsl]\{\Theta\}$

This lemma is again proved by induction on the depth of compound statements. But, since a subsidiary induction is required, the basis is sketched here. For the basis, it is assumed that no elements of *nsl* are compound statements. It is then possible to use induction on the length of *nsl*. If *nsl* is empty:

$$\begin{aligned}(\lambda\sigma,a.\underline{if}\ a=\underline{nil}\ \underline{then}\ \Theta(\sigma)\ \underline{else}\ (\sigma,a))\circ El[<>] &= \lambda\sigma.(\Theta(\sigma))\\ &= \Theta\\ &= Dl[<>]\{\Theta\}\end{aligned}$$

If *nsl* is not the empty list a case distinction is required. Assume:

$s\text{-}body(\underline{hd}nsl) \in Goto$

$E[mk\text{-}Goto(id)] = \lambda\sigma.(\sigma,id)$

$$\begin{aligned}El[nsl] &= (\lambda\sigma,a.\underline{if}\ a=\underline{nil}\ \underline{then}\ El[\underline{tl}nsl](\sigma)\ \underline{else}\ (\sigma,a))\circ E[mk\text{-}Goto(id)]\\ &= \lambda\sigma.(\sigma,id)\end{aligned}$$

$(\lambda\sigma,a.\underline{if}\ a=\underline{nil}\ \underline{then}\ \Theta(\sigma)\ \underline{else}\ (\sigma,a))\circ El[nsl] = \lambda\sigma.(\sigma,id)$

$$\begin{aligned}Dl[nsl]\{\Theta\} &= D[mk\text{-}Goto(id)]\{Dl[\underline{tl}nsl]\{\Theta\}\}\\ &= \lambda\sigma.(\sigma,id)\end{aligned}$$

Now, the only other possibility is that:

$s\text{-}body(\underline{hd}nsl) \in Assign$

$E[mk\text{-}Assign(vr,e)] = \lambda\sigma.(assign(vr,e)(\sigma),\underline{nil})$

$$\begin{aligned}El[nsl] &= (\lambda\sigma,a.\underline{if}\ a=\underline{nil}\ \underline{then}\ El[\underline{tl}nsl](\sigma)\ \underline{else}\ (\sigma,a))\\ &\quad \circ E[mk\text{-}Assign(vr,e)]\\ &= (\lambda\sigma.El[\underline{tl}nsl](assign(vr,e)(\sigma)))\end{aligned}$$

$$\begin{aligned}Dl[nsl]\{\Theta\} &= D[mk\text{-}Assign(vr,e)]\{Dl[\underline{tl}nsl]\{\Theta\}\}\\ &= \lambda\sigma.\{Dl[\underline{tl}nsl]\{\Theta\}\}(assign(vr,e)(\sigma))\end{aligned}$$

which, by induction hypothesis:

$= \lambda\sigma.(\lambda\sigma,a.\underline{if}\ a{=}\underline{nil}\ \underline{then}\ \Theta(\sigma)\ \underline{else}\ (\sigma,a))^{\circ}$
$El[\underline{tl}nsl](assign(vr,e)(\sigma))$

$= (\lambda\sigma,a.\underline{if}\ a{=}\underline{nil}\ \underline{then}\ \Theta(\sigma)\ \underline{else}\ (\sigma,a))^{\circ}El[nsl]$

Here again, the main result is a corollary of the lemma; for programs which are *Compound* statements:

$D[mk\text{-}Program(mk\text{-}Compound(nsl))]$
$= \underline{let}\ r = \ldots\ \underline{in}\ r^{\circ}Dl[nsl]\{\lambda\sigma.(\sigma,\underline{nil})\}$
$= \underline{let}\ r = \ldots\ \underline{in}\ r^{\circ}(\lambda(\sigma,a).(\sigma,\underline{nil}))^{\circ}El[nsl]$
$= \underline{let}\ r = \ldots\ \underline{in}\ r^{\circ}El[nsl]$
$= E[mk\text{-}Program(mk\text{-}Compound(nsl))]$

5.7 NORMAL CONTINUATIONS

As the reader may have noticed, the names of the semantic functions have been progressing back through the alphabet. The remaining task is to establish the connection between the *D* semantics of the preceding section and the original continuation semantics (*C*).

Here again, it is convenient to separate a lemma which relates *Dl* and *Cl*. With:

$cons = \lambda id.\lambda\sigma.(\sigma,id)$

the statement of the lemma is:

$r^{\circ}Dl[nsl]\{\Theta\} = Cl[nsl](r^{\circ}cons)\{r^{\circ}\Theta\}$

which shows that in order to perform *r* after the (*Dl*) meaning of *nsl*, it is necessary to compose *r* both with the passed continuation and with the environment entries. The proof follows the same pattern as that of the lemma in the preceding section. The final result can then be shown as follows:

$D[mk\text{-}Program(mk\text{-}Compound(nsl))]$
$= \underline{let}\ r = \ldots\ \underline{in}\ r^{\circ}Dl[nsl]\{\lambda\sigma.(\sigma,\underline{nil})\}$
$= \underline{let}\ r = \ldots\ \underline{in}\ Cl[nsl](r^{\circ}cons)\{r^{\circ}\lambda\sigma.(\sigma,\underline{nil})\}$
$= \underline{let}\ \rho = [id \mapsto Crest[id,nsl](\rho)\{\lambda\sigma.(\sigma,\underline{nil})\}\ |\ id\in labs(nsl)]\ \underline{in}$
$Cl[nsl](\rho)\ \{\lambda\sigma.(\sigma,\underline{nil})\}$

Since it has been shown above that the transformation always yields a <u>*nil*</u> second component, it is only necessary to make a systematic change to reduce the *ANS* domain to *STATE* and get:

C[mk-Program(mk-Compound(nsl))]

This concludes the chain of equivalence proofs:

$X = E = D = C$

A few remaining comments can be made about the comparison of the two definitions, *X* and *C*. The limitation of the current proof should be clearly understood. Two language definitions have been shown to be equivalent. This does not show that the two approaches (i.e. <u>*exit*</u>s and continuations) are equivalent. In fact, it would appear that definitions using <u>*exit*</u>s are less powerful in that they cannot (readily) be used to define features like coroutines where the essence is to pass a a continuation. There would appear to be an argument that a language definition is made more perspicuous if the domains exactly match the power of the language and this argument has been used to justify the choice of <u>*exit*</u>s to define "goto"-like exceptions. It should at least cause some hesitation to those who insist that "standard" semantics implies the use of continuations. An advantage of definition by continuations is that the *Answer* domain can be used to yield some final result other than (or as well as) the state. For example, [Gordon 79a] delivers the output file in this way. The definition of ALGOL 60 in Chapter 6 somewhat clouds the possible operations on output files. This deficiency can readily be overcome by a simple redefinition of the combinators.

One of the purposes of a formal definition is to provide a criterion for the correctness of implementations. Proofs have been based on both styles of definition but no detailed comparison has yet been published.

CHAPTER 6

ALGOL 60

ALGOL 60 has provided a reference point for many facets of computer science. It has been formally defined a number of times (e.g. [Lauer 68a, Allen 72a, Mosses 74a]). As such, the task of writing a definition of the language provides a convenient test of a definition method. The ALGOL 60 definition in this chapter provides the reader with a first example of a VDM definition of a real (as opposed to a contrived) problem. The text discusses the models of those language concepts not covered in chapter 4. One of the outcomes of constructing a definition is a list of "reservations" about the object under study: that is, comments on how the same effect could be achieved more simply. The only major problem left in the "Modified Language" ([de Morgan 76a]) is the incomplete type checking.

This definition shows that a powerful language can have a concise definition providing the language is well thought out. (This chapter is a revised version of [Henhapl 78a].) Other complete language definitions using VDM ideas are Pascal in chapter 7, PL/1 in [Bekić 74a], Ada in [Bjørner 80f] (see also [Ada 80c]), and CHILL [CCITT 80a].

CONTENTS

(*) Sect. 6.3.4 is treated in sect. 6.2.2; sect. 6.4.2 in sect. 6.2.1.

INTRODUCTION

For many years the official description of ALGOL 60 has been the "Revised Report" [Naur 63a]. Not only the language, but also its extremely precise description have been seen as a reference point. There were, however, a number of known unresolved problems and most of these have been eliminated by the recent modifications given in [de Morgan 76a]. A number of formal definitions exist for the language of the revised report: this paper presents a denotational defnition of the language as understood from the Modified ALGOL 60 Report (MAR).

Before making some introductory remarks on the definition, three points will be made about the language itself (as in MAR). Firstly the modifications have followed the earlier "*ECMA subset*" by making the language (almost) statically typed. Although all parameters must now be specified, there is still no way of fixing the dimensions of array parameters nor the required parameter types of procedure or function parameters (cf. ALGOL 68). In connection with this, it could be observed that the parameter matching rules of section 4.7.5.5 of MAR are somewhat difficult. In particular the definition given below assumes that, for "*by name*" passing of arithmetic expressions, the types must match exactly.

The third observation is one of surprise. The decision to restrict the control variable of a *<for statement>* to be a *<variable identifier>* (i.e. not a subscripted variable) may or may not be wise: but the argument that *<for statement>* can now be defined by expansion within ALGOL is surely dangerous. The definition given here would have had no difficulty treating the more general case because the concept of location has anyway to be introduced for other purposes.

Two of the major points resolved by the modifications are the meaning of *"own"* variables and the provision of a basic set of input-output functions: particular attention has been given to these points in the formal definition below. In fact, the treatment of own given here is more detailed than that for PL/1 static variables in [ULD69c]. Rather than perform name changes and generate dummy declarations in the outermost block, an extra environment component is used here to retain a mapping from (additional) unique names to their locations. This *own-env* is used in generating the denotations for "own" variables for insertion in the local *env*. The input-output functions are defined to change the "Channel" components of the *State*.

As discussed elsewhere in this volume, the definition of arbitrary order of evaluation has not been addressed: had it been, one would, for example, have to show that the elements of an expression can be evaluated in any order.

Neither the concrete syntax nor the translation to the abstract form are given in this definition.

6.0 BASIC DOMAINS

6.0.1 Static Environment

In order to define the context conditions (*WF*) a static environment is created. This same object facilitates the determination of the types of expressions etc.(*TP*). *Specifier* is defined in section 6.2.2 (see 6.7.2 for an Index).

$$STATICENV = Id \xrightarrow{m} Specifier$$

Note that a list of abbreviations is given in section 6.7.1.

Certain obvious steps have been taken to shorten the *WF* functions given below, for example if:

$$\theta :: \theta_1 \ \theta_2 \ \ldots \ \theta_n$$

then a rule (or part thereof) of the form:

$$WF[mk\text{-}\theta(\theta_1,\theta_2,\ldots,\theta_n)](env) \triangleq$$
$$\quad WF[\theta_1](env) \wedge WF[\theta_2](env) \wedge \ldots \wedge WF[\theta_n](env)$$

are omitted.

6.0.2 State

Central to the definition of the semantics is the *State* which contains the values for the (scalar) locations and for the input-output channels.

STATE :: STR :*STORE*
CHANS :*CHANNELS*

STORE = *SCALARLOC* $\underset{m}{\rightarrow}$ [*SCALARVAL*]

SCALARLOC Infinite set

SCALARVAL = *Int* | *Real* | *Bool*

CHANNELS = *Int* $\underset{m}{\rightarrow}$ $Char^*$

6.0.3 Environment

The denotations of (local) identifiers are contained in *env* which is a parameter to the meaning function (*M*).

ENV = *Id* $\underset{m}{\rightarrow}$ *DEN*

DEN = *TYPEDEN* | *ARRAYDEN* | *PROCDEN* | *ATVFNDEN* |
LABELDEN | *SWITCHDEN* | *BYNAMEDEN* | *String*

The denotation of (typed) scalar variables is a (scalar) location whose value is found in the *Store* part of the *State*.

TYPEDEN = *SCALARLOC*

Array variables denote maps from a dense (cf. *rect*) set of indices to scalar locations. Since each index denotes a separate location the mapping is one-one. As discussed in chapter 4, this mapping is part of the environment because elements of arrays can be passed as parameters "by location".

ARRAYDEN = $Int^+ \underset{m}{\leftrightarrow}$ *SCALARLOC*
constraint $(\exists ipl \in (Int \times Int)^+)(\underline{dom}\,aloc = rect(ipl))$

Procedure denotations are functions which yield transformations.

These transformations are of the abnormal, or *exit*, type. For function procedures, a scalar value may also be returned. The obvious parameter of a procedure denotation is the list of denotations for its actual parameters. A procedure denotation also depends on a set of activation identifiers. The use of such identifiers to uniquely identify labels is discussed in Chapter 4. The current set must be passed along the (dynamic) call chain in order to ensure that new names are chosen.

$$PROCDEN = (ACTPARMDEN^{*} \times AID\text{-}set) \rightarrow (STATE \xrightarrow{\sim} (STATE \times [LABELDEN] \times [SCALARVAL]))$$

The denotations of actual parameters include type information because, as pointed out above, the checking of actual formal parameter matching must be performed dynamically in ALGOL.

$$ACTPARMDEN :: s\text{-}v{:}DEN \quad s\text{-}tp{:}Specifier$$

A function procedure returns a value by assignment to a location associated with the name of the function. The denotation for an "activated" function procedure must therefore include such a scalar location.

$$ATVFNDEN :: s\text{-}loc{:}SCALARLOC \quad s\text{-}fn{:}PROCDEN$$

Label denotations include an activation identifier in order to ensure uniqueness.

$$LABELDEN :: Id \quad AID$$

AID Infinite set of *Tokens*

Switch denotations are very like those for procedures. It is important to realize that switches in ALGOL 60 do not damage the "stack property" of the language (that is no goto or call could ever refer to a completed block) - they do not provide the generality of PL/1 label variables.

$$SWITCHDEN = (Int \times AID\text{-}set) \rightarrow (STATE \xrightarrow{\sim} STATE \times [LABELDEN] \times LABELDEN)$$

ALGOL 60's "by name" parameter passing is very general and is modelled by something which can be seen to be like a parameterless procedure. It is necessary to distinguish below between those actual parameters which can be evaluated to a location since the corresponding formal parameter can then be used on the left of an assignment in parameter passing by location.

$$BYNAMEDEN = BYNAMELOCDEN \mid BYNAMEEXPRDEN$$
$$BYNAMELOCDEN :: AID\text{-}set \rightarrow (STATE \xrightarrow{\sim} (STATE \times LOC))$$
$$BYNAMEEXPRDEN :: AID\text{-}set \rightarrow (STATE \xrightarrow{\sim} (STATE \times SCALARVAL))$$

6.0.4 Auxiliary Semantic Objects

A special environment is created at the program level for own variables.

$$OWNENV = Ownid \underset{m}{\rightarrow} (TYPEDEN \mid ARRAYDEN)$$

Composite environments are used in the semantic functions (*M*) for statements and expressions.

$$STMTENV = OWNENV \times ENV \times AID\text{-}set$$
$$EXPRENV = ENV \times AID\text{-}set$$

Auxiliary objects are used in same type clauses

$$LOC \quad = SCALARLOC \mid ARRAYDEN$$
$$VAL \quad = SCALARVAL \mid LABELDEN$$

The *exit* transformations used in this definition are:

$$TR \quad = STATE \xrightarrow{\sim} (STATE \times [LABELDEN])$$

The following type clause abbreviations (~) are used:

$$M{:}\ D \Rightarrow \quad \sim \quad M{:}\ D \rightarrow TR$$
$$M{:}\ D \Rightarrow R \quad \sim \quad M{:}\ D \rightarrow STATE \xrightarrow{\sim} (STATE \times [LABELDEN] \times R)$$

6.1 PROGRAM LEVEL

6.1.1 Programs

Program :: *Programblock*
Programblock :: *Block*

Comment The Dummy *Programblock* can be thought of as defining the lifetime of the "own" declarations. It also contains the standard functions and procedures. Section 6.1.3 provides some meta-language definitions for standard functions which cannot be written in ALGOL.

Standard-proc-names = *Real-funct-names* | *Int-funct-names* | *Proc-names*

```
Real-Funct-names  = "abs"       | "sqrt"       | "ln"          | "exp" |
                    "sin"       | "cos"        | "arctan"      |
                    "maxreal"   | "minreal"    | "epsilon"

Int-funct-names   = "iabs"      | "sign"       | "entier"      |
                    "length"    | "maxint"

Proc-names        = "inchar"    | "outchar"    | "outstring"   |
                    "stop"      | "fault"      |
                    "inreal"    | "outreal"    |
                    "ininteger" | "outinteger" |  "outterminator"
```

Comment The quotes around the standard-procedure-names indicate the translated version of the identifiers.

```
WF[mk-Program(mk-Programblock(b))] ≜
  is-uniqueoids(b) ∧ is-constownbds(b) ∧
  (let senv₀ = [n ↦ mk-Typeproc(INT)  | n∈Int-funct-names] ∪
               [n ↦ mk-Typeproc(REAL) | n∈Real-funct-names] ∪
               [n ↦ PROC | n∈Proc-names] in
   WF[b](senv₀))
type Program → Bool
```

Comment $senv_0$ contains information about the language defined functions and procedures;

```
M[mk-Program(pb)](chanv) ≜
   let σ₀ = mk-STATE([],chanv) in
   CHANS(M[pb](σ₀))
type Program → (CHANNELS ⥲ CHANNELS)

M[mk-Programblock(b)] ≜
  let owns   = {d | is-within(d,b) ∧ d∈(Owntypedecl∪Ownarraydecl)} in
  def ownenv : [s-oid(d) ↦ M[d] | d∈owns];
  (tixe [ RET → I]
   in M[b](ownenv,[],{}));
  epilogue({s-id(d) | d∈owns})(ownenv)
type Programblock =>
```

6.1.2 Own Declarations

```
Owntypedecl  :: s-id:Id   s-oid:Ownid   s-desc:Type
Ownarraydecl :: s-id:Id   s-oid:Ownid   s-tp:Type   s-bdl:Boundpair+

WF[mk-Ownarraydecl(id,oid,tp,bdl)](senv) ≜
   (∀i∈inds bdl)(TP[s-bdl(bdl[i])](senv)∈Arithm ∧
                 TP[s-ubd(bdl[i])](senv)∈Arithm)

M[mk-Owntypedecl(id,oid,tp)] ≜
  def loc: M[mk-Typedecl(id,oid,tp)];
  if tp=BOOL then assign(FALSE,loc)
  else assign(0,loc);
  return(loc)
type Owntypedecl => TYPEDEN

M[mk-Ownarraydecl(id,oid,tp,bdl)] ≜
  def loc: M[mk-Arraydecl(id,oid,tp,bdl)]([ ],{ });
  if tp=BOOL then for all scl∈rng loc do assign(FALSE,scl)
  else for all scl∈rng loc do assign(0,scl);
  return(loc)
type Ownarraydecl => ARRAYDEN
Comment All own variables have a defined initial value.
```

6.1.3 Standard Functions and Transput

It is assumed that the translation of the standard functions and procedures are contained in the ("fictitious") outer block. The interpretation of their *proc-decl* follows the normal interpretation rules except in the cases where the body cannot be expressed in Algol. In these cases the state transition of the non-Algol part is explicitly listed below.

Note: Referencing the translated identifiers we use quotes. For the translation of the identifier inreal we thus get: *"inreal"*

(1) In procedure *stop:*

"goto Omega" → *exit*(RET)

(2) In procedure *inchar*, *s-body* contains:

```
def chv    : contents(env("channel"));
let str    = env("str") in
def int    : M[mk-Simplevarbn("int")](exenv);
def chans : dom c CHANS;
if chv∈chans
then (def chan : (c CHANS)(chv);
      if chan=<> then error
      else (let char = hdchan in
            let ind  = (if (∃i∈indsstr)(str[i]=char)
                        then (Δi∈indsstr)(str[i]=char∧
                                    (∀k∈{1:i-1})(str[k]≠char)))
                        else 0) in
            CHANS := c CHANS + [chv ↦ tlchan];
            assign(ind,int)))
else error
```

(3) In procedure *outchar*:

```
def chv    : contents(env("channel"));
let str    = env("str") in
def int    : contents(env("int"));
let char   = str(int)   in
def chans : dom c CHANS;
if chv∈chans then CHANS := c CHANS + [chv ↦ (c CHANS)(chv)^<char>]
else error
```

(4) In procedure *outterminator*: *s-body* contains:

```
def chv    : contents(env("channel"));
def chans : dom c CHANS;
if chv∈chans then CHANS := c CHANS + [chv ↦ (c CHANS)(chv) ^
                                         <implementation   defined
                                          symbol, depending  on the
                                          state   of   the   channel>]
else error
```

Procedures *maxint*, *minreal*, *maxreal* and *epsilon* have bodies which return the appropriate implementation defined constants.

6.2 SCOPE DEFINITION

6.2.1 Blocks

```
Block :: Decl-set   Stmt*

WF[mk-Block(dcls,stl)](senv) ≜
   let labl = contndll(stl) in
   is-uniquel(labl) ∧
   is-disjointl(<elemslabl, {s-id(d) | d∈dcls}>) ∧
   (let lenv = [s-id(d) ↦ SPEC(d) | d∈dcls] ∪
               [lab ↦ LABEL | lab∈elemslabl] in
    let renv = senv \ domlenv in
    let nenv = senv + lenv    in
    (∀d∈dcls)((d∈Arraydecl ⊃ WF[d](renv))  ∧
              (d∈Proc      ⊃ WF[d](nenv))  ∧
              (d∈Switch    ⊃ WF[d](nenv))) ∧
    (∀st∈elemsstl)(WF[st](nenv)))
type Block → STATICENV → Bool
```

Comment It is important to notice the different (static) environments used to check parts of the *Block*. In particular, a reduced environment (*renv*) is used for *Arraydecls* because any contained expressions should not contain references to local variables of the *Block* (to interpret such references in *senv* would be counter to the scope concept).

```
M[mk-Block(dcls,stl)](ownenv,env,cas) ≜
  let aid ∈(AID - cas) in
  def nenv : env +
          ([s-id(d) ↦ ownenv(s-oid(d))
                        | d∈dcls ∧ d∈(Owntypedecl∪Ownarraydecl)] ∪
           [s-id(d) ↦ M[d]                 | d∈dcls ∧ d∈Typedecl]  ∪
           [s-id(d) ↦ M[d](env,cas)        | d∈dcls ∧ d∈Arraydecl] ∪
           [s-id(d) ↦ M[d](nenv)           | d∈dcls ∧ d∈Switch]    ∪
           [s-id(d) ↦ M[d](ownenv,nenv)    | d∈dcls ∧ d∈Proc]      ∪
           [lab     ↦ mk-LABELDEN(lab,aid) | lab∈contndls(stl)]);
  let stenv = (ownenv,nenv,cas∪{aid}) in
  always epilogue({s-id(d) | d∈dcls ∧ d∈(Typedecl ∪ Arraydecl)})(nenv)
  in (tixe [mk-LABELDEN(tlab,aid) ↦ Mcue[tlab,stl](stenv)
                                  | tlab∈contndls(stl)] in
      for i=1 to lenstl do M[s-sp(stl[i])](stenv))
  type Block → STMTENV =>
```

6.2.2 Procedures

```
Proc        :: s-id :Id                     s-tp  :(Type | PROC)
               s-fpl:Id*                    s-vids:Id-set
               s-spm:Id ⇸ Specifier         s-body:(Block | Code)

Specifier =    Type | Typearray | Typeproc |PROC|LABEL|STRING|SWITCH
Typearray ::   Type
Typeproc  ::   Type
Code           Implementation defined
```

```
WF[mk-Proc(id,tp,fpl,vids,spm,b)](senv) ≜
   is-uniquel(fpl) ∧  ¬(id∈elemsfpl)                   ∧
   vids⊆elemsfpl ∧ domspm=elemsfpl                     ∧
   (∀id∈vids)(spm(id)∈(Type∪Typearray∪{LABEL}))        ∧
   WF[b](senv + spm)
type Proc → STATICENV → Bool
```

Comment the "Revised" version of ALGOL requires specification of all formals.

```
M[mk-Proc(id,tp,fpl,vids,spm,b)](oenv,env) ≜
  let f(denl,cas) =
   (if lendenl≠lenfpl ∨
        (∃i∈indsfpl)(¬is-parmmatch(denl[i],spm(fpl[i]),fpl[i]∈vids))
    then error
    else (def nenv : env +
              ([fpl[i] ↦ s-v(denl[i]) | i∈indsfpl ∧ ¬(fpl[i]∈vids)] ∪
               [fpl[i] ↦ M[spm(fpl[i])](s-v(denl[i]),cas)
                     | i∈indsfpl ∧ fpl[i]∈vids]);
          def nfenv : if tp=PROC then nenv
                      else (def rloc : genscden();
                                nenv + [id ↦ mk-ATVFNDEN(rloc,env(id))]);
          M[b](oenv,nfenv,cas);
          epilogue({fpl[i] | i∈indsfpl ∧ fpl[i]∈vids ∧
                               spm(fpl[i])∈(Type∪Typearray)});
          def rv : if tp=PROC then nil
                   else (let mk-ATVFNDEN(rloc,) = nfenv(id) in
                         contents(rloc);
                         STR := c STR - {rloc});
          return(rv))) in f
 type: Proc → (OWNENV × ENV) → PROCDEN
```

Comment note that the set of *AIDs* used in the evaluation of the body is passed from the (dynamic) call.

Comment for a function procedure, *rloc* is the location into which assignments to the function name (for return) are made.

```
is-parmmatch(mk-Actparmden(den,spa),spf,bv) ≜
  if bv then
    (spa = spf)                         v
    (spf∈Arithm∧spa∈Arithm) v
    (spf∈Typearray∧spa∈Typearray∧s-type(spf)∈Arithm∧s-type(spa)∈Arithm)
  else
    (spa=spf)                           v
    (spf=PROC∧spa∈Typeproc) v
    (spf∈Typeproc∧spa∈Typeproc∧s-type(spa)∈Arithm∧s-type(spf)∈Arithm)
type  Actparmden × Specifier × Bool → Bool
```

Comment This check has to be dynamic because of the incomplete specification of arrays and procedures.

Comment The third parameter signifies whether the parameter passing is "by value" (*true*) or "by name" (*false*).

```
M : Specifier → (DEN × AID-set) => DEN
```

Comment Obtains value for "by value" actuals:

```
M[mk-Typearray(tp)](den,cas) ≜
   def aloc: genarrayden(domden);
   for all esscl∈domden do (def v: contents(den(esscl));
                            assign(v,aloc(esscl)));
   return (aloc)

M[tp](den,cas) ≜
   def v : if den∈BYNAMEEXPRDEN then den(cas)
           else (def l : den(cas); contents(l));
   let vc = conv(v,tp) in
   def l  : genscden();
   assign(vc,l);
   return(l)
```

```
M[LABEL](den,cas) ≜ den(cas)

M : Code → STMTENV =>
M[c](senv) ≜   Implementation defined
```

6.3 DECLARATIONS

```
Decl  =  Typedecl | Arraydecl    | Switchdecl   |
         Proc     | Owntypedecl  | Ownarraydecl

Spec: Decl → Specifier  - obvious function
```

6.3.1 Type Declarations

```
Typedecl :: s-id:Id   s-desc:Type
Type      =  Arithm | BOOL
Arithm    =  INT | REAL

M[mk-Typedecl(id,tp)] ≜ genscden()
type Typedecl => TYPEDEN

genscden() ≜
   def ulocs: dom c STR;
   let l ∈ (SCALARLOC - ulocs) in
   STR := c STR ∪ [l ↦ NIL];
   return(l)
type => SCALARLOC

epilogue(ids)(env) ≜
   let sclocs = {env(id) |  id∈ids ∧ env(id)∈TYPEDEN} ∪
                union{rng(env(id)) | id∈ids ∧ env(id)∈ARRAYDEN} in
   STR := c STR\sclocs
type Id-set → ENV =>
```

6.3.2 Array Declarations

```
Arraydecl :: s-id:Id   s-tp:Type   s-bdl:Boundpair+
Boundpair :: s-lbd:Expr   s-ubd:Expr
```

The use of one *<bound pair list>* to define several *<array identifiers>*

is expanded by the translator. Notice that this can not be justified from *MAR* and, with side-effect producing function references in the bound pair list, is strictly wrong.

```
WF[mk-Arraydecl(,,bdl)](senv) ≜
 (∀bdp∈elems bdl)
   (TP[s-lbd(bdp)](senv)∈Arithm ∧ TP[s-ubd(bdp)](senv)∈Arithm)
```

```
M[mk-Arraydecl(,tp,bdl)](exenv) ≜
   def ebds  : <M[bdl[i]](exenv) | 1≤i≤len bdl>;
   let indes = rect(ebds)  in
   def aloc  : genarrayden(indes);
   return(aloc)
type: Arraydecl → EXPRENV => ARRAYDEN
```

```
M[mk-Boundpair(lbd,ubd)](exenv) ≜
   def lbdv  : M[lbd](exenv);
   def ubdv  : M[ubd](exenv);
   let lbdvc : conv(lbdv,INT) in
   let ubdvc : conv(ubdv,INT) in
   if ubdvs<lbdvc then error else return(lbdvc,ubdvc)
type: Boundpair → EXPRENV => (Int × Int)
```

Comment The generation of an array with no elements (for a dimension) is defined here to be in error. This shows the error prior to reference;

```
genarrayden(inds) ≜
   def aloc: [indl ↦ genscden() | indl∈inds];
   return(aloc)
type: (Int+)-set => ARRAYDEN
```

Comment Assumes index set is dense.

Comment One-one property of denotation ensured.

```
rect: (Int × Int)+ → (Int+)-set
pre:  No lower bound exceeds the corresponding upperbound.
```

Comment Generates the (dense) set of valid index lists.

6.3.3 Switch Declarations

Switchdecl :: s-id:Id   s-exl:Expr⁺

WF[mk-Switchdecl(,exl)](senv) $\underline{\Delta}$
    *(∀ex∈elemsexl)(TP[ex](senv)=*LABEL*)*
type: Switchdecl → STATICENV → Bool

M[mk-Switchdecl(,exl)](env) $\underline{\Delta}$
  let f(ind,cas) = (if 1≤ind≤lenexl
                 then M[exl[ind]](env,cas) else error)
  in f
type: Switchdecl → ENV → SWITCHDEN

Comment Notice that the expressions of the *Switchdecl* are evaluated when referenced (dynamically). The static environment (that of declaration) is used.

6.3.4 Procedure Declarations -- already treated in sect. 6.2.2

6.4 STATEMENTS

Stmt   :: s-lp:Id-set   s-sp:Unlabstmt
Unlabstmt = Compstmt | Block | Assign | Goto |
*   Dummy | Condstmt | For | Procstmt*

"Standard" types:

WF: Unlabstmt → STATICENV → Bool
M: Unlabstmt → STMTENV =>

6.4.1 Compound Statements

*Compstmt :: Stmt**

M[mk-Compstmt(stl)](stenv) $\underline{\Delta}$
  for i=1 to lenstl do M[s-sp(stl[i])](stenv)

6.4.2 Blocks -- already treated in sect. 6.2.1

6.4.3 Assignment Statements

```
Assign    :: s-lp:Destin+    s-rp:Expr
Destin    :: s-tg:Leftpart   s-tp:Type
Leftpart   = Var | Atvfnid
Atvfnid   :: Id
```

Comment The return of a value from a function procedure is achieved by an assignment to a destination with the name of the function. Such names are called activated function identifiers (*atvfnid*).

```
WF[mk-Assign(dl,e)](senv) ≜
    let etp = TP[e](senv) in
    (∀i∈indsdl)(WF[dl[i],etp](senv))

WF[mk-Destin(lp,tp),etp](senv) ≜
    compattps(tp,etp) ∧
    (lp∈Var ∧ is-scalar(lp,senv) ∧ tp=TP[lp](senv) ∨
     lp∈Atvfnid ∧ mk-Typeproc(tp)=senv(s-id(lp)))
type: Destin × Type → STATICENV → Bool

TP[mk-Atvfnid(id)](senv) ≜ let mk-Typeproc(tp)=senv(id) in tp

M[mk-Assign(dl,e)](,env,cas) ≜
    def edl : <M[dl[i]](env,cas) | 1≤i≤lendl>;
    def v   : M[e](env,cas);
    for i=1 to lenedl do (let vc = conv(v,s-tp(dl[i])) in
                                   assign(vc,edl[i]))
```

Comment Order of evaluation defined to resolve non-determinism.

```
M[mk-Destin(lp,tp)](exenv) ≜ M[lp](exenv)
type: Destin → EXPRENV => SCALARLOC
```

Comment The context conditions ensure that the location corresponding to a variable will be a member of *SCALARLOC*.

```
M[mk-Atvfnid(id)](env,cas) ≜ let mk-ATVFNDEN(loc,)=env(id) in loc
type: Atvfnid → EXPRENV → SCALARLOC
```

6.4.4 Goto Statements

Goto :: Expr

WF[mk-Goto(e)](senv) ≜ *TP[e](senv)=*LABEL

M[mk-Goto(e)](,env,cas) ≜ def *ld : M[e](env,cas);* exit*(ld)*

The possibility of branching (by goto) into phrase structures in reflected by providing appropriate *Mcue* functions. These functions deliver denotations (of *TR*) which correspond to the execution of a phrase structure from some label to the end of (or abnormal exit from) the phrase. Notice that *tixe* is only used at the *Block* level in this definition.

```
Mcue[lab,mk-Stmt(labs,sp)](stenv) ≜
  if lab∈labs then M[sp](stenv) else Mcue[lab,sp](stenv)
type: Id × Stmt → STMTENV =>
pre:  lab ∈ contndls(mk-Stmt(labs,sp))

Mcue[lab,mk-Compstmt(stl)](stenv) ≜ Mcue[lab,stl](stenv)
type: Id × Compstmt → STMTENV =>

Mcue[lab,stl](stenv) ≜
  let i = index(lab,stl) in
  Mcue[lab,stl[i]](stenv);
  for j=i+1 to lenstl do M[s-sp(stl[j])](stenv)
type: Id × Stmt* → STMTENV =>
pre:  lab ∈ contndls(stl)

Mcue[lab,mk-Condstmt(,th,el)](stenv) ≜
  if lab∈contndls(th) then Mcue[lab,th](stenv)
  else Mcue[lab,el](stenv)
type: Id × Condstmt → STMTENV =>
pre:  lab ∈ (contndls(th) ∪ contndls(el))
```

6.4.5 Dummy Statements

Dummy :: DUMMY

*M[mk-Dummy(*DUMMY*)](stmtenv)* ≜ I_{STATE}

6.4.6 Conditional Statements

Condstmt :: s-test:Expr   s-th:Stmt   s-el:Stmt

The else statement is always present, if necessary the translator inserts a null statement.

```
WF[mk-Condstmt(e,th,el)](senv) ≜ TP[e](senv)=BOOL

M[mk-Condstmt(e,th,el)](stmtenv) ≜
    let (,env,cas) = stmtenv in
    def b          : M[e](env,cas);
    if b then M[s-sp(th)](stmtenv) else M[s-sp(el)](stmtenv)
```

6.4.7 For Statements

```
For            :: s-cv:Simplevar s-cvtp:Arithm s-fl:Forelem+ s-b:Block
Forelem        =  Exprelem | Whileelem | Stepuntilelem
Exprelem       :: Expr
Whileelem      :: s-in:Expr   s-wh:Expr
Stepuntilelem  :: s-in:Expr   s-st:Expr   s-un:Expr
```

The body of the abstract form of a for statement is always a block; if not present in the concrete form it is generated by the translator.

```
WF[mk-For(cv,cvtp,fl,b)](senv) ≜
    is-scalar(cv,senv) ∧ cvtp=TP[cv](senv)

WF[mk-Exprelem(e)](senv) ≜ TP[e](senv)∈Arithm

WF[mk-Whileelem(in,wh)](senv) ≜
    TP[in](senv)∈Arithm ∧ TP[wh](senv)=BOOL

WF[mk-Stepuntilelem(in,st,un)](senv) ≜
    TP[in](senv)∈Arithm ∧ TP[st](senv)∈Arithm ∧ TP[un](senv)∈Arithm

M[mk-For(cv,cvtp,flel,b)](stenv) ≜
    for i=1 to lenflel do M[flel[i],cv,cvtp,b](stenv)
```

Types for remainder of this sub-section:

```
M: Forelem × Var × Type × Block → STMTENV =>
```

```
M[mk-Exprelem(e),cv,cvtp,b](stmtenv) ≜
    let (,env,cas) = stenv           in
    def v          : M[e](env,cas);
    let vc         = conv(v,cvtp)    in
    def l          : M[cv](env,cas);
    assign(vc,l);
    M[b](stmtenv)

M[mk-Whileelem(in,wh),cv,cvtp,bd](stmtenv) ≜
    let (,env,cas) = stmtenv         in
    def v          : M[in](env,cas);
    let vc         = conv(v,cvtp)    in
    def l          : M[cv](env,cas);
    assign(vc,l);
    def b          : M[wh](env,cas);
    if b then (M[bd](stmtenv);
               M[mk-Whileelem(in,wh),cv,cvtp,bd)(stmtenv))
    else I_STATE
```

Comment Re-evaluation of initial expression (*in*) required by language.

```
M[mk-Stepuntilelem(in,st,un),cv,cvtp,bd](stenv) ≜
    let (,env,cas) = stenv             in
    let exenv      = (env,cas)         in
    def vin        : M[in](exenv);
    let vinc       = conv(vin,cvtp)    in
    def l          : M[cv](exenv);
    assign(vinc,l);
    step(st,un,cv,cvtp,bd)(stenv)

step(st,un,cv,cvtp,b)(stenv) ≜
    let (,env,cas) = stenv         in
    let exenv      = (env,cas)     in
    def vst        : M[st](exenv);
    def b          : M["cv-un"](exenv)*(sign(vst)≤0);
    if b then (M[b](stenv);
               def l     : M[cv](exenv);
               def vcur  : contents(l)+vst;
               let vcurv = conv(vcur,cvtp) in
               assign(vcurv,l);
               step(st,un,cv,cvtp,b)(stenv))
    else I_STATE
```

6.4.8 Procedure Statements

```
Procstmt     :: (Procdes | Functdes)
Procdes      :: s-pn:Id   s-app:Actparm*
Actparm      :: s-v:Actparmval   s-tp:Specifier
Actparmval    = Parmexpr | Arrayname | Switchname | Procname | String
Parmexpr     :: Expr
Arrayname    :: Id
Switchname   :: Id
Procname     :: Id
String       :: Char*
Char            Implementation defined set
```

```
WF[mk-Procdes(id,apl)](senv) ≜ env(id)=PROC
type: Procdes → STATICENV → Bool
```

```
WF[mk-Actparm(v,sp)](senv) ≜
    TP[v](senv) = sp                               ∧
    (sp∈Type                      ⊃ v∈Parmexpr)    ∧
    (sp∈Arraytype                 ⊃ v∈Arrayname)   ∧
    (sp∈(Typeproc ∪ {PROC}        ⊃ v∈Procname)    ∧
    (sp=LABEL                     ⊃ v∈Parmexpr)    ∧
    (sp=STRING                    ⊃ v∈String)      ∧
    (sp=SWITCH                    ⊃ v∈Switchname)
```

```
TP: Actparmval → STATICENV → (Type | LABEL) Similar to TP of Expr
```

```
M[mk-Procstmt(des)](,env,cas) ≜
    if des∈Procdes then M[des](env,cas)
    else (def v : M[des](env,cas); I_STATE)
```

Comment When a function procedure is invoked by a *Procstmt* the returned value is discarded

```
M[mk-Procdes(id,apl)](env,cas) ≜
    def denl : <M[apl[i]](env) | 1≤i≤lenapl>;
    let f     = env(id) in
    f(denl,cas)
type: Procdes → EXPRENV => VAL
```

M[mk-Actparm(v,tp)](env) $\triangleq$
  let *d = M[v](env)* **in** *mk-Actparmden(d,tp)*
type: *Actparm → ENV → DEN*

The rest of the functions in this section are of type:

M: Actparmval → ENV → DEN

M[mk-Parmexpr(e)](env) $\triangleq$
  if *e∈Varref* **then** (**let** *f(cas)=M[e](env,cas)* **in** *mk-BYNAMELOCDEN(f)*)
  else (**let** *f(cas) = M[e](env,cas)* **in** *mk-BYNAMEEXPRDEN(f)*)

Comment The calling information does not determine whether "byname" or "byvalue" mode is to be used so the "byname" parameters are genrated and evaluated when necessary within the called procedure. The distinction between whether evaluation can be used to determine a location is, however, made here.

M[mk-Arrayname(id)](env) $\triangleq$ *env(id)*

M[mk-Switchname(id)](env) $\triangleq$ *env(id)*

M[mk-Procname(id)](env) $\triangleq$ *env(id)*

M[mk-String(s)](env) $\triangleq$ *s*

6.5 EXPRESSIONS

Expr = Typeconst | Varref | Labelconst | Switchdes |
Functdes | Prefixexpr | Infixexpr | Condexpr

Comment The order of evaluation, which is governed in the concrete syntax by operator priority and parenthesis, is captured by the structure of abstract expressions.

Comment The various forms of expressions have been brought together in one abstract syntax. Context conditions are defined which, for example, limit the form of label expressions to use conditionals (there are no infix or prefix operators on *LABELDEN*).

Within this section (unless otherwise indicated):

WF: Expr → *STATICENV* → *Bool*

TP: Expr → *STATICENV* → *(Type* | LABEL*)*

M: Expr → *EXPRENV* => *VAL*

6.5.1 Arithmetic Constants

Typeconst :: *Booleconst* | *Arithmconst*

Boolconst :: *Bool*

Arithmconst = *Realconst* | *Intconst*

Realconst :: *Real*

Intconst :: *Int*

Comment The abstract syntax contains the semantic objects rather than their representations.

TP[mk-Boolconst(bv)](senv) = BOOL

TP[mk-Realconst(rv)](senv) = REAL

TP[mk-Intconst(iv)](senv) = INT

M[mk-Boolconst(bv)](exenv) $\underline{\underline{\Delta}}$ *bv*

M[mk-Realconst(rv)](exenv) $\underline{\underline{\Delta}}$ *represent(rv)*

M[mk-Intconst(iv)](exenv) $\underline{\underline{\Delta}}$ *test(iv)*

6.5.2 Variable References

Varref :: *Var*

Var = *Simplevar* | *Subscrvar*

Simplevar = *Simplevarbn* | *Simplevarv*

Simplevarbn :: *s-nm:Id*

Simplevarv :: *s-nm:Id*

Subscrvar = *Subscrvarbn* | *Subscrvarv*

Subscrvarbn :: *s-nm:Id* *s-sscl:Subscrs*

Subscrvarv :: *s-nm:Id* *s-sscl:Subscrs*

Subscrs :: $Expr^+$

Comment The distinction is made between references to "byname" (*bn*) formal parameters and values (*v*). The latter class includes "byvalue" formal parameters and normal variables.

WF[mk-Simplevarbn(id)](senv) $\underline{\underline{\Delta}}$ *senv(id)*∈*Type*

WF[mk-Simplevarv(id)](senv) $\underline{\underline{\Delta}}$ *senv(id)*∈*Type*

```
WF[mk-Subscrvarbn(id,sscl)](senv) Δ
   senv(id)∈Typearray ∧ (∀i∈indssscl)(TP[sscl[i]](senv)∈Arithm)

WF[mk-Subscrvarv(id,sscl)](senv) Δ
   senv(id)∈Typearray ∧ (∀i∈indssscl)(TP[sscl[i]](senv)∈Arithm)
```

Comment The check that "byname" references are used exactly for "by-name" parameters is not shown formally. To do so would require a minor extension to the *STATICENV*.

```
TP[mk-Simplevarbn(id)](senv) Δ senv(id)
TP[mk-Simplevarv(id)](senv)  Δ senv(id)

M[mk-Varref(var)](env,cas) Δ
   if var∈(Simplevarv∪Subscrvarv) ∨ env(s-nm(var))∈BYNAMELOCDEN
      then (def l    : M[var](env,cas);   contents(l))
      else (let bned = env(s-nm(var)) in bned(cas))
```

The remainder of the functions in this sub-section are of type:

```
M: Var → EXPRENV => LOC

M[mk-Simplevarbn(id)](env,cas) Δ
   let bnd = env(id) in
   if bnd∈BYNAMELOCDEN then bnd(cas) else error

M[mk-Simplevarv(id)](env,) Δ env(id)

M[mk-Subscrvarbn(id,sscl)](env,cas) Δ
   def esscl : M[sscl](env,cas);
   let bnd   = env(id) in
   if bnd∈BYNAMELOCDEN
      then (def aloc : bnd(cas);
            if esscl∈domaloc then return(aloc(esscl)) else error)
      else error

M[mk-Subscrvarv(id,sscl)](env,cas) Δ
   def esscl : M[sscl](env,cas);
   let aloc  = env(id) in
   if esscl∈domaloc then return(aloc(esscl)) else error
```

```
M[mk-Subscrs(sscl)](exenv) ≜
    def esscl: <(def essc   : M[sscl[i]](exenv);
                 let esscv = conv(essc,INT)  in
                 esscv) | 1≤i≤lensscl>;
    return(esscl)
type: Subscrs → EXPRENV => Int⁺
```

Comment Order of evaluation defined to resolve non-determinacy

6.5.3 Label Constants

```
Labelconst :: Id

WF[mk-Labelconst(id)](senv)    ≜ senv(id)=LABEL

TP[mk-Labelconst(id)](senv)    ≜ LABEL

M[mk-Labelconst(id)](env,cas) ≜ env(id)
```

6.5.4 Switch Designators

```
Switchdes :: s-id:Id    s-ssc:Expr

WF[mk-Switchdes(id,ssc)](senv) ≜
    senv(id)=SWITCH ∧ TP[ssc](senv)∈Arithm

TP[mk-Switchdes(id)](senv) ≜ LABEL

M[mk-Switchdes(id,ssc)](env,cas) ≜
    def essc   : M[ssc](env,cas);
    let esscv = conv(essc,INT) in
    let swden = env(id)        in
    def ld     : swden(esscv,cas);
    return(ld)
```

6.5.5 Function Designators

```
Functdes :: s-nm:Id    s-app:Actparm*

WF[mk-Functdes(id,app)](senv) ≜ senv(id)∈Typeproc
```

```
TP[mk-Functdes(id,app)](senv) ≜ s-type(senv(id))

M[mk-Functdes(id,app)](env,cas) ≜
    def denl: <M[app[i]](env) | 1≤i≤lenapp>;
    let f    = env(id)    in
    def v    : f(denl,cas);
    return(v)
```

6.5.6 Prefix Expressions

```
Prefixexpr :: s-opr:Prefixopr    s-op:Expr
Prefixopr    = REALPLUS | REALMINUS | INTPLUS   | INTMINUS   | NOT
```

Comment Type information is inserted into the tree form of expressions, this permits the insertion of appropriate operators.

```
WF[mk-Prefixexpr(opr,expr)](senv) ≜
    if opr=NOT then TP[expr](senv)=BOOL
    else TP[expr](senv)∈Arithm

TP[mk-Prefixexpr(opr,expr)](senv) ≜
    if opr=NOT then BOOL
    else if opr∈{REALPLUS,REALMINUS} then REAL else INT

M[mk-Prefixexpr(opr,expr)](exenv) ≜
    def v: M[expr](exenv);
    M[opr](v)
```

using:

```
M: Prefixopr → SCALARVAL => SCALARVAL

M[NOT](v)          ≜ ¬v
M[REALPLUS](v)     ≜ v
M[INTPLUS](v)      ≜ v
M[REALMINUS](v)    ≜ -v
M[INTMINUS](v)     ≜ -v
```

6.5.7 Infix Expressions

```
Infixexpr :: s-op1:Expr    s-opr:Infixopr    s-op2:Expr
```

```
Infixopr  =  REALADD | REALSUB      | REALMULT | REALDIV |
             INTADD  | INTSUB       | INTMULT  | INTDIV  |
             REALEXP | REALINTEXP   | INTEXP   |
             LT | LE | EQ   | NE    | GE | GT |
             IMPL    | EQUIV        | AND | OR

WF[mk-Infixexpr(e1,opr,e2)](senv) ≜
    let tp1 = TP[e1](senv) in
    let tp2 = TP[e2](senv) in
    (opr∈{REALADD,REALSUB,REALMULT}∧ REAL∈{tp1,tp2}⊆Arithm          ∨
     opr=REALDIV∧{tp1,tp2}⊆Arithm                                   ∨
     opr=REALEXP∧tp1∈Arithm∧tp2=REAL                                ∨
     opr=REALINTEXP∧tp1=REAL∧tp2=INT                                ∨
     opr∈{INTADD,INTSUB,INTMULT,INTDIV,INTEXP}∧tp1=tp2=INT          ∨
     opr∈{LT,LE,EQ,NE,GE,GT}∧{tp1,tp2}⊆Arithm                       ∨
     opr∈{IMPL,EQUIV,AND,OR}∧tp1=tp2=BOOL)

TP[mk-Infixexpr(e1,opr,e2)](senv) ≜
    opr∈{INTADD,INTSUB,INTMULT,INTDIV,INTEXP}                        → INT,
    opr∈{REALADD,REALSUB,REALMULT,REALDIV,REALEXP,REALINTEXP}        → REAL,
    T                                                                → BOOL

M[mk-Infixexpr(e1,opr,e2)](exenv) ≜
    def v1: M[e1](exenv);
    def v2: M[e2](exenv);
    M[opr](v1,v2)
```

Comment Evaluation is shown here as being left to right in order to resolve the non-determinism.

Using:

```
M: Infixopr → (SCALARVAL × SCALARVAL) => SCALARVAL

M[REALADD](v,w)  ≜ represent(v+w)

M[REALSUB](v,w)  ≜ represent(v-w)

M[REALMULT](v,w) ≜ represent(v*w)

M[REALDIV](v,w)  ≜ if w=0 then fault1 else represent(v*represent(1/w))
```

```
M[REALEXP](v,w)     ≜ if  v>0 then value of the standard function exp
                                applied on represent(v * value of the
                                standard function ln applied on w)
                            else if v=0∧w>0 then 0 else fault2

M[REALINTEXP](v,w) ≜
    if v=0 ∧ w=0 then fault3
    else (let expn(n) = if n=0 then 1 else represent(expn(n-1)*v) in
          if w≥0 then expn(w) else represent(1/expr(-w)))

M[INTADD](v,w)   ≜ test(v+w)

M[INTSUB](v,w)   ≜ test(v-w)

M[INTMULT](v,w)  ≜ test(v*w)

M[INTDIV](v,w)   ≜ if w=0 then fault1 else test(v/w)

M[INTEXP](v,w)   ≜ if w<0 ∨ v=0 ∧ w=0 then fault4
                     else (let expi(n) = if n=0 then 1

                                      else text(expi(n-1)*v) in
                          return(expi(w)))

M[LT](v,w)        ≜ return(v < w)
M[LE](v,w)        ≜ return(v ≤ w)
M[EQ](v,w)        ≜ return(v = w)
M[NE](v,w)        ≜ return(v ≠ w)
M[GE](v,w)        ≜ return(v ≥ w)
M[GT](v,w)        ≜ return(v > w)
M[IMPL](v,w)      ≜ return(v ⊃ w)
M[EQUIV](v,w)     ≜ return(v = w)
M[AND](v,w)       ≜ return(v ∧ w)
M[OR](v,w)        ≜ return(v ∨ w)
```

Comment *fault1* corresponds to *fault('division by zero',v)*
fault2 corresponds to *fault('expr undefined',v)*
fault3 corresponds to *fault('expn undefined',v)*
fault4 corresponds to *fault('expi undefined',v)*

6.5.8 Conditional Expressions

Condexpr :: s-dec:Expr   s-th:Expr   s-el:Expr

WF[mk-Condexpr(dec,th,el)](senv) $\underline{\Delta}$
  *TP[dec](senv)=*BOOL ∧ *is-compattps(TP[th](senv),TP[el](senv))*

is-compattps(tp1,tp2) $\underline{\Delta}$ *tp1=tp2* ∨ *{tp1,tp2}⊆Arithm*
*type: (Type|*LABEL*) × (Type|*LABEL*) → Bool*

TP[mk-Condexpr(dec,th,el)](senv) $\underline{\Delta}$
  let tp1 = TP[th](senv) in
  let tp2 = TP[el](senv) in
  if tp1=tp2 then tp1 else REAL

M[mk-Condexpr(dec,th,el)](exenv) $\underline{\Delta}$
  def decv : M[dec](exenv);
  if decv then M[th](exenv) else M[el](exenv)

6.6 AUXILIARY FUNCTIONS

is-uniqueoids: Block → Bool

checks that the *oid* components of any pair of *Owntypedecl* or *Ownarraydecl within* the block are distinct from each other.

is-constownbds: Block → Bool

checks that all expressions in the *s-bdl* component of *Ownarraydecl*'s *within* the block are integer constants.

is-within: Phrase × Block → Bool

tests whether a phrase (of any syntactic class) is contained (at any nesting depth) within a block.

is-scalar(v)(senv) $\underline{\Delta}$
  env(s-nm(v))∈Type ∨ *v∈Subscrvar* ∧ *env(s-nm(v))∈Typearray*

contndls: $Stmt^* \to Id\text{-}set$
contndll: $Stmt^* \to Id^*$

Two obvious functions for gathering the labels of a list of statements (labels within nested blocks are not collected). The list version is required to preserve duplicates so that a test for redefinition can be made:

index: $Id \times Stmt^* \xrightarrow{\sim} Nat$

For identifiers in the *contndls*, this function finds the index of that statement which contains the identifier as a label.

is-uniquel: $Object^* \to Bool$ -- true iff no duplicates

is-disjointl: $(Object\text{-}set)^* \to Bool$ -- true iff sets are pair-wise disjoint

conv(v,tp) $\triangleq$ if tp=INT then *test*("rounded value of v") else v
type: $Scalar \times Type \to SCALARVAL$
pre: $(v \in Bool \supset tp = \text{BOOL}) \wedge (v \in Real \supset tp \in Arithm)$

contents(l) $\triangleq$ def v:(c STR)(l); if v=nil then error else return(v)
type: $Scalar \Rightarrow SCALARVAL$

assign(v,l) $\triangleq$ STR := c STR + $[l \mapsto v]$
type: $SCALARVAL \times SCALARLOC \Rightarrow$

test(i) $\triangleq$ if -MAXINT<i<MAXINT then return(i) else error
type: $Int \Rightarrow Int$

represent(r) $\triangleq$ if $-MAXREAL < r < -MINREAL \wedge MINREAL < r < MAXREAL \vee r=0$
then return("implementation defined approximation to r")
else error
type: $Real \Rightarrow Real$

compattps: $Type \times Type \to Bool$, true if types compatible for assignment

6.7 SUPPORT INFORMATION

This section offers two aids to reading the ALGOL definition.

6.7.1 Abbreviations

Object names have been abbreviated systematically as shown below. (Local values within functions are further abbreviated.)

Abnormal component	constant	operator
actual	declaration	parameter
activation identifier	denonation	procedure
activated	designator	reference
arithmetic	descriptor	specification
assignment	destination	statement
by-name	element	subscripted
Boolean	environment	transformation
by-value	expression	unlabelled
character	function	value
compound	identifier	variable
conditional	integer	

6.7.2 Index

This index includes objects and functions. The functions *(M, TP, WF)* are defined by cases on their phrases (Split), and can be found by locating the phrase.

CHAPTER 7

PASCAL

This chapter again provides a VDM definition of an actual programming language. In some senses this definition of standard Pascal is very revealing. The sheer length of the definition in comparison to that of ALGOL 60 requires some comment. The type definition facility in Pascal accounts for much of the length of the static semantics. But in many cases (e.g. variant records) one is forced to the conclusion that features of the language do not always fit together in a natural way. The language is, however, held in very high regard especially for teaching purposes. The resolution of this apparent contradiction appears to be that simple programs normally function in a "natural" way but that the combination of language features often leads to complexity. The text explains the models of those language concepts not discussed in chapter 4 and makes more detailed comments on the language. The chapter provides an example of how a formal definition can be used to study and criticize a language.

CONTENTS

7.1 INTRODUCTION

This chapter is an attempt to give a complete, formal definition of the Pascal programming language. Until recently, the "official" definition of Pascal was the "grey book" [Jensen 75a]. This definition is incomplete in that much of the fine detail of the language is undefined because the document attempts to be both a tutorial introduction and a definition. In 1979 it was proposed that Pascal should be officially standardized, and a BSI (British Standards Institute) document has been published to this effect. The standard goes a long way towards removing ambiguities and lack of rigor of the grey book, but being written in English, it still leaves some questions unanswered.

Several formal definitions of Pascal exist [Hoare 73d, Tennent 80a], but these do not address the complete language as defined in the BSI standard. The definition that follows covers all of the Pascal language, including conformant arrays and variant records.

The main difference between Pascal and the simple programming language in Chapter 4 is the addition of declared data-types and records. Both extensions are large, but can easily be handled, though there are some problems with Pascal variant records. There are also several other smaller extensions which need to be considered, but these do not fundamentally change the approach to the formal definition of a programming language.

One of the first major decisions to be made is the form of the abstract syntax. This definition has chosen to use one which is fairly close to the concrete syntax of Pascal. This has the advantage of making the relationship between the two more obvious; it also also has several disadvantages which will be discussed below.

Each additional tool which is necessary for the definition will be introduced under an appropriate heading.

7.1.1 Comments on Static Semantics

Static Environment

The static environment contains all global information necessary to prove harmony between the declaration and the context of an applied occurence of an identifier. Therefore the static environment contains the declarations of all known identifiers. In addition to declarative information, some restrictions of Pascal require extra information to be present. For example, the control variable of a *for* loop must be declared in the block in which it used, and it cannot be passed by reference. This extra information is collected in components of the static environment, the selector names of which are suffixed by *-info*.

According to the different needs, the static environment is not simply a map, but a tuple of maps and sets. To facilitate mental a grasp of context condition formulas, access to the static environment is modelled by sets of functions: *in-X(id)*ρ and *out-X(id)*ρ. *in-X(id)*ρ checks for the occurrence of *id* in the *X*-component of the static environment ρ. *out-X(id)*ρ yields the value of *id* in the *X*-component of ρ.

Entering a new scope, local information is added to the static environment by the set of functions *merge-X(°)*ρ. According to the visibility rules, however, all information redefined in the inner scope must first be eliminated by the function *erase*.

Type Concept

Equality of types in Standard Pascal is based either on type equations relating them, or on them being the same required type or constructed type and on their structural equality. Depending on the context, type evaluation of components requires either the name or the structure of the type. Functions yielding the name of a type are prefixed by *T* (for type), and functions yielding the structure are prefixed *NT* (for new type). For example:

type *A* = *array* ... ;
type *B* = *A*;
var *C* : *B*;

The type name evaluation of the component *C* gives the type name *B*. The new type evaluation of *C* gives *array* ... .

Some expressions do not posses a type name. Their type is either a required type (*Real*, *Integer*, *Boolean*, *Char*) or a constructed type (a type constructed by the 'string' or 'set' constructor or the 'nil' type). The constructed types are the main cause of complexity in the formulae below.

7.1.2 Comments on Dynamic Semantics

Passing Information to the Program

The Pascal Standard does not define how actual parameters are associated with the formal parameters of a program. The actual parameters could be passed by value, by reference, or by some other parameter-passing mechanism. This definition uses a value-result type mechanism; the actual parameters are described as a map from identifier into values, and results are returned by the same map. Providing that no side-effects occur while the program is running (e.g. the passing mechanism is by reference, and the operating system causes a change in an argument location) the value-result model is adequate.

Environments

The Block-environment is made up of three components, the type environment, the (static) environment, and the active identifier set. It contains all the information necessary for the declaration of identifiers, and the association of identifiers with their meaning. Type identifiers can be distinguished syntactically; all other identifiers can only have interpretations associated with them if it is known how they were declared. It is, in general, impossible to determine the meaning from the context of an identifier within a block. The type environment is used to map type identifiers into the associated type information. The static environment maps all other identifiers as appropriate: variables to their denotations, constants to their values.

The decision was made to represent Pascal programs by an abstract syntax very similar to the concrete syntax. Information that could have been associated with a node of the abstract syntax tree is in one of the maps of the Block-environment. Associating type information with the appropriate node of the program representation would remove the need for the type environment, and also remove some elements from the domain of the static environment, but at the expense of a more complicated abstract syntax. With the current choice of abstract syntax, the well-formed conditions can be more easily related to the semantic checking part of a compiler.

As type definitions have scope rules which are identical to the rules for variables, it is necessary that dynamically allocated storage (storage obtained by the procedure *new*, and buffers) should use the correct environment. Because of this requirement, pointers and buffers have type and static environment information associated with them.

The *s-aid* component is used as in the simple language of Chapter 4.

Hops and Jumps and Goto's

The use of goto is heavily restricted in Pascal. It is only permissible to jump out of programming constructs. If the target of the goto is out of a procedure, the target statement must not be contained within any other statement of the procedure containing the target. These restrictions allow a straight-forward handling of gotos.

Jumps out of a procedure block are dealt with by the usual tixe mechanism. *cue-i-statement-list* is used to pick up the interpretation from the target statement. For a local goto, it is just necessary to "guard" the interpretation of a *flow-of-control* structure with a tixe statement whose domain is all the "immediate" labels. Again *cue-i-statement-list* can be used to pick-up the interpretation from the correct point (see chapter 5 or 6).

Records

Records which do not contain variant components are easily modelled. For example the record:

var r: record a: At; b: Bt; c: Ct end;

is modelled in the environment map by a component:

$\ldots, r \mapsto [a \mapsto loca, b \mapsto locb, c \mapsto locc], \ldots$

The storage mapping will map *loca,locb,* and *locc* into values. An access to a location, for example *r.a*, is given by *env(r)(a)*. The semantics of the *with* statement are defined by overwriting the current environment map with the range element of *env* corresponding to the identifier of the with statement. For example *with r do* ... will change the environment:

$nenv = env + env(r)$

Within the statement part of the *with* statement, the updated environment is used. A reference to the variable *a* will deliver the location *loca*.

If variant records are to be modelled, an extra complication occurs. Consider the following Pascal program fragments:

```
var r: record
         a: Int;
         case b: Colour of
            red:    (w: Int);
            yellow: (x: Char; y: Int);
            green:  (z: Real)
       end;
...
r.b := red;
r.w  = 4;
...
r.b  = green;
```

After the first assignment the integer location *w* is active - an integer value can be assigned to it. The other two locations corresponding to *x*, *y*, and *z* cannot be referenced. After the assignment of the value *green* to *r.b*, the value in the integer location, *r.w* is lost (and also, perhaps, the location). The *real* location corresponding to *r.z* now becomes active (and useable) but the value contained within it is undefined. A reference to the location *r.w* is now illegal, the location has "vanished". A valid implementation could be to allocate storage for a component of a variant record that became active, and free the storage of a component that becomes inactive. This may cause a different integer location to be allocated for *w* when, in the above example, the tag location is reset to the value *red*. This is not what happens in most implementations of Pascal. (Unlike PL/I, there is no way of detecting the address of a location in a variant record in Pascal, as there does not exist a function to exextract the address of a location.)

If the full implications are considered, the following problem occurs. The environment map associates an identifier with its location and, within a procedure, should be static - constructed on procedure entry, and remaining unchanged until procedure exit. If the environment is to deal with variant records, it must model the (possible) allocation and de-allocation of storage within a variant record, and this violates the static nature of the environment map within a procedure. (The environment should be "read-only"; the state is designed to contain "changeable" information.)

It can be argued that it is unnecessary to model storage to this level of detail, but this would bias the definition towards an implementation that allocated all the storage of a variant record and re-used that storage as necessary. An implementation that wanted to allocate and free variant record storage as required (for space reasons, perhaps) would need to show that this equivalent to one which re-used storage; this may be difficult. A definition should be general enough to allow either implementation, and make it easy to show both are valid.

Having chosen to model variant records with storage allocated and freed as necessary, a solution to the environment problem is to split it into a static part, which remains unchanged during the life-time of a procedure, and a dynamic part which models the changes that can occur across an assignment to the tag field. Since the changes occur across a statement, the obvious place for the dynamic part of the environment to reside is in the state.

The model for variant records, then, is as follows. The static environment contains the identifiers associated with their (fixed) denotations; those which are part of a variant component have linking information to the dynamic environment. The association of the identifiers of the variant components with their denotation is in the dynamic environment. For the program above the static environment would contain:

$$\ldots\ r \mapsto [a \mapsto loca, b \mapsto \ldots, w \mapsto did,$$
$$x \mapsto did,\ y \mapsto did, z \mapsto did], \ldots$$

where *did* is an identifier. The dynamic environment would contain, if the value in *b* was *yellow*:

$$\ldots, did \mapsto [\ x \mapsto locx, y \mapsto locy], \ldots$$

ignoring for the moment what the tag denotation would.

The environment is now a mapping from <u>Id</u>entifiers into <u>Den</u>otations (for all except varient records, in which case it maps to a <u>D</u>ynamic environment <u>Id</u>entifier (so that the correct component of the dynamic environment can be found):

Env: Id $\underset{m}{\rightarrow}$ *(Den | Did)*
Denv: Did $\underset{m}{\rightarrow}$ *Env*

Now it is time to consider the denotation of the tag field. If the value in tag location is changed, then the storage associated with the old active component of the variant record needs to be freed, and new locations allocated for the new active component. The dynamic environment contains sufficient information for the de-allocation step, and will need to be updated to reflect the changes. Information as to what storage needs to be allocated is required, and this is best associated with the tag denotation in the static environment. The following tag denotation will allow this.

t ↦ *mk-Tag-den(loc,did,type-information)*

The first component is the *tag* location, which contains the current tag value, and the *did* is the dynamic environment identifier which is used to obtain the appropriate part of the dynamic environment. The *type-information* is necessary so that the storage can be allocated; it is the variant-component from the abstract syntax.

A further complication occurs in Pascal because it is possible to have a tag field with no associated identifier. The rules for this type of variant record need to be understood:

```
var r: record
         a: A;
         case colour of
           red:   (c:X);
           green: (y:Y;z:Z)
       end;
```

On entry to the procedure containing this declaration, the location for *a* is allocated, but nothing can be done yet, with the variant part. Assignment to *x* makes the *red* component active, and assignment to *y* or *z* makes the *green* component active.

This causes further problems because there is now a tag location with no associated identifier. There is no natural home for this location - in either the static or dynamic environment. Further thought indicates that it is not necessary to have a location for the tag. There are other implications - whereas if there is a tag location which has an associated identifier, it is only an assignment to the tag that causes the dynamic environment to change. Assignment to any component of a variant record which does not have a tag identifier can cause the dynamic environment to change (or become invalid). This can be solved by adding a second component to the dynamic environment which contains information about potentially valid references (which could cause storage to be allocated and de-allocated).

Consider the following declaration:

```
var r: record
        a: A;
        case colour of red:   (w:W);
                       green: (x:X;
                               case sex of male:   (y:Y);
                                           female: (z:Z))
      end;
```

On entry to the procedure containing this declaration, the static environment from the *Block-env* component and the dynamic and variant environments of the state look like:

Static: ..., $r \mapsto [a \mapsto loca, w \mapsto did, x \mapsto did,$
$y \mapsto did,\ z \mapsto did],\ \ldots$

Dynamic: ..., $did \mapsto [\,],\ \ldots$

```
Variant: ..., did ↦ [w ↦ [red   ↦ ("w:W"),
                          green ↦ ("x:X;
                                   cases sex of ...")],
                     x ↦ (...),
                     y ↦ (...),
                     z ↦ (...)]
```

with x, y, and z mapped to the same value as w.

An assignment to z produces the following changes to the dynamic and variant environemnts, note that the static environment remain unchanged:

$z := 1$

```
Dynamic:      did  ↦ [x ↦ locx,y ↦ did',z ↦ did ]
              did' ↦ [z ↦ locz]

Variant: ..., did  ↦ [ as before ],
              did' ↦ [y ↦ ("case sex of ..."),
                      z ↦ ("case sex of ...")]
```

The static and dynamic environments together give the locations which are currently active, those that could have values in them if initialized. The variant environment gives those components which are potentially active (no locations, and hence no values) but they can be assigned to. This can be seen with the following:

```
var r: record
         a: A;
         case c: colour of red:    (x:X)
                           green: (case sex of male:   (y:Y);
                                               female: (z:Z)
       end;
```

If *r.c* contains *red*, the three environment components look like:

```
Static:   ..., r ↦ [a ↦ loca,c ↦ (locc,didc,...),x ↦ didc,
                    y ↦ didc,z ↦ didc], ...

Dynamic:  ..., didc ↦ [x ↦ locx], ...

Variant:  ...
```

Note that *y* and *z* do not appear in the variant environment since as the value *red* is in the tag location *c*, assignment to either of the values is illegal.

If *r.c* contains *green*, and a value has been assigned to *r.z*, the dynamic and variant environment look like:

```
Dynamic:  ..., didc ↦ [y ↦ vdidc,z ↦ locz], ...

Variant:  ..., vdidc ↦ [y ↦ ("case sex of ..."),
                        z ↦ ("case sex of ...")], ...
```

Assignment to *r.y* is now valid, and there is sufficient information in the two environment mappings to allocate storage for *r.y*.

For a reference in an expression, or a similar context, it is the static and dynamic environment which give all the information. For a reference on the left-hand side of an assignment statement, or a similar context, it is the three environments together which combine to give the necessary information. If the information is not present, then the reference is illegal. The two operations, *lhs-apply* and *rhs-apply*, resolve this.

The advantage of this model is that variant record problems have been localized, and the simple treatment of the *with* statement need not be altered; the (static) environment can be changed locally as before. There are other solutions which can disguise the variant record problem. These code all the information in a structured form in the (static) environment, but *with* is not defined in such a natural way. There is also the problem of passing active locations by reference; the associated tag has to be marked as read-only.

The *allocated-den* component of the Semantic Domain is used to diagnose a restriction on record assignment: it is illegal to have a variant record on either (or both) sides of an assignment statement if it was created by the version of the *new* procedure which allows tag values to be specified.

Pascal allows a component of a record to be another record. This is modelled in the definition by *Record-den* being a subset of *Loc* objects.

Arrays

The storage model for arrays is easier for Pascal than for the simple language. The reason for this is that Pascal defines multidimensional arrays to be an array of an array of an ∘∘∘ . Even though Pascal allows the use of any ordinal type as indices, rather than restricting them to be integers, this leads to a simpler model.

type colour = (red,blue,green,yellow);
var a: array [colour] of Integer

The array declared in the Pascal program fragment above can be represented by a mapping:

a: Colour $\underset{m}{\rightarrow}$ *Integer*

with a simple condition that the domain of the mapping is the set colour. A multi-dimensional array such as:

var b: array [colour,1..20] of Integer

is defined to be a syntactic short hand notation for:

var b: array [colour] of array [1..20] of Integer;

This array can be represented by a mapping of Colour into Objects which are *arrays [1..20] of Integer*, thus:

b: *Colour* $\underset{m}{\rightarrow}$ *Array*
Array: *{1:20}* $\underset{m}{\rightarrow}$ *Integer*

Note that there is a requirement that all range elements are the same type.

The model for arrays simplifies to:

Array-den: Ordinal $\underset{m}{\rightarrow}$ *Den*

where *Den* is any object that can be stored in an array, including another array.

Conformant Arrays

One of the major criticisms of the original Pascal language was the inability to write a general procedure or function which took array arguments, such as one to calculate the length of a vector. The bounds of an array are part of its type, and so a procedure needed to be written for each possible array size. Standard Pascal has extended the class of arguments to allow arrays to be passed to a procedure with information on their bounds. The bounds are declared as part of the parameter description. When the procedure is called, the identifiers corresponding to the array bounds are set to the correct value. Note that these identifiers have the same properties as the identifiers declared in the const part of a block.

Input-Output

The definition should allow implementations which free and allocate buffers after certain operations. The reason for modelling this is again for easier proof of correctness of a compiler. If the definition did not specify this possibility, it would be necessary to prove that an implementation that did free and reallocate buffers was valid. Note that I/O operations are not allowed file whose buffer has been passed by reference, since the buffer could be freed.

Invalid references

The problem of the "dangling reference" must be handled by the definition. This occurs when a program frees a storage location while there is still a reference to it. Either the storage must not be freed, or access to it through the reference must be an error. This problem can occur in PASCAL in several ways. A file buffer can be passed by reference to a procedure, and an I/O operation is performed on that file. As PASCAL allows the buffer to be freed and re-allocated, a reference to the original buffer is invalid. A component of a variant record can be passed by reference; changing the tag value will cause the invalid reference problem to occur. There is also the familiar problem of the *dispose* operation on a storage location to which there exists a (separate) reference.

The definition detects these problems by allocating and freeing storage for both buffers and variant record components as required. Whenever a new storage location is allocated, it will have a new identifier. Hence any reference to storage which has been freed will be in error, as the storage identifier will not be in the domain of the storage map. Where Pascal specifically forbids an action that could cause the invalid reference problem, this definition has chosen to record what would happen if it were allowed. This avoids additional complexity in the definition.

Conclusions

This definition of Pascal is long in comparison to that of the ALGOL 60 definition of chapter 6. Much of the additional length is concerned with the extra features of Pascal, and the associated problems.

The concept of user-defined types, adds considerably to the semantic checks which need to be done. For a larger, typed language, such as Ada, it would be better to have two abstract syntaxes. The first would be close to the concrete syntax of the language being defined. The second would be suitable for use by the dynamic semantics. Pascal is not large enough to warrant this extra complication.

The type mechanism of Standard Pascal allows all type checking to be done at compile time, unlike grey book Pascal and ALGOL 60. In both these languages the matching of arguments, which are procedures or functions to their parameter declarations, has to be a run-time chack. Unfortunately, the rules in Standard Pascal are too restrictive in this case; a procedure cannot be passed as an argument to itself.

The added complexity of of the storage model, and environment information necessary to deal with types, especially variant records, adds considerably to the size of the definition compared to that of ALGOL 60. The problems caused by variant records, both in the definition and in a "safe" implementation of Pascal, imply that they are not a good concept. ALGOL 68 style unions, perhaps with the option of visible tagfield, seem a better way to give similar facilities. With unions most of the required checking can be done at compile time, or at run time with simple code. The ability to pass a component of a variant record by reference will cause difficulties for a safe compiler (which would trap all errors). This is not allowed with ALGOL 68 unions. Variant records without a tag field identifier allow a "hole" in the type-checking for communicating with a non-Pascal environment. This is best done by code procedures as in ALGOL 60;

Finally, in ALGOL 60 most of the I/O is defined by procedures, while in Pascal it is defined by the same mechanism as the rest of the language. This implies that a definition claiming to be complete should include a formal definition of the appropriate operations.

The current definition shows that Pascal is not a simple language. Any compiler generating safe code, would need to include much run-time checking if all error situations are to be diagnosed. Much thought needs to be put into the design of a programming language; and a formal definition should be done against an abstract syntax as a way of testing designs. Much work has been done to show that the flows-of-control constructs of a programming language can benefit from using a formal approach. Building a (mathematical) storage model would benefit the other component of a programming language - the data.

7.2 SYNTACTIC DOMAINS

```
Program                  ::  s-name  :Id
                             s-args  :Id-set
                             s-block :Block

Block                    ::  s-decls :Declarations
                             s-stl   :Statement*

Declarations             ::  s-labels     :Label-set
                             s-constants  :(Id →m Constant)
                             s-types      :(Id →m Type)
                             s-variables  :(Id →m Type-id)
                             s-procedures :(Id →m Procedure)
                             s-functions  :(Id →m Function)

Statement                ::  s-label :[Label]
                             s-st    :Unlabelled-statement

Unlabelled-statement     =   Compound-statement    |
                             Assignment-statement  |
                             Procedure-statement   |
                             If-statement          |
                             Case-statement        |
                             While-statement       |
                             Repeat-statement      |
                             For-statement         |
                             With-statement        |
                             Goto-statement        |
                             NULL-STATEMENT

Compound-statement       ::  Statement*

Assignment-statement     ::  s-lp:Target   s-rp:Expression

Target                   =   Variable-access | Function-id

Function-id              ::  s-id:Id

Procedure-statement      ::  s-nm:Id   s-apl:Actual-parm*
```

```
If-statement            :: s-expr :Expression
                           s-th   :Statement
                           s-el   :[Statement]

Case-statement          :: s-expr:Expression  s-cc:Case-component+
Case-component          :: s-cs:Constant-set  s-st:Statement

While-statement         :: s-expr:Expression  s-st:Statement

Repeat-statement        :: s-st:Statement+    s-expr:Expression

For-statement           :: s-id          :Id
                           s-from        :Expression
                           s-direction   :(TO|DOWNTO)
                           s-to          :Expression
                           s-st          :Statement

With-statement          :: s-var:Variable-access  s-st:Statement

Goto-statement          =  Local-goto | Nonlocal-goto

Local-goto              :: Label

Nonlocal-goto           :: Label

Expression           =  Constant-expression | Variable-expression |
                        Function-designator | Prefix-expression   |
                        Infix-expression    | Set-constructor

Constant-expression     =  Scalar-const | String-const | NIL-VALUE

Scalar-const            =  Real-const | Integer-const |
                           Char-const | Id-const

Real-const              :: Real

Integer-const           :: Integer

Char-const              :: Char

Id-const                :: Id
```

```
String-const            ::  Char+

Variable-expression     ::  Variable-access

Variable-access         =   Id                   | Component-variable |
                            Reference-variable   | Buffer-variable

Component-variable      =   Indexed-variable     | Field-designator

Indexed-variable        ::  s-nm:Variable-access   s-expr:Expression

Field-designator        ::  s-nm:Variable-access   s-id:Id

Reference-variable      ::  Variable-access
Buffer-variable         ::  Variable-access

Function-designator     ::  s-nm:Id   s-apl:Actual-parm*

Actual-parm             =   Variable-access | Expression     |
                            Function-parm   | Procedure-parm |
                            Read-parm       | Write-parm

Function-parm           ::  Id
Procedure-parm          ::  Id

Write-parm              =   Default-write-parm | Width-write-parm |
                            Fixed-write-parm

Default-write-parm      ::  s-expr :Expression

Width-write-parm        ::  s-expr:Expression   s-len:Expression

Fixed-write-parm        ::  s-expr :Expression
                            s-len  :Expression
                            s-frac :Expression

Read-parm               ::  s-target :Variable-access
                            s-type   :{Integer,Real,Char}

Prefix-expression       ::  s-op:Prefix-op   s-opr:Expression

Prefix-op               =   Sign | not
```

Sign	=	real-plus | real-minus | integer-plus | integer-minus
Infix-expression	::	*s-lp:Expression* *s-op:Infix-op* *s-rp:Expression*
Infix-op	=	and | or | real-add | real-sub | real-mult | real-div | integer-add | integer-sub | integer-div | integer-mod | integer-mult | eq | ne | lt | le | ge | gt | union | intersection | difference | super-set | sub-set | in
Set-constructor	::	*Member**
Member	::	*Expression* | *Interval*
Interval	::	*s-low:Expression* *s-high:Expression*
Constant	=	*Prefix-const* | *String-const* | *Scalar-const*
Prefix-const	::	*Sign* *Id*
Type	=	*Domain-type* | *Structured-type* | *Packed-type* | *Reference-type*
Domain-type	=	*Type-id* | *Enumerated-type* | *Subrange-type*
Type-id	::	*s-id:Id*
Enumerated-type	::	Id^+
Subrange-type	::	*s-first:Constant* *s-last:Constant*
Structured-type	=	*Record-type* | *Array-type* | *File-type* | *Set-type*

```
Record-type                  ::  s-fp :(Id ⇸m Type-id)
                                 s-vp :[Variant-part]

Variant-part                 ::  s-tag  :[Id]
                                 s-tagt :Type-id
                                 s-evp  :(Constant ⇸m Record-type)

Array-type                   =   s-dtype:Type-id   s-rtype:Type-id

File-type                    ::  Type-id
Set-type                     ::  Type-id
Reference-type               ::  Type-id

Packed-type                  ::  s-type :Structured-type

Procedure                    ::  s-parms:Parameters  s-body:Block

Function                     ::  s-parms  :Parameters
                                 s-body   :Block
                                 s-return :Type-id

Parameters                   ::  s-ids  :Formal-parameter*
                                 s-type :(Id ⇸m Parameter-type)

Formal-parameter             =   Id+

Parameter-type               =   Var-formal-parameter         |
                                 Value-formal-parameter       |
                                 Function-formal-parameter    |
                                 Procedure-formal-parameter   |
                                 Var-array-formal-parameter   |
                                 Value-array-formal-parameter

Var-formal-parameter         ::  Type-id

Value-formal-parameter       ::  Type-id

Function-formal-parameter    ::  s-parms:Parameters   s-return:Type-id

Procedure-formal-parameter   ::  s-parms:Parameters
```

Var-array-formal-parameter :: *s-schema:Conformant-array-schema*

Value-array-formal-parameter :: *s-schema:Conformant-array-schema*

Conformant-array-schema = *P-array-schema* | *Array-schema*

P-array-schema :: *s-ind:Index-type-spec* *s-type:Type-id*

Array-schema :: *s-ind :Index-type-spec*
s-type :Array-type-info

Array-type-info = *Conformant-array-schema* | *Type-id*

Index-type-spec :: *s-low:Id* *s-high:Id* *s-type:Type-id*

Auxiliary Definition

Required-type = {Integer,Real,Char,Boolean}

Notes on Concrete to Abstract Translation

Although the concrete syntax of Pascal and the translation algorithms from concrete to abstract syntax are not given here, a number of points about the translation mechanism need to be made.

- Concrete delimiters (e.g. ";", and ",") and comments are dropped.
- Within expressions, brackets and operator precedence are used to determine the appropriate abstract tree structure of an expression.
- Array declaration abbreviations are removed, e.g.:

  var a : array[1..3,1..4] of integer;

  is expanded to:

  var a : array[1..3] of array[1..4] of integer;

- Certain concrete syntax constructions are considered as abbreviations and are not represented by the abstract syntax. Thus:

  var id_1, id_2, ... , id_n: *new-type-desc*

is considered to be an abbreviation for:

```
type typeid = new-type-desc;
var id1      : typeid,
    id2      : typeid,
    ...        ...
    idn      : typeid;        -- where typeid is not used elsewhere.
```

- Each structured type only has *Type-ids* describing the types of its components
- All type identifiers of a program are distinct
- I/O file abbreviations are completed:

write(x,y)

is expanded to the:

mk-Procedure-statement("output",< ... "x" ... >)

7.3 STATIC SEMANTICS

7.3.1 Static Semantic Domains

```
Static-env :: s-local-labels  : Label-set
              s-global-labels : Label-set
              s-constants     : Id ⇸ (Constant | Required-value)
              s-types         : Id ⇸ (Type | Required-type)
              s-variables     : Id ⇸ (Type-id | Conformant-array-schema)
              s-procedures    : Id ⇸ (Procedures |
                                          required-procedure-heading)
              s-functions     : Id ⇸ (Function-heading |
                                          required-function-heading)
              s-for-info      : Id-set
              s-function-info : Id-set
              s-tag-info      : Id-set
              s-packed-info   : Id-set

Required-type         = Real | Integer | Boolean | Char | Text
```

```
Required-value          =  Bool

Function-heading        :: Parameters  Type

All-type                =  Type | Required-type | nil-type | empty-set-type
                           constructed-set-type | constructed-string-type

Constructed-set-type    :: Domain-type

Constructed-string-type :: Integer
```

Test Functions of Static Environment

```
in-local-labels(lab)ρ   ≜ lab∈s-local-labels(ρ)
in-global-labels(lab)ρ  ≜ lab∈s-global-labels(ρ)
in-constants(id)ρ       ≜ id∈dom(s-constants(ρ))
in-types(id)ρ           ≜ id∈dom(s-types(ρ))
in-variables(id)ρ       ≜ id∈dom(s-variables(ρ))
in-procedures(id)ρ      ≜ id∈dom(s-procedures(ρ))
in-functions(id)ρ       ≜ id∈dom(s-functions(ρ))
in-schema-info(id)ρ     ≜ id∈dom(s-schema-info(ρ))
in-for-info(id)ρ        ≜ id∈s-for-info(ρ)
in-function-info(id)ρ   ≜ id∈s-function-info(ρ)
in-tag-info(id)ρ        ≜ id∈s-tag-info(ρ)
in-packed-info(id)ρ     ≜ id∈s-packed-info(ρ)

in-bounds(id)ρ          ≜ (∃id1∈Id)(in-variables(id1)ρ) ∧
                            let tid=s-variables(ρ)(id1) in
                            mk-Index-type-spec(id,,)∈bounds-of(tid) ∨
                            mk-Index-type-spec(,id,)∈bounds-of(tid)

in-enumerated(id)ρ      ≜ (∃id1∈doms-types(ρ))
                              (is-Enumerated-type(s-types(ρ)(id1))∧
                               let mk-Enumerated-type(list)=s-types(ρ)(id1)
                               in (∃i∈indslist)(id=list[i]))
```

Access Functions of Static Environment

```
out-constants(id)ρ    ≜ s-constants(ρ)(id)
out-types(id)ρ        ≜ s-types(ρ)(id)
out-variables(id)ρ    ≜ s-variables(ρ)(id)
```

```
out-procedures(id)ρ  ≜ s-procedures(ρ)(id)

out-functions(id)ρ   ≜ cases s-functions(ρ)(id):
                           mk-function-heading(parms,rtype) → parms,
                           T → required-function-heading

out-return-type(id)ρ ≜ cases s-functions(ρ)(id):
                           mk-function-heading(parms,rtype) → rtype,
                           T → required-return-type

out-bounds(id)ρ      ≜ let type∈Somain-type be s:t:
                         (∃id1∈Id)(in-variables(id1)ρ) ∧
                         let tid∈s-variables(ρ)(id1) in
                         mk-Index-type-spec(id,,type)∈bounds-of(tid) ∨
                         mk-Index-type-spec(,id,type)∈bounds-of(tid))
                       in type

out-enumerated(id)ρ  ≜ let id1∈Id be s:t: id1∈doms-types(ρ)        in
                       let mk-Enumerated-type(l)=s-types(ρ)(id1) in
                       (∃i∈indsl)(id=l[i])
```

Transformation Functions of Static Environment

```
merge(mk-Declarations(,constm,typem,varm,procm,functm))ρ ≜
  mk-Static-env(s-local-labels(ρ),
                s-global-labels(ρ),
                s-constants(ρ)  ∪ constm,
                s-types(ρ) ∪ typem,
                s-variables(ρ)  ∪ varm,
                s-procedures(ρ) ∪ [id ↦ parms |
                                     mk-Procedure(parms,)=procm(id)],
                s-functions(ρ)  ∪ [id ↦ mk-Function-heading(parms,rtype) |
                                  mk-Function(parms,,rtype)=functm(id)],
                s-for-info(ρ),
                s-function-info(ρ),
                s-tag-info(ρ),
                s-packed-info(ρ))

merge-X(Y)ρ ≜  let ρ' be s:t: s-X(ρ')=s-X(ρ)∪Y
                               ∩ (other components unchanged) in ρ'
```

Note: The *Static-env*, ρ, has been restricted before the above *merge* functions are called.

*erase(ids,labst)*ρ $\triangleq$ all *id*∈*ids* are erased from all components of type *Id* $\underset{m}{\rightarrow}$ *X* or *Id-set*, all *labels* ∈ *labs* are erased from the *local-labels* and *global-labels* components of the *Static-enf*

Initialization

```
required-static-env =
   mk-Static-env(s-local-labels : {},
                 s-global-labels: {},
                 s-constant      : ["maxint" ↦
                                     mk-Integer-constant(maxint),
                                    "true"  ↦ true,
                                    "false" ↦ false],
                 s-types         : ["Boolean" ↦ Boolean,
                                    "Integer" ↦ Integer,
                                    "Real"    ↦ Real,
                                    "Char"    ↦ Char,
                                    "Text"    ↦ Text],
                 s-variables     : ["input"   ↦ Text,
                                    "output"  ↦ Text],
                 s-procedures    : ["dispose" ↦ required-proc-heading,
                                   also for "get","new","pack","put",
                                            "read", "readln" "reset",
                                            "rewrite", "unpack","write"
                                            "writeln" ],
                 s-functions     : ["abs" ↦ required-function-heading,
                                   also for "sqr","sin","cos","exp",
                                            "ln","sqrt", "arctan","chr",
                                            "trunc","round","ord","succ",
                                            "pred","odd","eof","eoln"],
                 s-for-info      : {},
                 s-function-info: {},
                 s-tag-info      : {},
                 s-packed-info   : {})
```

7.3.2 Context Condition Functions

Function Abbreviations

WF-	Well-formedness of a:	*WFP*	- Program
WFVA	- Variable Access	*WFDP*	- Parameter Declaration
WFB	- Block	*WFSCH*	- Conformant Array Schema
WFBD	- Block Declaration	*TE*	Type of an Expression
WFD	- Declarations	*TVA*	Type of a Variable Acces
WFSL	- Statement List	*NTE*	New Type of an Expression
WFUS	- Unlabelled Statement	*NTVA*	New Type of a Variable Access
WFE	- Expression	*NTT*	New Type of a Type

Function Definitions

```
WFP: Program → Bool
WFP[mk-Program(,args,block)] ≜
   is-unique-declarations(<>,[],block) ∧ is-unique-labels(block) ∧
   (let ids = all-local-id(<>,[],block) in
   (∀i∈indsargs)(let id = args[i] in
                 if id∈{"input","output"}  then id∉ids
                 else id∈doms-variables(s-decls(block))) ∧
    WFB[block]erase(ids,{})required-static-env

WFB: Block → Static-env → Bool
WFB[mk-Block(decls,stl)]ρ ≜
   all-for-id(stl) ⊆ doms-variables(decls)        ∧
   let ρ' = merge(decls)ρ in
   WFBD[decls]merge-global-labels(labels(stl))ρ' ∧
   WFSL[stl]ρ'

WFBD: Declarations → Static-env → Bool
WFBD[mk-Declarations(,constm,typem,varm,procm,functm)]ρ ≜
   (∀id∈domconstm)(WFD[constm(id)]ρ) ∧ (∀id∈domtypem)(WFD[typem(id)]ρ)  ∧
   (∀id∈domvarm)(WFD[varm(id)]ρ)     ∧ (∀id∈domprocm)(WFD[procm(id)]ρ)  ∧
   (∀id∈domfunctm)(WFD[functm(id)]merge-function-info({id})ρ)

WFSL: Statement* → Static-env → Bool
WFSL[sl]ρ ≜
   let ρ' = merge-local-labels(labels(sl))ρ in
   (∀i∈indssl)(WFUS[s-st(sl[i])]ρ')
```

```
WFUS: Unlabelled-statement → Static-env → Bool

WFUS[mk-Compound-statement(sl)]ρ ≜ WFSL(sl)ρ

WFUS[mk-Procedure-statement(id,apl)]ρ ≜
    in-procedures(id)ρ ∧
    cases out-procedures(id)ρ:
       required-procedure-heading →
          is-required-procedure-correspondence(id,apl)ρ
       mk-Parameters(idl,type)     →
          is-corresponding(idl,type,apl)ρ

WFUS[mk-Assignment-statement(target,exp)]ρ ≜
    if is-Function-id(target)
       then let id = s-id(target) in
            in-functions(id)ρ ∧ in-function-info(id)ρ ∧
            WFE[exp]ρ ∧
            is-assignment-compatible(out-return-type(id)ρ,TE[exp]ρ)ρ
       else WFVA[target]ρ ∧
            WFE[expr]ρ     ∧
            (is-Id(target) ⊃ ¬in-for-info(target)ρ) ∧
             is-assignment-compatible(TVA[target]ρ,TE[exp]ρ)ρ

WFUS[mk-If-statement(exp,th,el)]ρ ≜
   WFE[exp]ρ  ∧  WFSL[<th>]ρ  ∧  (el≠nil ⊃ WFSL[<el>]ρ)  ∧
   NTE[exp]ρ=Boolean

WFUS[mk-Case-statement(exp,ccl)]ρ ≜
   WFE[exp]ρ ∧
   let type = TE[exp]ρ in is-ordinal(type)ρ ∧
   (∀i∈indsccl)(let mk-Case-component(cs,sp) = ccl[i] in
                (∀c∈cs)(WFC[c]ρ ∧ is-same(type,TE[c]ρ)ρ) ∧
                WFSL[<sp>]ρ) ∧
   (∀i,j∈indsccl)(s-cs(ccl[i])∩s-cs(ccl[j])≠{} ⊃ i=j)

WFUS[mk-While-statement(exp,st)]ρ ≜
   WFE[exp]ρ  ∧  WFSL[<st>]ρ  ∧   NTE[exp]=Boolean

WFUS[mk-Repeat-statement(sl,exp)]ρ ≜
   WFSL[sl]ρ  ∧  WFE[exp]ρ  ∧  NTE[exp]= Boolean
```

```
WFUS[mk-For-statement(id,from,,to,st)]ρ ≜
    in-variables(id)ρ ∧ ¬in-for-info(id)ρ ∧ is-ordinal(NTVA[id]ρ)ρ ∧
    WFE[from]ρ  ∧  WFE[to]ρ  ∧  WFSL[<st>]merge-for-info({id})ρ ∧
    is-compatible(TVA[id]ρ,TE[from]ρ) ∧ is-compatible(TVA[id]ρ,TE[to]ρ)

WFUS[mk-With-statement(vs,st)]ρ ≜
    WFVA[vs]ρ ∧
    let type = NTVA[vs]ρ in
    let type1  =  if  is-Packed-type(type)  then  s-type(type)  else  type  in
    is-Record-type(type1) ∧
    WFSL[<st>]merge-variables(all-fields(type1))
              merge-tag-info(all-tags(type1))
              merge-packed-info(if is-Packed-type(type)
                                   then all-fields(type1) else {})
              erase(all-fields(type1),{})ρ

WFUS[mk-Local-goto(id)]ρ  ≜ in-local-labels(id)ρ

WFUS[mk-Global-goto(id)]ρ ≜ in-global-labels(id)ρ

WFE: Expression → Static-env → Bool

WFE[mk-Constant-expression(exp)]ρ ≜
    cases exp:
        mk-Real-constant()        → true
        mk-Integer-constant(i)  → -maxint<i<maxint
        mk-Char-constant()        → true
        mk-Id-constant(id)        → in-constants(id)ρ ∨ in-bounds(id)ρ
        mk-String-constant(cl)  → lencl>1
        nil-value                 → true

WFE[mk-Set-constructor(mk)]ρ ≜
    mk=<> ∨
    let es = union{if is-Expression(mk[i]) then {mk[i]}
                     else {s-low(mk[i]),s-high(mk[i])} | i∈indsmk} in
    (∀e1,e2∈es)
        (let t1 = NTE[e1]ρ in
         let t2 = NTE[e2)ρ in
         is-ordinal(t1)ρ ∧ t1=t2)
```

```
WFE[mk-Prefix-expression(op,exp)]ρ  Δ
    WFE[exp]ρ  ∧
    let t = NTE[exp]ρ  in
    cases op:
        real-plus,real-minus        → t = Real
        integer-plus,integer-minus  → t = Integer
        not                         → t = Boolean

WFE[mk-Infix-expression(exp1,op,exp2)]ρ  Δ
    WFE[exp1]ρ  ∧ WFE[exp2]ρ  ∧
    let t1 = NTE[exp1]ρ  in
    let t2 = NTE[exp2]ρ  in
    cases op:
        and,or                      → t1=Boolean  ∧ t2=Boolean
        real-add,real-sub,
        real-mult,real-div          → t1=Real     ∧ t2=Real ∨
                                      t1=Integer  ∧ t2=Real ∨
                                      t1=Real     ∧ t2=Integer
        integer-add,integer-sub,
        integer-mult, integer-mod,
        integer-div                 → t1=Integer  ∧ t2=Integer
        eq,ne                       → (is-simple(t1)ρ                 ∨
                                        is-Reference-type(t1)         ∨
                                        is-all-set-type(t1)           ∨
                                        is-all-string-type(t1)ρ)        ∧
                                      (is-compatible(t1,t2)ρ          ∨
                                        t1=Real     ∧ t2=Integer ∨
                                        t1=Integer  ∧ t2=Real )
        lt,gt,le,ge                 → (is-simple(t1)ρ                 ∨
                                        is-all-string-type(t1)ρ)        ∧
                                      (is-compatible(t1,t2)ρ          ∨
                                        t1=Real     ∧ t2=Integer ∨
                                        t1=Integer  ∧ t2=Real )
        union,intersection,dif-
        ference,super-set,sub-set   → is-all-set-type(t1) ∧
                                      is-all-set-type(t2) ∧
                                      is-compatible(t1,t2)ρ
        in                          → is-ordinal(t1)ρ ∧ is-all-set-type(t2)∧
                                      is-compatible
                                          (NTE[mk-Set-constructor
                                                   (<mk-Member(exp1)>)]ρ,t2)ρ
```

```
WFE[mk-Variable-expression(va)]ρ ≜ WFVA[va]ρ

WFE[mk-Function-designator(id,apl)]ρ ≜
  in-functions(id)ρ ∧
  cases out-functions(id)ρ:
    required-function-heading →
             is-required-function-correspondence(id,apl)ρ
    mk-Parameters(idl,type)   →
             is-corresponding(idl,type,apl)ρ

WFVA: Variable-access → Static-env → Bool

WFVA(id)ρ ≜ in-variables(id)ρ

WFVA[mk-Indexed-variable(va,exp)]ρ = ≜
   WFVA[va]ρ ∧ WFE[exp]ρ ∧
   let tva = NTVA[va]ρ in
   let tva1 = if is-Packed-type(tva) then s-type(tva) else tva in
   is-Array-type(tva1) ∧
   is-assignment-compatible(s-dtype(tva1),NTE[exp]ρ)ρ

WFVA[mk-Field-designator(va,id)]ρ ≜
   WFVA[va]ρ ∧
   let tva = NTVA[va]ρ in
   let tva1 = if is-Packed-type then s-type(tva) else tva in
   is-Record-type(tva1) ∧ id∈domall-fields(tva1)

WFVA[mk-Reference-variable(va)]ρ ≜
   WFVA[va]ρ ∧ is-Reference-type(NTVA[va]ρ)

WFVA[mk-Buffer-variable(va)]ρ ≜
   WFVA[va]ρ ∧
   let tva = NTVA[va]ρ in
   let tva1 = if is-Packed-type(tva) then s-type(tva) else tva in
   is-File-type(tva1)

WFD: (Constant | Type | Procedure | Function) → Static-env → Bool

WFD[mk-Prefix-constant(sign,id)]ρ ≜
   in-constants(id)ρ ∧
   WFE[mk-Prefix-expression(sign,mk-Id-const(id))]ρ
```

```
WFD[mk-Real-const()]ρ                ≜ true
WFD[mk-Integer-const(i)]ρ            ≜ -maxint<i<maxint
WFD[mk-Char-const()]ρ                ≜ true
WFD[mk-Id-const(id)]ρ                ≜ in-constants(id)ρ
WFD[mk-String-const(cl)]ρ            ≜ lencl > 1
WFD[mk-Type-id(id)]ρ                 ≜ in-type(id)ρ
WFD[mk-Enumerated-type(idl)]ρ        ≜ true

WFD[mk-Subrange-type(f,l)]ρ ≜
    WFE[f]ρ ∧ WFE[l]ρ ∧ is-ordinal(TE[f]ρ)ρ ∧
    is-same(TE[f]ρ,TE[l]ρ)ρ ∧
    values(mk-subrange-type(f,l))ρ≠{}

WFD[mk-Array-type(dt,rt)]ρ           ≜ is-ordinal(NTT[dt]ρ)ρ ∧ WFD[rt]ρ

WFD[mk-Record-type(fp,vp)]ρ ≜
    is-unique-fields(mk-Record-type(fp,vp),vp)  ∧
    (∀id∈domfp)(WFD[fp(id)]ρ) ∧
    vp≠nil ⊃ (let mk-Variant-part(,tid,evp) = vp in
              let nt = NTT[tid]ρ                  in
              (∀c∈domevp)(WFE[c]ρ ∧ is-compatible(tid,NTE[c]ρ)ρ ∧
               WFD[evp(c)]ρ) ∧ values(nt)ρ=domevp)

WFD[mk-Set-type(dt)]ρ                ≜ is-ordinal(NTT(dt)ρ)ρ

WFD[mk-File-type(t)]ρ                ≜ is-not-containing-file-type(t)ρ

WFD[mk-Reference-type(mk-Type-id(id))]ρ ≜ in-types(id)ρ

WFD[mk-Packed-type(t)]ρ              ≜ WFD[t]ρ

WFD[mk-Procedure(parms,block)]ρ ≜ is-wf-function-procedure(parms,block)ρ

WFD[mk-Function(parms,block,type)]ρ ≜
    let t = NTT[type] in
    (is-simple(t)ρ ∨ is-Reference-type(t)) ∧
     is-wf-function-procedure(parms,block)ρ

WFDP: Parameter-type → Static-env → Bool

WFDP[mk-Var-formal-parameter(type)]ρ ≜ in-types(s-id(type))ρ
```

```
WFDP[mk-Value-formal-parameter(type)]ρ Δ
   in-types(s-id(type))ρ ∧ is-not-containing-file-type(NTT[type]ρ)ρ

WFDP[mk-Var-array-formal-parameter(schema)]ρ Δ
   WFSCH[schema]ρ

WFDP[mk-Value-array-formal-parameter(schema)]ρ Δ
   is-not-containing-file-type(schema)ρ ∧ WFSCH[schema]ρ

WFSCH: Conformant-array-schema → Static-env → Bool

WFSCH[mk-P-array-schema(index-type,type)]ρ Δ
   in-types(s-id(s-type(index-type)))        ∧
   is-ordinal(NTT[s-type(index-type)]ρ)ρ ∧
   in-types(s-id(type))ρ

WFSCH[mk-Array-schema(index-type,schema)]ρ Δ
   in-types(s-type(index-type))ρ              ∧
   is-ordinal(NTT[s-type(index-type)]ρ)ρ ∧
   if is-Id(schema)
      then in-types(schema)ρ
      else WFSCH[schema]ρ

TE: Expression → Static-env → All-type

TE[mk-Real-const()]ρ               Δ Real
TE[mk-Integer-const()]ρ            Δ Integer
TE[mk-Char-const()]ρ               Δ Char
TE[mk-String-const(cl)]ρ           Δ mk-Constructed-string-type(len cl)
TE[mk-Variable-expression(va)]ρ Δ TVA[va]ρ

TE[mk-Set-constructor(ml)]ρ Δ
   if ml=<>
      then empty-set-type
      else mk-Constructed-set-type(if is-Expression(ml[1])
                                       then NTE[ml[1]]ρ
                                       else NTE[s-low(ml[1])]ρ)

TE[nil]ρ Δ nil-type
```

```
TE[mk-Prefix-expression(op,)]ρ ≜
   cases op:
      real-plus,real-minus          → Real
      integer-plus,integer-minus    → Integer
      not                           → Boolean

TE[mk-Id-const(id)]ρ ≜
   if in-constants(id)ρ
      then if in-enumerated(id)ρ
              then out-enumerated(id)ρ
              else let const = out-constants(id)ρ in
                   if const∈Bool then Boolean  else TE[const]ρ
      else out-bounds(id)ρ

TE[mk-Infix-expression(opr1,op,opr2)]ρ ≜
   cases op:
      real-add,real-sub,real-mult,real-div          → Real
      integer-add,integer-sub,integer-mult,
      integer-div,integer-mod                       → Integer
      eq,ne,le,ge,gt,and,or,in,superset,subset      → Boolean
      union,intersection,difference                 → TE[opr1]ρ

TE[mk-Function-designator(id,apl)]ρ ≜
   let t = out-return-type(id)ρ in
   if t=required-return-type
      then cases id:
              "abs","sqr","pred","succ"                      → NTE[apl[1]]ρ
              "sin","cos","exp","ln","sqrt","arctan"         → Real
              "trunc","round","ord"                          → Integer
              "chr"                                          → Char
              "odd","eof","eoln"                             → Boolean
      else t

TVA: Variable-access → Static-env → (Type | Required-type)

TVA[id]ρ ≜ out-variables(id)ρ

TVA[mk-Indexed-variable(va,)]ρ ≜
   let t = NTVA[va]ρ in
   if is-Packed-type(t) then s-rtype(s-type(t)) else s-rtype(t)
```

```
TVA[mk-Field-designator(va,id)]ρ ≜
   let t = NTVA[va]ρ in
   let t1 = if is-Packed-type(t) then s-type(t) else t in
   all-fields(t1)(id)

TVA[mk-Reference-variable(va)]ρ ≜
   let mk-Reference-type(type) = NTVA[va]ρ in type

TVA[mk-Buffer-variable(va)]ρ ≜
   let t = NTVA[va]ρ in
   let t1 = if is-Packed-type(t) then s-type(t) else t in
   if t1=Text then Char else t1

NTE: Expression → Static-env → (All-type | Generated-type)
NTE[exp]ρ ≜ let t = TE[exp]ρ in if is-Type-id(t) then NTT[t]ρ else t

NTVA: Variable-access → Static-env → (Type | Required-type)
NTVA[va]ρ ≜ let t = TVA[va]ρ if is-Type-id(t) then NTT[t]ρ else t

NTT: Type → Static-env → (Type | Required-type)
NTT[type]ρ ≜ cases type: mk-Type-id(id) → NTT[out-types(id)ρ]ρ
                         T              → type
```

7.3.3 Auxiliary Functions

is-unique-declarations: $Id^{**} \times (Id \underset{m}{\rightarrow} Type\text{-}id) \times [Block] \rightarrow Bool$

is-unique-declarations(idll,parm-decl,block) ≜

all identifiers occurring
- in *idll*,
- in *mk-Index-type-spec* at *s-low* or *s-high* position in *parm-decl*,
- in *doms-constants(s-decl(block))*,
- in *doms-types(s-decl(block))*,
- in *doms-variables(s-decl(block))*,
- in *doms-procedures(s-decl(block))*,
- in *doms-functions(s-decl(block))*,
- in *mk-enumerated-type* in *s-types(s-decl(block))* are different and

all identifers occurring in *idll* occur in *domparm-decl*, and there is no cyclic definition in *s-constants(block)* and each cyccyclic definition in *s-types(block)* contains at least one *mk-Reference-type*

*all-local-id: Id** × (Id $\underset{m}{\rightarrow}$ Type-id) × [Block] → Id-set*
all-local-id(idll,parm-decl,block) $\underline{\Delta}$ all identifiers tested above

is-unique-labels: Block → Bool
is-unique-labels(block) $\underline{\Delta}$
s-labels(s-decl(block)) is equal to the set of labels occurring in *s-stl(block)* and no label occurs more than once in *s-stl(block)*

```
all-tags: Record-type → Id-set
all-tags(mk-Record-type(,vp)) Δ
  if vp=nil then {} else let mk-Variant-part(tag,,evp) = vp in
                            union {all-tags(evp(c)) | c ∈ dom evp} ∪
                            if tag=nil then {}   else {tag}
```

```
is-unique-fields: Record-type → Bool
is-unique-fields(mk-Record-type(fp,vp)) Δ
    all identifiers occurring
      in domfp,
      in mk-variant-part at s-tag position and
      in dom(s-fp(mk-Record-type())) in vp
    are different
```

```
all-for-id: Statement-list → Id-set
all-for-id (stl) Δ
    all identifiers occurring in mk-For-statement at s-id position.
```

```
is-variant-constants: Record-type×Actual-parm-list → Static-env → Bool
is-variant-constants(mk-Record-type(,vp),apl)ρ Δ
    vp≠nil ∧ is-Constant(hdapl) ∧ WFE[hdapl]ρ ∧
    let mk-Variant-part(,,evp) = vp in
    hdapl∈domevp ∧
    (tlapl≠<> ⊃ is-variant-constants(evp(hdapl),tlapl)ρ)
```

```
all-fields: Record-type → Id-set
all-fields(mk-Record-type(fp,vp)) Δ
    domfp ∪ if vp=nil
             then {}
             else let mk-Variant-part(tag,,evp) = vp in
                  union {all-fields(evp(c) | c∈domevp} ∪
                  if tag=nil then {}  else {tag}
```

```
values: Domain-type → Static-env → Constant-set
values(type)ρ ≜
  cases type:
     mk-Subrange-type(f,l) →
        cases NTE[f]ρ:
           mk-Enumerated(idl) → {mk-Id-const(idl[i]) |
                                          (∃j,k∈indsidl)
                                             (idl[j]=f∧ idl[k]=l ∧ j≤i≤k)}
           Integer → let mk-Integer-const(f1) = f in
                     let mk-Integer-const(l1) = l in
                     {mk-Integer-const(i) | f≤i≤l}
           Char    → Implementation defined set of Char-const
           Boolean → if f-mk-Const-id("true") ∧ l=mk-Id-const("false")
                       then {} else {f,l}
     mk-Enumerated(idl) → {mk-Id-const(idl[i]) | i∈indsidl}
     Integer →   {mk-Integer-const(i) |-maxint<i<maxint∧
     Char    →   Implementation defined set of Char-const
     Boolean →   {mk-Id-const("false"),mk-Id-const("true")}

is-not-containing-file-type: (Type | Conformant-array-schema) →
                                              static-env → Bool
is-not-containing-file-type(type)ρ ≜
     is-File-type(type) ∧
     for all id's occurring in mk-Type-id in type:
        is-Reference-type(out-types(id)ρ) ∨
        is-not-containing-file-type(out-types(id)ρ) holds.

is-same: All-type × All-type → Static-env → Bool
is-same(t1,t2)ρ ≜
   is-Type-id(t1) ∧ is-Type-id(t2) ∧
   (t1=t2 ∨ is-same(s-id(t1),t2)ρ ∨ is-same(t1,s-id(t2))ρ)

is-ordinal: All-type → Static-env → Bool
is-ordinal(t)ρ ≜
   let nt = NTT(t)ρ in
   nt=Integer ∨ nt=Char ∨ nt=Boolean ∨
   is-Enumerated-type(nt)

is-simple: All-type → Static-env → Bool
is-simple(t)ρ ≜
   is-ordinal(t)ρ ∨ NTT[t]ρ=Real
```

```
is-compatible: All-type × All-type → Static-env → Bool
is-compatible(t1,t2)ρ ≜
   is-same(t1,t2)ρ ∨
   let nt1 = NTT[t1]ρ in
   let nt2 = NTT[t2]ρ in
   (is-Subrange-type(nt1) ∧ is-Subrange-type(nt2) ∧
       is-compatible-subranges(nt1,nt2)ρ) ∨
   (is-all-set-type(t1) ∧ is-all-set-type(t2) ∧
       is-compatible-sets(nt1,nt2)ρ)        ∨
   (is-all-string-type(t1)ρ ∧ is-all-string-type(t2)ρ ∧
       is-compatible-strings(nt1,nt2)ρ) ∨
   is-compatible-references(nt1,nt2)

is-compatible-subranges: Subrange-type×Subrange-type→Static-env → Bool
is-compatible-subranges((mk-Subrange-type(f1,),mk-Subrange-type(f2,))ρ ≜
   let t1 = NTE[f1]ρ in
   let t2 = NTE[f2]ρ in
   t1=t2 ∨ is-same(t1,t2)ρ

is-compatible-sets: All-type × All-type → Static-env → Bool
is-compatible-sets(t1,t2)ρ ≜
  cases t1:
   empty-set-type                       → true
   mk-Constructed-set-type(base1)       →
     cases t2:
       mk-Constructed-set-type(base2)       → is-compatible(base1,base2)ρ
       mk-Set-type(base2)                   → is-compatible(base1,base2)ρ
       mk-Packed-type(mk-Set-type(base2))   → is-compatible(base1,base2)ρ
       T                                    → is-compatible-sets(t2,t1)
   mk-Set-type(base1)                   →
     cases t2:
       mk-Set-type(base2)                   → is-compatible(base1,base2)ρ
       mk-Packed-type()                     → false
       T                                    → is-compatible-sets(t2,t1)ρ
   mk-Packed-type(mk-Set-type(base1)) →
     cases t2:
       mk-Packed-type(mk-Set-type(base2))   → is-compatible(base1,base2)ρ
       T                                    → is-compatible-sets(t2,t1)ρ
```

```
is-all-set-type: All-type → Bool
is-all-set-type(t) ≜
   is-Set-type(t) ∨ is-Packed-type(t) ∧ is-Set-type(s-type(t)) ∨
   t=empty-set-type ∨ is-Constructed-set-type(t)

is-all-string-type: All-type → Static-env → Bool
is-all-string-type(t)ρ ≜
   is-Constructed-string-type(t) ∨
   let nt = NTT[t] in
   cases nt:
      mk-Packed-type(mk-Array-type(dt,ct)) →
         let ndt = NTT[dt] in
         let nct = NTT[ct] in
         is-Subrange-type(ndt) ∧
         (∃l∈Integer)(ndt=mk-Subrange(mk-Integer-const(1),
                                       mk-Integer-const(l)))∧nct=Char
      T                                       → false

is-compatible-strings: All-type × All-type → Static-env → Bool
is-compatible-strings(t1,t2)ρ ≜
  cases t1:
    mk-Constructed-string-type(l1)
      → cases t2:
          mk-Constructed-string-type(l2)  → l1=l2
          T                               → l1=string-length(t2)ρ
    T → cases t2:
          mk-Constructed-string-type()    → is-compatible-strings(t2,t1)ρ
          T                               → string-length(t1)ρ=
                                            string-length(t2)ρ

string-length: Packed-type → Static-env → Integer
string-length(mk-Packed-type(mk-Array-type(dt,))ρ =
   let mk-Subrange-type(,l) = NTT[dt]ρ in l

is-compatible-references: All-type × All-type → Static-env → Bool
is-compatible-references(t1,t2) =
   (is-Reference-type(t1) ∨ t1 = nil-type) ∧
    t2 = nil-type ∨
    is-compatible-references(t2,t1)
```

```
is-assignment-compatible: All-type × All-type → Static-env → Bool
is-assignment-compatible(t1,t2)ρ ≜
   is-same(t1,t2)ρ ∧ is-not-containing-file-type(t1)ρ ∨
   let nt1 = NTT[t1] in
   let nt2 = NTT[t2] in
   nt1=Real ∧ nt2=Integer ∨ is-compatible(nt1,nt2)ρ

is-corresponding: Id** × (Id →m Parameter-type) ×
                          Actual-parm-list → Static-env → Bool
is-corresponding(idll,parm-decl,apl)ρ ≜
   apl=<> ∧ idll=<> ∨
   apl≠<> ∧ idll≠<> ∧
   let l = len hdidll in
   lenapl≥l ∧
   (is-Var-array-formal-parameter(parm-decl(hd hd idll)) ∨
    is-Value-array-formal-parameter(parm-decl(hd hd idll)) ⊃
    (∀i,j∈{1:l})(is-same(TE[apl[i]]ρ,TE[apl[j]]ρ)ρ))  ∧
    (∀i∈{1:l})(is-element-corresponding(parm-decl(hdidll[i]),apl[i])ρ)∧
     is-corresponding(tlidll,parm-decl,<apl[i] | i∈{l+1:lenapl}>)ρ

is-element-corresponding: Parameter-type×Actual-parm → Static-env → Bool
is-element-corresponding(pt,ap)ρ ≜
   cases pt:
      mk-Value-formal-parameter(id)               →
         is-Expression(ap) ∧ WFE[ap]ρ ∧
         is-assignment-compatible(mk-Type-id(id),TE[ap]ρ)ρ
      mk-Var-formal-parameter(id)                 →
         is-Variable-access(ap) ∧ WFVA[ap]ρ ∧
         (is-Id(ap) ⊃ ¬in-for-info(ap)ρ ∧ ¬in-tag-info(id)ρ ∧
                 ¬in-packed-info(id)ρ) ∧ ¬is-tag-access(ap)ρ ∧
                 ¬is-packed-component(ap)ρ ∧
          is-same(mk-Type-id(id),TVA[ap]ρ)ρ
      mk-Procedure-formal-parameter(parms)        →
         is-Procedure-parm(ap) ∧
         let mk-Procedure-parm(id) = ap in
         in-procedures(id)ρ ∧ is-congruous(out-procedures(id)ρ,parms)ρ
      mk-Function-formal-parameter(parms,type) →
         is-Function-parm(ap) ∧
         let mk-Function-parm(id) = ap in
         in-functions(id)ρ ∧ is-same(out-return-type(id)ρ,type)ρ ∧
         is-congruous(out-functions(id)ρ,parms)ρ
```

```
    mk-Var-array-formal-parameter(cas)          →
       is-Variable-access(ap) ∧ WFVA[ap]ρ ∧
       ¬is-packed-component(ap)ρ           ∧
       is-conformable(cas,NTVA[ap]ρ)ρ
    mk-Value-array-formal-parameter(cas)        →
       is-Expression(ap) ∧ WFE[ap]ρ ∧ ¬is-conformant-array(ap)ρ
       is-conformable(cas,NTE[ap]ρ)ρ

is-packed-component: Variable-access → Static-env → Bool
is-packed-component(va)ρ ≜
   cases va:
      mk-Indexed-variable(va1,)  → is-Packed-type(NTVA[va1])ρ
      mk-Field-designator(va1,)  → is-Packed-type(NTVA[va1])ρ
      mk-Buffer-variable(va1)    → is-Packed-type(NTVA[va1])ρ
      T                          → false

is-tag-access: Variable-access → Static-env → Bool
is-tag-access(va)ρ ≜ is-Field-designator(va)∧s-Id(va)∈all-tags(NTVA[va]ρ)

is-congruous: Parameters × Parameters → Static-env → Bool
is-congruous(mk-Parameters(idll1,p1),mk-Parameters(idll2,p2))ρ ≜
   lenidll1=lenidll2 ∧
   (∀i∈indsidll1)(lenidll1[i]=lenidll2[i] ∧
   let t1 = p1(hdidll1[i]) in
   let t2 = p2(hdidll2[i]) in
   cases <t1,t2>:
     <mk-Value-formal-parameter(t1),mk-Value-formal-parmeter(t2)>,
     <mk-Var-formal-parameter(t1),mk-Var-formal-parameter(t2)>
          →  is-same(t1,t2)ρ
     <mk-Procedure-formal-parameter(parms1),
      mk-Procedure-formal-parameter(parms2)>
          →  is-congruous(parms1,parms2)ρ
     <mk-Function-formal-parameter(parms1,type1),
      mk-Function-formal-parameter(parms2,type2)>
          →  is-same(type1,type2)ρ ∧ is-congruous(parms1,parms2)ρ
     <mk-Value-array-formal-parameter(cas1),
      mk-Value-array-formal-parameter(cas2)>,
     <mk-Var-array-formal-parameter(cas1),
      mk-Var-array-formal-parameter(cas2)>
          →  is-equivalent-schema(cas1,cas2)ρ
     T    →  false)
```

```
is-equivalent-schema: Conformant-array-schema × Conformant-array-schema
                                          → Static-env → Bool
is-equivalent-schema(cas1,cas2)ρ ≜
    cases <cas1,cas2>:
      <mk-P-array-schema(mk-Index-type-spec(,,dt1),t1),
       mk-P-array-schema(mk-Index-type-spec(,,dt2),t2) >→
          is-same(dt1,dt2)ρ ∧ is-same(t1,t2)ρ
      <mk-Array-schema(mk-Index-type-spec(,,dt1),t1),
       mk-Array-schema(mk-Index-type-spec(,,dt2),t2)>    →
          is-same(dt1,dt2)ρ ∧
          (is-Type-id(t1) ∧ is-Type-id(t2) ∧
           is-same(t1,t2)ρ ∨
          is-Conformant-array-schema(t1) ∧
          is-Conformant-array-schema(t2) ∧
          is-equivalent-schema(t1,t2))
      T                                                   → false

is-conformable: Conformant-array-schema × Type → Static-env → Bool
is-conformable(cas,t)ρ =
    cases <cas,t>:
      <mk-P-array-schema(mk-Index-type-sepc(,,dt1),ct1),
       mk-Packed-type(mk-Array-type(dt2,ct2))> →
          is-compatible(dt1,dt2)ρ ∧ is-same(ct1,ct2)ρ
      <mk-Array-schema(mk-Index-type-spec(,,dt1),ct1),
       mk-Array-type(dt2,ct2))>                 →
          is-compatible(dt1,dt2)ρ           ∧
          (is-Id(s-id(ct1)) ∧ is-same(ct1,ct2)ρ ∨
           is-conformable(ct1,ct2))
      T                                         → false

labels: Statement* → Label-set
labels(sl) ≜
    {lab | i∈indssl ∧
           mk-Statement(lab,)=sl[i] ∧
           lab≠nil}
```

```
is-required-procedure-correspondence: Id × Actual-parm* →
                                            Static-env → Bool

is-required-procedure-correspondence(id,apl)ρ ≜
  cases id: "rewrite","put"
            "reset","get"    → lenapl=1 ∧
                               is-Variable-access(apl[1]) ∧
                               WFVA[apl[1]]ρ              ∧
                               let t = NTVA[apl[1]]       in
                               is-File-type(t) ∨ is-Packed-type(t) ∧
                               is-File-type(s-type(t))
            "read"           → lenapl≥2 ∧
                               is-Variable-access(apl[1]) ∧
                               NTVA[apl[1]]ρ=Text         ∧
                               (∀i∈indsapl - {1})
                                 (is-Read-parm(apl[i])    ∧
                                  let mk-Read-parm(va,t) = apl[i] in
                                  NTVA[va]ρ=t)
            "write"          → lenapl≥2 ∧
                               is-Variable-access(apl[1]) ∧
                               NTVA[apl[1]]ρ=Text         ∧
                               (∀i∈indsapl - {1})
                                 cases apl[i]:
                                   mk-Default-write-parm(exp)
                                     → check-write-expr(exp)ρ,
                                   mk-Width-write-parm(exp1,exp2)
                                     → check-write-expr(exp1)ρ ∧
                                       check-write-expr(exp2)ρ,
                                   mk-Fixed-write-parm(exp1,exp2,exp3)
                                     → check-write-expr(exp1)ρ ∧
                                       check-write-expr(exp2)ρ ∧
                                       check-write-expr(exp3)ρ,
            "new","dispose"  → lenapl≥1 ∧
                               let t = NTVA[hd apl] in
                               is-Reference-type(t) ∧
                               lenapl>1 ⊃
                               let t1=if is-Packed-type(t)
                                        then s-type(t) else t in
                               is-Record-type(t1) ∧
                               is-variant-constants(t1,tlapl)ρ
```

```
          "pack"              → len apl=3 ∧
                                check-pack(apl[1],apl[2],apl[3]),
          "unpack"            → len apl=3 ∧
                                check-pack(apl[3],apl[1],apl[2])

check-write-expr: Expression → Static-env → Bool
check-write-expr(e)ρ ≜
    WFE[e]ρ ∧ let nt=NTE[e]ρ in nt∈Required-type ∨ is-all-string-type(nt)

check-write-fields: Expression → Static-env → Bool
check-write-fields(e)ρ ≜ WFE[e]ρ ∧ NTE[e]=Integer

check-pack: Actual-parm × Actual-parm × Actual-parm → Static-env → Bool
check-pack(upk,i,pk)ρ≜
   is-Variable-access(upk) ∧ WFVA[upk]ρ ∧
   is-Expression(i)        ∧ WFE[i]ρ     ∧
   is-Variable-access(pk)  ∧ WFVA[pk]ρ   ∧
   let upkt = NTVA[upk]ρ,
        pkt = NTVA[pk]ρ in
   is-Array-type(upkt)   ∧
   is-Packed-type(pkt)   ∧
   let mk-Array-type(dt,rt) = upkt in
   is-same(rt,pkt)       ∧
   is-assignment-compatible(dt,NTE[i]ρ)

is-required-function-correspondence: Id × Actual-parm-list →
                                                        Static-env → Bool
is-required-function-correspondence(id,apl) ≜
   len apl=1 ∧
   is-Expression(apl[1]) ∧ WFE[apl[1]]ρ ∧
   let nt = NTE[apl[1]]ρ in
   cases id:
      "abs","sqr"                               → nt ∈ {Integer,Real}
      "sin","cos","exp","ln","sqrt","arctan",
      "trunc","round"                           → nt = Real
      "ord","succ","pred"                       → is-ordinal(nt)ρ
      "chr","odd"                               → nt = Integer
      "eof"                                     → is-File-type(nt) ∨
                                                  is-Packed-type(nt) ∧
                                                  is-File-type(s-type(nt))
      "eoln"                                    → nt = Text
```

```
is-wf-function-procedure: Parameters × Block → Static-env → Bool
is-wf-function-procedure(parms,block)ρ ≜
   let mk-Parameters(ids,type) = parms in
   is-unique-declarations(ids,type,block) ∧
   is-unique-labels(block)                ∧
   let ρ1 = erase(all-local-ids(ids,type,nil),{})ρ in
   (∀id∈domtype)(WFDP[type(id)]ρ1)       ∧
   let ρ2 = erase(all-local-ids(<>,[],block),{})ρ1  in
   let ρ3 = merge-variables([id ↦ t | id∈domtype])  ∧
             (type(id) = mk-Var-formal-parameter(t)          ∨
              type(id) = mk-Value-formal-parameter(t)        ∨
              type(id) = mk-Var-array-formal-parameter(t)    ∨
              type(id) = mk-Value-array-formal-parameter(t)])ρ2 in
   let ρ4 = merge-procedures([id ↦ t | id∈domtype]) ∧
              type(id) = mk-Procedure-formal-parameter(t)])ρ3   in
   let ρ5 = merge-functions([id ↦ t | id∈domtype])  ∧
              type(id) = mk-Function-formal-parameter(t)])ρ4    in
   WFB[block]ρ4
```

```
bounds-of: (Type-id | Conformant-array-schema) → Index-type-spec-set
bounds-of(tid) ≜
   cases tid:
      mk-P-array-schema(its,)      → {its}
      mk-Array-schema(its,ati)     → {its} ∪ bounds-of(ati)
      T                            → {}
```

7.4 DYNAMIC SEMANTICS

7.4.1 Semantic Domains

```
External-values        =    Id ⇸m (Value | Value*)

Tr                     =    State ⥲ State × [Label-den]

State                  ::   STORE   :(Sc-loc ⇸m [Sc-value])
                            FILES   :(File-id ⇸m File)
                            DENV    :(Did ⇸m Env)
                            VENV    :(Did ⇸m (Id ⇸m Variant-inf))
```

Sc-value = *Int* | *Real* | *Bool* |
Char | *Enumerated* | *Set* | *Pointer*

Enumerated :: *s-value:Id* *s-order:Id*$^{+}$

Set = *Ordinal-set*
Pointer = *Loc* | <u>NIL-VALUE</u>

File :: *s-buffer :Buffer*
s-lpart :[Value**]*
s-rpart :[Value**]*
s-access :[Mode]

Buffer :: *s-loc :[Loc]*
s-type :Type
s-senv :Storage-env

Mode = <u>inspection</u> | <u>generation</u>
Env = *Id* $\xrightarrow{m}$ *(Den* | *Did)*
Variant-inf :: *s-varc :Variant-Component*
s-senv :Storage-env

Variant-component = *Constant* $\xrightarrow{m}$ *Record-type*

Den = *Sc-loc* | *Array-den* | *Record-den*
| *Tag-den* | *File-den* | *Pointer-den*
| *Proc-den* | *Fun-den* | *Subrange-den*
| *Label-den* | *Simple-value* | *Allocated-den*

Array-den = *Ordinal* $\xrightarrow{m}$ *Loc*

Constraint: $(\forall ad \in Array\text{-}den)(\forall rx, ry \in \underline{rng}\ ad)(is\text{-}same\text{-}loc\text{-}type(rx,ry))$

Record-den :: *(Id* $\xrightarrow{m}$ *Record-component)*

Tag-den :: *s-loc :Sc-loc*
s-did :Did
s-type :Variant-inf

File-den :: *File-id*

```
Pointer-den              ::  s-loc  :Sc-loc
                             s-type :Type
                             s-senv :Storage-env

Proc-den                 ::  (Actual-parms* × Aid-set) ⥲ Tr

Fun-den          ::  s-den:(Actual-parms* × Aid-set ⥲ (State → State ×
                                           [Label-den]  ×  Sc-value))
                     s-result-loc:Sc-loc

Actual-parms             =   Loc | Value | Proc-den | Fun-den |
                             Actual-read-parm | Actual-write-parm

Subrange-den             ::  s-loc:Sc-loc    s-range:Interval
Label-den                ::  Label  [Aid]
Allocated-den            ::  s-den:Record-den

Value                    =   Sc-value      | Array-value |
                             Record-value |  Set-value

Array-value              =   Ordinal -m-> Value
Record-value             =   Id -m-> Value
Set-value                =   Ordinal-set

Actual-read-parm         ::  s-loc:Sc-loc    type:{Integer,Real,Char}

Actual-write-parm        ::  s-val   :Sc-value
                             s-width :[Int]
                             s-frac  :[Int]
```

<u>Auxiliary Objects</u>

```
Ordinal                  =   Int  | Bool  | Char | Enumerated

Storage-loc              =   Sc-loc        | Array-den   | Record-den
                           | Pointer-den   | Subrange-den

Loc                      =   Storage-loc   | File-den

Record-component         =   Simple-value | Tag-den     | Loc   | Did
```

```
Block-env                  :: s-type :Type-env
                              s-env  :Env
                              s-aid  :Aid-set

Type-env                   =  Id ⇀ Type
Simple-value               =  Ordinal | Real
Storage-env                =  Type-env × Env

Aid,Did,File-id,Id,Label,Sc-loc :   Disjoint Infinite Sets

Passed-by-denotation       =  Var-formal-parameter              |
                              Function-formal-parameter         |
                              Procedure-formal-parameter        |
                              Var-array-formal-parameter

Passed-by-value            =  Value-formal-parameter            |
                              Value-array-formal-parameter

Array-parameter            =  Value-array-formal-parameter      |
                              Var-array-formal-parameter
```

7.4.2 Semantic Elaboration Functions

Meaning Function Abbreviations

MP	*Meaning of a Program*	*MSL*	*Meaning of a Statement List*
MB	*Meaning of a Block*	*MS*	*Meaning of a Statement*
MBD	*Meaning of Block Declarations*	*MUS*	*Meaning of an Unlabelled Statement*
MD	*Meaning of a Declaration*	*E*	*Meaning of an Expression*

Other Common Abbreviations

arg	argument	*exp*	expression	*op*	operator
const	constant	*id*	identifier	*parm*	parameter
decl	declaration	*nm*	name	*st*	statement
				stl	*statement-list*

Semantic Functions

```
i-program  :  Program → (External-values → External-values)
i-program[p](extv) ≜
   (let σ = mk-State([],[],[],[]) in
    MP[p](extv)σ)
```

```
MP  :  Program → External-values → (State → State × [Label-den] ×
                                                  External-values)
MP[mk-Program(,args,block)](extv) ≜
   (let t          = required-types                        in
    let ρ          = required-declarations                 in
    let mk-block(decls,stl) = block                        in
    def δ          : MBD[decls]mk-Block-env(t,ρ,{});
    bind[args](extv,δ);
    MSL[stl]δ;
    def result : unbind[args]δ;
    epilogue[decls](δ);
    return(result))

required-types  =  ["Integer" ↦ Integer,
                    "Boolean" ↦ Boolean,
                    "Real"    ↦ Real,
                    "Char"    ↦ Char,
                    "Text"    ↦ mk-File-type(Char)]

required-declarations =
   ["abs"     ↦ abs-denotation,          "page"    ↦ page-denotation,
    "arctan"  ↦ arctan-denotation,       "pred"    ↦ pred-denotation,
    "chr"     ↦ chr-denotation,          "put"     ↦ put-denotation,
    "cos"     ↦ cos-denotation,          "read"    ↦ read-denotation,
    "dispose" ↦ dispose-denotation,      "readln"  ↦ readln-denotation,
    "eof"     ↦ eof-denotation,          "reset"   ↦ reset-denotation,
    "eoln"    ↦ eoln-denotation,         "rewrite" ↦ rewrite-denotation,
    "exp"     ↦ exp-denotation,          "round"   ↦ round-denotation,
    "false"   ↦ false                    "sin"     ↦ sin-denotation,
    "get"     ↦ get-denotation,          "sqr"     ↦ sqr-denotation,
    "input"   ↦ mk-File-den(finput),     "sqrt"    ↦ sqrt-denotation,
    "maxint"  ↦ maxint-denotation,       "succ"    ↦ succ-denotation,
    "new"     ↦ new-denotation,          "true"    ↦ true
    "odd"     ↦ odd-denotation,          "trunc"   ↦ trunc-denotation,
    "ord"     ↦ ord-denotation,          "unpack"  ↦ unpack-denotation,
    "output"  ↦ mk-File-den(foutput)     "write"   ↦ write-denotation,
    "pack"    ↦ pack-denotation,         "writeln" ↦ writeln-denotation]
```

Note: When referencing the translated identifiers (members of the set *Id*), quotes are used (e.g. *"Integer"* for the translation of the identifier *Integer*.)

```
bind  :   Id-set → External-values × Block-env =>
bind[ids](extv,mk-Block-env(t,ρ,)) ≜
  for all id∈ids do
      if ρ(id)∈File-den
         then let mk-File-den(fid) = ρ(id)        in
              let buffer =
                  if id="input" ∨ id="output"
                     then mk-Buffer(nil,mk-File-type(Char,(t,ρ))
                     else buffer-of(ρ(id))        in
              let lp,rp ∈ Value* s.t. lp^rp=extv(id) in
              FILES := c FILES + [fid ↦ mk-File(buffer,lp,rp,nil)];
              (id="input"   → reset(ρ(id)),
               id="output" → rewrite(ρ(id)))
         else assign(ρ(id),extv(id))


unbind: Id-set → Block-env => External-values
unbind[ids](δ) ≜  [id ↦ unbind-val[id]δ | id∈ids]


unbind-val: Id → Block-env => (Value | Value*)
unbind-val[id](mk-Block-env(,ρ,)) ≜
   if ρ(id)∈File-den
      then let mk-File-den(fid) = ρ(id)            in
           def mk-File(,lp,rp,) : (c FILES)(fid)    ;
           return (lp^rp)
      else contents(ρ(id))


MB: Block × Block-env =>
MB[mk-block(decls,stl)]δ ≜
   def δ': MBD[decls]δ;
   always epilogue[decls]δ' in MSL[stl]δ'


epilogue: Declarations → Block-env =>
epilogue[decls]mk-Block-env(,ρ,) ≜
   let vdecls = s-variables(decls)     in
   let vdens  = {ρ(x) | x∈domvdecls}   in
   deallocate(vdens)
```

```
MBD: Declarations → Block-env => Block-env
MBD[mk-Declarations(labs,constm,typem,varm,procm,funm)]δ ≜
    let mk-block-env(t,ρ,cas) = δ  in
    let aid∈Aid - cas in
    let t' = t + [id ↦ typem(id) | id ∈ dom typem]  in
    def ρ' : ρ + ([id ↦ mk-Label-den(id,aid)   | id ∈ labs]          ∪
                  [id ↦ MD[constm(id)](t',ρ') | id ∈ dom constm]  ∪
                  [id ↦ MD[varm(id)](t',ρ')     | id  ∈  dom  varm  ]    ∪
                  [id ↦ MD[procm(id)](t',ρ')    | id  ∈  dom  procm]    ∪
                  [id ↦ MD[funm(id)](t',ρ')     | id  ∈  dom  funm]     ∪
                  enumerated-values(rng varm ∪ rng typem,t');
    return(mk-Block-env(t',ρ',cas ∪ {aid}))


MSL: Statement* → Block-env =>
MSL[stl]δ ≜
   let ρ = s-env(δ)  in
   tixe [ρ(lab) ↦ cue-i-statement-list[lab,stl]δ | lab∈labels-of[stl]] in
   i-statement-list[stl]δ

cue-i-statement-list: Label × Statement* → Block-env =>
cue-i-statement-list[lab,stl]δ  ≜
    let n = index(lab,stl) in
    for i=n to lenstl do MS[s-st(stl[i])]δ


MS: Statement  → Block-env =>
MS[mk-Statement(lab,st)]δ ≜
    let ρ = s-env(δ)  in
    tixe [l ↦ MUS[st]δ | l ∈ if lab=nil then {} else {l}] in
    MUS[st]δ


MUS: Unlabelled-statement  → Block-env =>

MUS[mk-Compound-statement(stl)]δ ≜ i-statement-list[stl]δ

i-statement-list: Statement* → Block-env =>
i-statement-list[stl]δ ≜
    tixe [lab ↦ cue-i-statement-list[lab,stl]δ | is-dcont(lab,stl)] in
    for i=1 to len stl do MS[s-st(stl[i])]δ
```

```
MUS[mk-Assignment-statement(target,exp)]δ ≜
    def rhs: E[exp]δ;
    def lhs: e-left-reference[target]δ
    assign(lhs,rhs)

MUS[mk-Procedure-statement(id,apl)]δ ≜
    def denl : <e-actual-parameter[apl[i]]δ | 1≤i≤lenapl>;
    let f     = s-env(δ)(id)
    in f(denl,s-aid(δ))

MUS[mk-If-statement(exp,th,el)]δ ≜
    def v: E[exp]δ;
    if v then MS[th]δ else if el≠nil then MS[el]δ else I

MUS[mk-Case-statement(exp,ccl)]δ ≜
    def cv: E[exp]δ;
    if cv∈union{s-cs(ccl(i)) | i∈indsccl}
       then let s=(Δi)(c∈s-cs(cll(i))) in MS[ccl[i]]δ
       else error

MUS[mk-While-statement(exp,st)]δ ≜ while E[exp]δ do MS[st]δ

MUS[mk-Repeat-statement(stl,exp)]δ ≜
   MSL[stl]δ; while E[exp]δ do i-statement-list[stl]δ

MUS[mk-Local-goto(id)]δ ≜ exit(id)

MUS[mk-Nonlocal-goto(id)]δ ≜ exit(s-env(δ)(id))

MUS[mk-For-statement(id,from,direction,to,st)]δ ≜
   let next    = if direction=TO then succ else pred in
   def initial : E[from]δ;
   def final   : E[to]δ;
   if ftest(initial,final,direction)
      then (let control = mk-Variable-access(id) in
              assign(control,initial);
              MS[st]δ)
      else I;
   while contents(control)≠final do
      (assign(control,next(control));
       MS[st]δ)
```

```
ftest: Sc-value × Sc-value × {TO,DOWNTO} → Bool
ftest(v1,v2,dir) ≜
   (dir = TO       ↦ v1≤v2
    dir = DOWNTO ↦ v1≥v2)

MUS[mk-With-statement(vs,st)]δ ≜
   def wρ : e-left-reference(vs]δ;
   let mk-Block-env(t,ρ,aid) = δ        in
   let δ' = mk-Block-env(t,ρ+wρ,aid)  in
   MS[st]δ'

e-left-reference: Target → Block-env → Den
e-left-reference[d]δ ≜
   (d∈Variable-access → e-reference(d,δ,lhs-apply)
    d∈Function-id      → let fden = s-env(δ)(s-id(d))  in
                          s-result-loc(fden))

assign:  Den × Value =>
assign(den,value) ≜
   cases den:
      mk-Array-den(d)              →
         for all i∈dom d do assign(d(i),value(i)),
      mk-Record-den(d)             →
         for all id∈dom d do assign(lhs-apply(d,id),value(id)),
      mk-Subrange-den(loc,range) →
         if s-low(range)≤value≤s-high(range)
            then assign(loc,value)
            else error,
      mk-Tag-den(loc,did,vinf)    →
         if contents(loc)≠value
            then let mk-Variant-inf(vc,senv) = vinf in
                     deallocate({did});
                     assign(loc,value);
                     DENV := c DENV + [did ↦ MD[vc(value)](senv)]
            else I,
      mk-Pointer-den(loc)           → assign(loc,value),
      T    → if den∈dom c STORE
                 then STORE := c STORE + [den ↦ value]
                 else error

MUS[NULL-STATEMENT] ≜ I
```

```
E: Expression → Block-env => Value

E[mk-Variable-expression(va)]δ ≜
    def den : e-reference[va](δ,rhs-apply);
    if ¬(den∈Allocated-den) then contents(den) else error

E[mk-Constant-expression(exp)]δ ≜
    (cases exp:
        mk-Real-constant(r)         → represent(r),
        mk-Integer-constant(i)      → test(i),
        mk-Char-constant(c)         → return(c),
        mk-Id-constant(i)           → return(s-env(δ)(i)),
        mk-String-constant(s)       → return([i → s(i) | i∈inds s]),
        NIL-VALUE                   → return(NIL-VALUE)

E[mk-Function-designator(id,apl)]δ ≜
    def denl : <e-actual-parameter[apl[i]]δ | 1≤i≤len apl>;
    let f    =  s-env(δ)(id)  in
    def v    : f(denl,s-aid(δ));
    return(v)

E[mk-Prefix-expression(op,exp)]δ ≜
    def value: E[exp]δ;
    apply-prefix-operation(op,value)

E[mk-Infix-expression(lexp,op,rexp)]δ ≜
    def lvalue : E[lexp]δ;
    def rvalue : E[rexp]δ;
    apply-infix-operation(lvalue,op,rvalue)

E[mk-Set-constructor(ml)]δ ≜ union{e-member(ml(i),δ) | i∈indsml}

apply-prefix-operation: Prefix-opr × Value => Value
apply-prefix-operation(op,value) ≜
    cases op:
        integer-plus,real-plus → return(value)
        integer-minus          → return(-value)
        real-minus             → represent(-value)
        not                    → return(¬value)
```

```
apply-infix-operation: Value × Infix-op × Value => Value
apply-infix-operation(v,op,w) ≜
   cases op:
       real-add      → represent(v + w)
       real-sub      → represent(v - w)
       real-mult     → represent(v * w)
       real-div      → if w ≠ 0
                          then represent(v / w)
                          else error
       integer-add   → test(v + w)
       integer-sub   → test(v - w)
       integer-mult  → test(v * w)
       integer-div   → if w≠0
                          then let d be s.t. (∃r∈Integer)(0≤r<w∧v=d*w+r)
                                  in test(d)
                          else error
       integer-mod   → if w≠0
                          then let r be s.t. 0≤r<w ∧
                                              (∃d∈Integer)(d>0 ∧ v=d*w+r)
                                  in test(r)
                          else error
       lt            → return(v < w)
       le            → return(v ≤ w)
       eq            → return(v = w)
       ne            → return(v ≠ w)
       ge            → return(v ≥ w)
       gt            → return(v > w)
       union         → return(v ∪ w)
       intersection  → return(v ∩ w)
       difference    → return(v - w)
       super-set     → return(v ⊇ w)
       sub-set       → return(v ⊆ w)
       in            → return(v ∈ w)
       and           → return(v ∧ w)
       or            → return(v ∨ w)
```

The six relational operators <, ≤, =, ≠, ≥, > have been extended to the sets *Bool*, *Char*, and *Enumerated* as follows:

Bool	is given the order: *false*, *true*
Char	is given an implementation-defined order.
Enumerated	are ordered according to the associated value list.

```
e-member: Set-constructor → Block-env => Ordinal-set
e-member[m]δ  ≜
   if m∈Expression
      then {E[m]δ}
      else let mk-Interval(l,h) = m in
            def lv : E[l]δ;
            def hv : E[h]δ;
      return( {x | lv≤x≤hv} )

represent: Real => Real
represent(r) ≜
   if -maxreal<r<-minreal ∨ minreal<r<-maxreal ∨ r=0
      then return(an implementation defined approximation of r)
      else error

test: Int => Int
test(i) ≜ if -maxint≤r≤maxint then return(i) else error

e-reference: Variable-access → Block-env × (Env × Id → Den) => Den
e-reference[va](δ,apply) ≜
   cases va:
      mk-Index-variable(ar,exp)  →
         (def mp    : e-reference[ar](δ,apply);
          def index : E[exp]δ;
          if index ∈ dom mp then return(mp(index)) else error),
      mk-Field-designator(re,id) →
         (def r  : e-reference[re](δ,apply);
          let mp = if r∈Allocated-den then s-den(r) else r in
          apply(mp,id)),
      mk-Reference-variable(rv)  →
         (contents(e-reference[rv](δ,apply))),
      mk-Buffer-variable(br)      →
          def fid  : e-reference[rv](δ,apply);
          def file : (c FILES)(fid);
          return(s-loc(s-buffer(file))),
      T → apply(s-env(δ),id)

rhs-apply: Env × Id => Den
rhs-apply(m,id) ≜ if id∈dom m then let r = m(id) in
                                        r∈Den → return(r),
                                        r∈Did → rhs-apply((c DENV)(r),id))
                                  else error
```

```
lhs-apply: Record-component × Id => Den
lhs(m,id) ≜ if id∊dom m then let r = m(id) in
                                (r∊Den → return(r),
                                 r∊Did → cont-apply(r,id))
                             else error

cont-apply: Did × Id => Den
cont-apply(did,id) ≜
   def m : (c VENV)(did) + (c DENV)(did);
   let r = m(id) in
  (r ∊ Den            → return(r),
   r ∊ Did            →  cont-apply(r,id),
   r ∊ Variant-inf    →  (set-up(did,id); cont-apply(did,id)))

set-up: Den × Id =>
set-up(did,id) ≜
   def mk-Variant-inf(vc,senv) : (c VENV)(did)(id);
   deallocate(rng((c DENV)(did)));
   let ntag∊Constant be s.t. id∊ids-of(vc(ntag)) in
   DENV := c DENV + [did ↦ MD[vc(ntag)]senv]

contents: Loc => Value
contents(d) ≜
 cases d:
   mk-Array-den(ad)         → [i ↦ contents∘ad(id) | i∊domad] ,
   mk-Record-den(rd)        → [id ↦ contents∘rhs-apply(rd,id) | id∊domrd] ,
   mk-Pointer-den(loc,,)    → contents(loc),
   mk-Subrange-den(loc,)    → contents(loc),
   mk-Tag-den(loc,,)        → contents(loc),
   T                        → if d∊dom(c STORE)
                                 then (c STORE)(d)
                                 else error

e-actual-parameter: Actual-parm → Block-env => Actual-parms
e-actual-parameter[ap]δ ≜
 (ap ∊ Variable-access           → e-left-reference[ap]ρ,
  ap ∊ Expression                → E[ap]δ,
  ap = mk-Function-parm(id)      → return(s-env(δ)(id)),
  ap = mk-Procedure-parm(id)     → return(s-env(δ)(id)),
  ap ∊ Write-parm                → return(e-write-parm(ap,δ)),
  ap ∊ Read-parm                 → return(e-read-parm(ap,δ))
```

```
e-write-parm: Write-parm → Block-env => Actual-write-parm
e-write-parm[ap]δ ≜
    (let exp = s-expr(ap)  in
    def ev   : E[exp]δ;
    cases ap:
       mk-Default-write-parm()          →
           mk-Actual-write-parm(ev,nil,nil)
       mk-Width-write-parm(,e1)         →
           def v1 : E[e1]δ;
           mk-Actual-write-parm(ev,v1,nil)
       mk-Fixed-write-parm(,e1,e2)   →
           def v1 : E[e1]δ;
           def v2 : E[e2]δ;
           mk-Actual-write-parm(ev,v1,v2)

e-read-parm: Read-parm → Block-env => Actual-read-parm
e-read-parm[ap]δ ≜
    let d    = s-target(ap) in
    let t    = s-type(ap)   in
    def loc : e-left-reference[l]δ;
    mk-Actual-read-parm(loc,t)

MD: Type → Storage-env =>Den  Unless otherwise stated

MD[mk-Constant(cn)](t,ρ) ≜
    cases cn:
       mk-Prefix-const(sign,id) → def v = MD[mk-Constant(id)](t,ρ);
                                  if sign=PLUS then v else - v,
       mk-String-const(sc)      → sc,
       mk-Real-constant(r)      → represent(r),
       mk-Integer-constant(i)   → test(i),
       mk-Char-constant(c)      → c,
       mk-Id-constant(id)       → ρ(id)

MD[mk-Type-id(id)](t,ρ)             ≜ MD[t(id)](t,ρ)

MD[mk-Enumerated-type(idl)](t,ρ) ≜ generate-sc-loc()

MD[mk-Record-type(fp,vp)](t,ρ) ≜
    def f : e-fixed-part(fp,(t,ρ));
    def v : e-variant-part(vp,(t,ρ));
    return(f∪v)
```

```
MD[mk-Subrange-type(fc,lc)](t,ρ) ≜
    let fv  = ρ(fc) in
    let lv  = ρ(lc) in
    def loc : generate-sc-loc();
    return(mk-Subrange-den(loc,mk-interval(fv,lv)))

MD[mk-Array-type(dt,rt)](t,ρ)  ≜
    def array : elements(dt,(t,ρ));
    return([d ↦ MD[rt](t,ρ) | d ∈ array])

elements: Type × Storage-env => Ordinal-set
elements(type,(t,ρ)) ≜
    let atype = type-of(type) in
   (atype ∈  Enumerated-type   →  let {dt} = collect-values(atype,t)  in
                                   return (elems dt),
    atype ∈ Subrange-type      →  let mk-Subrange(f,l) = atype in
                                   def fc : MD[f](t,ρ);
                                   def lc : MD[l](t,ρ);
                              return({x | x∈values(fc) ∧ fc≤x≤lc}))

MD[mk-File-type(ft)](t,ρ) ≜
    let buffer = mk-Buffer(nil,ft,(t,ρ))       in
    let file    = mk-File(buffer,nil,nil,nil) in
    def fid ∈ File-id - dom c FILES;
    FILES := c FILES + [fid ↦ file];
    return(mk-File-den(fid))

MD[mk-Set-type(dt)](t,ρ)          ≜ generate-sc-loc()

MD[mk-Packed-type(type)](t,ρ)  ≜ MD[type](t,ρ)

MD[mk-Reference-type(tp)](t,ρ) ≜
    def loc : generate-sc-loc();
    return(mk-Pointer-den(loc,tp,(t,δ)))

MD[rt](t,ρ) ≜ generate-sc-loc()

e-fixed-part: (Id → Type-id) × Storage-env => Den
e-fixed-part(fp,(t,ρ)) ≜ [id ↦ MD[fp(id)](t,ρ) | id∈domfp]
```

```
e-variant-part: Variant-part × Storage-env => Den
e-variant-part(vp,(t,ρ)) ≜
   if vp=nil then return([] )
   else def did ∈ Did - dom c DENV;
        DENV := c DENV + [did ↦ []];
        def td : e-tag-part(vp,did,(t,ρ))
        let v  = [id ↦ did | id∈ids-of(s-evp(vp))] in
        return(td∪v)

e-tag-part: Variant-part × Did × Storage-env => Den
e-tag-part(vp,did,(t,ρ)) ≜
   let mk-Variant-part(tid,ttype,vc) = vp  in
   let vinf = mk-Variant-inf(vc,(t,ρ))     in
   if tid≠nil then def tden : MD[ttype](t,ρ);
                   return([id ↦ mk-Tag-den(tden,did,vinf)] )
   else let venv = build-venv(vinf) in
        VENV := c VENV + [did ↦ venv];
        return([] )

build-venv: Variant-Inf → (Id ⩦ Variant-component)
build-venv(vi) ≜ merge{build-each-venv(rt,vi) | rt∈rngs-varc(vi)}

build-each-venv: Record-type × Variant-inf → (Id → Variant-inf)
build-each-venv(rt,vi) ≜
   let mk-Record-type(fp,vp) = rt  in
       [id ↦ vi | id∈domfp] +
        if vp=nil then []
        else let mk-Variant-part(tid,,lvc) = vp  in
             if tid=nil then build-venv(mk-Variant-inf(lvc,s-senv(vi)))
             else [tid ↦ vi]

generate-sc-loc: => Sc-loc
generate-sc-loc() ≜  def loc ∈ Sc-loc - Used-storage();
                     STORE := c STORE ∪ [loc ↦ nil];
                     return(loc)

MD[mk-Procedure(parms,block)](t,ρ) ≜
   let f(apl,cas) = def ρ' : ρ + build-parm-env(parms,apl,t,ρ');
                    MB[block](mk-Block-env(t,ρ',cas);
                    deallocate-parameter-locs[parms]ρ'
   in f
```

```
deallocate-parameter-locs: Parameters → Env =>
deallocate-parameter-locs[parms]ρ ≜
   deallocate({ρ(id) | id∈elems s-ids(parms)})

MD[mk-Function(parms,block,return)](t,ρ) ≜
   let f(apl,cas) =
      def ρ'     : ρ + build-parm-env(parms,apl,(t,ρ'));
      def rloc   : MD[return](t,ρ);
      i-block[block](mk-Block-env(t,ρ',cas);
      def result : contents(rloc);
      deallocate-parameter-and-return-locs[parms](rloc)ρ';
      return(result)
   in mk-Function-den(f,rloc)

deallocate-parameter-and-return-locs: Parameters → Den → Env =>
deallocate-parameter-and-return-locs[parms](rloc)ρ ≜
   deallocate({ρ(id) | id∈elems s-ids(parms)}∪{rloc})

build-parm-env: Parameters × Actual-parm* × Storage-env → Env
build-parm-env(mk-parameters(fpl,type),apl,(t,ρ)) ≜
   let idl = conc fpl in
   [idl(i) ↦ apl(i)
          | i∈indsapl ∧ type(idl[i])∈Passed-by-denotation]  ∪
   [idl(i) ↦ e-value-parameter(apl[i],type(idl[i]),(t',ρ))
          | i∈indsapl ∧ type(idl[i])∈Passed-by-value]       ∪
   merge{set-bounds(apl(i),cas)
          | i∈indsapl ∧ type(idl[i])∈Array-parameter) ∧
            cas=s-schema(type(idl[i]))}

e-value-parameter: Value × Type × Storage-env => Den
e-value-parameter(val,type,(t,ρ)) ≜
   cases type:
      mk-Value-formal-parameter(pt)        →
         def loc : MD(pt)(t,ρ);
         assign(loc,value);
         return(loc)
      mk-Value-array-formal-parameter(pt) →
         let at = construct-array-type(pt,ρ) in
         e-value-parameters(val,at,(t,ρ))
```

```
construct-array-type: Conformant-array-schema × env → Array-type
construct-array-type(cas,ρ) ≜
   let its = s-ind(cas)                                  in
   let mk-Index-type-spec(lid,hid,type) = its            in
   let l   = ρ(lid)                                      in
   let h   = ρ(hid)                                      in
   let dt  = mk-Subrange-type(l,h)                       in
   cases cas: mk-P-array-schema(,type) → mk-Array-type(dt,type)
              mk-Array-schema(,type)   →
                 let rt = if type∈Conformant-array-schema
                             then construct-array-type(type,δ)
                             else type
                 in mk-Array-type(dt,rt)

set-bounds: Actual-parameter × Conformant-array-schema → Env
set-bounds(d,cas) ≜
   let its = s-ind(cas)                                  in
   let mk-Index-type-spec(lid,hid,)    = its             in
   let lbound = mins(dom d)                              in
   let hbound = maxs(dom d)                              in
   let m = [lid ↦ lbound, hid ↦ hbound]                  in
   cases cas: mk-Array-schema(,type)   →
                 if type∈Conformant-array-schema
                    then let nl∈rng d in set-bounds(nl,type) + m
                    else m,
              mk-P-array-schema(,type) → m

enumerated-values: Type-set × Type-env → (Id → Simple-value)
enumerated-values(types,t) ≜
   let tev = union{collect-values(type,t) | type∈types} in
   [id → mk-Enumerated(id,idl) | id∈elemsidl ∧ idl∈tev]

collect-values: Type × Type-env → Id⁺-set
collect-values(type,t) ≜
   cases type:
      mk-Type-id(id)             → collect-values(t(id),t)
      mk-Enumerated-type(idl)    → {idl}
      mk-File-type(ft)           → collect-values(ft)
      mk-Set-type(st)            → collect-values(st)
      mk-Packed-type(pt)         → collect-values(pt)
```

```
mk-Record-type(fp,vp)      →
    union{collect-values(tp) | (∃x∈fp)(tp=s-type(x))} ∪
    if vp=nil then {}
    else union{collect-values(tp) | tp∈rng s-evp(vp)}
mk-Array-type(dt,rt)       → collect-values(dt) ∪ collect-values(rt)
mk-Reference-type(rt)      → collect-values(rt)
T                          → {}
```

Denotations for Standard Procedures and Functions

The denotations for the functions and procedures *abs*, *arctan*, *cos*, *exp*, *maxint*, *odd*, *pack*, *readin*, *round*, *sin*, *sgr*, *sgrt*, *trunc* and *unpack* are Pascal programs that return the appropriate values. The denotations for the other functions and procedures are all of the form:

xxx-denotation $\triangleq$ *let xxx(arguments) in xxx*

where the *xxx* is given below:

chr

```
chr: Int → Char
chr(x) = an implementation-defined character
```

dispose

```
dispose: Pointer-den[Value*] =>
dispose(pden,vl) =
    if vl=nil
       then let mk-Pointer-den(loc,,)=pden in deallocate({contents(loc)})
       else check-tags(pden,vl); dispose(pden,nil)

check-tags: Pointer-den × Value* → Bool
check-tags(p,vl) ≜
    let mk-Pointer-den(loc,type,) = p              in
    let rd = allocated-type(type,vl)               in
    def mk-Allocated-den(locs) : contents(loc);
    rd = domlocs
```

```
allocated-type: Type × Value* → Id-set
allocated-type(type,vl) ≜
   if vl=<>
      then ids-of(type)
      else let mk-Record-type(fp,vp) = type in
           ids-of(mk-Record-type(fp,nil)) ∪
           (let mk-Variant-part(id,,evp) = vp in
            if id=nil then {id}
            else {id} ∪ allocated-type(evp(hdvl),tlvl))
```

eof

```
eof: File-den => Bool
eof(mk-File-den(fid)) ≜
   if is-file-defined(fid)
      then s-rpart((c FILES)(fid))=<>
      else error
```

eoln

```
eoln: File-den => Bool
eoln(mk-File-den(fid)) ≜
   if ¬eof(mk-File-den(fid)) ∧ is-text(fid) ∧ is-file-defined(fid)
      then hds-rpart((c FILES)(fid))=end-of-line
      else error
```

get

```
get: File-den =>
get(mk-File-den(fid)) ≜
   if pre-get(fid)
      then def mk-File(buffer,lp,rp,mode) : (c FILES)(fid);
           def buffer'                    : re-allocate(buffer);
           FILES := c FILES + [fid ↦ mk-File(buffer',lp^<hd rp>,
                      tl rp,inspection)];
           assign(buffer',hd rp)
      else error
```

```
pre-get: File-id => Bool
pre-get(fid) ≜
    is-file-defined(fid) ∧
    (def mk-File(,,rp,mode) : (c FILES)(fid);
     rp=<> ∧ mode=inspection )

is-file-defined: File-id => Bool
is-file-defined(fid) ≜
    def mk-File(,lp,rp,) : (c FILES)(fid);
    lp≠nil ∧ rp≠nil
```

new

```
new: Pointer-den × [Value*] =>
new(pden,vl) =
    let mk-Pointer-den(ploc,type,senv) = pden in
    def den : allocate-new(type,senv,vl);
    let rden = if vl=nil then den else mk-Allocated-den(den) in
    STORE := c STORE + [ploc ↦ rden]

allocate-new: Type × Store-env × Value* => Den
allocate-new(type,senv,vl) ≜
    if vl=nil
       then MD(type)(senv)
       else let mk-Record-type(fp,vp) = type in
            MD(fp)(senv)
            +(let mk-Variant-part(id,ttype,evp) = vp in
              if id=nil then [] else [id ↦ hdvl]
              + allocate-new(evp(hdvl),senv,tlvl))
```

ord

```
ord: Value → Integer
ord(v) ≜ v ∈ Integer     → v,
         v ∈ Boolean     → if v then 1 else 0
         v ∈ Char        → let i∈Integer be s.t. v=chr(i) in i
         v ∈ Enumerated  → let mk-Enumerated(id,idl) = v  in
                           (Δi∈indsidl)(idl[i]=id)-1
```

page

```
page: File-den =>
page(mk-File-den(fid)) ≜ if pre-put(fid) ∧ is-text(fid)
                            then def mk-File(,lp,,) : (c FILES)(fid);
                                 if lp(len lp)≠end-of-line
                                    then put-char(fid,end-of-line);
                                    else I;
                                 put-char(fid,end-of-page)
                            else error
```

pred

```
pred: Ordinal → Ordinal
pred(x) ≜ if mins(values(x))<x
             then (Δr∈values(x))(ord(r)=ord(x)-1)
             else undefined
```

put

```
put: File-den =>
put(mk-File-den(fid)) ≜
   if pre-put(fid)
      then def ch : contents(buffer-of(fid));
               put-char(fid,ch)
      else error

put-char: File-Id × Char =>
put-char(fid,ch) ≜
   def mk-File(buffer,lp,rp,mode) : (c FILES)(fid);
   def buffer'                    : re-allocate(buffer);
   FILES := c FILES + [fid ↦ mk-File(buffer',lp^<ch>,<>,generation)

pre-put: File-id => Bool
pre-put(fid) ≜
   def mk-File(,lp,rp,mode) : (c FILES)(fid);
   return(lp≠nil ∧ rp=<> ∧ mode=generation)
```

read

```
read: File-Id × Actual-read-parm =>
read(fid,arp) ≜
   let mk-Actual-read-parm(loc,type) = arp  in
   cases type:
      Integer → def v: get-value(fid,Integer);
                   assign(loc,v)
      Char    → def buffer : buffer-of(fid);
                   assign(loc,contents(buffer));
                   get(fid)
      Real    → def v : get-value(fid,Real);
                   assign(loc,v)

get-value: File-id × {Integer,Real} => Value
get-value(fid,type) =
   def mk-File(buffer,lp,rp,) : (c FILES)(fid);
   let i,j∈{0:lenrp} be s.t.
        i≥1 ∧
        check-syntax(subl(rp,i,j),type) ∧
        (¬∃k>j)(check-syntax(subl(rp,i,k),type) ∧
        (∀n∈{1:i-1})(rp(n)∈{BLANK,end-of-line) in
   if j≠0
      then def buffer' : re-allocate(buffer);
           FILES := (c FILES + [fid ↦ mk-File(buffer',
                                              lp^subl(rp,i,j),
                                              rest(rp,j+1),
                                              generation)];
           assign(buffer',rp(j+1));
           return(numeric-rep-of(subl(rp,i,j))
      else error

check-syntax: Char-list × {Integer,Real} → Bool
```

The result of *check-syntax(clist,type)* is *TRUE* if the characters in *clist* correspond to the syntax of a signed-integer, if *type* is Integer, or to a signed-number, if *type* is Real. Otherwise it is *FALSE*.

reset

```
reset: File-den =>
reset(mk-File-den(fid)) Δ
    if is-file-defined(fid)
       then def mk-File(buffer,lp,rp,) : (c FILES)(fid);
            let file-value = complete-file(lp^rp,s-type(buffer)) in
            def buffer'     : re-allocate(buffer);
            FILES := c FILES + [fid ↦ mk-File(buffer',<>,file-value,
                                                        inspection)]
            if file-value≠<> then assign(buffer',hd file-value) else I
       else I

complete-file: Value-list × Type → Value-list
complete-file(vl,type) Δ
    type≠Char ∨ vl=<>          → vl
    vl(len vl)=end-of-line     → vl
    T                          → vl^end-of-line
```

rewrite

```
rewrite: File-den =>
rewrite(mk-file-den(fid)) Δ
    def buffer  : buffer-of(mk-File-den(fid));
    def buffer' : re-allocate(buffer);
    FILES := (c FILES + [fid ↦ mk-File(buffer',<>,<>,generation)]
```

succ

```
succ: Ordinal → Ordinal
succ(x) Δ if x<maxs(values(x))
             then (Δr∈values(x))(ord(r)=ord(x)+1)
             else undefined
```

<u>write</u>

```
write: File-den × Actual-write-parameter =>
write(mk-File-den(fid),awp) ≜
   let val = s-value(awp) in
   let s∈String be s.t.
      (cases val:
          val ∈ Char     → is-character-rep(s,awp)
          val ∈ Integer  → is-integer-rep(s,awp)
          val ∈ Real     → is-real-rep(s,awp)
          val ∈ String   → is-string-rep(s,awp)
          val ∈ Boolean  → is-boolean-rep(s,awp)) in
   if pre-put(fid) ∧ is-text(fid)
      then def mk-File(buffer,lp,rp,mode) : c FILES;
           def buffer' : re-allocate(buffer);
           FILES := c FILES + [fid ↦ mk-File(buffer',lp^s,
                                              <>,generation)]
      else error
```

The functions: *is-character-rep*, *is-integer-rep*, *is-real-rep*, *is-string-rep*, *is-boolean-rep*, *is-fixed-rep*, and *is-floating-rep*

all have type: *String × Actual-write-parm → Bool*

```
is-character-rep(s,awp) ≜
   let field-width = check-width(awp)         in
   let value       = s-val(awp)               in
   let lead        = max(0,field-width - 1)   in
   let spaces      = {1:lead}                 in
   lens=field-width ∧ (∀i∈spaces)(s[i]=BLANK) ∧ s[lens]=value

is-integer-rep(s,awp) ≜
   let field-width = check-width(awp)                                 in
   let value       = s-val(awp)                                       in
   let lead        = max(0,field-width - (intsize(value) + 1))        in
   let zeros       = {1:lead}                                         in
   lens=field-width ∧ (∀i∈zeros)(s[i]=BLANK) ∧
   (if value≥0 then s[lead + 1]=BLANK else s[lead + 1]=MINUS) ∧
   numeric-rep-of(rest(s,lead + 2))=abs(value)
```

```
is-real-rep(s,awp) ≜
    s-frac(awp)=nil → is-floating-rep(s,awp),T → is-fixed-rep(s,awp)

is-string-rep(s,awp) ≜
    let field-width = check-width(awp)                    in
    let value       = s-val(awp)                          in
    let lead        = max(0,field-width - lenvalue)       in
    let spaces      = {1:lead}                            in
    lens=field-width ∧ (∀i∈spaces)(s[i]=BLANK) ∧
    rest(s,lead+1)=subl(value,1,min(lenvalue,lens - lead))

is-floating-rep(s,awp) ≜
    let field-width = check-width(awp)                   in
    let value       = s-val(awp)                         in
    let dec-places  = field-width - expdigits - 5        in
    let x,y ∈ Int be s:t: if value=0 then x=0 ∧ y=0
                                     else 10>x≥1 ∧
                                          dec-places-of(x)=dec-places ∧
                                          is-approximation(value,x,y) in
    lens=field-width ∧
    (if value>0 then s[1]=BLANK else s[1]=MINUS) ∧
    numeric-rep-of(s[2])=trunc(x) ∧
    s[3]=POINT ∧
    numeric-rep-of(subl(s,4,dec-places))=x-trunc(x) ∧
    s[4 + dec-places]=EXPON ∧
    s[5 + dec-places]=(y≥0 → PLUS,T → USCORE) ∧
    numeric-rep-of(rest(s,6 + dec-places))=y
```

Comment: *expdigits* is an implementation-defined integer value representing the number of digit characters written in an exponent.

```
is-fixed-rep(s,awp) ≜
    let (field-width,frac-width) = check-width(awp)                   in
    let value                    = s-val(awp)                         in
    let sign                     = if value>0 then 0 else 1           in
    let min-width                = intsize(value)+frac-width+sign+1   in
    let x∈Int be s.t. if value=0 then x=0
                      else dec-place-of(x)=frac-width ∧
                           is-approximation(value,x,0)                in
    let lead                     = max(0,field-width - min-width)     in
    let zeros                    = {1:lead}                           in
```

```
    lens=field-with ∧ (∀i∈zeros)(s[i]=BLANK) ∧
    value<0 ⊃ s[lead + 1]=MINUS  ∧
    numeric-rep-of(subl(s,lead+sign+1,intsize(x))=trunc(x) ∧
    s[lead+sign+intsize(x)+1))= POINT ∧
    numeric-rep-of(rest(s,lead+sign+intsize(x)+2))=x - trunc(x)

is-boolean-rep(s,awp) ≜
    let field-width = check-width(awp)                                in
    let value       = s-val(awp)                                      in
    let result      = if value then <T,R,R,U,E> else <F,A,L,S,E>      in
    is-string-rep(s,mk-Actual-write-parm(result,field-width,nil))

check-width: Actual-write-parm → (Int | Int × Int)
check-width(mk-Actual-write-parm(v,tw,fw)) ≜
    v∈Char              → let aw = if tw=nil then 1 else tw in
                          if aw≥1 then aw
                          else undefined,
    v∈Integer           → let aw = if tw=nil then intw else tw in
                          if aw≥1 then max(intsize(v)+1,aw)
                          else undefined,
    v∈Real ∧ fw=nil     → let aw = if tw=nil then realw else tw in
                          if aw≥1 then max(expdigits+6,aw)
                          else undefined,
    v∈Real ∧ fw≠nil     → let sign = if v>0 then 0 else 1               in
                          let mchs = sign+intsize(v)+1+dec-digits-of(v) in
                          let aw   = if tw=nil then mchs else tw        in
                          if aw≥1 ∧ fw≥1 then (max(aw,mchs),fw)
                          else undefined,
    v∈Bool              → let aw = if tw=nil then boolw else tw in
                          if aw≥1 then aw else undefined
    v∈String            → let aw = if tw=nil then lenv else tw in
                          if aw≥1 then aw else undefined
```

Comment: *intw*, *realw*, and *boolw* are implementation-defined integer values representing the number of characters written out for *Integer*, *Real* or *Boolean*, respectively.

numeric-rep-of: $Char^*$ → *Int* | *Real*

numeric-rep-of converts a *Char-list* into a implementation defined value which the character string is a representation of.

```
intsize: Real → Int
intsize(x) ≜ if x=0 then 1
             else let r be s.t. 10**(r-1)≤abs(x)<10**r in r

is-an-approximation: Real × Real × Integer → Bool
is-an-approximation(x,y,z) ≜
   rep-of(x-0.5*10**-dec-places-of(x),y)
   ≤ abs(r) <
   rep-of(x+0.5*10**+dec-places-of(x),y)

rep-of: Real × Integer → Real
rep-of(x,y) ≜ x*10**y
```

writeln

```
writeln: File-den =>
writeln(mk-File-den(fid)) ≜
     if pre-put(fid) ∧ is-text(fid)
        then put-char(fid,end-of-line)
        else error
```

7.4.3 Auxiliary Functions

```
deallocate: Den-set =>
deallocate(ds) =
    def locs : union{sc-locs-of(d) | d∈ds} ;
    STORE := c STORE \ locs;
    def files : union{files-of(d) | d∈ds} ;
    FILES := c FILES \ files;
    def dids : {x | x∈Did∧(∃y∈rng((cDENV)(x)))(sc-locs-of(y)⊆locs)} ;
    DENV  := c DENV \ dids;
    VENV  := c VENV \ dids

sc-locs-of: Storage-loc => Sc-loc-set
sc-locs-of(x) ≜
    (x ∈ Sc-loc          → {x},
     x ∈ Array-den       → union{sc-locs-of(r) | r ∈ rng x},
     x ∈ Record-den      → union{sc-locs-of(r) | r ∈ rng x},
     x ∈ File-den        → def mk-File(buf,,,,) : (c FILE)(x);
                           sc-locs-of(buf),
```

```
      x ∈ Pointer-den  → let mk-Pointer-den(l,,) = x in {l},
      x ∈ Subrange-den → let mk-Subrange-den(l,) = x in {l},
      x ∈ Tag-den      → let mk-Tag-den(l,,) = x in {l},
      x ∈ Did          → union{sc-locs-of(r) | r ∈ rng((c DENV)(x))},
      x = nil          → {})

files-of: Structural-den => Fil-id-set
files-of(x) ≜
   (x ∈ File-den   → {s-id(x)},
    x ∈ Array-den  → union{files-of(r) | r ∈ rng(x)},
    x ∈ Record-den → union{files-of(r) | r ∈ rng(x)},
    x ∈ Did        → union{files-of(r) | r ∈ rng((c DENV)(x))},
    T              → {})

buffer-of: File-den => Den
buffer-of(mk-File-den(fid)) ≜
   def mk-File(buffer,,,) : (c FILES)(fid); s-loc(buffer)

labels-of: Statement* → Label-set
labels-of(stl) = {s-label(stl(i)) | i∈indsstl} - {nil}

used-storage: => Sc-loc-set
used-storage() ≜
   dom c STORE ∪  union{sc-locs-of(y) | y∈rng(c STORE) ∩  Storage-loc}

re-allocate: Buffer => Buffer
re-allocate(buffer) ≜
   let mk-Buffer(loc,type,senv) = buffer in
   if loc≠nil then de-allocate({loc}) else I;
   def loc' : MD[type](senv);
   mk-Buffer(loc',type,senv)

ids-of: Record-type → Id-set
ids-of(rt) ≜
   let mk-Record-type(fp,vp) = rc in
   if vp=nil
      then dom fp
      else let mk-Variant-part(tag,,vc) = vp  in
           dom(fp)∪ (if tag=nil then {} else{tag})
           ∪ union{ids-of(rts) | rts∈rngvc}
```

```
is-dcont: Label × Statement-list → Bool
is-dcont(lab,sl) ≜ (∃i∈inds sl)(lab=s-label(sl[i]))

index: Label × Statement-list → Nat
index(lab,stl) ≜ (Δi∈inds stl)(lab = stl[i])

values: Ordinal → Ordinal-set
values(x) ≜ x∈Integer     → {i | -maxint≤i≤maxint },
            x∈Bool        → { Bool},
            x∈Char        → { Char},
            x∈Enumerated  → let mk-Enumerated(,idl) = x in
                            {mk-Enumerated(e,idl) | e∈elemsidl}

type-of: Type × Type-env → Type
type-of(t,tρ) ≜ if t∈Type-id then type-of(tρ(s-id(t)),tρ) else t

is-text: File-id => Bool
is-text(fid) ≜ def file : (c FILES)(fid);
               let mk-Buffer(,t,(tρ,)) = s-buffer(file) in
               type-of(t,tρ)=mk-File-type(Char)

maxs: Ordinal-set → Ordinal
maxs(s)      ≜ let e∈s in if cards=1 then e else max(e,maxs(s-{e}))
pre-maxs(s) ≜ s≠{}

mins: Ordinal-set → Ordinal
mins(s)      ≜ let e∈s in if cards=1 then e else min(e,mins(s-{e}))
pre-mins(s) ≜ s≠{}
```

Comment: *min* and *max* can be extended to *Ordinals* using the extended definition of ≥.

```
subl: X* × Int × Int → X*
subl(l,i,n)      ≜ l=<> ∨ n=0 → <>
                   i=1        → hdl^subl(tll,1,n-1)
                   T          → subl(tll, i-1, n
pre-subl(l,,n) ≜ i∈indsl ∧ n≥0

rest: X* × Int → X*
rest(l,i)        ≜ subl(l,i,lenl - i+1)
pre-rest(l,i)  ≜ i∈indsl
```

is-same-loc-type: Loc × Loc → Bool
is-same-loc-type(l1,l2) $\underline{\underline{\Delta}}$
  (l1,l2∈File-den) ∨ *(l1,l2∈Sc-loc)* ∨ *(l1,l2∈Array-den)* ∨
  (l1,l2∈Record-den ∧ *<u>dom</u>l1=<u>dom</u>l2)* ∨
  (l1,l2∈Subrange-den ∧ *s-range(l1)=s-range(l2)*

7.5 INDEXES

7.5.1 Static Semantics Functions and Objects

7.5.2 Dynamic Semantics Functions and Objects

CHAPTER 8

COMPILER DESIGN

The process of developing programs from their specifications is described in chapter 10. This chapter discusses the special problem of using a denotational language definition in the design of a compiler. In particular, the examples show that a VDM definition can be used to justify a mapping from the source language to sequences of instructions of the object machine. Such a mapping can then be used as a specification of the translation process: the techniques of chapter 10 being applicable to the development of a translator. One can see such a compiler design approach as isolating the use of the semantics to the first stage. As normal with such proposals, the top-down description is an over-simplification: it provides a documentation structure rather than a constraint on thinking. The examples are taken from the language of chapter 4. The proofs are not given at a very formal level.

This chapter is a rewritten version of [Jones 78c]. Other relevant references are [McCarthy 67a, Lucas 68a, Jones 71a] (this last paper contains further references to the early Vienna work in this area), [Jones 76a, Milne 76a, Morris 73a] and [Mosses 76a].

CONTENTS

8.1 INTRODUCTION

A definition of a language is written in terms of semantic objects (e.g. state) which are abstract in the sense that they possess only properties which are essential to the semantics. The first task in compiler design is to choose how these objects are to be represented on the target machine. Just as in conventional "data refinement" the representation is likely to have extra information, necessary to manipulate data efficiently, which are not present in the abstraction. In the ideal case, the representation can be related to the abstraction using a "retrieve function" (chapter 10 contains a detailed explanation of data refinement proofs).

The semantics of the language can be redefined in terms of the chosen representation. The proof of correctness of this alternative definition is given by relating it to the original semantics as shown in Fig. 1.

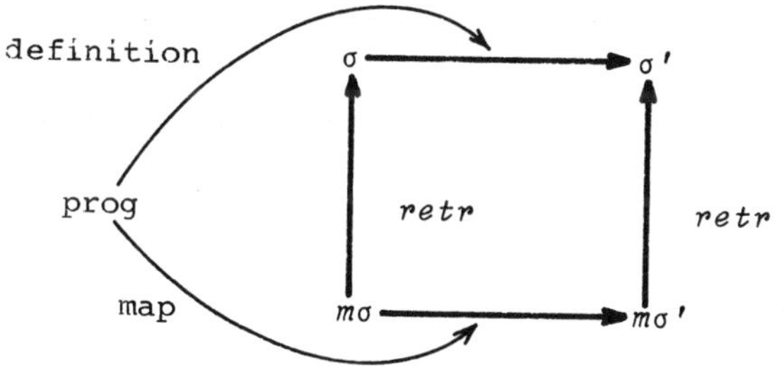

Fig. 1: First Stage of Compiler Correctness

The original definition maps abstract programs into state transformations (σ, σ' are members of the abstract states). The chosen state representation ($m\sigma$, $m\sigma'$ as typical members) is related to the abstract state by a retrieve function (*retr*). It is necessary to establish that this diagram commutes in the sense that the state transformation on the representation states is the same, when viewed under the retrieve function, as that on the abstract states. This form of justification should be decomposed to treat one language "concept" at a time.

At the end of the first stage, it is known what transformations are to be made in the target machine for particular language constructs. The next task is to choose sequences of target machine instructions which realize these transformations. Given an understanding of the semantics of the object machine instructions, the correctness of a translator specification is illustrated in Fig. 2.

This shows that the state transformations which are required on the object machine should be identical with the effect of the sequences of object machine instructions generated. Once again, such an argument must be decomposed.

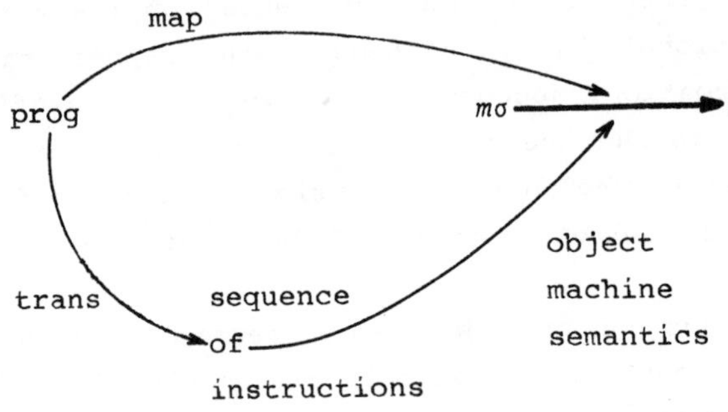

Fig. 2: Translator Correctness

The understanding of the object machine would not normally have to be recorded in a complete formal semantics. However, for an unconventional machine, it may be necessary to record assumptions on its architecture in terms of a state.

As with most descriptions of "top-down" design, the above is a simplification. It would clearly be unwise to choose a representation of the state without considering the instruction set of the target machine. Such a lack of foresight could result in choosing transformations which could only be realized inefficiently on the object machine. Clearly, a compiler designer will often sketch "instruction sequences" for sample programs as one of the first attempts to understand the translation problem. The structure described above is, then, one for presenting clear documentation (including correctness argument) rather than a constraint on thinking.

Compiler design documentation thus breaks into three major parts. The design of the object time environment solves the problem of representing abstract state objects (e.g. mappings) on the chosen object machine. This "object machine" may be an extension of the hardware to include commonly required service routines. The choice of the (extended) machine instructions to achieve the required transformations gives rise to a translator specification. The development of the translator itself is not covered here but is discussed in Chapter 9.

The program as so far described would only be practical for very small languages. For an actual programming language, it is essential that the design is decomposed so that different "language concepts" can be treated independently. This desirable separation is not fully formalized. However, the monolithic proof of [Jones 76a] has been decomposed to consider the following concepts separately:

i) Expression evaluation
ii) Location reference
iii) Environment handling
iv) Statement sequencing
v) Input/Output

The first of these concepts has been described by several authors and is presented as the first example below. The example gives the opportunity to discuss the topic of different forms of optimization. Location reference and Environment handling have often been grouped together as in [Henhapl 70a]. The former concept provides the second example in this chapter and shows how an implementation might resolve non-determinacy in the specification. Environment handling (or "reference to automatic variables") has been extensively studied by the Vienna group (see [Lucas 68b, Henhapl 70a, Jones 71a]). Statement sequencing is discussed in [Zimmerman 70a] & [Bjørner 78a]. Input/Output -- as always the poor relation -- is not normally the subject of papers because of the reliance on details of the chosen operating system interface.

8.2 EXPRESSION EVALUATION - LANGUAGE

The denotational semantics of expression evaluation avoids the issue of allocation of space for intermediate values. This is quite proper in the semantics, but it is an important issue which must be resolved in the design of the object time state. The parts of the language of chapter 4 which are of concern here are given by the following abstract syntax:

$$
\begin{array}{lll}
\mathit{Assign} & :: & \mathit{Varref} \quad \mathit{Expr} \\
\mathit{Expr} & = & \mathit{Infixexpr} \mid \mathit{Rhsref} \\
\mathit{Infixexpr} & :: & \mathit{Expr} \quad \mathit{Op} \quad \mathit{Expr} \\
\mathit{Op} & = & \mathit{Intop} \mid \mathit{Boolop} \mid \mathit{Comparisonop} \\
\mathit{Rhsref} & :: & \mathit{Varref} \\
\mathit{Varref} & :: & \mathit{Id} \quad [\mathit{Expr}^{+}] \\
\mathit{Scalartype} & = & \underline{\mathrm{INT}} \mid \underline{\mathrm{BOOL}}
\end{array}
$$

The relevant context conditions from chapter 4 are also assumed, as is the auxiliary function *SCTP*. Notice that two different ways of isolating this language concept are being used. The detailed list of operators is not discussed. This relies on the tacit assumption that the target machine has an adequate set of instructions. If, for example, there were no division instruction, the control of temporaries for the expanded code would probably have to be considered here. Another "interface" to the expression evaluation concept is the calculation of addresses for elements of arrays (see below): although this can be set aside, the implications for the use of temporaries must be considered here. It is for this reason that the use of array references on the left of assignment statements is included in the language fragment.

The relevant semantic objects (again taken from chapter 4) are:

$$
\begin{array}{lll}
STATE & :: & \mathrm{STR}{:}STORE\ \ldots \\
STORE & = & SCALARLOC \xrightarrow[m]{} [SCALARVALUE] \\
SCALARVALUE & = & Bool \mid Int \\
ENV & = & Id \xrightarrow[m]{} DEN \\
DEN & = & LOC \mid \ldots \\
LOC & = & ARRAYLOC \mid SCALARLOC \\
ARRAYLOC & = & Nat^{+} \xrightarrow[m]{} SCALARLOC^{+}
\end{array}
$$

Elements of *ARRAYLOC* are one-one mappings and their domains form a rectangle:

$$rect\colon\ Nat^{*} \to (Nat^{*})\text{-}set$$

The relevant semantic functions are:

$$
\begin{array}{l}
M[mk\text{-}Assign(vr,e)](\rho)\ \underline{\Delta} \\
\quad \underline{def}\ l : Mloc[vr](\rho); \\
\quad \underline{def}\ v : M[e](\rho); \\
\quad \mathrm{STR} := \underline{c}\ \mathrm{STR} + [l \mapsto v]
\end{array}
$$

$$
\begin{array}{l}
M[mk\text{-}Infixexpr(e1,op,e2)](\rho)\ \underline{\Delta} \\
\quad \underline{def}\ v1 : M[e1](\rho); \\
\quad \underline{def}\ v2 : M[e2](\rho); \\
\quad \underline{return}(M[op](v1,v2))
\end{array}
$$

$$M[mk\text{-}Rhsref(vr)](\rho)\ \underline{\Delta}\ (\underline{def}\ l : Mloc[vr](\rho);\ contents(l))$$

```
Mloc[mk-Varref(id,sscl)](ρ) ≜
   if sscl=nil then return(ρ(id))
   else let aloc  = ρ(id) in
        def esscl : <M[sscl[i]](ρ) | i∈indsscl>;
        if ¬(esscl∈domaloc) then error else return(aloc(esscl)))

contents(l) ≜ def v : (c STR)(l);
              if v=nil then error else return(v)
```

There are two places above where a program can be in error in a way which cannot be detected statically. In both cases, the design chosen below does not detect the error. This is a design decision and has nothing to do with the development method. Those who consider the decision too dangerous to be acceptable might choose to outline an alternative design.

8.3 EXPRESSION EVALUATION - TARGET MACHINE

The representation of store (as a byte string) is discussed in the second example below. Here this problem is avoided by showing the *STORE* in its abstract form. What cannot be postponed is providing space for the temporaries which are implied by *let vi* in the semantics. In a typical von Neumann computer such temporaries are most conveniently stored in registers. The initial development assumes that there are "enough" such registers and the problems posed by a paucity are discussed as optimization. With some care in the description, it is possible to leave open the possibility that the same registers are used for other purposes (e.g. address calculation). The use of registers is, however, assumed to be on "stack" basis.

The state of the target machine is then:

```
STATEm :: STR:  STORE  ...
          REGS: (Regno →m SCALARVALUE)
```

In order to defer decisions about address calculation, a function is assumed which computes locations given store references and registers:

```
sr:  STOREREF × (Regno →m SCALARVALUE) → SCALARLOC
```

In a machine with registers and store there are likely to be a range of instructions. Taking something like an IBM System/360 as a model, there might be register to register, register to store, and store to store instructions.

As is observed above, the specific instructions available have a great influence on the way in which the (alternative) definition based on target machine states is defined. Had there been three address instructions available, a different transformation would have been defined. The case distinctions given here are rather coarse and give rise to somewhat pessimistic code; the subject of optimization is considered below. A function for choosing new registers is defined:

```
newreg: Regno-set → Regno
newreg(rs)=r  ⊃  ¬(r∈rs)
```

The semantic functions for the machine state might be (*tgi* indicates that a target is provided and that an integer expression is being evaluated - cf. [Jones 76a] for all cases):

```
Mc[mk-Assign(vr,e)](δ,rs) ≜
    def (ref,rs') : MCloc[vr](δ,rs);
    if SCTP[vr] = INT then let nr = newreg(rs') in
                          MCtgi[e](δ,nr,rs');
                          def l : sr(ref,c REGS);
                          STR := c STR + [l ↦ (c REGS)(nr)]
    else ...

MCtgi[mk-Infixexpr(e1,op,e2)](δ,r,rs) ≜
    let nr = newreg(rs∪{r}) in
    MCtgi[e1](δ,r,rs);
    MCtgi[e2](δ,nr,rs∪{r});
    REGS := c REGS + [r ↦ M[op]((c REGS)(r),(c REGS)(nr))]

MCtgi[mk-Rhsref(vr)](δ,r,rs) ≜
    def (ref,rs') : MCloc[vr](δ,rs);
    def l         : sr(ref,c REGS);
    REGS := c REGS + [r ↦ contents(l)]
```

These functions use a dictionary which provides statically determinable information about identifiers:

$$\delta \in DICT = Id \underset{m}{\to} DICTINF$$

The retrieve function which relates the semantic objects here with those of the definition is of type:

$$retr: DICT \times STATE_m \to ENV \times STATE$$

with:

$$retr(\delta,\sigma m) \triangleq (retrENV(\delta,REGS(\sigma m)),retrSTATE(\sigma m))$$

$$retrENV: \quad DICT \times (Regno \underset{m}{\to} SCALARVALUE) \to ENV$$
$$retrSTATE: \; STATE_m \to STATE$$

The details of these functions need not be given here. The overall result to be shown for assignment statements is:

$$((\rho,\sigma) = retr(\delta,\sigma m)) \supset (\underline{let}\ \sigma m' = MC[asn](\delta,rs)(\sigma m)\ \underline{in}$$
$$\underline{let}\ \sigma' = M[asn](\rho)(\sigma)\ \underline{in}$$
$$(\sigma' = retrState(\sigma m')) \wedge regs(rs,\sigma m,\sigma m'))$$

where *regs* is a predicate which checks that two states agree over a given register set:

$$regs(rs,\sigma m,\sigma m') = \mathrm{REGS}(\sigma m)|rs = \mathrm{REGS}(\sigma m')|rs$$

This predicate is used to define the stack nature of register use.

Consulting the *M* and *MC* semantics for assignment statements, it is clear that something must be assumed about the computation of locations. In addition to the obvious properties requiring that Fig. 1 commutes and the location "corresponds" the overall proof requires that no registers are "freed":

$$(\rho,\sigma)=retr(\delta,\sigma m) \supset (\underline{let}\ (\sigma m',ref,rs') = MCloc[vr](\delta,rs)(\sigma m)\ \underline{in}$$
$$\underline{let}\ (\sigma', l) = Mloc[vr](\rho)(\sigma)\ \underline{in}$$
$$\sigma' = retrSTATE(\sigma m') \wedge rs \subseteq rs' \wedge$$
$$l = sr(ref,\mathrm{REGS}(\sigma m') \mid rs') \wedge regs(rs,\sigma m,\sigma m'))$$

This assumption documents one of the interfaces of the expression evaluation language concept. A related property about expression evaluation itself is required to prove the overall result about assignment. It is:

$$((\rho,\sigma)=retr(\delta,\sigma m) \wedge \neg(r\epsilon s) \wedge (SCTP[e]=\underline{\text{INT}})) \supset$$
$$(\underline{let}\ (\sigma m',vm) = MCtgi[e](\delta,r,rs)(\sigma m)\ \underline{in}$$
$$\underline{let}\ (\sigma',v) = M[e](\rho)(\sigma)\ \underline{in}$$
$$\sigma'=retrState(\sigma m') \wedge v=\text{REGS}(\sigma m')(r) \wedge regs(rs,\sigma m,\sigma m'))$$

From this, and the fact that:

$$rs' \supseteq rs$$

the assignment result follows without difficulty.

The proof of the required result about expressions can be performed by structural induction over the syntactic structure of *Expr*. For elements of *Infixexpr*, the proof relies on the preservation of the registers given the hypotheses:

$$\neg(r\epsilon rs)$$
$$\neg(nr \in rs\cup\{r\})$$

and the type matching which results from the context conditions.

For elements of *Rhsref*, the assumption about *MCloc* and an obvious property of *retrSTATE* are required.

As indicated above, the transformations shown, and thus the implied code, are "pessimistic". With small expressions the superfluous "LOAD" instructions become very wasteful. Consider the following example:

```
MC[x:=a+b](...) ≜
    (def refx : MCloc[x](...);
     def refa : MCloc[a](...);
     def la   : sr(refa, c REGS);
     REGS     := c REGS + [r ↦ contents(la)]
     def refb : MCloc[b](...);
     def lb   : sr(refb, c REGS);
     REGS     := c REGS + [nr ↦ contents(lb)];
     REGS     := c REGS + [r  ↦ (c REGS)(r)+(c REGS)(nr)];
     def lx   : sr(refx,c REGS);
     STR      := c STR + [l ↦ (c REGS)(r)]
```

obviously the sequence *corresponding to:*

RS(LOAD,nr,refb); RR(ADD,r,nr)

should be combined to use:

*RS(*ADD*,r,refb)*

This is an example of a class of optimization which can be defined in a natural way over the structure of a program. The necessary case distinction can be defined as follows:

```
MCtgi[mk-Infixexpr(e1,op,e2)](δ,r,rs) ≜
  MCtgi[e1](δ,r,rs);
  if e2∈Infixexpr then
   (let nr = newreg(rs∪{r}) in
    MCtgi[e2](δ,nr,rs∪{r});
    REGS   := c REGS + [r1 ↦ M[op]((c REGS)(r1),(c REGS)(r2)]))])
  else
   (def (ref,rs') : MCloc[e2](dict,rs);
    def l   :  sr(ref,c REGS);
    REGS   := c REGS + [r ↦ M[op]((c REGS)(r),(c STR)(l))])
```

There are a number of examples of this class of optimization: [Jones 76a] shows a similar approach to handling comparison in conditional statements and the ubiquitous: $x := x + c$ type of assignment could be handled in the same way.

There are other classes of optimization which are better handled by an extra, equivalence preserving, pass. An example of this class is the allocation of actual registers to the "virtual" registers allocated by *MC*. The development of such translator structure is discussed in Chapter 9.

8.4 EXPRESSION EVALUATION - CODE SEQUENCES

The previous section redefined the semantics of (a part of) the language on a more baroque state. The correctness argument shows that this and the original language semantics correspond. It is now possible to proceed to the step invisaged in Fig. 2. In this simple example the transformations match obvious machine instructions. Thus:

```
Instr =  RR | RS | SS
RR    :: (LOADREGISTER | Op)    Regno      Regno
RS    :: (LOAD | STORE | Op)    Regno      Storeref
SS    :: (MOVE | ...)           Storeref   Storeref
```

The semantics of the register-to-register and register-to-store instructions is given by:

```
MC[mk-RR(op,r1,r2)] ≜
  if op = LOADREGISTER then
          REGS := c REGS + [r1 ↦ (c REGS)(r2)]
  else if op ∈ Intop then
          REGS := c REGS + [r1 ↦ M[op]((c REGS)(r1),(c REGS)(r2))]
  else ...

MC[mk-RS(op,r,sref)] ≜
   def l : sr(sref,c REGS);
   if op = STORE then STR := c STR + [l ↦ (c REGS)(r)]
   else if op = LOAD then REGS := c REGS + [r ↦ contents(l)]
   else ...
```

It is a straightforward task to rewrite to *MC* semantics using these operations. (But the reader should bear in mind the warning given above that a careless choice of transformations may only be realizable by very inefficient sequences of instructions.) For example, the final version of *MCtg* becomes:

```
Ttgi[mk-Infixexpr(e1,op,e2)](δ,r,rs) ≜
     MCtgi[e1](δ,r,rs);
     if e2 ∈ Infixexpr then
       (let nr = newreg(rs∪{r}) in
        MCtgi[e2](δ,nr,rs∪{r});
        MC[mk-RR(op,r,nr)])
     else
       (def (ref,rs') : MCloc[e2](δ,rs);
        MC[mk-RS(op,r,ref)])
```

The correctness of this transition *Ttgi* can be checked by expansion to agree with *MCtgi*.

Having reached the stage of machine-like operations, it is now possible to reinterpret the *T* functions: rather than mapping programs into functions, they can now be viewed as mapping into sequences of instructions. It should be observed that there are two sorts of case distinctions made in the *T* function. The static distinction like *e2∈Infixexpr* and dynamic distinction like the value of the Boolean expression in a conditional statement. The static distinctions depend on the text alone and govern a form of macro-expansion into the required instruction sequences. This view results in a specification of a mapping from (abstract) programs to sequences of instructions.

The total translator should, of course, not rely on programs being given in a convenient tree form. The task of relating the forms to something like "reverse Polish" is a simple case of data refinement. Suppose that the concrete syntax for the internal form of expression is:

```
Iexpr      ::=  Iinfexpr | Ivarref
Iinfixexpr ::=  Iexpr   Iexpr   Op
Ivarref    ::=  ...
```

The relevant retrieve function:

$retrExpr : Iexpr \to Expr$

This can be defined by a standard stack algorithm. In order to sketch how this would work a function

$convert: (Ivarref \mid Op)^* \times Expr^* \to Expr$

is defined which must initially be called with a first argument which satisfies the concrete syntax of *Iexpr* and a second argument which is an empty list.

```
convert(tokenl,stack) ≜
  if hdtokenl∈Op then
      let e2 = hdstack    in
      let e1 = hdtlstack  in
      convert(tltokenl,<mk-Expr(e1,hdtokenl,e2)>^tltlstack)
  else
      convert(tltokenl,<hd tokenl>^stack)
```

If the actual infix expressions were to be taken as input, one of the "two stack" algorithms could be used to express the retrieve function. In this case there would be more than one representation for each abstract tree. For an indication of how this method of documentation an interface works for a large language like PL/I, see [Weissenböck 75a].

8.5 LOCATION REFERENCES - LANGUAGE

This second example of relating design to the semantic definition concerns the computation of locations. It illustrates both data refinement and the resolution of non-determinacy in the semantics.

The part of the language of interest concerns the declaration of variables. The relevant abstract syntax definition from chapter 4 is:

```
Block       :: s-dclm:(Id -m-> Type)  ...
Type        :: Scalartype   [Expr+]
Scalartype  =  INT | BOOL
```

The relevant semantic objects are:

```
STORE    = SCALARLOC -m-> [SCALARVALUE]
ARRAYLOC = Nat+ -m-> SCALARLOC
```

where members of *ARRAYLOC* are one-to-one mappings whose domain forms a rectangle of natural numbers. The relevant semantic functions are:

```
M[mk-Block(dclm, ...)](ρ) Δ ...
   def ρ' : ρ + ([id ↦ M[dclm(id)](ρ) | id∈domdclm] ∪ ... );
   always (let sclocs =  ...  in
           STR          := c STR \ sclocs; ...) in ...

M[mk-Type(sctp,bdl)](ρ) Δ
   if bdl=nil then (def l∈SCALARLOC - dom c STR;
                    STR := c STR ∪ [l ↦ nil];
                    return(l))
   else (def ebdl : ...;
         if ... then error
         else (let al∈ARRAYLOC s:t: domal = rect(ebdl) ∧
                                        is-disjl(<rngal,dom cSTR>);
               STR  := c STR ∪ [scl ↦ nil | scl∈rngal];
               return(al)))
```

```
Mloc[mk-Varref(id,sscl)](ρ) ≜
    if sscl=nil then return (ρ(id))
    else (let aloc = ρ(id) in
          def esscl : <M[sscl[i]](ρ) | i∈indsscl>;
          if ¬(esscl∈domaloc) then error else return(aloc(esscl)))
```

Locations are constrained only in some respects by this *M* semantics. Care is taken in the semantics of *Type* to define a non-deterministic choice of *SCALARLOC*s. Although particular implementations will presumably provide a deterministic algorithm for selecting locations, the algorithm is not precisely determined by the semantics. (Strictly, this has lifted the whole definition from denotations which are functions to relations as denotations. The fact that the actual choice does not affect the outcome of a program could be formally proved.) The advantage of this freedom can now be felt. Here the chosen implementation reuses locations in a "stack" style; alternative implementations could always select new locations or or could perform dynamic garbage collection. Each such implementation could be shown to be a different specialization of the choice given in the *M* semantics. If, on the other hand, the semantics had prescribed a choice function, it would be necessary - for some implementations - to become involved in a cumbersome equivalence proof.

8.6 LOCATION REFERENCES - TARGET MACHINE

The standard von Neumann machine architecture does not support mappings as general as those used in "Store". The representation chosen here is of a byte string. Furthermore, not all *Scalarvalues* require the same amount of space. Here, integers are allocated four bytes (aligned on a four-byte boundary) and Boolean values one (whole!) byte. Arrays are mapped so that left-hand indices vary most rapidly. Array locations are represented by a base value and a list of multipliers. The bytes are used as a stack with a stack pointer (*PTR*) to indicate the next, unused, byte. Scalar locations are modelled by natural numbers which, in machine terms, are indices into the byte string.

By defining only constraints on the use of store (beyond the stack pointer), it is possible to have freedom for other information to be inserted in the stack. This freedom could be used to store a "display" and/or a "static chain" (cf.[Henhapl 70a]). Another implementation decision made here is to ignore the checking of subscript range. The semantics defines it to be on *error* if the subscript is out of bounds -- this leaves an implementation free to do as it pleases. (A different implementation which avoided the danger of computing addresses outside on array could equally well be proved correct.) Thus:

$STATE_m$ :: STR: $Byte^*$ ...
PTR: *Nat*

SCALARLOC = *Nat*

$ARRAYLOC_m$ :: *s-base: Nat0*
s-mults: Nat^+

There are obvious constraints which prohibit variables from overlapping. In a normal data refinement proof (cf. chapter 10) the next step would be to relate the representation to the abstraction by a retrieve function. In the current example, this is not possible because the representation lacks some of the information in the abstraction. In particular, the maximum bound information is not stored with the values. This information would have been required only to support the elided test. There are two possible ways of handling such a problem: [Jones 76a] followed [Lucas 68a] in using "ghost variables". Here, a relation between abstraction and representation is used rather than a retrieve function:

$Rstore \subseteq (SCALARLOC \underset{m}{\to} SCALARVALUE) \times Byte^+$
$Rstore(sm,bl) = sm = [l \mapsto value(l,type(l),bl) \mid l \in \underline{dom}\, sm]$

$type: SCALARLOC \to Scalartype$
$value: SCALARLOC \times Scalartype \times Byte^* \to SCALARVALUE$

$Raloc(arloc,mk\text{-}Arraylocm(b,ml)) =$
$\quad arloc = [sscl \mapsto arref(b,ml,sscl) \mid sscl \in \underline{dom}\, arloc]$

$arref(b,ml,sscl) = b + sum(1,\underline{len}\, ml, ml[i]+sscl[i])$

The semantics, expressed in terms of $STATE_m$ etc. is:

$MC[mk\text{-}Block(dclm,...)](\rho) \triangleq$

...
<u>def</u> *oldp* : <u>c</u> PTR;
<u>def</u> ρ' : $\rho + ([id \mapsto MC[dclm(id)](\rho) \mid id \in \underline{dom}\, dclm] \cup ...)$;
<u>always</u> (PTR := *oldp*; ...)
<u>in</u> (...)

```
MC[mk-Type(sctp,bdl)](ρ) ≜
   if bdl=nil then if sctp=BOOL
                   then (def l∈Nat s:t: l ≥ c PTR;
                              PTR := l+1;
                              return(l))
                   else (def l∈Nat s:t: l ≥ c PTR ∧ mod(l,4)=0;
                              PTR := l+4;
                              return(l))
   else (def ebdl : ...;
         if sctp = BOOL then (def l∈Nat s:t: l ≥ c PTR - 1;
                                  let ml =  mults(ebdl,1) in
                                  PTR    := 1+arref(1,ebdl,ml)+1;
                                  return mk-Arrayloсm(l,ml))
         else ... )
```

Notice that the check on valid bounds has been omitted. Furthermore, there should strictly be a check on the exhaustion of store - this has not been shown here. The other functions are:

```
mults(ubdl,m) ≜ if len ubdl=1 then <m>
                else (let tml=mults(tlubdl,m) in
                      <hdtlubdl * hdtml> ^ tml)
```

for:

```
MCloc[mk-Varref(id,sscl)](ρ)
```

in the scalar case, the address must be located and the array case the base address and multipliers used by *arref* to compute the address of the element. The addresses and multipliers would actually be located via a "display".

The *MC* semantics can be seen to conform to the constraints in the *M* semantics from the following observations:

- locations chosen beyond the stack pointer (PTR) are disjoint from existing locations
- consistency (non-overlap etc.) is preserved
- array locations correspond (under *Raloc*) to one:one mappings with rectangular domains.

CHAPTER 9

RIGOROUS DEVELOPMENT OF INTERPRETERS AND COMPILERS

This chapter again tackles the problem of compiler development. The language considered is SAL, a Simple Applicative Language, which is not that simple: it handles functions as values - including such delivered out of their defining scope. Thus it illustrates the so-called FUNARG property [Moses 70a, Weizenbaum 68a]. The intermediate steps use imperative constructs of the meta-language (e.g. declarations) which are described in the Glossary of Notation. The example is used to illustrate the step to compiling algorithms and uses 'attribute semantics'. (The chapter is a rewritten, abbreviated version of [Bjørner 77b].)

CONTENTS

9.1 INTRODUCTION

Starting with a denotational semantics definition of a simple applicative language, SAL, we systematically develop the specifications of a compiler for SAL. We do so by presenting, in a unifying framework -- and steps of increasing concretization -- the commonly known semantics definition styles of the 1960's and 1970's:

i. denotational semantics
ii. first-order functional semantics
iii. abstract state machine operational semantics
iv. concrete state machine operational semantics
v. attribute semantics.

The first four semantics styles are employed in the definition of an interpetive semantics, whilst the fifth style is engaged in the final description of a compiling algorithm. The target machine for which the compiler is to generate code is likewise interpretively defined.

The double aim of this chapter is to advocate a different approach to the teaching of compiler design; and to illustrate that the spectrum of semantics definition methods of the 1960s fit into a development hierarchy. The main content of the chapter is seen as the exemplification of a disciplined software development methodology, especially as applicable to programming language design and compiler development, and the demonstration of its feasibility. The implied, derived and constituent aspects of the chapter are then these: the design of a hierarchy of meta-languages for expressing levels of abstraction and concretization; and the placement in a proper context, blending and exploitation of a number of seemingly diverse software techniques. These latter include the conscious choice and/or mixture of levels of representational and operational abstraction, configurational (bottom-up) and hierarchical (top-down) abstraction, and functional (applicative) versus state (imperative) programming.

We believe, seemingly contrary to all textbooks on compiler design, that the very initial stages of any compiler development must concentrate first on precise descriptions of the source and the target languages; to be followed by a precise description of the compiling algorithm. That is: of the compiler's input/output relation: source program texts into target code sequences. We also believe that an activity such as the one whose initial steps have been outlined above, can be meaningfully embedded within a more generally applicable software development methodology.

The borderline between modelling the source language abstractly for purposes of language design and compiler and program development are these: the language designer experiments with different models in attempts to understand, discover, purify, generalize and simplify language constructs. The compiler developer uses the final abstraction document as a basis for implementation of the compiler. And the source language programmer refers to the mathematical semantics definition when proving correctness of source programs. In this paper we shall exemplify only the compiler developer's view.

9.2 INFORMAL DESCRIPTION OF SAL

Syntax:

SAL is a simple applicative language. Its programs are expressions. There are eight expression categories:

*Const*ants	k
*Var*iables	id
Infix expressions	e1 + e2
*Cond*itional expressions	if et then ec else ea
Simple *Let* Blocks	(let id = ed in eb)
*Rec*ursive Functions	(letrec g(id) = ed in eb)
*Lamb*da Functions	λid.ed
*Appl*ications	ef(ea)

(Most of our elaboration functions, incidentally, will be expressed in a simple language like SAL.) Blocks with multiple definitions can be "mimicked" by multiply nested simple (*Let*) blocks. Multiple, mutually recursive functions, however, cannot be explicitly defined other than through the use of formal function arguments.

Data Types:

Constants stand for Natural numbers, Booleans, etc. The infix operators are then the usual ones: ADDition, SUBtraction, AND etc.

Comment:

SAL may seem awfully trivial to those who are used to programming with an ample supply and type variety of assignable variables -- but its realization illustrates most of the more intricate aspects of interpreter, that is runtime code, and compiler design. The main reason for this should be seen in SALs ability to yield FUNction VALues out of their defining scope (that is the so-called FUNARG property [Moses 70a, Weizenbaum 68a]). In addition, our development concentrates on implementing the block-structure and function invocation aspects.

Semantics:

SAL programs express only three kinds of VALues: Natural numbers, truth valued Booleans, and FUNction VALues, that is objects which are functions from VALues to VALues, these again including FUNctions, etc.. The DENotation, that is VALue, of a variable identifier, 'id', is that of the possibly recursively defined) defining expression: 'ed' (respectively: 'Yλg.λid.ed') of the lexicographically youngest incarnation, that is the "outwardgoing" statically closest containing block. Y is the fixed point finding function which when applied to 'λg.λid.ed' yields the "smallest" solution to the equation: 'g(id)=ed', in which 'g' occurs free in 'ed'. Infix and conditional expression VALues are as you expect them to be. The VALue of a block is that of the expression body, 'eb', in which all free occurences of the 'id' of a let, respectively the 'g' of a letrec, block header definition have been replaced (or: substituted) by their VALues. That is: 'ed' is evaluated in an environment, *env'*, which is exactly that extension of the block-embracing environment, *env*, which binds 'id' (respectively 'g') to its VALue, and otherwise binds as *env*. The VALue of a lambda-expression, 'λid.ed', is the FUNction of 'id' that 'ed' denotes in the environment in which it is first encountered, that is defined. Finally: the VALue of an application, 'ef(ea)', is the result of applying the FUNction VALue that 'ef' denotes to the VALue denoted by 'ea'.

9.3 INTERPRETIVE SEMANTICS DEFINITIONS

Four styles will be given. In the first definition we express the semantics of SAL in terms of mathematical functions. Thus the semantics of a compound syntactic object is expressed as the (homomorphic) function that is as functional composition) of the semantics of the individual, proper components. The denoted functions are themselves expressed in terms of so-called semantic domains, and these are again functional. The remaining definitions are increasingly more 'computational', that is can best be understood as specifying sequences of computations given an input, that is an initial binding of variables to their meaning.

The last, fourth, interpretive definition "unzips" user-defined functions by permitting a compiletime macro-expansion of the definition, pre-processing SAL program-defined functions into label/goto "bracketed" meta-language texts, and calls of these functions into (branch and link-like) gotos to such texts. The principles of properly saving, updating (that is "setting-up") and restoring (that is "taking-down" & "re-installing") calling and defining environments form a more detailed version than any of the preceding definitions, and of otherwise published accounts of this so-called static (environmentally preceding) and dynamic (call) activation chain mechanisms.

9.3.1 Denotational Semantics (I)

Without much further ado we now present the first in a series of seven specifications of SAL (I-IV,VI-VIII).

I.1 Syntactic Domains

(1) *Prog* = *Expr*

(2) *Expr* = *Const* | *Var* | *Infix* | *Cond* | *Let* | *Rec* | *Lamb* | *Appl*

(3) *Const* :: *Int*

(4) *Var* :: *Id*

(5) *Infix* :: *Expr Op Expr*

(6) *Cond* :: *Expr Expr Expr*

(7) *Let* :: *Id Expr Expr*

(8) *Rec* :: *Id Lamb Expr*

(9) *Lamb* :: *Id Expr*

(10) *Appl* :: *Expr Expr*

(11) *Id* ⊂ *Token*

(12) *Op* = ADD | SUB | AND | ...

I.2 Semantic Domains

(13) *ENV* = *Id* $\underset{m}{\rightarrow}$ *VAL*

(14) *VAL* = *Int* | *Bool* | *FUN*

(15) *FUN* = *VAL* $\tilde{\rightarrow}$ *VAL*

I.3 Elaboration Functions

```
(16) type: eval-prog:  Prog → VAL
(17) type: eval-expr:  Expr → (ENV → VAL)
(18) type: eval-fun:   Lamb → (ENV → FUN)

16. eval-prog[e] ≜ eval-expr[e]([])

18. eval-fun[mk-Lamb(id,e)]env ≜ λa.eval-expr[e](env+[id ↦ a])

17. eval-expr[e]env ≜
  .1  cases e: mk-Const(k)        → k,
  .2           mk-Var(id)         → env(id),
  .3           mk-Infix(e1,o,e2)  → (let v1 = eval-expr[e1]env,
  .4                                     v2 = eval-expr[e2]env in
  .5                                 cases o: ADD→v1+v2,SUB→v1-v2,...)),
  .6           mk-Cond(t,c,a)     → if eval-expr[t]env
  .7                                   then eval-expr[c]env
  .8                                   else eval-expr[a]env,
  .9           mk-Let(id,d,b)     → (let env'=env+[id ↦ eval-expr[d]env] in
  .10                                eval-expr[b]env'),
  .11          mk-Rec(g,d,b)      → (let env'=env+[g ↦ eval-fun[d]env'] in
  .12                                eval-expr[b]env'),
  .13          mk-Lamb( , )       → eval-fun[e]env,
  .14          mk-Appl(f,a)       → (let fun = eval-expr[f]env,
  .15                                    val = eval-expr[a]env     in
  .16                                if is-FUN(fun)
  .17                                  then fun(val) else undefined
```

9.3.2 First-Order Applicative Semantics (II)

By a first-order applicative semantics definition we mean one whose semantic domains are non-functional, but which is still referentially transparent. Hence, if we were given, as a basis, a denota tional semantics we would have to object transform its functional components into such objects which by means of suitable "simulations" can mimic the essential aspects of the denotational definition. In the case of SAL two kinds of objects are to ve transformed: $ENV = Id \xrightarrow{m} VAL$ and, among *VAL*ues: $FUN = VAL \xrightarrow{\sim} VAL$. The former objects were constructed by means of expressions:

I.18. *env' = env + [id ↦ a]*

I.17.9 *env' = env + [id ↦ eval-expr[d]env]*

I.17.11 *env' = env + [g ↦ eval-fun[d]env']*

The latter objects were denoted by an expression basically of the lambda form:

I.18. *λa.(eval-expr[e](env +[id ↦ a]))*

We shall not motivate the transformation choices further (see [Reynolds 72a]), nor state general derivation principles, but rather present the transformed objects as "faits-accomplis": *ENV* objects, which are MAPs ($\overrightarrow{m}$), as *ENV1* objects of the tuple type, with extensions accomplished in terms of concatenations (^), and functional application (*()*) as directed, linear searches (*look-up1*). The mathematical functions, *fun*, denoted by lambda-expressions are then realized as so-called *closures* -- these are 'passive' structures, which pairs the expression, *d*, to be evaluated, with the defining environment, *env'*, so that when *fun* is to be applied, *fun(val)*, then a simulation of *clos* with the transformed counterpart, *arg*, of *val*, is performed: *apply1(clos,arg)*.

Instead of now presenting the more concrete, first-order functional elaboration functions we first present arguments for why we believe that our choices will do the job. Those arguments are stated as *retrieve* functions, *retr-ENV* and *retr-VAL*, which apply to the transformed objects and yield the more abstract "ancestors" from which they were derived. We next observe that the definition is still functional, as was the denotational. All arguments are explicit, there is no reference to assignable/declared variables. And we finally note that we cannot, given a specific expression, *e*, 'stick' it into the *m1-eval-expr* (together with an initial, say empty environment) and by macro-substitution eliminate all references to *m1-eval-expr*. The reason for this "failure" will be seen in our "stacking" closures whose subsequent application requires *m1-eval-expr*.

II.1 Syntactic Domains - as in I.1

II.2 Semantic Domains

(1)	*ENV1 = IdVal**	(4)	*REC :: Id Lamb*
(2)	*IdVAL = SIMP | REC*	(5)	*VAL1 = Int | Bool | CLOS*
(3)	*SIMP :: Id VAL1*	(6)	*CLOS :: Lamb ENV1*

II.2.1 Retrieve Functions

```
(7) type: retr-ENV:  ENV1 → ENV
(8) type: retr-VAL:  VAL1 → VAL

7.0 retr-ENV(env1) ≜
 .1  if env1=<>
 .2   then [],
 .3   else
 .4    (let env = retr-ENV(tl env1) in
 .5     cases hd env1:
 .6       mk-SIMP(id,val1) → env + [id ↦ retr-VAL(val1)],
 .7       mk-REC(g,d)      → (let env' = env + [g ↦ eval-fun[d]env'] in
 .8                           env')))

8.0 retr-VAL(val1) ≜
 .1  cases val1: (mk-CLOS(l,env1) → eval-fun[l](retr-ENV(env1)),
 .2               T               → val1)
```

II.2.2 Auxiliary Function

```
(9) type: look-up1:  Id × ENV1 → VAL1

9.0 look-up1(id,env1) ≜
 .1  if env1=<>
 .2     then undefined
 .3     else cases hd env1: mk-SIMP(id,val1) → val1,
 .4                         mk-REC(id,lamb)  → mk-CLOS(lamb,env1),
 .5                         T                → look-up1(id,tl env1)
```

II.3 Elaboration Functions

```
(10) type: m1-eval-prog:  Prog          ⥲ VAL1
(11) type: m1-eval-expr:  Expr → (ENV1 ⥲ VAL1)
(12) type: apply1:        CLOS × VAL1   ⥲ VAL1

10.0 m1-eval-prog[e] ≜ m1-eval-expr[e](<>)

11.0 m1-eval-expr[e](env1) ≜
  .1  cases e: mk-Const(k)     → k,
  .2           mk-Var(id)      → look-up1(id,env1),
```

```
.3     mk-Infix(e1,o,e2) → (let v1 = m1-eval-expr[e1](env1),
.4                              v2 = m1-eval-expr[e2](env1)      in
.5                          cases o:
.6                            ADD → v1+v2, SUB → v1-v2, ...)),
.7     mk-Cond(t,c,a)    → if m1-eval-expr[t](env1)
.8                            then m1-eval-expr[c](env1)
.9                            else m1-eval-expr[a](env1),
.10    mk-Let(id,d,b)    → (let v     = m1-eval-expr[d](env1)    in
.11                         let env1' = <mk-SIMP(id,v)>^env1     in
.12                         m1-eval-expr[b](env1')),
.13    mk-Rec(g,d,b)     → (let env1' = <mk-REC(g,d)>^env1       in
.14                         m1-eval-expr[b](env1')),
.15    mk-Lamb(,)        → mk-CLOS(e,env1),
.16    mk-Appl(f,a)      → (let clos = m1-eval-expr[f](env1),
.17                               arg  = m1-eval-expr[a](env1)   in
.18                         apply1(clos,arg))
```

```
12.0 apply1(clos,arg) ≜
  .1  cases clos:
  .2   mk-CLOS(mk-Lamb(id,d),ρ1) → (let ρ1'=<mk-SIMP(id,arg)>^ρ1 in
  .3                                  m1-eval-expr[d](ρ1')),
  .4   T                          → undefined
```

9.3.3 Abstract State Machine Semantics (III)

By an abstract state machine semantics we understand a definition which typically employs (globally) declared variables of abstract, possibly higher-level, type. It expresses the semantics (not in terms of applicatively defined, "grand" transformations on this state, but) in terms of statement sequences denoting a computational process of individual, "smaller" state transformations.

In the SAL case we choose to map the semantic *ENV1* arguments onto a globally declared variable, *env2*, thereby removing these arguments from the elaboration function references. By doing so we must additionally mimic the meta-language's own recursion capability which is exploited e.g. in lines II.11.3-4,7-9, ... Thus the type of *env2* is to become a stack of stacks, that is: *ENV2=ENV1**, where *ENV1=IdVal**. Each cenv2 element is that stack of *Id*'s and their values, which when *looked-up* properly (cf. *retr-ENV*) reflects the bindings of the so-called "lexicographically youngest incarnations" of each identifier in the static scope, that is:

in going outwards from the identifier use through embracing blocks towards the outermost program expression level. As long as no let or rec defined function is being *Appl*ied, the 'env2' will contain exactly one *ENV1* element. As soon as a defined function is *Appl*ied, the calling environment is dumped on the 'env2' stack. On its top is pushed the *ENV1* environment current when the function was defined.

In addition we choose to mechanize the recursive stacking of temporaries (e.g. II.11.3-4, 10, 16-17) by means of a global stack, *STK*. We could have merged *STK* into *ENV2*, but decide not to at present. Hence this abstract machine definition also requires further decomposition of the *look-up1* operation. As before, we state our beliefs as to why we think the present development is on a right track, by presenting *retr*ieve functions.

The abstract state machine semantics definition is said to be operational, or to be a mechanical semantics definition, since it specifies the meaning of SAL by describing the operation of a machine effecting the computation of the desired value. Such definitions rather directly suggests, or are, realizations. They do not possess, or involve, implicit, implementation language processor controlled, but explicit state machine semantics definer determined allocation and freeing. We refer to: ^, respectively *tl*. The allocation and freeing is of otherwise recursively nested (that is stacked) objects. The definition, however, still requires the presence, at run-time, of *m2-eval-expr* (III.23.8). It still cannot be completely factored out of the definition for any given, non-trivial expression. Thus there still cannot be an exhaustive, macro-substitution process which completely eliminates the interpretive nature of the definition. The reason is as before: *CLOS*ures are triplets of a function definition bound variable, *id*, a function 'body', *d*, and the recursive, defining environment, *env2'*. Together they represent, but are not, the function, *fun* (I.18). It must instead be mimicked; hence the required presence of *m2-eval-expr*.

III.1 Syntactic Domains -- as in I.1

III.2 Semantic Domains

(1)	*ENV2*	=	*ENV1**	
(2)	*ENV1*	=	*IdVal**	
(3)	*IdVal*	=	*SIMP* | *REC*	
(4)	*SIMP*	::	*Id*	*VAL1*
(5)	*REC*	::	*Id*	*Lamb*
(6)	*VAL1*	=	*Int* | *Bool* | *CLOS*	
(7)	*CLOS*	::	*Lamb*	*ENV1*
(8)	*STK*	=	*VAL1**	

```
(9)   Σ      =    (env2 →m ENV2) ∪ (stk →m STK)
```

III.2.1 State Initialization

```
(10)  dcl env2 := <<>> type ENV2,
(11)      stk  := <>   type STK;
```

III.2.2 Retrieve Functions

```
(12)  type: retr-ENV1:  Σ → ENV1     retr-ENV1() Δ hd c env2
(13)  type: retr-VAL1:  Σ → VAL1     retr-VAL1() Δ hd c stk
```

III.2.3 Auxiliary Function

```
(14)  type: look-up2:  Id → (Σ ⥲ Σ)

14.0 look-up2(id) Δ
  .1    (trap exit() with I in
  .2     for j=1 to len hd c env2 do
  .3       cases hd c env2[j]:
  .4         mk-SIMP(id,val2)
  .5             → (stk := <val2> ^ c stk;
  .6                exit),
  .7         mk-REC(id,e)
  .8             → (def env2' : <(hd c env2)[k] | j ≤ k ≤ len hd c env2>;
  .9                stk := <mk-CLOS(e,env2')> ^ c stk;
  .10               exit)
  .11        T    → I);
  .12    error)
```

III.3 Elaboration Functions

```
(15)  type: m2-eval-prog:  Prog → (Σ ⥲ Σ  VAL1)
(16)  type: m2-eval-expr:  Expr → (Σ ⥲ Σ)

15.0 m2-eval-prog[e]                 Δ (env2) := <<>>;
  .1                                    m2-eval-expr[e];
  .2                                    env2 := tl c env2;
  .3                                    return(hd c stk))

16.0 m2-eval-Const[mk-Const(k)]      Δ  stk := <k>^c stk
```

```
17.0 m2-eval-Var[mk-Var(id)]            Δ look-up2(id)

18.0 m2-eval-Infix[mk-Infix(e1,o,e2)] Δ
  .1        (m2-eval-expr[e1];
  .2         m2-eval-expr[e2];
  .3         stk := <hd tl c stk  cases o: ADD → +, SUB → -,...  hd c stk>
  .4              ^ tl tl c stk)

19.0 m2-eval-Cond[mk-Cond(t,c,a)]       Δ (m2-eval-expr[t];
  .1                                      def b: hd c stk;
  .2                                      stk := tl c stk;
  .3                                      if b then m2-eval-expr[c]
  .4                                           else m2-eval-expr[a])

20.0 m2-eval-Lamb[e] Δ  stk := <mk-CLOS(e,hd c env2)> ^ c stk

21.0 m2-eval-Let[mk-Let(id,d,b)]        Δ
  .1        (m2-eval-expr[d];
  .2         env2 := <<mk-SIMP(id,hd c stk)> ^ hd c env2> ^ tl c env2;
  .3         stk  := tl c stk;
  .4         m2-eval-expr[b];
  .5         env2 := <tl hd c env2> ^ tl c env2)

22.0 m2-eval-Rec[mk-Rec(g,d,b)]         Δ
  .1        (env2 := <<mk-REC(id,d)> ^ hd c env2> ^ tl c env2;
  .2         m2-eval-expr[b];
  .3         env2 := <tl hd c env2> ^ tl c env2)

23.0 m2-eval-Appl[mk-Appl(f,a)] Δ
  .1        (m2-eval-expr[a];
  .2         m2-eval-expr[f];
  .3         if is-CLOS(hd c stk)
  .4            then (def mk-CLOS(mk-Lamb(id,e'),env2') : hd c stk;
  .5                  env2 := <<mk-SIMP(id,hd tl c stk)>^env2'>^c env2;
  .6                  stk  := tl tl c stk;
  .7                  m2-eval-expr[e'];
  .8                  env2 := tl c env2)
  .9            else error)
```

9.3.4 Concrete State Machine Semantics (IV)

By a concrete state machine semantics we understand a definition which again exploits globally declared variables, but now of more concrete, efficiently realizable type. We shall in particular mean such forms which model, or rather closely exhibit, the actual run-time structure of for example such objects as activation stacks, but such that the definition is still interpretable within, at this time, an extended meta-language. It is observed that the borderline between the definition styles is smooth, and thus that too rigid delineations serve no purpose. In the abstract state machine semantics of SAL we observe a number of storagewise inefficient object representations; these are caused almost exclusively by our choice to stay with the CLOSure representation of FUNctions as first derived in sect. 9.3.2. Closures "drag" along with them, not only the function body text, but also the entire defining environment. This generally results in extensive duplication of dynamic scope information being kept "stored" in *ENV2*. The basic object transformation objective therefore, of this development step, is now to keep only nonredundant environment information in the transformed activation stack. We shall achieve this by "folding" the *ENV2* stack of *ENV1* stacks "back into" a tree structured activation stack (*STG*). Each "path" from a leaf to the root signifies a chain of dynamically preceding activations, with one of these chains signifying the current, all others those of defining, environment chains of FUNARG functions. Each chain is statically and dynamically linked, corresponding to the subchain of environmentally preceding, lexicographically youngest, that is most recent, incarnations of statically embracing blocks; respectively the complete chain of dynamically (call/invocation) preceding activations. Our definition thus entails a complete, self-contained description of a commonly used variant of the so-called DISPLAY variable referencing scheme first attributed to Dijkstra [Dijkstra 62a]. We can, however, only succeed in achieving this realization of activations if, at the same time we refine *CLOS*ures into pairs of resulting program *lab*el points, *lfct*, and defining environment activation stack pointers, *cp*. From *lfct* we are able to ***retr***ieve the *Lamb*da expression, and from *cp* we are able to ***retr***ieve the defining *env*ironment.

Compiler-Compilers:

To realize this goal we also, in this step, refine *CLOS*ures by macro-expansion compilation of SAL texts, ***e***, into extended meta-language texts.

texts. It is thus we have chosen here to introduce, somewhat belatedly, but - we think - in an appropriate context, the issue of viewing a meta-language expressed definition of some source language construct as specifying a compilation of source language texts into meta-language texts. By a meta-language, <u>macro-substitution</u>, <u>compiled</u> (interpretive) <u>semantics</u> we basically understand a definition in the meta-language not containing any references to specifier defined elaboration functions. We shall, however, widen the above to admit forms, which contain such references, but where these now are to be thought of as references to <u>elaboration macros</u>, hence implying a <u>pre-processing</u> stage, called compiling, prior to interpretation of 'pure' meta-text, that is metatext free from references to specifier defined functions. We are given input source texts in the form of arguments to elaboration functions. To achieve an extended meta-language definition, which can be so macro-expanded, recursive definitions of objects (like for example *env'* I.17.9) and functions must be eliminated. We do so either by taking their fixed points, or by "unzipping" them into mechanical constructions. Taking fixed points, for example results in:

$$\underline{let}\ env' = Y\lambda\rho.(env + [id \rightarrow eval\text{-}expr(d)\rho])$$

but that doesn't help us very much when we come to actual, effective realizations on computers - it is, or may be, beautiful in theory, but "costly" in practice. Even though computers may be claimed to possess fixed point finding instructions, Y, they would have to be general enough to cater for the most complex case. Instead we unravel each individual use of recursion separately, and so-far by hand. In the case of *env'* by providing suitable stacks, pointer initializations and manipulations. The guiding principle being: to derive, from the more abstract definition, to each occurrence of an otherwise recursive definition a most fitting, efficient and economical realization. In the next five subsections (A-B-C-D-E) we now go into a characterization of the resulting definition at this stage. Again we present it as a "fait-accompli", leaving to other treatments the formulation of (and partial, theoretical support for) the general derivation techniques applied.

The definition represents two intertwined efforts: the further concretization of run-time objects, here the *ENV2* stack into the Σ complex, and the further decomposition of elaboration function definitions so that we can come to the point where references such as *m3-int-Expr*, can be successively eliminated.

A: The Environmentally Preceding Activation *(EPA)* & Variable Referencing Scheme, and the Run-Time State

The *ENV2* and *STK* of III is merged into the separately allocated *DSA*s (Dynamic Storage Areas) of *STG*. These are chained together: dynamic chains by *CP* (for: Calling Pointer), lexicographic chains to (defining) youngest incarnations by *EP* (for: Environment Pointer). The exact functioning of this *EPA* scheme is precisely described by the formulae. Hence it will not be informally described here. Our objective in presenting the formulae (IV.1-IV.32) is twofold: (1) to indicate a stepwise refinement process which leads to their derivation and the possibility now of a correctness proof with respect to a far shorter definition, and (2) to show that, even when starting with the concrete, which most textbooks unfortunately still do, and then invariably only very incompletely, one can indeed achieve a complete yet terse formulation.

B: Macro-Expansion

A conditional (*Cond*) expression, for example, results in all of the text corresponding to IV.26.1,4-5 being generated first, in a pre-processing 'compile' stage. A simple *Let* defining block expression, for example, results in all of the text corresponding to IV.27.1,.3 being expanded before any elaboration. Etcetera. Thus lines IV.21.1, -28.5,.12, -31.4 etc., do not denote themselves, that is run-time references to *m3-int-Expr*, but the text resulting from similar expansions. One may choose to do likewise for the auxiliary functions *Pop* and *Push*, or one may wish to keep these as standard run-time routines.

C: Realization of *CLOS*ures

Note the *Rec* or *Lamb* cases: 'letrec g(id)=d in b' respectively: '$\lambda id.id$'. Upon evaluation of a *Rec* or a *Lamb* their defined function bodies, *d*, are not elaborated (until actually *Appl*ied). Since we have decided to macro-expand these texts "in-line" with the text in which they were defined, and since we are not to execute this text when otherwise elaborating the two definition cases, we shall (i) *lab*el their expansions, (ii) *lab*el the text immediately following these expansions, (iii) precede the expansion with a (meta-language) *GOTO* around the thus expanded text, (iv) and terminate the expanded text itself with a *GOTO* intended to return to the caller, who, it is expected, "dropped" a suitable return address in a global 'Ra' branch label register before *GO*ing *TO* the *lab*el of the expanded function text. All this is "performed" in functions IV.30, respectively IV.29. So what is left in the *EPA* of the former *CLOS*ures? The answer is: just the "barebones". Enough to reconstruct (that is *retrieve*) the *id*, the *d*, and their defining *env*ironment: the former two from *lab(fct)*, the *env*ironment from c'p' (IV.3.4, IV.30.8). Thus, in this definition, a function *CLOS*ure has been realized as a *FCT* pair: (*fct*, *ptr*). This solution closely mirrors the way in which procedures are realized in actual programming language systems.

D: The Compiler State

We observe that *Labels* had to be generated for each *Lamb*, *Appl* and *Rec* (actually its *Lamb* part), and since we describe only once (in IV.30 and IV.29) what meta-language text to be generated, that is how to schematically elaborate these, we shall have to view the formulae (IV.21-31) as subject to (as already mentioned) a two stage process: the 'compiler' stage which macro-expands the SAL program into "pure" meta-text, and the 'interpreter' which executes the expanded text. Thus 11 lines of the formulae, namely those with lower case *let* and *def*, are 'executed' at compile-time, all *dict* (in *DICT*) objects are likewise compile-time computed, and all references to *m3*- functions are eliminated by the compile-time macrosubstitution process already mentioned. All upper-case *LET* and *DEF*s, are then to be executed at "run-time", that is in the interpreter stage. Thus the abstract compiler, whose "working behavior" will not be formalized in this paper, performs three actions: it generate labels; it computes, distributes and uses dictionaries; and it generates *META-IV* texts. Whereas in *ENV1* and *ENV2* *VAL*ues of *id*s were explicitly paired with these, in *DSA*s only the *VAL*ues are left, but in fixed positions (*VR*). Consider any variable, *id*. It is defined at block depth *n*, and uniquely so. And it is used, for example at block depth *ln*, where: $0 \leq n \leq ln$. The *DICT* components serve exactly this singular purpose (at least in this sample definition): for all *id*s in some context, to map them into the static block depth, *n*, at which they were defined. Since the static chain also touches exactly the embracing blocks, *ln*-*n* denotes the number of levels one has to chain back to get to the *VAL*ue corresponding to *id* (IV.24.4). In fact, that is the whole, singular purpose of the static (*EP*) chain. Since it is furthermore observed (IV.24.1) that the only place *dict* is used, is in the compile stage, any reference to *dict* is seen also to be eliminated. Finally observe, that the unique label objects denoted by *lfct*, *lbyp* and *lret* shall be substituted into respective uses (IV.30.4,.8; IV.30.3,.7; IV.29.9,.11).

E: Execution

The result of of executing a SAL program is to be found on top of the temporary list (IV.19.2), about which we can assert a length of exactly one in line (IV.21.2)! So *m3-int-Expr* places (*m3-push*es) the result of any expression elaboration on top of the current *DSA*'s *TL* -- with the working register, Ur, invariably holding this result too at the instance of *push*ing. A simple *Let Expr* is executed by first finding the *VAL*ue of the locally defined variable, *id*, in the environment in which the *Let* is encountered. Then a new activation is set up to elaborate the body, *b*, of the *Let*. Working register Ur is used to store the result temporarily while the activation is terminated, but not necessarily disposed off. The result is *push*ed on the *TL* of the invoking activation's *DSA*. Since the *VAL*ue so yielded might be a function which was "concocted" by the activation just left, and since that *FunCT*ion may depend on its locally defined *Var*iable *VAL*ues, we cannot, in general, dispose of the activation. This "story" then shall account for our use of the (--) dashed line around the reclamation of *ST*or*age* shown in (IV.31.9, IV.28.17). The yielded *FunCT*ion *VAL*ue would be (realized as) a pair: *mk-FCT(lfct,ptr)* where *ptr* is a *pointer* to that, or a contained, activation. This is again the FUNARG situation previously mentioned. By not disposing (IV.31.9) of the *DSA* we are later able to "reactivate" the *FunCT*ion defining activation. We leave it to the reader to "exercise" remaining aspects of the definition.

IV.1 Syntactic Domains -- as in I.1

IV.2 Semantic Domains

IV.2.1 Run-Time State Components

(1) $\Sigma t = (\mathrm{Stg} \xrightarrow{m} STG) \cup (\mathrm{Cp} \xrightarrow{m} [Ptr]) \cup (\mathrm{Ep} \xrightarrow{m} [Ptr]) \cup (\mathrm{Br} \xrightarrow{m} [Lbl]) \cup (\mathrm{Ra} \xrightarrow{m} [Lbl]) \cup (\mathrm{Ur} \xrightarrow{m} [VAL2]) \cup (\mathrm{Wr} \xrightarrow{m} [VAL2])$

(2,3,4) $P, EP, CP = [Ptr]$

(5,6) $BR, RA = [Lbl]$

(7) $STG = Ptr \xrightarrow{m} DSA$

(8,9) $Ptr, Lbl \subset Token$

(10) $DSA :: CP\ EP\ RA\ VR\ TL$

(11) $VR = [VAL2]$

(12) $TL = VAL2^*$

(13) $VAL2 = Int \mid Bool \mid FCT$

(14) $FCT :: BR\ \ EP$

Initial State

```
(15)    LET ptr     ∈ Ptr;
(16)    DCL Stg    := [ptr ↦ mk-DSA(nil,nil,nil,nil,<>)],  type STG,
            Cp     := ptr                                   type [Ptr],
            Ep     := ptr                                   type [Ptr],
            Br     := nil                                   type BR,
            Ra     := nil                                   type RA,
            Ur,Wr  := nil                                   type [VAL2];
```

IV.2.2 Compiler State

```
Global:  (32)   Σc       =   Ls ⇸ Lbl-set

         (33)   dcl Ls  :=   {}  type Lbl-set;

Local:   (34)   LN       =   Nat
         (35)   DICT     =   Id ⇸ Nat
```

IV.3 Elaboration Functions

Function Types:

```
(21)  m3-int-Prog:   Prog                          → ((Σc→Σc) → (Σt→Σt))
(22)  m3-int-Expr:   Expr  → ((DICT × LN) → ((Σc→Σc) → (Σt→Σt)))
(23)  m3-int-Const:  Const → ((DICT × LN)                → (Σt→Σt))
(24)  m3-int-Var:    Var   → ((DICT × LN) → ((Σc→Σc) → (Σt→Σt)))
(25)  m3-int-Infix:  Infix → ((DICT × LN) → ((Σc→Σc) → (Σt→Σt)))
(26)  m3-int-Cond:   Cond  → ((DICT × LN) → ((Σc→Σc) → (Σt→Σt)))
(27)  m3-int-Let:    Let   → ((DICT × LN) → ((Σc→Σc) → (Σt→Σt)))
(28)  m3-int-Rec:    Rec   → ((DICT × LN) → ((Σc→Σc) → (Σt→Σt)))
(29)  m3-int-Appl:   Appl  → ((DICT × LN) → ((Σc→Σc) → (Σt→Σt)))
(30)  m3-int-Lamb:   Lamb  → ((DICT × LN) → ((Σc→Σc) → (Σt→Σt)))
(31)  m3-int-Block:  Expr  → ((DICT × LN) → ((Σc→Σc) → (Σt→Σt)))

(18)  m3-Pop:    ref VAL2          → (Σt→Σt)
(19)  m3-Push:   ref VAL2          → (Σt→Σt)

(20)  make-Lbl:             → (Σc→Σc)
```

IV.3.1 Auxiliary Functions

Run-Time Functions:

```
18.0 m3-Pop(ref) ≜
  .1     (DEF mk-DSA(c,e,a,v,tl) : (c Stg)(c Cp);
  .2      Stg := c Stg + [c Cp ↦ mk-DSA(c,e,a,v,tl tl)];
  .3      ref := hd tl)

19.0 m3-Push(ref) ≜
  .1     (DEF mk-DSA(c,e,a,v,tl) : (c Stg)(c Cp);
  .2      Stg := c Stg + [c Cp ↦ mk-DSA(c,e,a,v,<c ref> ^ tl)])
```

Compile-Time Functions:

```
20.0 make-lbl() ≜
  .1     (def l∈Lbl\c Ls;
  .2      Ls := c Ls ∪ {l};
  .3      return(l))
```

IV.3.2 Compile/Execute Functions

```
21.0 m3-int-Prog[e] ≜
  .1    (m3-int-Expr[e]([],0);
  .2     Ur := hd(s-TL((c Stg)(c Cp)));
  .3     c Ur)

22.0 m3-int-Expr[e](dict,ln) ≜
  .1    is-Cons(e)   → m3-int-Const[e],
  .2    is-Var(e)    → m3-int-Var[e](dict,ln),
  .3    is-Infix(e)  → m3-int-Infix[e](dict,ln),
  .4    is-Cond(e)   → m3-int-Cond[e](dict,ln),
  .5    is-Let(e)    → m3-int-Let[e](dict,ln),
  .6    is-Rec(e)    → m3-int-Rec[e](dict,ln),
  .7    is-Lamb(e)   → m3-int-Lamb[e](dict,ln),
  .8    is-Appl(e)   → m3-int-Appl[e](dict,ln)

23.0 m3-int-Const[mk-Const(k)] ≜
  .1    Ur := k; m3-Push(Ur)
```

```
24.0 m3-int-Var[mk-Var(id)](dict,ln) △
  .1    (let n = dict(id) in
  .2     Ep := c Cp;
  .3     FOR i=1 TO ln-n DO Ep := s-EP((c Stg)(c Ep));
  .4     Ur := s-VR((c Stg)(c Ep));
  .5     m3-Push( Ur);
  .6     Ep := c Cp)

25.0 m3-int-Infix[mk-Infix(e1,o,e2)](dict,ln) △
  .1    (m3-int-Expr[e1](dict,ln);
  .2     m3-int-Expr[e2](dict,ln);
  .3     m3-Pop(Ur);
  .4     m3-Pop(Wr);
  .5     Ur := c Ur  (cases o: ADD → +, SUB → -,...)  c Wr;
  .6     m3-Push(Ur))

26.0 m3-int-Cond[mk-Cond(t,c,a)](dict,ln) △
  .1    (m3-int-Expr[t](dict,ln);
  .2     m3-Pop(Ur);
  .3     IF c Ur
  .4        THEN m3-int-Expr[c](dict,ln)
  .5        ELSE m3-int-Expr[a](dict,ln))

27.0 m3-int-Let[mk-Let(id,d,b)](dict,ln) △
  .1    (m3-int-Expr[d](dict,ln);
  .2     m3-Pop(Ur);
  .3     m3-int-Block[b](dict + [id ↦ ln+1],ln+1))

30.0 m3-int-Lamb[mk-Lamb(id,d)](dict,ln) △
  .1    (def lfct : make-lbl(),
  .2         lbyp : make-lbl();
  .3     GOTO lbyp;
  .4     LAB(lfct);
  .5        m3-int-Block[d](dict + [id ↦ ln+1],ln+1);
  .6        GOTO c Ra;
  .7     LAB(lbyp):
  .8     Ur := mk-FCT(lfct,c Cp);
  .9     m3-Push(Ur))
```

```
31.0 m3-int-Block[b](dict,ln) ≜
 .1    (DEF ptr ∈ Ptr - dom c Stg;
 .2     Stg    := c Stg ∪ [ptr ↦ mk-DSA(c Cp,c Ep,c Ra,c Ur,<>)];
 .3     Cp,Ep := ptr;
 .4     m3-int-Expr[b](dict,ln);
 .5     m3-Pop(Ur);
 .6     Ep    := s-EP((c Stg)(c Cp));
 .7     Ra    := s-RA((c Stg)(c Cp));
 .8     Cp    := s-CP((c Stg)(c Cp));

 .9     ┌─────────────────────┐
        │ Stg := c Stg\{ptr}; │
        └─────────────────────┘

 .10    m3-Push(Ur))

28.0   m3-int-Rec[mk-Rec(g,mk-Lamb(id,d),b)](dict,ln) ≜
 .1     (def lfct: make-lbl(),
 .2          lbyp: make-lbl();
 .3      GOTO lbyp;
 .4      LAB(lfct):
 .5         m3-int-Block[d](dict + [g ↦ ln+1,id ↦ ln+2],ln+2);
 .6         GOTO c Ra;
 .7      LAB(lbyp):
 .8      DEF ptr∈Ptr\dom c Stg;
 .9      Ur     := mk-FCT(lfct,ptr);
 .10     Stg    := c Stg ∪ [ptr ↦ mk-DSA(c Cp,c Ep,c Ra,c Ur,<>)];
 .11     Cp,Ep := ptr;
 .12     m3-int-Expr[b](dict + [g ↦ ln+1],ln+1);
 .13     m3-Pop(Ur);
 .14     Ep := s-EP((c Stg)(c Cp));
 .15     Ra := s-RA((c Stg)(c Cp));
 .16     Cp := s-CP((c Stg)(c Cp));

 .17    ┌──────────────────────┐
        │  Stg := c Stg\{ptr}; │
        └──────────────────────┘

 .18     m3-Push(Ur))
```

```
32.0 m3-int-Appl[mk-Appl(f,a)](dict,ln) Δ
  .1  (def lret: make-lbl();
  .2   m3-int-Expr[a](dict,ln);
  .3   m3-int-Expr[f](dict,ln);
  .4   m3-Pop(Ur);
  .5   IF is-FCT(c Ur)
  .6      THEN (Br := s-BR(c Ur);
  .7            Ep := s-EP(c Ur);
  .8            m3-Pop(Ur);
  .9            Ra := lret;
  .10           GOTO c Br;
  .11           LAB(lret):
  .12           I)
  .13     ELSE ERROR)
```

9.4 COMPILING ALGORITHMS AND ATTRIBUTE SEMANTICS

In this section we shall arrive at a specification of SAL in terms of the combination of two separate definitions: a compiling algorithm which to any SAL construct specifies its translation, not into the meta-language, but into actual ("physically existing") machine code; and a suitably abstracted definition of the target machine architecture, that is its semantic domains (working registers, condition code, storage, input/output etc.) and instruction repertoire: formats and meaning. The structure of the section is as follows: in subsect. 9.4.1 we give the pair of definitions: target machine, TM, and the compiling algorithm form SAL to TM. The latter is directly derived from the last, concrete definition of SAL in sect. 9.3.4. In subsect. 9.4.2 we then restate the compiling algorithm of sect. 9.4.1, but now in terms more familiar to afecionados of attribute semantics. And in sect. 9.4.3 we give a similar attribute semantics definition of a compiling algorithm from SAL into TM. This latter algorithm is based on the separation of activation and temporary stacks first shown in the abstract machine of sect. 9.3.2. The purpose of showing the attribute semantics is to demonstrate, finally, how such are formally derivable from denotational semantics definitions. The reason why we state two independent attribute sematics definitions is to illustrate the distinctions between synthesized and inherited attributes, and their relation to questions about single- and multipass compilers. The latter will be discussed in sect. 9.5.

9.4.1 A Target Machine and a Compiling Algorithm (V-VI)

-- THE TARGET MACHINE, TM (V)

V.1 Syntactic Domains

```
(1)  Code  =  Ins*
(2)  Ins   =  Sim | St  | Lim | Ld  | Fct | Jmp |
              Cjp | Mov | Adj | Pck | Unp | Pr  | ...
(3)  Sim   :: Adr  (Int | Bool | ...)
(4)  St    :: Adr  Reg  Nat1
(5)  Lim   :: Reg  (Int | Bool | Lbl | ...)
(6)  Ld    :: Reg  Nat1  Adr
(7)  Fct   :: Reg  Op  (Reg | Adr)
(8)  Op    =  ADD|SUB|MPY|DIV|AND|OR|NOT|XOR|LOW|LEQ|EQ|NEQ|HI|HEQ|...
(9)  Jmp   :: (Lbl | Reg)
(10) Cjp   :: Reg  Cmp  (Lbl | ...)
(11) Cmp   =  TRUE | FALSE | ZERO | NOTFCT | ...
(12) Pr    :: (Reg | Quot)
(13) Adj   :: Reg  Int
(14) Mov   :: Reg  Reg
(15) Pck   :: Reg  Reg  Reg
(16) Unp   :: Reg  Reg  Reg
(17) Reg   =  Nat1
(18) Adr   :: Base  Displ
(19) Base  =  Reg
(20) Displ =  Int
(21) Lbl   ⊂  Token
```

V.2 Semantic Domains

```
(22) Σm    =  (Stg ⇀m STG) ∪ (Reg ⇀m REG) ∪ (Out ⇀m OUT) ∪ ...
(23) STG   =  LOC ⇀m VAL
(24) REG   =  Nat ⇀m VAL
(25) VAL   =  Int | Bool | Lbl | LOC | FCT
(26) LOC   =  Int
(27) FCT   :: Lbl  LOC
(28) OUT   =  VAL*
```

-- leaving a number of machine components undefined.

Global State Initialization:

```
(29) dcl Stg := [i → undefined | -2**s<i<2**s] type STG,
(30)     Reg := [i → undefined | -2**r<i<2**r] type REG;
```

V.3 (Micro-Program) Elaboration Functions

```
(31) type int-code: Code          → (Σm → Σm)
(32) type int-insl: Ins* (Nat1    → (Σm → Σm))
(33) type int-ins:  Ins           → (Σm → Σm)
(34) type eval-adr: Adr           → (Σm → Σm)

31.0 int-code[c] ≜
  .1     (tixe [lbl ↦ int-insl[c'](i) | (let c' = c^<mk-Lbl(ERROR)>  in
  .2                                       i = (Δj∈indsc')(c'[j]=lbl)]  in
  .3      int-insl[c](1))

32.0 int-insl[c](i) ≜
  .1      if i>lenc then I else (int-ins[c[i]];int-insl[c](i+1))

33.0 int-ins[ins] ≜
  .1    cases ins:
  .2      mk-Lbl(lbl)      → I,
  .3      mk-Sim(a,k)      → (def ea :  eval-adr[a];
  .4                            Stg    := c Stg + [ea ↦ k]),
  .5      mk-St(a,r,n)     → (def ea : eval-adr[a];
  .6                            for i=0 to n-1 do
  .7                                Stg := c Stg + [(ea+i) ↦ (c Reg)(r+i)]),
  .8      mk-Lim(r,k)      → Reg := c Reg + [r ↦ k],
  .9      mk-Ld(r,n,a)     → (def ea :  eval-adr[a];
  .10                           for i=0 to n-1 do
  .11                               Reg := c Reg + [(r+1) ↦ (c Stg)(ea+i)]),
  .12     mk-Fct(r,o,ar) →
  .13             (def v : is-Adr(ar) → (c Stg)(eval-adr[ar]),
  .14                      T            (c Reg)(ar);
  .15              cases o: ADD → Reg := c Reg + [r ↦ (c Reg)(r)+v],
  .16                       SUB → Reg := c Reg + [r ↦ (c Reg)(r)-v],
  .17                       ...
  .18                       HI  → Reg := c Reg + [r ↦ (c Reg)(r)>v],
  .19                       ...),
```

```
.20   mk-Jmp(l)       → exit(l),
.21   mk-Cjp(r,c,l)   → if cases c: TRUE    → (c Reg)(r),
.22                                 FALSE   → ¬(c Reg)(r),
.23                                 ...
.24                                 NOTFCT  → ¬is-FCT((c Reg)(r)),
.25                                 ...
.26                                 ZERO    → (c Reg)(r)=0,
.27                                 ...
.28                        then (is-Lbl(l) → exit(l),
.29                                   T        → exit((c Reg)(l)))
.30                        else I,
.31   mk-Adj(r,i)     → Reg := c Reg + [r  ↦ (c Reg)(r)+i],
.32   mk-Mov(r1,r2)   → Reg := c Reg + [r1 ↦ (c Reg)(r2)],
.33   mk-Pck(r,l,a)   → if is-Lbl((c Reg)(l)) ∧ is-LOC((c Reg)(a))
.34                          then (def f: mk-FCT((c Reg)(l),(c Reg)(a));
.35                                Reg := c Reg + [r ↦ f])
.36                          else exit(mk-Lbl(ERROR)),
.37   mk-Upk(l,a,r)   → if is-FCT((c Reg)(r))
.38                          then (def l': s-Lbl((c Reg)(r)),
.39                                    d :  s-LOC((c Reg)(r));
.40                                Reg  := c Reg + [l ↦ l',a ↦ a'])
.41                          else exit(mk-Lbl(ERROR)),
.42   mk-Pr(rq)       → (def q : is-Reg(rq) → (c Reg)(rq),
.43                                 T          → rq;
.44                         Out := c Out^<q>),
      ...

34.0 eval-adr[mk-Adr(b,d)] ≜
  .1     (def il : (c Reg)(b);
  .2      if is-LOC(il) ∨ is-Int(il)
  .3         then (let ea = d+il  in
  .4               if -2^8 < ea < +2^8
  .5                  then return(ea)
  .6                  else exit(mk-Lbl(ERROR)))
  .7         else exit(mk-Lbl(ERROR)))
```

-- THE COMPILING ALGORITHM

Having now examined the target machine, TM, architecture, that is the semantics of the machine language, independently of SAL, we now turn to the specification of what *Code* to generate for each SAL construct. We are seeking a definition, *c-prog*, *c-expr*, etc., which again is to be understood in just one, the compiling phase, way. *DICT*ionaries are used as before, and so is *LN*. An extra (compiletime) object is passed to any macro invocation of *c-expr*. It represents the current stack index to the target machine realization of the *TL*s of *DSA*s. Since storage cannot (in general) be reclaimed when a *Block* body *VAL*ue has been computed, and since in this version we have decided to stick with the merge of the control information of the activations *(CP,EP,RA)* not only with local *VAR*iable (*VR*), but also with temporaries (*TL*), we shall have to set aside, in linear storage, the maximum amount of storage cells needed in any expression elaboration, and let that be the over-cautious realization, at this stage, of *TL*. To that end a crude compiler function, *depth*, is defined. It computes the number of temporaries, *de*, needed to compute any expression, but takes into account that embedded *Let*s and *Rec*s lead to new activations for which separate stacks, *TL*, are set aside. We say that *depth* is crude since optimizing versions are easy to formulate, but would, in this example, lead to an excessive number of formulae lines. The disjoint *DSA*s of the previous (IV) definition are now mapped onto a linear ('cell') storage. Each 'new' *DSA* realization consists of 4 + *de* cells: *CP*, *EP*, *RA*, *VR*, respectively *TL*.

VI Compiling Algorithm

VI.1 Compiler Domains

VI.1.1 Syntactic Domains -- as in I.1

VI.1.2 Compiler Components

(1) Σ_c = Ls $\underset{m}{\rightarrow}$ *Lbl-set*
(2) *DICT* = *Id* $\underset{m}{\rightarrow}$ *LN*
(3) *LN* = *Nat0*
(4) *Lbl* ⊂ *Token* | ERROR

VI.2 Auxiliary Compiler Functions

(5) *dcl* Ls := {ERROR} *type* *Lbl-set*;

(6) *type: make-lbl:* → $(\Sigma_c \rightarrow \Sigma_c \times Lbl)$

(7) *type: depth:* *Expr* → *Nat1*

```
6.0  make-lbl() ≜
        (def l∈Lbl -c Ls;
         Ls := c Ls ∪ {l};
         return(l))

7.0  depth(e) ≜
        cases e:
          mk-Const()        → 1,
          mk-Var()          → 1,
          mk-Infix(e1,e2)   → max(depth(e1),depth(e2)) + 1,
          mk-Cond(t,c,a)    → max(depth(t),depth(c),depth(a)) + 1,
          mk-Let(,d,)       → depth(d),
          mk-Rec(,,)        → 1,
          mk-Lamb(,)        → 1,
          mk-Appl(f,a)      → max(depth(f),depth(a)) + 1
```

VI.3 Translator Specifications

VI.3.1 Global Constant Definitions

```
(8)   let p          = 0,
(9)       ep         = 1,
(10)      ra         = 2,
(11)      vr,pm,u,j  = 3,
(12)      top        = 4,
(13)      br         = 5,
(14)      t          = 4,
(15)      error      = ERROR;
```

VI.3.2 Compiling Specifications

```
(17)     type: c-prog:   Θ                → (Σc → Σc × Ins*)
(18)     type: c-const:  Θ            STK → Ins*
(19-27)  type: c-expr:   Θ DICT LN STK    → (Σc → Σc × Ins*)
```

where Θ stands for the syntactic category name, i.e.: *c-prog* ⊃ Θ =*prog*, *c-expr* ⊃ Θ =*expr*, etc.

(17)

```
c-Prog[e] ≜
   (def lexit : make-lbl();
    let de    = depth(e) in
    <mk-Lim(p,0),
     mk-Lim(cp,0),
     mk-Lim(top,t+de)>^
     c-Expr[e]([],0,t)^
    <mk-Ld(u,1,mk-Adr(p,t)),
     mk-Pr(u),
     mk-Jmp(lexit),
     error,
     mk-Br(error),
     lexit>)
```

(18)

```
c-Const[mk-Const(k)](stk) ≜
   <mk-Sim(mk-Adr(p,stk),k),
    mk-Lim(u,k)>
```

(20)

```
c-Infix[mk-Infix(e1,o,e2)](δ,ln,stk) ≜
   (c-Expr[e2](δ,ln,stk)^
    c-Expr[e1](δ,ln,stk+1)^
   <mk-Ld(u,1,mk-Adr(p,stk+1))
    mk-Fct(u,o,mk-Adr(p,stk)),
    mk-St(mk-Adr(p,stk),u,1)>)
```

(22)

```
c-lamb[mk-Lamb(id,d)](δ,ln,stk) ≜
   (def lfct: make-lbl();
        lbyp: make-lbl();
    <mk-Jmp(lbyp),
     lfct>^
     c-Block[d](δ+[id↦ln+1],ln+1,stk)
    <mk-Jmp(ra),
     lbyp,
     mk-Lim(u,lfct),
     mk-Pck(u,u,p),
     mk-St(mk-Adr(p,stk),u,1)>)
```

(19)

```
c-Var[mk-Var(id)](δ,ln,stk) ≜
   (let n = δ(id) in
    def lloop: make-lbl(),
        lload: make-lbl();
    <mk-Lim(j,ln-n),
     lloop,
     mk-Cjp(j,ZERO,lload),
     mk-Ld(ep,1,mk-Adr(ep,ep)),
     mk-Adj(j,-1),
     mk-Jmp(lloop),
     lload,
     mk-Ld(u,1,mk-Adr(ep,vr)),
     mk-St(mk-Adr(p,stk),u,1),
     mk-Mov(ep,p)>)
```

(21)

```
c-Cond[mk-Cond(t,c,a)](δ,ln,stk) ≜
   (def lalt: make-lbl(),
        lout: make-lbl();
     c-Expr[t](δ,ln,stk)^
    <mk-Ld(u,1,mk-Adr(p,stk)),
     mk-Cjp(u,FALSE,lalt)>^
     c-Expr[c](δ,ln,stk)^
    <mk-Jmp(lout),
     lalt>^
     c-Expr[a](δ,ln,stk)^
    <lout>)
```

(23)

```
c-appl[mk-Appl(f,a)](δ,ln,stk) ≜
   (def lret: make-lbl();
    c-expr[a](δ,ln,stk)^
    c-expr[f](δ,ln,stk+1)^
    <mk-Ld(u,1,mk-Adr(p,stk+1)),
     mk-Cjp(u,NOTFCT,error),
     mk-Unp(br,ep,u),
     mk-Lim(ra,lret),
     mk-Ld(pm,1,mk-Adr(p,stk)),
     mk-Jmp(br),
     lret>)
```

```
(24)
c-Let[mk-Let(id,d,b)](δ,ln,stk) ≜
    (c-Expr[d](δ,ln,stk)⌢
    <mk-Ld(u,1,mk-Adr(p,stk))>⌢
     c-Block[b](δ+[id↦ln+1],ln+1,stk)
```

```
(25)
c-Rec[mk-Rec(g,lf,b)](δ,ln,stk) ≜
   (let mk-Lamb(id,d) = lf in
    def lfct: make-lbl(),
        lbyp: make-lbl();
    let db = depth(b) in
    <mk-Jmp(lbyp),
     lfct>⌢
     c-Block[d](δ + [g↦ln+1,id↦ln+2],
                ln+2,stk)
   ⌢<mk-Jmp(ra),
     lbyp,
     mk-Lim(u,lfct),
     mk-St(mk-Adr(top,p),p,t-1),
     mk-Pck(u,u,top),
     mk-St(mk-Adr(top,u),u,1),
     mk-Mov(p,top),
     mk-Mov(ep,top),
     mk-Adj(top,t+db)>⌢
     c-Expr[b](δ + [g↦ln+1],ln+1)⌢
    <mk-Ld(u,1,mk-Adr(p,t)),
     mk-Ld(p,t-1,mk-Adr(p,p)),
     mk-St(mk-Adr(p,stk),u,1)>)
```

```
(26)
c-Block[bl](δ,ln,stk) ≜
   (let dbl = depth(bl) in
    <mk-St(mk-Adr(top,p),p,t),
     mk-Mov(p,top),
     mk-Mov(ep,top),
     mk-Adj(top,t+dbl)>⌢
     c-Expr[bl](δ,ln+1,t)⌢
    <mk-Ld(u,1,mk-Adr(p,t)),
     mk-Ld(p,t-1,mk-Adr(p,p)),
     mk-St(mk-Adr(p,stk),u,1)>)
```

```
(27)
c-Expr[e](δ,ln,stk) ≜
   (is-Const[e] → c-Const[e](stk),          is-Let[e]  → c-Let[e](δ,ln,stk),
    is-Var[e]   → c-Var[e](δ,ln,stk),       is-Rec[e]  → c-Rec[e](δ,ln,stk),
    is-Infix[e] → c-Infix[e](δ,ln,stk),     is-Lamb[e] → c-Lamb[e](δ,ln,stk),
    is-Cond[e]  → c-Cond[e](δ,ln,stk),      is-Appl[e] → c-Appl[e](δ,ln,stk))
```

9.4.2 An Attribute Semantics (VII)

By an attribute semantics definition of a source language is normally understood a set of (usually concrete, BNF) syntax rules defining the source language's character string representations; an association of so-called attributes to each syntactic category (that is distinct rule); and to each pairing of a left-hand side (or: non-terminal) with a right-hand side alternative, a set of action clusters, one per attribute associated with non-terminals of either the leftor the right-hand sides. The action clusters are statement sequences, and their purpose is to assign values to the attributes. The meaning of such an attribute semantics definition is as follows: consider a source text and its corresponding ('annotated') parse tree. To each tree node allocate an attribute variable corresponding to each of the attributes of the node category. Then compute the values of these according to the attribute semantics definition action clusters. Two extreme cases arise: the value of an attribute is a function solely of the attribute values of the immediate descendant, or ascendant-node(s). We say that the attribute is synthesized, respectively inherited. Obviously nonsensical attribute semantics definitions can be constructed for which their computation for arbitrary or certain parse trees is impossible due for example to circularity. Some such possibilities, for example that of circularity, can, however, be statically checked, that is without recourse to parse trees.

We first choose the same basic realization as up till now, but, for sake of notational variety, and perhaps also your increased reading ability, express the compiled target code in "free form". Hence the meaning is intended to be identical, down to individual computation sequences. The reader will otherwise observe a close resemblance between this, and the immediately preceding definition. In fact their only difference is one of style. Either could equally rightfully be called an attribute semantics.

Annotation:

A concrete, BNF-like grammar is given below. To each category is then associated a small number of attributes. The *depth* attribute, *d*, computes, as did the *depth* function (VI.7), the maximum length of the temporary list - and does so bottom-up; hence it is a synthesized attribute. The *stack*, *level number* and *dictionary* attributes: *stk*, *ln*, *dict* are all passed down from the parse tree root, and are thus inherited. Finally the *code* attribute is synthesized and stores the generated *Codetext* strings. We have not shown a formal (say BNF-) grammar for these strings, but really ought to have done. Subsect. VII.3 finally gives the actual action cluster rules for each grammar rule/production.

Note:

Note also our distinction, in VII.3 formulae between *italic* and roman formulae text parts. The latter denotes *Code-text* to be generated, the former auxiliary quantities whose values are to be resolved in the *code* attribute computation process. Thus in for example VII.8.4 *cde* is to be computed and its arabic numeral representation then to be inserted. Similarly for lines VII.8.10, 10.5 and 10, where appropriately roman unique label identifiers are to be inserted in lieu of the *italic* label identifiers. The result of a parse tree computation is finally accumulated in *code* of the root node.

VII Synthesized and Inherited Attribute Semantics Compiling Algorithm

VII.1 Concrete BNF-like Grammar

```
(1)    Prog   ::=  Expr

(2.1)  Expr   ::=  k
  .2          ::=  id
  .3          ::=  ( Expr + Expr )
  .4          ::=  if Expr then Expr else Expr fi
  .5          ::=  let id = Expr ; Block end
  .6          ::=  rec g = Lamb ; Block end
  .7          ::=  Lamb
  .8          ::=  apply Expr ( Expr )

(3)    Block  ::=  Expr

(4)    Lamb   ::=  fun ( id ) = Block end
```

where we have abbreviated the classes of identifiers, constants and operators to just id, k and +.

VII.2 Node Attributes

(5)	Prog	*code*	<u>type</u> *Code-text*	<u>*synthesized*</u>
(6)	Expr	*code*	<u>type</u> *Code-text*	<u>*synthesized*</u>
	Lamb	*ln*	<u>type</u> *Nat*	<u>*inherited*</u>
		dict	<u>type</u> *Id* $\overrightarrow{m}$ *Nat*	<u>*inherited*</u>
		stk	<u>type</u> *Nat1*	<u>*inherited*</u>
		d	<u>type</u> *Nat1*	<u>*synthesized*</u>
(7)	Block	*code*	<u>type</u> *Code-text*	<u>*synthesized*</u>
		ln	<u>type</u> *Nat*	<u>*inherited*</u>
		dict	<u>type</u> *Id* $\overrightarrow{m}$ *Nat*	<u>*inherited*</u>

VII.3 Action Cluster Rules

```
(8)     Progp ::= Expre
  .1    def lexit: make-lbl();
  .2    code_p := "R[p] := 0;
  .3                R[ep] := 0;
  .4                R[top] := t + cde;
  .5               "^ccode_e^"
  .6                R[u] := cS[cR[p] + t];
  .7                Out := cR[u];
  .8                goto lexit;
  .9                lerr:
  .10               Out := ERROR;
  .11               lexit:
  .12              ";
  .13   ln_e    := 0;
  .14   dict_e  := [];
  .15   stk_e   := t;

(9)     Expre ::= k
  .1    de      := 1;
  .2    code_e  := "S[cR[p]+ cstk_e] := k;
  .3                R[u] := k;
  .4               ";

(10)    Expre ::= id
  .1    def lloop: make-lbl(),
  .2        lload: make-lbl();
  .3    de      := 1;
  .4    code_e  := R[j]                  := cln_e - cdict_e(id);
  .5               lloop:
  .6               if cR[j] = 0 then goto lload;
  .7               R[ep]                 := cS[cR[ep] + ep];
  .8               R[j]                  := cR[j] - 1;
  .9               goto lloop;
  .10              lload:
  .11              R[u]                  := cS[cR[ep] + vr];
  .12              S[cR[p] + cstk_e]     := cR[u];
  .13              R[ep]                 := cR[p];
  .14             ";
```

(11) $Expre ::= (Expre1 + Expre2)$

- .1 $de := \underline{max}(\underline{c}de^1, \underline{c}de^2) + 1;$
- .2 $ln_{e1}, ln_{e2} := \underline{c}ln_e;$
- .3 $stk_{e2} := \underline{c}stk_e;$
- .4 $stk_{e1} := \underline{c}stk_e + 1;$
- .5 $dict_{e1}, dict_{e2} := \underline{c}dict_e;$
- .6 $code_e := \underline{c}code_{e2}$ ^
- .7 $\underline{c}code_{e1}$ ^
- .8   "R[u] $:= \underline{c}S[\underline{c}R[p] + \underline{c}stk_e];$
- .9   R[u] $:= \underline{c}R[u] + \underline{c}S[\underline{c}R[p] + \underline{c}stk_e];$
- .10 $S[\underline{c}R[p] + \underline{c}stk_e] := \underline{c}R[u];$
- .11   ";

(12) $Expre ::= \underline{if}\ Exprt\ \underline{then}\ Exprc\ \underline{else}\ Expra$

- .1 $\underline{def}\ lalt: make\text{-}lbl(),$
- .2 $lout: make\text{-}lbl();$
- .3 $de := \underline{max}(\underline{c}d_t, \underline{c}d_c, \underline{c}d_a) + 1;$
- .4 $ln_t, ln_c, ln_a := \underline{c}ln_e;$
- .5 $stk_t, stk_c, stk_a := \underline{c}stk_e;$
- .6 $dict_t, dict_c, dict_a := \underline{c}dict_e;$
- .7 $code_e := \underline{c}code_t$ ^
- .8   "R[u] $:= \underline{c}S[\underline{c}R[p] + \underline{c}stk_e];$
- .9 $\underline{if}\ \neg\underline{c}R[u]\ \underline{then}\ \underline{goto}\ lalt;$
- .10   "^$code_c$ ^"
- .11-.14 $\underline{goto}\ lout;\ lalt:$ "^$\underline{c}code_a$ ^" $lout:$
- .15   ";

(13) $Expre ::= \underline{let}\ id = Exprd\ ;\ Blockb\ \underline{end}$

- .1 $d_e := \underline{c}d_b;$
- .2 $ln_a := \underline{c}ln_e;$
- .3 $ln_b := \underline{c}ln_e + 1;$
- .4 $stk_d := \underline{c}stk_e;$
- .5 $dict_d := \underline{c}dict_e;$
- .6 $dict_b := \underline{c}dict_e + [id \mapsto \underline{c}ln_e + 1];$
- .7 $code_e := \underline{c}code_d$ ^"
- .8   R[u] $:= \underline{c}S[\underline{c}R[p] + \underline{c}stk_e];$
- .9   "^$\underline{c}code_b$^"
- .10   ";

```
(14)  Expre ::= rec g =  fun ( id ) = Blockd end ; Blockb  end
  .1  def lfct: make-lbl(),
  .2      lbyp: make-lbl();
  .3  d_e    := 1;
  .4  ln_d   := cln_e + 2;
  .5  ln_b   := cln_e + 1;
  .6  dict_d := cdict_e + [g ↦ ln+1, id ↦ ln+2];
  .7  dict_b := cdict_e + [g ↦ ln+1];
  .8  code_e := "goto lbyp;
  .9            lfct:
  .10          "^ccode_d^"
  .11           goto cR[ra];
  .12           lbyp:
  .13           R[u]                 := lfct;
  .14           R[u]                 := mk-FCT(cR[u],cR[top]);
  .15           S[cR[top] + p]       := cR[p];
  .16           S[cR[top] + ep]      := cR[ep];
  .17           S[cR[top] + ra]      := cR[ra];
  .18           S[cR[top] + vr]      := cR[u];
  .19           R[p]                 := cR[top];
  .20           R[ep]                := cR[top];
  .21           R[top]               := cR[top] + (t+cd_e);
  .22          "^ccode_b^"
  .23           R[ep]                := cS[cR[p] + ep];
  .24           R[ra]                := cS[cR[p] + ra];
  .25           R[u]                 := cS[cR[p] + t];
  .26           R[p]                 := cS[cR[p] + p];
  .27           S[cR[p] + cstk_e]    := cR[u];
  .28           ";

(16)  Expre ::= Lambl
  .1  d_e    := cd_l;
  .2  ln_l   := cln_e;
  .3  stk_l  := cstk_e;
  .4  dict_l := cdict_e;
  .5  code_e := ccode_l;
```

```
(15)  Lambe ::= fun ( id ) = Blockb  end
  .1  def lfct : make-lbl(),
  .2      lbyp : make-lbl();
  .3  d_e     := 1;
  .4  ln_b    := cln_e + 1;
  .5  dict_b  := cdict_e + [id ↦ cln_e + 1];
  .6  code_e  := "goto lbyp;
  .7              lfct:
  .8            "^ccode_b^"
  .9              goto cR[ra];
  .10             lbyp:
  .11             R[u]                := lfct;
  .12             R[u]                := mk-FCT(cR[u],cR[p]);
  .13             S[cR[p] + cstk_e]   := cR[u];
  .14           ";

(17)  Expre ::= apply  Exprf  ( Expra )
  .1  def lret : make-lbl();
  .2  d_e              := max(cd_f, cd_a) + 1;
  .3  ln_f, ln_a       := cln_e;
  .4  stk_a            := cstk_e;
  .5  stk_f            := cstk_e + 1;
  .6  dict_f, dict_a   := cdict_e;
  .7  code_e           := ccode_a^"
  .8                    "^ccode_f^"
  .9                      R[u]  := cS[cR[p] + (cstke+1)];
  .10                     IF NOTFCT(cR[u]) THEN GOTO lerr;
  .11                     R[br] := s-Lbl(cR[u]);
  .12                     R[ep] := s-LOC(cR[u]);
  .13                     R[ra] := lret;
  .14                     R[pm] := cS[cR[p] + cstk_e];
  .15                     GOTO cR[br];
  .16                     lret:
  .17                   ";

(18)  Blockb ::= Expre
  .1  ln_e    := cln_b + 1;
  .2  dict_e  := cdict_b;
  .3  stk_e   := t;
  .4  code_b  := "S[cR[top] + p]    := cR[p];
  .5              S[cR[top] + ep]   := cR[ep];
```

```
.6          S[cR[top] + ra]   := cR[ra];
.7          S[cR[top] + vr]   := cR[u];
.8          R[p]              := cK[top];
.9          R[ep]             := cR[p];
.10         R[top]            := cR[top] + (t+cd_e);
.11       "^ccode_e^"
.12         R[e]P             := cS[cR[p] + ep];
.13         R[ra]             := cS[cR[p] + ra];
.14         R[u]              := cS[cR[p] + t];
.15         R[p]              := cS[cR[p] + p];
.16         S[cR[p] + cstk_e] := cR[u];
.17         ";
```

9.4.3 Another Attribute Semantics (VIII)

The language defined by the concrete BNF grammar given in 9.4.2 (VII.1) for SAL is both bottom-up and topdown analyzable. That didn't matter very much in section 9.4.2, since attribute variable value computations still required the presence of the entire parse tree before any *Code-text* could be generated. In this section we present an attribute semantics specification of another compiling algorithm, which, based on a top-down parse process, is capable of generating *Code-text* simultaneously with parsing. Again we shall not argue how we choose a/the solution. Instead we ask you to recall the twin stack abstract machine of section 9.3.3. Now all *DSA* realizations fit exactly into four (*t*) positions: (*CP*, *EP*, *RA*, *VR*) with temporaries allocated to a global, contiguous stack, *STK*'s direct implementation. Since SAL is simply applicative (it permits for example no GOTOs) this poses no special problems as concerns correct indices into stack tops. The *STK* has been realized in 'core' "below" the activation stack: think of the target machine addressing being "wrapped around" zero address to maximum available core storage address - and you get a scheme which was very common in the earlier days on mono-processing. One crucial, final note: to cope with known *Code-text* to be "delay"-generated a global 'attribute' (also) called *code*, is introduced. It is treated as a stack. Push corresponds to concatenation, pop to taking the head off -- leaving the tail. Pushing occurs for all *Code-texts* known when recognizing the initial prefix string, as one does in top-down analysis, of a composite expressing: if, let, rec, apply, (and fun. Popping of one part occurs when any expression has been completely analyzed: k, id, fi, end, end, end,), and end, respectively.

VIII Inherited Attribute Semantics Compiling Algorithm

VIII.1 Syntactic Domains -- as in VII.1

VIII.2 Node & Global Attributes

```
(5) Expr   ln    type Nat0           inherited
    Lamb   dict  type Id →m Nat0     inherited
    Block

(6) Prog   code   type Code-text   stack
           print  type Code-text   output
```

VIII.3 Attribute Rules

```
(7)      Progp ::= Expre
  .1     def lexit: make-lbl();
  .2     print "R[p]   := 0;
  .3           R[ep]  := 0;
  .4           R[top] := t;
  .5           R[stk] := -1;";
  .6     code := <"R[u] := cS[-1];
  .7              Out  := cR[u];
  .8              goto lexit;
  .9              lerr:
  .10             Out  := ERROR;
  .11             lexit: ">;
  .12    ln_e   := 0;
  .13    dict_e := [];

(8)      Expre ::= k
  .1     print "S[cR[stk]] := k;
  .2           R[u]       := k;
  .3           R[stk]     := cR[stk] + 1;
  .4          "^hd c code;
  .5     code := tl c code;

(9)      Expr ::= id
  .1     def lloop : make-lbl(),
  .2         lload : make-lbl();
  .3     print "R[j] := cln_e - (cdict_e)(id);
```

```
.4          lloop:
.5          if cR[j] = 0 then goto lload;
.6          R[ep] := cS[cR[ep] + ep];
.7          R[j]  := cR[j] - 1;
.8          goto lloop
.9          lload:
.10         R[u]  := cS[cR[ep] + vr];
.11         S[cR[stk]] := cR[u];
.12         R[stk] := cR[stk] - 1;
.13         R[ep]  := cR[p];
.14      "^hd c code;
.15  code := tl c code;
```

(10) $\text{Expre} ::= (\text{Expr}^1 + \text{Expr}^2)$

```
.1   ln_e1,ln_e2      := cln_e;
.2   dict_e1,dict_e2 := cdict_e;
.3   code            := <"">^
.4                     <"R[u]        := cS[cR[stk]];
.5                       R[u]        := cR[u] + cS[cR[stk] + 1];
.6                       R[stk]      := cR[stkP + 1];
.7                       S[cR[stk]] := cR[u];
.8                     ">^ccode;
```

(11) $\text{Expre} ::= \underline{if}\ \text{Expr}t\ \underline{then}\ \text{Expr}c\ \underline{else}\ \text{Expr}a\ \underline{fi}$

```
.1   def lalt : make-lbl(),
.2       lout : make-lbl();
.3   ln_t,ln_c,ln_a      := cln_e;
.4   dict_t,dict_c,dict_a := cdict_e;
.5   code                := "R[u]    := cS[cR[stk]];
.6                           R[stk] := cR[stk] + 1;
.7                           if ¬cR[u] then goto lalt;
.8                         ">^
.9                     <"goto lout;
.10                     lalt:
.11                     ">^
.12                     <"lout:
.13                     ">^ccode;
```

```
(12)  Expre ::= let id = Exprd ; Blockb end
  .1  ln_d    := cln_e;
  .2  ln_b    := cln_e + 1;
  .3  dict_d  := cdict_e;
  .4  dict_b  := cdict_e + [id ↦ cln_e + 1];
  .5  code    := <"R[u]   := cS[cR[stk]];
  .6              R[stk] := cR[stk] + 1;
  .7             ">^
  .8             <"">^ccode;

(13)  Expre ::= rec g =  fun ( id ) = Blockd end ; Blockb end
  .1  def lfct : make-lbl(),
  .2      lbyp : make-lbl();
  .3  ln_d    := cln_e + 2;
  .4  ln_b    := cln_e + 1;
  .5  dict_d  := cdict_e + [id ↦ cln_e + 2, g ↦ cln_e + 1];
  .6  dict_b  := cdict_e + [g  ↦ cln_e + 1];
  .7  print "goto lbyp;
  .8             lfct:
  .9        ";
  .10 code := <"goto cR[ra];
  .11           lbyp:
  .12           R[u]                := lfct;
  .13           R[u]                := mk-FCT(cR[u],cR[top]);
  .14           S[cR[top] + p]      := cR[p];
  .15           S[cR[top] + ep]     := cR[ep];
  .16           S[cR[top] + ra]     := cR[ra];
  .17           S[cR[topP + vr]     := cR[u];
  .18           R[p]                := cR[top];
  .19           R[ep]               := cR[top];
  .20           R[top]              := cR[top] + t;
  .21         ">^<"
  .22           R[ep]               := cS[cR[p] + ep];
  .23           R[ra]               := cS[cR[p] + ra];
  .24           R[u]                := cS[cR[p] + t];
  .25           R[p]                := cS[cR[p] + p];
  .26           S[cR[stk]]          := cR[u];
  .27           R[stk]              := cR[stk] + 1;
  .28         ">^ccode;
```

```
(14)  Expre ::= Lambd
  .1  lnd    := clne;
  .2  dictd  := cdicte;

(15)  Lambe ::= fun ( id ) = Blockb end
  .1  def lfct : make-lbl(),
  .2      lbyp : make-lbl();
  .3  lnb    := clne + 1;
  .4  dictb  := cdicte + [id ↦ clne + 1];
  .5  code   := "goto cR[ra];
  .6             lbyp:
  .7             R[u]         := lfct;
  .8             R[u]         := mk-FCT(cR[u],cR[p]);
  .9             S[cR[stk]]   := cR]u];
  .10            R[stk]       := cR[stk] - 1;
  .11           ">^ccode;
  .12 print "goto lbyp;
  .13        lfct:
  .14       ";

(16)  Expre ::= apply Exprf ( Expra )
  .1  def lret : make-lbl();
  .2  lnf,lna      := clne;
  .3  dictf,dicta  := cdicte;
  .4  code         := <"">^
  .5                  <"R[u] := cS[cR[stk] - 1];
  .6                    if NOTFCT(cR[u])
  .7                       then goto lerr;
  .8                    R[br]  := s-Lbl(cR[u]);
  .9                    R[ep]  := s-LOC(cR[u]);
  .10                   R[ra]  := lret;
  .11                   R[pm]  := cS[cR[stk]];
  .12                   R[stk] := cR[stk] - 2;
  .13                   goto cR[br];
  .14                   lret:
  .15                 ">^ccode;
```

```
(17)  Blockb ::= Expre
 .1   ln_e   := cln_b + 1;
 .2   dict_e := cdict_b;
 .3   print "S[cR[top] + p]   := cR[p];
 .4          S[cR[top] + ep]  := cR[ep];
 .5          S[cR[top] + ra]  := cR[ra];
 .6          S[cR[top] + vr]  := cR[u];
 .7          R[p]             := cR[top];
 .8          R[ep]            := cR[top];
 .9          R[top]           := cR[top] + t;
 .10         ";
 .11  code := <"R[ep]       := cS[cR[p] + ep];
 .12             R[ra]       := cS[cR[p] + ra];
 .13             R]u]        := cS[cR[p] + t];
 .14             R[p]        := cS[cR[p] + p];
 .15             S[cR[stk]]  := cR[u];
 .16             R[stk]      := cR[stk] + 1;
 .17             ">^ccode;
```

9.5 COMPILER STRUCTURES

From the compiling algorithm specifications of section 9.3.2-3 we can now read properties other than just the source text input vs. target machine code output itself. Thus the compiling algorithm determines first level structures of the compiler itself. That is, it answers questions such as: "Is it a two, or can it be a single-pass compiler?"; "What information is put in the dictionary, and when?"; "How is the dictionary realizable: as part of the intermediate text of a multi-pass compiler, with the *dict*ionary components 'scattered' over this intermediate text; or necessarily as a 'global' component, 'disjoint' from any intermediate text or parse tree?".

Single- and Multi-Pass Compilers

If all attributes can be computed in a synthetic manner then a single-pass compiler based on a bottom-up parse can always be realized. This is so since any deterministic language can always be so (in fact LR(K)) parsed. Similarly, if the language can be top-down (for example LL(K)) parsed (possibly using some recursive descent method), and a compiling algorithm given by a purely inherited attribute semantics, then a single-pass compiler is again possible. If, however, as for example suggested by our first SAL attribute semantics compiling algorithm (9.3.2), some attributes, like the local, temporay list stack pointer, and the block/body level number, and *dictionary*, are inherited, while others, the maximum local stack depth and the generated *code*, are synthesized, then a multi-pass compiler with at least two passes cannot be avoided. If the inherited and synthesized attributes of such a compiling algorithm solely derive from constants emanating from respectively the root and leaves, then a two-pass compiler can result. This is in fact the case with the VI and VII specifications. The exact minimum number of logical, that is intrinsically required, passes, is a function of the semantics and syntax of the language - with the semantics property eventually showing up in the intricate web-like relationships between synthesized and inherited attributes. Of course: silly, unnecessarily complicated, attribute semantics, that is such as those involving nonintrinsical combinations of inherited and synthesized attribute value computations, would then indicate a higher (minimum) number of passes than strictly required. Only calm scrutiny, a careful analysis and a complete mastering of the language semantics and specification tools will eventually lead to optimal realizations.

So what is then the difference between the two compiling algorithms: VII and VIII? One leads to a two-pass-, the other to a single-pass compiler for one and the same language (semantics). Is not a minimum pass compiler always to be preferred? Well, the gain in compilation speed in the latter has been obtained at the expense of slower execution speed, since -- as in usually the case with pure, stack-oriented execution -- a temporary stack index, R[stk], must now be dynamically adjusted: at the worst once per 'popping', and once per 'pushing'. This being in contrast to the fixed-offset addressing possible by our two-pass compilation, which - in turn - causes possibly excessive storage to be (pre-)allocated.

Compiler Object Realizations

Whilst the purpose of 'mapping' the denotational semantics into successively lower-order, increasingly more concrete/intricate semantics definitions, was one of eliminating higher-order, functional objects -- as well as the run-time presence of elaboration routines -- we now suddenly see the re-appearance, in for example the attribute semantics definitions, of higher order objects: the functional dictionaries, and even the (non-functional, but) varying string length (*Code-text*) obobjects. The input/

output relationships of a compiler have been specified. Now we must object transform abstractly described compiler objects, and operation decompose the likewise implicitly specified primitive operations on these. In fact, we must also take issue, at long last, with the internal realization of abstract SAL programs. But note this: nothing has been lost in postponing this decision till now. On the contrary: we may now be able to design exactly that internal representation which best suits the code-generation parse-tree walking algorithm. The techniques of 'mapping' such abstractions into concrete implementations using methods akin to those of this papers' specialized, run-time structure-oriented ones, will not be further dealt with here.

9.6 COMPILING CORRECTNESS

Time has finally come to take issue with the problem of correctness. In this section we shall illustrate only one such proof. We prove that the development I → II is correct. Subsequent development stages are proved correct using essentially the same technique, but becoming, first increasingly more cumbersome (to report and read), and with III → IV also somewhat more complex.

Correctness Criterion:

-- Theorem (Thm)

$$
\begin{aligned}
&(\forall env \in ENV,\ \forall env1 \in ENV1)\\
&\quad (env = retr\text{-}ENV(env1))\\
&\qquad \supset\ (\forall e \in expr)(eval\text{-}expr[e]env\\
&\qquad\qquad = retr\text{-}VAL(m1\text{-}eval\text{-}expr[e](env1)))
\end{aligned}
$$

Annotation:

For all such abstract, *env*, and concrete, *env1*, environments which correspond, it shall be the case that evaluating any expression, *e*, using the abstract interpreter on *env* will yield the same value as is retrievable from evaluating that same expression *e* using the more concrete interpreter on *env1*.

The statement of this criterion, as well as its actual, detailed proof, is new.

The structure of Thm can be pictured:

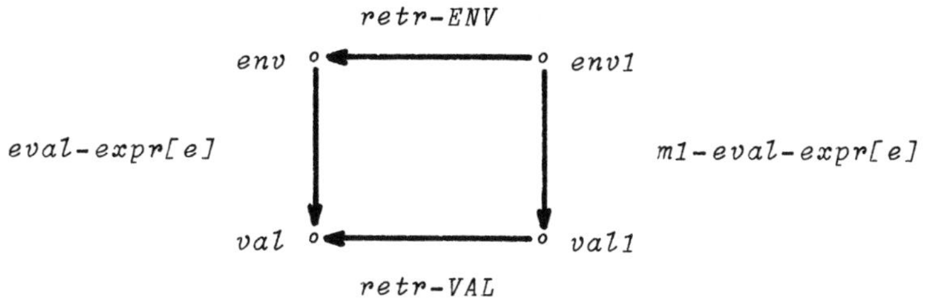

It is derived from the general idea of 'simulation' of one program by another (executing one algebra on another).

Proof of Correctness

Our task of proving that *m1-eval-expr* (in the sense of the criterion above) does the same, to any expression, as *eval-expr*, that is delivers comparable results, can be broken into two steps. Firstly we plan the proof. We look for a strategy, a proof technique, which, with the least amount of effort, will achieve the proof. Secondly we carry through the actual details of all parts of the proof, as structured in the first step above. The strategy to be followed here is that of proof by structural induction. That is: since the criterion calls for all expressions, we naturally look for a way of proving it for a finite set of representative examples. The selection of these is guided by the structure (and alternatives) of the syntactic domain abstract syntax, and by the corresponding structure and alternatives of the elaboration functions. The structure of the semantic domains here play a lesser rôle (than might otherwise be the case -- for for example III → IV). The abstract syntax for expressions determined the major structure of the elaboration functions, as is natural for denotational semantics definitions. Therefore we shall now structure the proof according to the cases of alternative syntactic categories, and by induction due to the recursive definition of *Expr*.

Legend:

Thm., abbreviates 'theorem', Asm. 'assumption', Lm. 'lemma', QED 'proved'; the lemma is displayed after the proof.

<u>case</u> <u>1</u>: *e = mk-Const(k)*

1.	*eval-expr[mk-Const(k)](env)*	= *k*	
2.	*m1-eval-expr[mk-Const(k)](env1)*	= *k*	
3.	*retr-VAL(k)*	= *k*	

<u>case</u> <u>2</u>: *e = mk-Var(id)*

0.	<u>assumption</u>: *env = retr-ENV(env1)*		Thm.
1.	*eval-expr[mk-Var(id)](env)*	= *env(id)*	
2.	*m1-eval-expr[mk-Var(id)](env1)*	= *look-up(id,env1)*	
3.	*retr-VAL(look-up1(id,env1))*	= *env(id)*	Lm., QED.

<u>case</u> <u>4</u>: *e = mk-Cond(t,c,a)*

0.	<u>assumption</u>: *env = retr-ENV(env1)*		Thm.
1.	*eval-expr[mk-Cond(t,c,a)](env)*	= <u>*if*</u> *eval-expr[t](env)* <u>*then*</u> *eval-expr[c](env)* <u>*else*</u> *eval-expr[a](env)*	
2.	*m1-eval-expr[mk-Cond(t,c,a)](env1)*	= <u>*if*</u> *m1-eval-expr[t](env1)* <u>*then*</u> *m1-eval-expr[c](env1)* <u>*else*</u> *m1-eval-expr[a](env1)*	
3.	<u>induction</u> <u>hypothesis</u>		Thm.
.1	*eval-expr[t](env) ~ m1-eval-expr[t](env1)*		
.2	*eval-expr[c](env) ~ m1-eval-expr[c](env1)*		
.3	*eval-expr[a](env) ~ m1-eval-expr[a](env1)*		
4.	*m1-eval-expr[t](env1) ∈ Bool*		
5.	*eval-expr[t](env) = m1-eval-expr[t](env1)*		
6.	<u>subcase</u> <u>1</u>		
.0	*eval-expr[t](env)*	= <u>*true*</u>	Asm.
.1	*eval-expr[mk-Cond(t,c,a)](env)*	= *eval-expr[c](env)*	
.2	*m1-eval-expr[mk-Cond(t,c,a)](env1)*	= *m1-eval-expr[c](env1)*	
.3	8.1 = 8.2 follows from 5.2		QED.
7.	<u>subcase</u> <u>2</u> -- as 6.		QED.

<u>case</u> <u>5</u>: *e = mk-Lamb(id,d)*

0.	<u>assumption</u>: *env = retr-ENV(env1)*		Thm.

```
1.   eval-expr[mk-Lamb(id,d)]env         = eval-fun[mk-Lamb(id,d)]env
2.   m1-eval-expr[mk-Lamb(id,d)](env1)   = mk-CLOS(mk-Lamb(id,d),env1)
3.   retr-VAL(mk-CLOS(mk-Lamb(id,d),env1)
 .1  = eval-fun[mk-Lamb(id,d)](retr-ENV(env1))
 .2  = eval-fun[mk-Lamb(id,d)]env
QED  follows from 2. = 5.2
```

case 6: *e = mk-Appl(f,a)*

```
0.   assumption: env = retr-ENV(env1)
1.   eval-expr[mk-Appl(f,a)]env = (eval-expr[f]env)(eval-expr[a]env)
2.0  m1-eval-expr[mk-Appl(f,a)](env1)
 .1  = (let clos = m1-eval-expr[f](env1),
 .2            arg  = m1-eval-expr[a](env1) in
 .3       apply1(clos,arg))

3.   induction,hypothesis                                          Thm.
 .1  eval-expr[f]env ~ m1-eval-expr[f](env1)
 .2  eval-expr[a]env ~ m1-eval-expr[a](env1)

4.0  eval-expr[f]env ∈ FUN ⊃                                       Asm.
 .1  (∃mk-Lamb(id,d),∃env' ∈ ENV)
 .2     (eval-expr[f]env = eval-fun[mk-Lamb(id,d)](env)
```

The above should be expressed in terms of a "recursively defined predicate", see [Milne 77a, Tennent 82a]. The idea of that predicate transpires, however from the above & below predicates.

-- Considering only a "good" case:

```
5.0  m1-eval-expr[f](env1) ∈ CLOS ⊃
 .1  (...,∃env1' ∈ ENV1)
 .2     (env' = retr-ENV(env1'))
 .3    ∧(m1-eval-expr[mk-Lamb(id,d)](env1') = m1-eval-expr[f](env1)

6.  m1-eval-expr[mk-Lamb(id,d)](env1')
 .1  = mk-CLOS(mk-Lamb(id,d),env1')
 .2  = m1-eval-expr[f](env1)
 .3  = clos
```

```
7.  apply1(clos,arg)
 .1  = apply1(mk-CLOS(mk-Lamb(id,d),env1'),arg)
 .2  = (let env1" = <mk-SIMP(id,arg)>^env1'
        m1-eval-expr[d](env1"))

8.  (eval-expr[f]env)(eval-expr[a]env)
 .1  = eval-fun[mk-Lamb(id,d)](env')(eval-...|
 .2  = λx.(let env" = env' + [id ↦ a] in |..-expr[a]env)
           eval-expr[d]env")(eval-expr[a]env)
 .3  = (let env" = env' + [id ↦ eval-expr[a]env];
        eval-expr[d]env")

9.  env" = retr-ENV(env1")                              follows from:
 .1       retr-ENV(env1') = env'
 .2    ∧ env1" = <mk-SIMP(id,arg)>^env1'
 .3    ∧ env"  = env' + [id ↦ eval-expr[a]env]
 .4    ∧ arg   = m1-eval-expr[a](env1)
 .5    ∧ retr-ENV definition
 .6    ∧ eval-expr[a]env = retr-VAL(arg)

10.  induction,hypothesis:
  .1  eval-expr[d]env" ~ m1-eval-expr[d](env1")              Thm.

11.  QED then follows
```

case 7: *e = mk-Rec(g,mk-Lamb(id,d),b)*

```
0.   assumption: env = retr-ENV(env1)
1.   eval-expr[mk-Rec(g,mk-Lamb(id,d),b)]env
2.   = (let env' = env + [g ↦ eval-fun[mk-Lamb(id,d)]env] in
        eval-expr[b]env')
3.   m1-eval-expr[mk-Rec(g,mk-Lamb(id,d),b)](env1)
4.   = (let env1' = <mk-REC(g,mk-Lamb(id,d))>^env1 in
        m1-eval-expr[b](env1'))
5.   env1' = retr-ENV(env')                              follows from:
 .1       env'  = env + [g ↦ eval-fun[mk-Lamb(id,d)]env']
 .2    ∧ env1' = <mk-REC(g,mk-Lamb(id,d))>^env1
 .3    ∧ env   = retr-ENV(env1)
 .4    ∧ retr-ENV(env1')
6.   (5)  ⊃ eval-expr[b]env'
            = retr-VAL(m1-eval-expr[b](env1'))                QED.
```

Lemma:

$(env=retr\text{-}ENV(env1)) \supset (\forall id \in \underline{dom}\ env)(env(id)=retr\text{-}VAL(look\text{-}up1(id,env1)))$

The lemma is (for example) proved by induction on the length of *env1*. Two cases form the basis step: the *SIMP*le and the *REC*ursive header. We leave the proof as an exercise.

9.7 SUMMARY

We have shown the systematic derivation, from a denotational semantics definition, of an implementation of a Simple Applicative Language featuring both a block-structure and the procedure concept. The derivation proceeded in a number of increasingly concrete, more detailed, run-time-oriented styles, Hence we were able to illustrate how run-time structures such as DISPLAYs could be orderly developed, eventually proven correct. The various definition styles were basically those current during the 1960's, and we have thus shown how they relate.

9.8 BIBLIOGRAPHY

Chapter 1 surveys the roots of denotational semantics definitions. Our example language, SAL, is taken from [Reynolds 72a], as is the next stage of development.

The first first-order applicative semantics was that of LISP1.5 [McCarthy 62b]. (A denotational semantics study of LISP 1.5 was carried out by Gordon [Gordon 73a].) The 1960's saw further exercises in first-order functional semantics, notably among which we find the IBM Vienna Lab. series of PL/I definitions: ULD versions 1,2,3: [ULD66, ULD68, ULD69], Reynolds' GEDANKEN [Reynolds 70a], and the sketches of Lockwood Morris [Morris 70a]. Common to all, however, is the fact that none were derived from other semantic definitions (except perhaps in an intuitive sense those of [Morris 70a]); but marked the only available 'abstraction'. The present derivation of SAL.I into SAL.II is essentially that of [Reynolds 72a], the statement of the retrieve functions and the (proof of the) theorem (sect. 9.6) is ,however, new.

Abstract state machine semantics definitions were first reported by

Landin [Landin 64a], and received their full development with the IBM Vienna Lab. series of PL/I definitions, ULD versions 1,2,3 (Universial Lanuage Descriptions, as expressed in the so-called VDL, Vienna Definition Language [ULD66, ULD687, ULD69]. Whereas Landin's definition of an even simpler applicative expression language, AE, than SAL was also paired with a denotational definition, no attempt was then reported on proving their 'equivalence', let alone deriving the former systematically from the latter. Landin's mechanical version was since referred to as the SECD, Stack/Environment/Control/Dump, machine specification style, since the structure was amenable to a variety of language definitions. The VDL based definitions [ULD66, ULD68, ULD69, Lauer 68a, Zimmerman 69a, Allen 72a] too, were free-standing, in that no abstract model was used as a departure point. The recent PL/I ANS/ECMA standards proposal [ANSI 76a] is basically a derivative of the ULD/VDL style of semantics, as also explained in [Beech 73a]. [Lauer 73a - Hoare 74a, Marcotty 76a] presents examples of abstract state machine semantics, with [Lauer 73a - Hoare 74a] proving equivalence among several variants of these and also axiomatically stated versions.

Historically attribute semantics originated with E.T. Irons' work on ALGOL 60 compilers - and we still find that the technique is mostly used in compiling algorithm specification, including statically checkable context condition/constraint testing. In contrast hereto: to specify the semantics of a source language one usually introduces a parse tree 'walking' function which in addition to the local attributes, also work on, that is manipulate, global objects, thus effecting desired computations.

Attribute semantics definitions received their purifying, individualizing treatment from Knuth, Lewis/Stearns/Rosenkrantz, Wirth/Weber and others; Irons started the whole thing [Irons 61a, Irons 63a, Wirth 66b, Knuth 68a, Knuth 71a, Lorho 75a, Neel 74a, Bochmann 76a, Wilner 72a, Kennedy 74a].

The idea of proving correctness "by commuting diagrams", that is by simulating one machine by another was reported by [McCarthy 67a, Landin 72a, Milner 71a-b, Weyhrauch 72a, Morris 73a, Lucas 72a, Goguen 75a, Goguen 78a], see also [Jones 80c, Ganzinger 80a, Gaudel 80a], and many others. The subject of compiler correctness proving is currently under intense study.

The idea of deriving target machine codes from source language specifications is reported in [Dommergaard 80a, Wand 80bc, Wand 82b, Mosses 81a].

PART III

VDM AND OTHER SYSTEMS

Part III includes some applications of VDM outside the area of programming languages. During the 1970's, there was a steady growth of interest in database work. Several large database systems were widely applied to commercial applications. Of deeper significance is the fact that these systems exhibited a range of different underlying "architectures" (relational, hierarchical, network). Clearly there was a need for some precise specifications. This challenge has been taken up by a number of groups (see chapter 12 for further references). Here chapters 12 and 13 discuss the definition and design of database systems. Chapters 10 and 11 provide useful examples which lead into applications to database architectures. Other applications of VDM include the specification of "generic office automation systems" by the Danish Datamatics Centre, and a number of IBM products.

The meta-language used in VDM is not closed. The earlier parts of this book have used a limited range of constructs in order to simplify reading. This part of the book uses some additional constructs and also shows a more "imperative" style of specification. The extra features of the meta-language are described in the Glossary.

CHAPTER 10

PROGRAM DESIGN BY DATA REFINEMENT

The case is made above for studying languages and their implementations. There is, however, a large body of material on program development relating to other application areas. This material frequently uses specification by pre-/post-conditions and abstract data types; the related design techniques are justified by rules about control constructs and data refinement. This chapter exemplifies the relevant parts of VDM. Special emphasis is put on the refinement of abstract data types to machine representations since this is the activity which is more relevant to the early stages of program development.

In this chapter, modules are isolated and developed separately. This focusses on a different area of VDM from that considered in earlier parts. So far attention has been on the order of actions as fixed by combinators; here the concern is with the individual actions. Clearly, both aspects must be considered in a development method.

The example considered is the access to data via keys. This is a problem which is of great importance to many computer applications and which relates to the topic of databases discussed later in this part of the book. The material here is derived from [Fielding 80a]. Full details of the "Rigorous Approach" to software developments are given in [Jones 80a] and overviews are available in [Jones 81b, Stoy 81a]. Another interesting application of this material is given in a recent UK Department of Industry survey of Program Design Methods in which VDM is applied to the definition of KAPSE (Kernel Ada Support Environment) (see also [Clemmensen 82a]).

CONTENTS

10.1 INTRODUCTION

Map data objects are used repeatedly in the specifications of systems. The retrieval of information via a key is also a widespread data processing problem. There are a large number of established methods to implement such maps (e.g. hashing). In this chapter both binary and, so-called, B-trees are developed as representations of abstract maps. These designs are given as examples of the development method rather than in an attempt to contribute new algorithms.

A binary tree can contain one key at each node (data may, optionally, be stored also in the node). The simplest update algorithms do not result in a balanced tree. A B-tree can contain different numbers of keys in different nodes. The number must, however, lie between bounds m (the "order" of the tree) and $2*m$. Furthermore, all "leaves" of a B-tree occur at the same depth. Algorithms exist for insertion and deletion which ensure that the tree remains balanced. The particular type of tree considered here is known as a Bplus-tree. It has the additional property that it can provide sequential access as well as random access via key.

The rigorous method of specification and development is described with the aid of the simpler problem of representing abstract maps as binary trees. This example enables the entire refinement process, from abstract specification down to corresponding program code, to be illustrated.

The B-tree development starts with the same abstract specification of a map from keys to data, with operations defined for finding, inserting and deleting a key. Then, two levels of refinement follow, which represent a map as a tree structure and have corresponding operations which model the operations of the initial specification. The first of these levels represents a tree as a set of nested sets, with the leaves of the tree consisting of mappings from keys to data. The second level represents the tree by using lists - each intermediate node consisting of an ordered list of keys and a list of nodes.

Each stage of the refinement is related to the preceding stage by a retrieve function and is shown to be correct with respect to the preceding stage in accordance with the conditions for the refinement of data types and operations given in [Jones 80a] and summarized in Section 2. No code is provided here for B-trees. A Pascal program is given in full detail in [Fielding 80a].

10.2 THE RIGOROUS METHOD OF SPECIFICATION AND DESIGN

In the "rigorous method", a specification is written as a constructive specification of a data type. Development can then proceed either by operation decomposition or by data refinement. What is described below is the terminology and notation used in "constructive specification" and development by "data refinement".

A program is considered to be an operation (or operations) on a "state" of a particular class. An "operation" can change the values of the components, that comprise a state, but cannot alter its structure. (The notation for operations etc. has been changed from the original in order to fit the current context.)

In order to specify a program, a class of states must be defined. It is best to design the structure of the states by choosing a data type which matches the problem as closely as possible. Such a data type is one which probably cannot be implemented directly, and is known as an "abstract data type" - it is considered to be characterized by its operations. The notation used in defining states is "abstract syntax" (for a description see Chapter 2). An example of a state description is:

$$Mkd = Key \underset{m}{\rightarrow} Data$$

(In contrast, a data type could be defined "implicitly", by using axioms to relate its operations to each other. The "constructive" approach, which is used here, specifies the effects of the operations in terms of the underlying abstract state.)

Operations are specified by using predicates (pre- and post-conditions) as this produces shorter specifications which embody the properties required without specifying how they are to be achieved.

An operation is specified by three clauses, in the following format:

1. $OP\colon A1 \times A2 \times \ldots \times An \Rightarrow R1 \times R2 \times \ldots \times Rm$

A class of states is associated with a group of operations. The types of any arguments accepted and results produced are shown explicitly.

2. $pre\text{-}OP\colon State \times A1 \times A2 \times \ldots \times An \rightarrow Bool$

This is a predicate which specifies over what subset of the class of states the operation should work.

3. $post\text{-}OP: State \times A1 \times A2 \times \ldots \times An \times State \times R1 \times R2 \times \ldots \times Rn \rightarrow Bool$

This is a predicate which defines the required relationship between the initial and final states. Examples of operation specifications are:

$FIND: Key \Rightarrow Data$
$pre\text{-}FIND(m,k) \quad \triangleq \; k \in \underline{dom}\, m$
$post\text{-}FIND(m,k,m',d) \; \triangleq \; m'=m \wedge d=m(k)$

(This operation works on the states shown above (Mkd) and returns the data item associated with the given key.)

$INSERT: Key \times Data \Rightarrow$
$pre\text{-}INSERT(m,k,d) \quad \triangleq \; \neg(k \in \underline{dom}\, m)$
$post\text{-}INSERT(m,k,d,m') \; \triangleq \; m'=m \cup [k \mapsto d]$

$DELETE: Key \Rightarrow$
$pre\text{-}DELETE(m,k) \quad \triangleq \; k \in \underline{dom}\, m$
$post\text{-}DELETE(m,k,m') \; \triangleq \; m'=m \setminus \{k\}$

Notice that the pre-conditions define these operations to be partial. Subsequent uses of post-conditions show how they can be used to define a range of valid results.

The state of a specification is chosen to be as abstract as possible providing it can be used to describe the required operations. The choice of a map (Mkd) satisfies this criterion. Assuming that the implementation language does not support such maps, development must now proceed by "data refinement". That is, a less abstract "representation" is chosen and new operations are defined in terms of the more concrete objects. Precise criteria are laid down for the correctness of such steps. Refinement may take place in several steps.

(The refinement process, like other "top-down" methods should be seen as providing a structure for documentation rather than an order of thought. One particular area where a designer may need to backtrack is in the choice of "data type invariants".)

One possible representation for *Mkd* is binary trees. If a tree is not empty, it consists of a node which contains a key, the associated data and two trees (either or both of which may be <u>*nil*</u>). Thus:

Bintree = [Binnode]

Binnode :: s-lt:Bintree s-k:Key s-d:Data s-rt:Bintree

One criterion for a good specification is the minimization of extra well-formedness conditions on the states. In [Jones 80a] these are referred to as "data type invariants". The definition of *Mkd* is ideal in that there is no need for a data type invariant; it is typical of representations that the invariants become increasingly complex. Here *Bintree* requires an invariant which states that only those trees for which all nodes have ordered keys are considered "valid":

invnd: Binnode → Bool
invnd(mk-Binnode(lt,k,d,rt)) $\triangleq$
  (∀lk∈collkeys(lt))(lk<k) ∧ (∀rk∈collkeys(rt))(k<rk)

collkeys: Bintree → Key-set
collkeys(t) $\triangleq$
  <u>*if*</u> *t=*<u>*nil*</u> <u>*then*</u> {}
  <u>*else*</u> *collkeys(s-lt(t))* ∪ {*s-k(t)*} ∪ *collkeys(s-rt(t))*

The set *Bintree* is now considered to contain only objects all of whose nodes are valid with respect to *invnd*.

The need to record a data type invariant arises because, although it may be evident from the operations, it is required explicitly in later development correctness proofs and will also prevent errors in future alterations to the specification. Each operation must be shown to preserve any data type invariant which might exist. The correctness condition for "preservation of validity" is:

(∀s∈Valids)(pre-OP(s,args) ∧ post-OP(s,args,s',res) ⊃ s'∈Valids)

Since, in the specification *Mkd* has no data type invariant, this is obvious for the operations *FIND, INSERT* and *DELETE*.

A "retrieve function" relates a representation to its abstraction and is the basis for data refinement proofs. Objects of a representation may contain more information than those of the abstraction and so a retrieve function operates on a state of the representation and retrieves the necessary information for the corresponding state in the abstraction.

The retrieve function for binary trees is:

retr: Bintree → Mkd
retr(n) $\triangleq$ <u>*if*</u> *n=*<u>*nil*</u> <u>*then*</u> [ ]
<u>*else*</u> (<u>*let*</u> *mk-Binnode(lt,k,d,rt) = n* <u>*in*</u>
<u>*merge*</u>(*[k ↦ d],retr(lt),retr(rt)*))

Having established the connection between the abstraction and the representation, the correctness of the latter can be considered. It is required that the retrieve function be defined on all valid (representation) states. In the case of *Bintree*, *invnd* ensures that the maps to be merged have disjoint domains and thus *retr* is total over valid binary trees. A more formal proof is given in [Fielding 80a] by showing by (structural) induction that:

<u>*dom*</u> *retr(t) = collkeys(t)*

The second correctness condition on the data type itself shows that there exists at least one (valid) representation for each (valid) abstract object; there may exist more than one. For the problem in hand this becomes:

$(\forall m \in Mkd)(\exists t \in Bintree)(retr(t)=m)$

A formal proof by induction on <u>*domm*</u> is given in [Fielding 80a].

Having checked the representation itself, the new operations which work on the representation must be considered. The operation equivalent to *FIND* is:

FINDBIN: Key => Data
pre-FINDBIN(t,k) $\triangleq$ $k \in collkeys(t)$
post-FINDBIN(t,k,t',d) $\triangleq$ $t'=t \wedge d=findb(t,k)$

findb: Bintree × Key $\overset{\sim}{\to}$ *Data*
pre-findb(t,k) $\triangleq$ $k \in collkeys(t)$

findb(mk-Binnode(lt,mk,md,rt),k) $\triangleq$
  if $k=mk$ then md else if $k<mk$ then *findb(lt,k)* else *findb(rt,k)*

Notice that *findb* is defined for valid trees because the data type invariant ensures that recursion is always into the appropriate sub-tree. The "preservation of validity" can now be considered: in this case *FINDBIN* is an identity on states so must preserve the invariant.

To establish that *FINDBIN* "models" (i.e. is correct with respect to) *FIND*, two conditions must be established.

The first condition, the "domain condition", shows that the pre-condition is sufficiently wide and has the form, for the binary tree example:

$$(\forall t \in Bintree)(pre\text{-}FIND(retr(t),k) \supset pre\text{-}FINDBIN(t,k))$$

Rewriting this using the definitions gives:

$$(\forall t \in Bintree)(k \in \underline{dom}\, retr(t) \supset k \in collkeys(t))$$

This can be proved by structural induction on *Bintree* - the details of the proof are not given here, but can be found in [Fielding 80a].

The second condition is known as the "results condition" and requires that given any state satisfying the pre-condition, and the result state after being operated on by the operation on the representation (i.e. a state satisfying the post-condition), this pair of states must satisfy the post-condition of the operation on the abstraction when viewed through the retrieve function. The form of this condition for this example is:

$$(\forall t \in Bintree)(pre\text{-}FIND(retr(t),k) \wedge post\text{-}FINDBIN(t,k,t',d) \supset$$
$$post\text{-}FIND(retr(t),k,retr(t'),d))$$

Expanding this gives:

$$(\forall t \in Bintree)(k \in \underline{dom}\, retr(t) \wedge t'=t \wedge d=findb(t,k) \supset$$
$$retr(t')=retr(t) \wedge d=(retr(t))(k))$$

Both operations are required to be identities on states so that it is only necessary to show:

$(\forall t \in Bintree)(k \in \underline{dom}\, retr(t) \wedge d = findb(t,k) \supset d = (retr(t))(k))$

This proof can again be done by structural induction and the details are given in [Fielding 80a].

The version of the *INSERT* operation which is to work on the binary tree representation is:

$INSERTBIN: Key \times Data \Rightarrow$
$pre\text{-}INSERTBIN(t,k,d) \quad \underline{\Delta}\ \neg(k \in collkeys(t))$
$post\text{-}INSERTBIN(t,k,d,t') \ \underline{\Delta}\ t' = insb(t,k,d)$

$insb: Bintree \times Key \times Data \xrightarrow{\sim} Bintree$
$pre\text{-}insb(t,k,d)\ \underline{\Delta}\ \neg(k \in collkeys(t))$
$insb(t,k,d)\ \underline{\Delta}$
$\quad \underline{if}\ t = \underline{nil}\ \underline{then}\ mk\text{-}Binnode(\underline{nil},k,d,\underline{nil})$
$\quad \underline{else}\ (\underline{let}\ mk\text{-}Binnode(lt,mk,md,rt) = t \quad \underline{in}$
$\qquad \underline{if}\ k < mk\ \underline{then}\ mk\text{-}Binnode(insb(lt,k,d),mk,md,rt)$
$\qquad \underline{else}\ mk\text{-}Binnode(lt,mk,md,insb(rt,k,d)))$

Since *INSERTBIN* actually changes the tree, it is necessary to show "preservation of validity". This proof is given in detail to illustrate a proof by structural induction. It is required to show that if *t* is valid (i.e. is in *Bintree*) then:

$\neg(k \in collkeys(t)) \wedge t' = insb(t,k,d) \supset$
$\qquad t' \in Bintree \wedge collkeys(t') = collkeys(t) \cup \{k\}$

As a basis, assume that:

$t = \underline{nil}$

then:

$insb(t,k,d)\ \underline{\Delta}\ mk\text{-}Binnode(\underline{nil},k,d,\underline{nil})$

The definition of *invnd* gives:

$invnd(mk\text{-}Binnode(\underline{nil},k,d,\underline{nil}))$
$= \ (\forall lk \in collkeys(\underline{nil}))(lk < k) \wedge (\forall rk \in collkeys(\underline{nil}))(k < rk)$
$= \ \underline{true}$

and:

collkeys(mk-Binnode(nil,k,d,nil)) = {*k*}

This base case is like the argument for zero in a proof by mathematical induction on the natural numbers. In a mathematical induction proof, the induction step is from *n-1* to *n*; with structural induction the step is from sub-trees to trees built from such sub-trees. As induction hypothesis it is assumed that *insb* applied to either *t1* or *t2* preserves validity and adds the given key. Then:

insb(mk-Binnode(t1,mk,md,t2),k,d) =
    if k<mk then mk-Binnode(insb(t1,k,d),mk,md,t2)
    else mk-Binnode(t1,mk,md,insb(t2,k,d))

Consider the case:

k<mk

by induction hypothesis:

insb(t1,k,d)∈Bintree ∧ *collkeys(insb(t1,k,d))=collkeys(t1)*∪{*k*}

Thus:

(∀lk∈collkeys(insb(t1,k,d)))(lk<mk)

because of the assumption of validity on the starting tree and the case assumption. Furthermore:

collkeys(mk-Binnode(insb(t1,k,d),mk,md,t2))
= *collkeys(insb(t1,k,d))* ∪ {*mk*} ∪ *collkeys(t2)*
= *collkeys(t1)* ∪ {*mk*} ∪ *collkeys(t2)* ∪ {*k*}
= *collkeys(mk-Binnode(t1,mk,md,t2))* ∪ {*k*}

as required. The other case (*mk<k*) is proved in the same way. Thus the preservation of validity follows for all trees.

Establishing that *INSERTBIN* models *INSERT* requires that the domain and result conditions be established. The domain condition requires:

(∀t∈Bintree)(pre-INSERT(retr(t),k,d) ⊃ *pre-INSERTBIN(t,k,d))*

which becomes:

$(\forall t \in Bintree)(\neg(k \in \underline{dom} retr(t)) \supset \neg(k \in collkeys(t)))$

which is proved exactly as for *FINDBIN*. The result rule becomes:

$$(\forall t \in Bintree)(pre\text{-}INSERT(retr(t),k,d) \wedge post\text{-}INSERTBIN(t,k,d,t') \supset post\text{-}INSERT(retr(t),k,d,retr(t')))$$

which expands to:

$$(\forall t \in Bintree)(\neg(k \in \underline{dom} retr(t)) \wedge t'=insb(t,k,d) \supset retr(t')=retr(t) \cup [k \mapsto d])$$

The reader can use this example to practice proof by structural induction. The final operation to be provided on binary trees is:

```
DELETEBIN: Key =>
pre-DELETEBIN(t,k)      ≜ k∈collkeys(t)
post-DELETEBIN(t,k,t')  ≜ t'=delb(t,k)

delb: Bintree × Key ⇀ Bintree
pre-delb(t,k) ≜ k ∈ collkeys(t)
delb(mk-Binnode(lt,mk,md,rt),k) ≜
    if k<mk then mk-Binnode(delb(lt,k),mk,md,rt)
    else if mk<k then mk-Binnode(lt,mk,md,delb(rt,k))
           else if lt=nil ∧ rt=nil then nil
                else if lt=nil
                     then (let (rk,rd,rt') = bringlo(rt) in
                              mk-Binnode(lt,rk,rd,rt'))
                     else (let (lk,ld,lt') = bringhi(lt) in
                              mk-Binnode(lt',lk,ld,rt))

bringlo: Bintree ⇀ Key × Data × Bintree
pre-bringlo(t) ≜ t≠nil
bringlo(mk-Binnode(lt,k,d,rt)) ≜
    if lt≠nil then (let (lk,ld,lt') = bringlo(lt) in
                   (lk,ld,mk-Binnode(lt',k,d,rt)))
    else if rt=nil then (k,d,nil)
         else (let (rk,rd,rt') = bringlo(rt) in
              (k,d,mk-Binnode(nil,rk,rd,rt')))
```

(The *bringhi* function is similar to *bringlo*.) It is interesting to observe that, even in the simple case of binary trees, deletion is more complex than insertion; this observation will apply with more force in the case of B-trees. The fact that *DELETEBIN* preserves validity can again be proved by structural induction. The base case must be a tree containing exactly the key to be deleted (i.e. $mk\text{-}Binnode(\underline{nil},k,d,\underline{nil})$) and a subsidiary proof is required to show that:

$$bringlo(t)=(k,d,t') \supset$$
$$\quad t'\in Bintree \wedge collkeys(t)=collkeys(t')\cup\{k\} \wedge$$
$$\quad d=retr(t)(k) \wedge (\forall k'\in collks(t'))(k<k')$$

The domain condition for *DELETEBIN* is similar to those above; the reader should be able to produce the appropriate results condition. (Another exercise for the interested reader is to design and justify a version of *DELETEBIN* which identifies the special case where exactly one subnode is nil and avoid the "bring" operation.)

The operations *FINDBIN*, *INSERTBIN* and *DELETEBIN* show the main techniques for manipulating binary trees. The *Binarytree* object, however, is not directly realizable in Pascal. A further step of refinement is needed to represent the tree-like structures using pointers and variables on the heap. The Pascal "heap" can be thought of as a mapping from pointers (*Ptr*) to node representations (*Binnoderep*); the root of the tree is an (optionally *nil*) pointer. Thus the state of the actual program is:

$$Bintreerep :: ROOT: [Ptr]$$
$$\qquad HEAP: (Ptr \underset{m}{\to} Binnoderep)$$

$$Binnoderep :: lptr: [Ptr]$$
$$\qquad key : Key$$
$$\qquad data: Data$$
$$\qquad rptr: [Ptr]$$

This representation requires an invariant stating that all non-*nil* pointers are defined and that the pointers define a tree structure (there are no joins or loops). The retrieve function (to *Bintree*) is obvious and is not given here. It is the essence of the "rigorous approach" to use formal definitions and proofs as appropriate. The knowledge of the formal basis makes it possible to complete details if necessary. The code corresponding to the above development is now given. The fact that the tree is updated in-place, makes some of the code simpler than the "functional programming" style used above. Code to trap situations where operations are used outside their pre-conditions has also been included.

```
program bintree;
type key  = integer;
     ptr  = ↑ node;
     node = record lptr: ptr;
                   key : key;
                   data: char;
                   rptr: ptr
            end;
var root: ptr;

function find(p:ptr; k:key): char;
begin
    if p=nil then writeln('error - not found')
    else with p↑ do
            begin
               if key=k then find := data
               else if k<key then find := find(lptr,k)
                    else find := find(rptr,k)
            end
end;

procedure add(var p:ptr; k:key; d:char);
begin
    if p=nil
       then begin
               new(p);
               with p↑ do
                  begin
                     key := k; data := d; lptr := nil; rptr := nil
                  end
            end
       else with p↑ do
               begin
                  if k<key then add(lptr,k,d)
                  else if key<k then add(rptr,k,d)
                       else writeln('error - not inserted',k)
               end
end;
```

```
procedure delete(var p:ptr; k:key);
   procedure bringlo(var p: ptr; var k:key; var d:char);
   begin
      with p↑ do
         if lptr<>nil then bringlo(lptr,k,d)
         else begin
                 k := key; d := data;
                 if rptr = nil then dispose(p)
                 else bringlo(rptr,key,data)
              end
   end;
   procedure bringhi(var p:ptr; var k:key; var d:char);
   begin
      with p↑ do
         if rptr<>nil then bringhi(rptr,k,d)
         else begin
                 k := key; d := data;
                 if lptr = nil then dispose(p)
                 else bringhi(lptr,key,data)
              end
   end;
begin
   if p=nil then writeln('error - key not found',k)
   else with p↑ do
      begin
         if k<key then delete(lptr,k)
         else if key < k then delete(rptr,k)
              else if (lptr=nil) ∧ (rptr=nil) then dispose(p)
                   else if  rptr<>nil  then  bringlo(rptr,key,data)
                        else bringhi(lptr,key,data)
      end
end { delete };
:
:
end.
```

The code given above is so close to the design on abstract trees that detailed proofs are not given. If, however, it were decided to avoid the use of recursion and program the operations via loops, the rules of operation decomposition of [Jones 80a] (using loop invariants etc.) could be used.

10.3 B-TREE OVERVIEW

B-trees provide a useful structure for storing maps from keys to data. There is minimal space overhead for small indexes while very large ones support fast information retrieval. As described in the preceding section, binary trees can become unbalanced. Although there is much work published on balancing binary trees, one of the attractions of B-trees is the relative simplicity of update algorithms which preserve balance. Perhaps the decisive reason for using B-trees is the ability to choose the "order" of the tree so that node size approximates to the physical block size of the storage medium on which the index is to be stored. For descriptions of B-trees see [Comer 79a, Knuth 75a, Wirth 76a].

If the degree of a node is defined to be the number of sons it has and a leaf is a terminal node which has no sons, then a B-tree of order m satisfies:

(a) The degree of a non-leaf node, other than the root, lies between bounds $m+1$ and $2m+1$.

(b) The degree of the root is between bounds 2 and $2m+1$, unless it is a leaf.

(c) If the root is a leaf, it may contain from 0 to $2m$ keys. Otherwise the number of keys contained in any node lies between bounds m and $2m$ and a non-leaf node with k sons will contain $k-1$ keys.

(d) All the leaves occur at the same depth (i.e. the tree is balanced).

In a B-tree the data associated with a key occurs in the node containing the key. However a Bplus-tree is a special form of B-tree which has all key-data pairs in the leaves and non-leaf nodes do not contain data. The keys in non-leaf nodes serve as separators and are usually copies of some of the keys which are the maximum keys of the leaf nodes. Deletion may sometimes cause non-key values to be left as separators.

The leaves of a Bplus-tree may be linked which facilitates sequential processing of the data by the "next" operation.

A description of the algorithms for performing the find, insert and delete operations on the Bplus-tree is given in section 4 below.

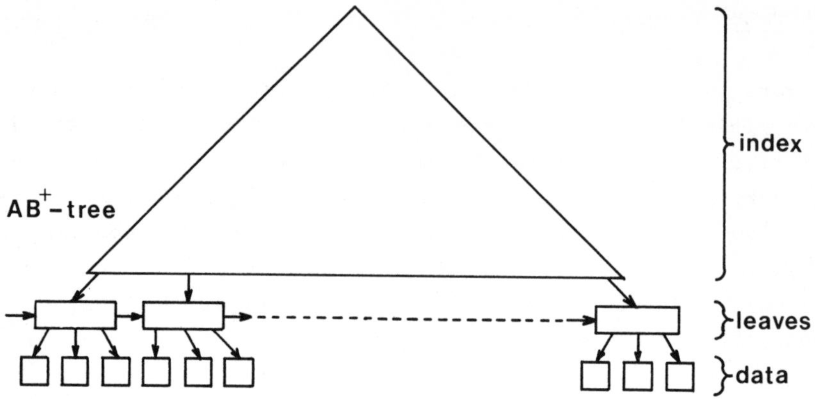

Fig. 1

The Bplus-tree is, of couse, a representation of the mapping (*Mkd*); the operations whose development is to be considered are already specified as *FIND*, *INSERT* and *DELETE*.

10.4 FIRST REPRESENTATION

An essential part of documenting a design is to decide on the order in which design decisions are to be recorded. This representation embodies the decision to use tree-like structures but does not consider issues of order of keys within sub-nodes (the choice between nodes can be thought of for now as being made by searching all sub-nodes!) The B-tree used in this section poses the main problems of node splitting, merging etc. but is sufficiently abstract to make these operations easier to comprehend and justify. It is interesting to note that proving preservation of validity by *INSERTB* and *DELETEB* is more difficult than showing that the individual operations model the specifications.

The "order" of the tree (m) is used in defining the size bounds on nodes. Rather than having an extra argument to most functions, m is referred to freely below. The overall structure of the representation considered in this section is:

$Btree = Node$

$invb(t) \triangleq t \in Inode \supset 2 \leq size(t) \wedge (\forall sn \in t)(invlosize(sn))$

$Node = Inode \mid Tnode$

Thus the *Node* at the root has rather looser lower bounds on size than other nodes. All nodes, however, share the same upper bounds.

$$Tnode = Key \underset{m}{\rightarrow} Data$$

$$invt(tn) \quad \triangleq \; invhisize(tn)$$

$$Inode = Node\text{-}set$$

$$invi(in) \quad \triangleq \; invhisize(in) \wedge balanced(in) \wedge disjks(in)$$

$$size(n) \quad \triangleq \; \underline{if}\ n \in Tnode\ \underline{then}\ \underline{card}\ \underline{dom} n\ \underline{else}\ \underline{card} n$$

$$invlosize(n) \quad \triangleq \; size(n) \geq minisize(n) \wedge (n \in Inode \supset (\forall sn \in n)(invlosize(sn)))$$

$$invhisize(n) \quad \triangleq \; size(n) \leq maxisize(n)$$

$$minisize(n) \quad \triangleq \; \underline{if}\ n \in Tnode\ \underline{then}\ m\ \underline{else}\ m+1$$

$$maxsize(n) \quad \triangleq \; \underline{if}\ n \in Tnode\ \underline{then}\ 2*m\ \underline{else}\ 2*m+1$$

A major aspect of the invariant for an *Inode* is that all *(Tnode)* leaves are at the same depth:

$$balanced(in) \quad \triangleq \; (\exists d \in Nat)(\forall sn \in in)(deptheq(sn,d))$$

$$deptheq(n,d) \quad \triangleq \; \underline{if}\ n \in Tnode\ \underline{then}\ d=1\ \underline{else}\ (\forall sn \in n)(deptheq(sn,d-1))$$

Although this representation is not fixing the way in which keys are split between nodes, it is necessary to ensure that keys are contained in at most one sub-node:

$$disjks(in) \quad \triangleq \; (\forall sn1, sn2 \in in)(sn1 = sn2 \vee is\text{-}disj(collks(sn1), collks(sn2)))$$

$$collks(n) \quad \triangleq \; \underline{if}\ n \in Tnode\ \underline{then}\ \underline{dom} n\ \underline{else}\ \underline{union}\{collks(sn) \mid sn \in n\}$$

$$is\text{-}disj(s1,s2) \; \triangleq \; \neg(\exists e)(e \in s1 \wedge e \in s2)$$

Whenever the sets (Btree, Node etc.) are referred to below, it is assumed that only "valid" objects which satisfy these invariants are to be considered.

The relation between *Btree* and *Mkd* is expressed by the following retrieve function:

$$retrn(n) \triangleq \underline{if}\ n \in Tnode\ \underline{then}\ n\ \underline{else}\ \underline{merge}\{retrn(sn) \mid sn \in n\}$$

The disjoint keys condition on *Inodes* ensures that *retrn* is defined for all (valid) *Btrees*.

The adequacy condition requires that:

$$(\forall m \in Mkd)(\exists t \in Btree)(m = retrn(t))$$

This can be proved by induction on $\underline{dom}m$ but notice that particular care is required with the basis: it is to permit the representation of small maps that *invlosize* is not applied to the root.

A useful function to aid readability of what follows is:

$$kof\colon Key \times Node \to Bool$$
$$kof(k,n) \triangleq k \in collks(n)$$

An immediate lemma, which can be proved by structural induction, is:

$$\underline{dom}retrn(n) = \{k \mid kof(k,n)\}$$

The *FINDB* operation can be explained in terms of Figure 2.

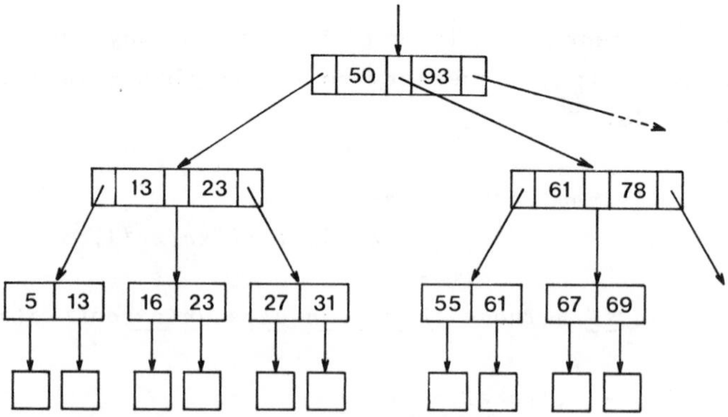

Fig. 2

Suppose that key *67* is to be found. The search starts at the root and 3 possible paths may be taken. For keys ≤ 50 the leftmost path would be taken; for keys > *50* and ≤ *93* the centre path is chosen and for keys > *93* the rightmost path is selected. This selection process is repeated at each node until a leaf is reached. If a match is not found in the leaf, then the key is not in the tree. The find must search all the way to a leaf as all the keys reside in the leaves, and the key values in non-leaf nodes simply serve as separators: these nodes do not contain data. (The keys used in examples indicate how selection is achieved in the final algorithm - in the current representation there are no keys in *Inodes*.)

Formally:

$FINDB: Key \Rightarrow Data$
$pre\text{-}FINDB(t,k) \quad \triangleq\ kof(k,n)$
$post\text{-}FINDB(t,k,t',d) \quad \triangleq\ t'=t \wedge d=find(k,t)$

$find: Key \times Node \xrightarrow{\sim} Data$
$pre\text{-}find(k,n) \quad \triangleq\ kof(k,n)$
$find(k,n) \quad \triangleq\ \underline{if}\ n \in Tnode\ \underline{then}\ n(k)\ \underline{else}\ find(k,sel(n,k))$

$sel: Inode \times Key \xrightarrow{\sim} Node$
$pre\text{-}sel(in,k) \quad \triangleq\ kof(k,in)$
$post\text{-}sel(in,k,n) \quad \triangleq\ n \in in \wedge kof(k,n)$

For valid nodes, a lemma relating *find* and *retrn* is:

$$kof(k,n) \supset find(k,n)=retrn(n)(k)$$

this can be proved by structural induction on the form of *Node*: for elements of *Tnode* the result is immediate; for elements of *Inode* the post-condition of *sel* is required.

The fact that *FINDB* preserves validity is immediate since it does not change the state. The domain condition follows immediately from the lemma on *retrn* and *kof*. The results condition follows immediately from the lemma relating *find* and *retrn*.

The *INSERTB* operation can be thought of as working in two stages. Firstly a find operation is carried out, which must progress all the way down to the correct leaf for insertion. The insertion takes place in the leaf and the balance of the tree is restored, if necessary, by a procedure which works up from the leaf to the root. If the find stops at a leaf that is not full, the new key and data are simply inserted. If however, the leaf is full (i.e. it contains *2m* keys) it must be "split" into two nodes. The smallest *m* keys and the associated data form one node; the largest *m* keys and data form the second node; a copy of the middle key is inserted into the keylist of the parent node to become a separator. If the parent node is not full, the key can be added and the insertion process completed. If the parent node is full, it must be split in a similar manner, but instead of only a copy of the middle key being promoted to the parent node, the actual key is promoted. If the splitting process propagates all the way to the root, and it also has to be split, then the tree increases one level in height: it grows from the root.

For example insertion in a tree of order 1. Consider insertion of the key *56* into:

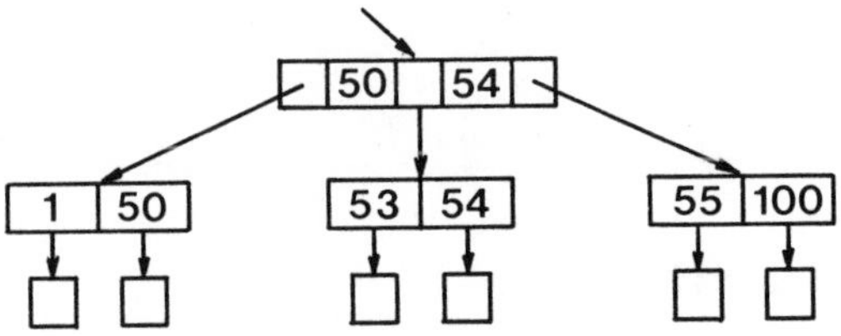

Fig. 3

yields:

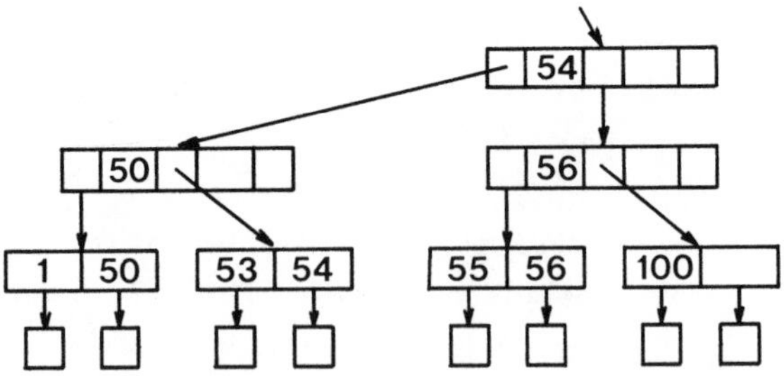

Fig. 4

Formally:

INSERTB: Key × Data =>

$pre\text{-}INSERTB(t,k,d) \triangleq \neg kof(k,n)$

$post\text{-}INSERTB(t,k,d,t') \triangleq \underline{let}\ ns' = insn(t,k,d)\ \underline{in}$
$\quad t' = \underline{if}\ \underline{card}ns'=1\ \underline{then}\ el(ns')\ \underline{else}\ ns'$

$insn: Node \times Key \times Data \xrightarrow{\sim} Node\text{-}set$

$pre\text{-}insn(n,k,d) \triangleq \neg kof(k,n)$

$insn(n,k,d) \triangleq \underline{if}\ n\in Tnode\ \underline{then}\ (\underline{let}\ n' = n \cup [k\mapsto d]\ \underline{in}$
$\quad \underline{if}\ invhisize(n')\ \underline{then}\ \{n'\}$
$\quad \underline{else}\ \{(n'|ks)\ |\ ks\in splits(\underline{dom}n')\})$
$\underline{else}\ (\underline{let}\ sn\in n\ \underline{in}$
$\quad \underline{let}\ sns' = insn(sn,k,d)\ \underline{in}$
$\quad \underline{let}\ n' = (n-\{sn\}) \cup sns'\ \underline{in}$
$\quad \underline{if}\ invhsize(n')\ \underline{then}\ \{n'\}$
$\quad \underline{else}\ splits(n')$

$el: X\text{-}set \xrightarrow{\sim} X$

$pre\text{-}el(s) \triangleq \underline{card}s = 1$

$post\text{-}el(s,e) \triangleq \{e\} = s$

$splits: X\text{-}set \rightarrow (X\text{-}set)\text{-}set$

$post\text{-}splits(s,p) \triangleq (\exists s1,s2)(p=\{s1,s2\} \wedge s1\cup s2=s \wedge is\text{-}disj(s1,s2) \wedge$
$\quad (\exists i\in Nat0)(\forall ss\in p)(i\leq \underline{card}ss\leq i+1)$

Notice the non-deterministic aspects of this description: the node in which new data is inserted is not determined nor is the rule for splitting keys between nodes. It is now necessary to show that *INSERTB* preserves validity of *Btree*. Once again, structural induction is used - but here it is desirable to separate the base case as three lemmas. For each of these lemmas, assume:

$tn\in Tnode,\quad \neg kof(k,tn),\quad ns'=insn(tn,k,d)$

The first lemma ensures basic validity and defines the resulting keyset:

$ns'\in Tnode\text{-}set \wedge 1<size(ns')<2 \wedge$
$disjks(ns') \wedge collks(ns')=collks(tn)\cup\{k\}$

the proof is as follows: $\underline{let}\ n' = tn \cup [k \mapsto d]$

consider the case: $invhisize(n')$
$\quad ns'=\{n'\}$

and all results are immediate. Alternatively:

$\neg invhisize(n')$
$ns' = \{(n'|ks) \mid ks \in splits(\underline{dom}\, n')\}$

from *splits* and *invhisize*:

$(\forall snm' \in ns')(invhisize(snm'))$
$disjks(ns')$
$\underline{card}\, ns' = 2$
$collks(ns') = collks(n')$
$\qquad = collks(tn) \cup \{k\}$

which concludes the proof.

The second lemma establishes preservation of *invlosize*:

$invlosize(tn) \supset (\forall nsm' \in ns')(invlosize(nsm'))$

The third lemma is:

$retrn(ns') = retrn(tn) \cup [k \mapsto d]$

The interested reader should find these proofs straightforward. The corresponding three lemmas for (general) elements of *Node* each assume:

$n \in Node, \quad \neg kof(k,n), \quad ns' = insn(n,k,d)$

The lemma on basic validity is:

$ns' \in Node\text{-}set \wedge 1 < size(ns') < 2 \wedge$
$(\forall nsn' \in ns')(deptheq(nsn',d) = deptheq(n,d)) \wedge$
$disjks(ns') \wedge collks(ns') = collks(n) \cup \{k\}$

The proof is by structural induction on *Node*. The basis is an immediate consequence of the corresponding lemma on *Tnodes*. For the induction step ($n \in Inode$):

$\underline{let}\ sn \in n$
$\underline{let}\ sns' = insn(sn, \dot{k}, d)$

By induction hypothesis:

$sns' \in Node\text{-}set \wedge 1 \leq size(sns') \leq 2 \wedge$
$(\forall snsn' \in sns')(deptheq(snsn',d) = deptheq(sn,d)) \wedge$
$disjks(sns') \wedge collks(sns') = collks(sn) \cup \{k\}$

__let__ $n' = (n - \{sn\}) \cup sns'$

so:

$n' \in Node\text{-}set \wedge size(n) \leq size(n') \leq size(n)+1 \wedge$
$(\forall nsn' \in n')(deptheq(nsn',d) = deptheq(n,d+1)) \wedge$
$disjks(n') \wedge collks(n') = collks(n) \cup \{k\}$

It is now only necesssary to consider cases defined by *invhisize* to conclude the proof.

The lemma on the lower bounds of size is:

$invlosize(n) \supset (\forall snm' \in ns')(invlosize(nsm'))$

and the final lemma on the result is:

$retrn(ns') = retrn(n) \cup [k \mapsto d]$

Both of these lemmas are proved by structural induction using the corresponding *Tnode* results for the basis.

The preservation of validity is an immediate consequence of the first two of the general lemmas. The domain condition follows from the original lemma relating *retrn* and *kof*. The results condition follows from the last lemma discussed.

The *DELETEB* operation is like insertion in that it occurs in two stages, starting with a find to locate the leaf containing the key to be deleted. After this key has been removed, if the leaf then has less than *m* keys, balance the leaf in question; if greater than *2m*, the keys of the two nodes are evenly divided between the nodes and the original separator key in the parent node is overwritten with a copy of the middle key of the two nodes concerned ("redistribution"). If the sum of the keys is less than *2m*, the leaves are "merged" (the opposite of splitting) and the separator key in the parent node is discarded.

Redistribution and merging are slightly different in non-leaf nodes. If the redistribution of two non-leaf nodes occurs, the separator key in the parent node is replaced by the middle key of the two nodes concerned. If a merge occurs in two non-leaf nodes, the separator key in the parent node is pulled down and added to the combined node. If merging propagates all the way up to the root the height of the tree can decrease by one level.

For example deletion in a B-tree of order 2:

(a) Redistribution in leaf nodes

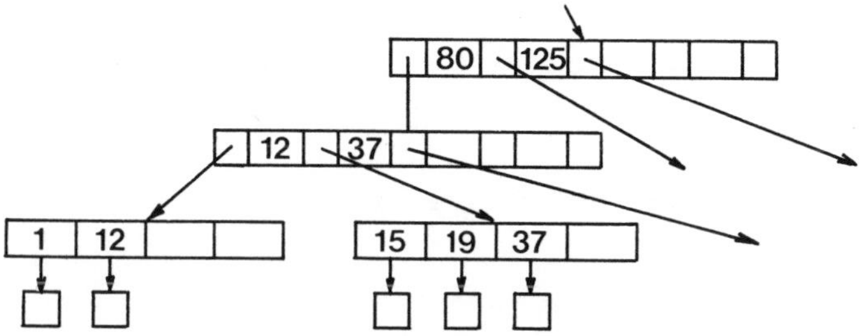

Fig. 5

Deleting key *12* produces:

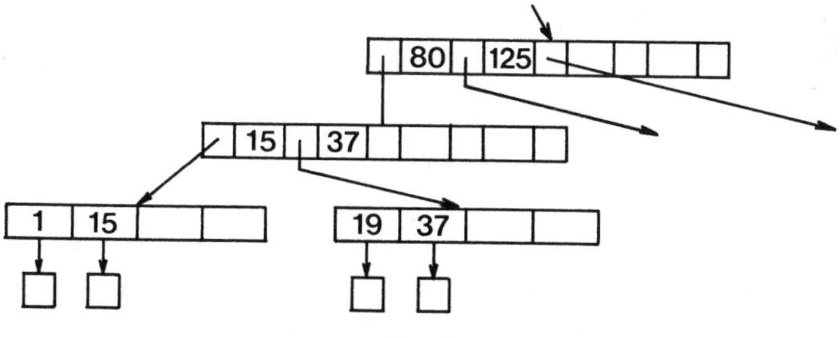

Fig. 6

(b) Merging in leaf nodes:

Now, deleting key *15* produces:

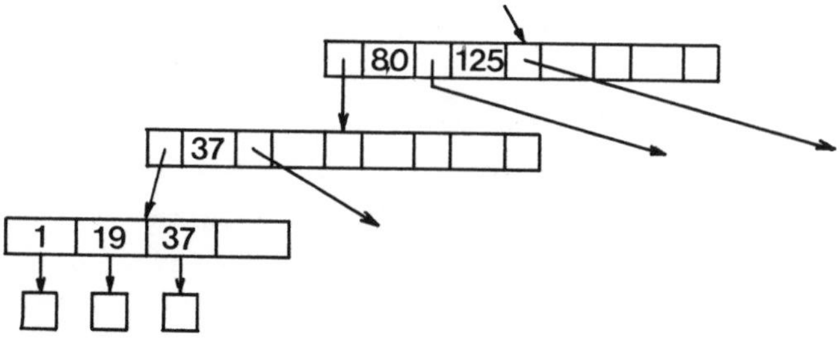

Fig. 7

(c) Redistribution in non-leaf nodes - starting with:

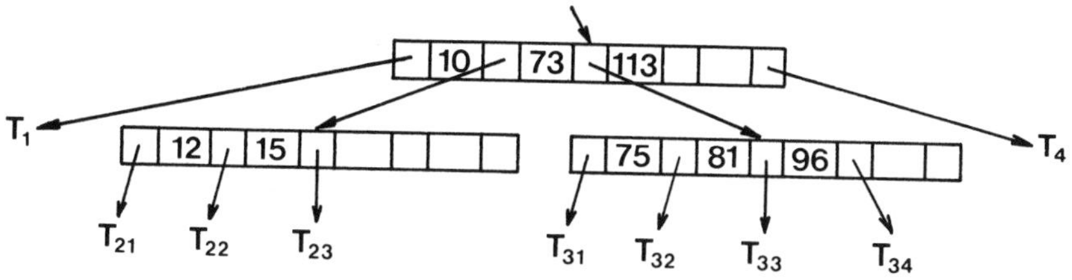

Fig. 8

Merging of nodes T_{22} and T_{23} causes redistribution:

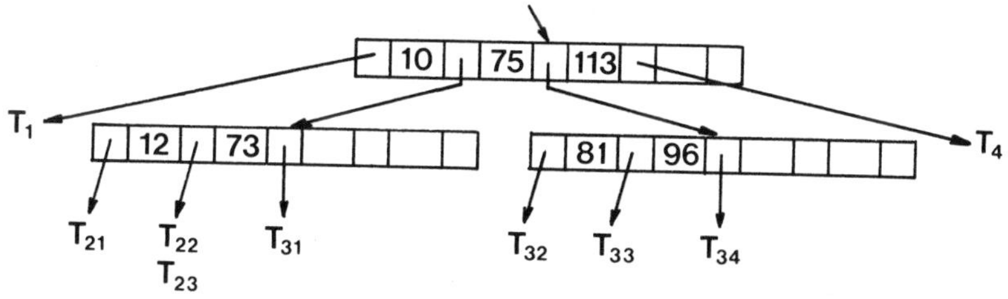

Fig. 9

(d) Merging in non-leaf nodes - a further merge of T_{33}/T_{34} results in:

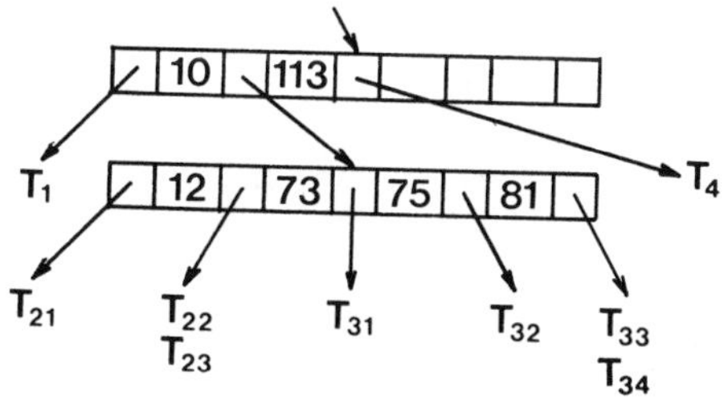

Fig. 10

Formally:

```
DELETEB: Key =>
pre-DELETEB(t,k)      ≜ kof(k,t)
post-DELETEB(t,k,t') ≜
    let rn = deln(t,k) in
    t' = if rn∈Tnode ∧ size(rn)=1 then el(rn) else rn

deln: Node × Key ⥲ Node
pre-deln(n,k) ≜ kof(k,n)
deln(n,k) ≜
    if n∈Tnode then n\{k}
    else (let cn = sel(n,k)  in
          let rn = del(cn,k) in
          if invlosize(rn) then (n-{cn})∪{rn}
          else (let nn∈n-{cn} in
                let rest = n-{cn,nn} in
                if size(rn)+size(nn)<2*minsize(rn) then rest∪{rn∪nn}
                else if cn ∈ Inode
                     then rest ∪ {nsn           | nsn∈splits(rn∪nn)}
                     else rest ∪ {((rn∪nn)|ks)  | ks∈splits(dom rn∪dom nn)}))
```

As with the correctness of the B-tree insert operation, the key to justifying *DELETEB* is a series of lemmas. Two lemmas concern *Tnodes* and assume:

$$tn \in Tnode, \quad kof(k,tn), \quad tn' = deln(tn,k)$$

The basic validity result is:

$$tn' \in Tnode \wedge size(tn') = size(tn) - 1 \wedge collks(tn') = collks(tn) - \{k\}$$

There is no guarantee about preserving the minimum size of a *Tnode*. The result is such that:

$$retrn(tn') = retrn(tn) \setminus \{k\}$$

Both of these lemmas are straightforward. Proofs by induction, using the above results, can be given for three lemmas on general nodes - for each assume:

$n \in Node$, $kof(k,n)$, $n'=deln(n,k)$

The three lemmas are:

$$n' \in Node \wedge size(n') < size(n) \wedge$$
$$(deptheq(n',d)=deptheq(n,d)) \wedge collks(n')=collks(n)-\{k\}$$

$$invlosize(n) \wedge n' \in Inode \supset (\forall sn' \in n')(invlosize(sn'))$$

$$retrn(n') = retrn(n) \setminus \{k\}$$

These lemmas make the proof both of preservation of validity and that *DELETEB* models *DELETE* straightforward.

10.5 SECOND REPRESENTATION

Having solved the crucial problem of balancing the trees, this stage of refinement can introduce the keys into *Inodes*. This makes it possible to remove the arbitrary selection of sub-nodes for insertion and the completely unrealistic specification of *sel*. The invariant of this representation can conveniently be split into those constraints already considered and those (e.g. order of the key lists) which could not have been stated earlier. (The authors of this paper are grateful to Lockwood Morris for proposing this split.) This division significantly simplifies the proof.

The definition of the new representation is:

$$
\begin{array}{ll}
Btreep & = Nodep \\
invp(t) & \triangleq invb(retrb(t)) \\
Nodep & = Tnodep \mid Inodep \\
Tnodep & = Key \underset{m}{\rightarrow} Data \\
invtp(tnp) & \triangleq invt(retrn(tnp)) \\
Inodep & :: \ s\text{-}keyl{:}Key^{+} \quad s\text{-}treel{:}Nodep^{+}
\end{array}
$$

$$
\begin{array}{ll}
invip(inp) & \triangleq invi(retrn(inp)) \wedge \\
& (\underline{let}\ mk\text{-}Inodep(kl,tl) = inp\ \underline{in} \\
& \ \underline{len}kl = \underline{len}tl-1 \wedge \\
& \ (\forall i \in \underline{inds}\ kl)(setle(collksp(tl[i]),\{kl[i]\}) \wedge \\
& \qquad setl(\{kl[i]\},collksp(tl[i+1]))))
\end{array}
$$

Notice, that it is a consequence of *invip* that the keylist should be ordered.

$$collksp(n) \triangleq \underline{if}\ n \in Tnode\ \underline{then}\ \underline{dom}\ n$$
$$\underline{else}\ \underline{union}\{collksp(sn) \mid sn \in \underline{elems}\, s\text{-}treel(n)\}$$

The relations between sets of keys are:

$$setle(ks1,ks2) \triangleq (\forall k1 \in ks1, k2 \in ks2)(k1 \leq k2)$$

$$setl(ks1,ks2) \triangleq (\forall k1 \in ks1, k2 \in ks2)(k1 < k2)$$

The necessary retrieve function is:

$$retrb: Nodep \to Node$$
$$retrb(np) \triangleq \underline{if}\ np \in Tnodep\ \underline{then}\ np$$
$$\underline{else}\ \{retrb(s\text{-}treel(np)[i]) \mid i \in \underline{inds}\, s\text{-}treel(np)\}$$

The development and justification of this stage is not pursued in detail. It is, however, worth noticing an unusual feature of this step of data refinement. Because of the freedom to place keys in any order in a *Btree*, not all elements can be represented by a *Btreep*. Strictly speaking, this violates the adequacy condition. There is an explanation in [Jones 80a] as to how to deal with this general problem. Here, however, it is easier to think of the algorithms at this level resolving non-determinacy of the higher level: since the *Btree* algorithms were proven without constraint, any algorithms which simply define the choice to be made are correct. The remaining part of the refinement (i.e. the addition of keylists) fits the usual scheme for data refinement.

Only the find operation is considered on this representation (see [Fielding 80a] for details of the others).

$$FINDP: Key \Rightarrow Data$$
$$pre\text{-}FINDP(tp,k) \triangleq kofp(k,tp)$$
$$post\text{-}FINDP(tp,k,tp',d) \triangleq tp'=tp \wedge d=findp(k,tp)$$

$$kofp(k,np) \triangleq k \in collksp(np)$$

$$findp: Key \times Nodep \xrightarrow{\sim} Data$$
$$pre\text{-}findp(k,np) \triangleq kofp(k,np)$$

$$findp(k,np) \quad \triangleq \; \underline{if}\ np \in Tnodep\ \underline{then}\ np(k)$$
$$\underline{else}\ (\underline{let}\ i = indexp(k, s\text{-}keyl(np))\ \underline{in}$$
$$findp(k, s\text{-}treel(np)[i]))$$

$$indexp\colon Key \times Key^{*} \rightarrow Nat$$
$$pre\text{-}indexp(k,kl) \quad \triangleq \; is\text{-}ordered(kl)$$
$$post\text{-}indexp(k,kl,i) \quad \triangleq \; k \le \underline{hd}\,kl \land i=1 \lor kl(\underline{len}\ kl) < k \land i = \underline{len}\,kl+1$$
$$\lor\ kl[i-1] < k \le kl[i]$$

$$is\text{-}ordered\colon Key^{*} \rightarrow Bool$$

Although the indirect definition of part of the invariant (via *retrb* and *invb*) simplifies the proof at this level, it would be necessary to "bring down" the invariant before proceeding to the next stage. This would involve defining functions such as *invhisizep*.

10.6 FURTHER DEVELOPMENT

The step of representing *Btreep* in, say, Pascal is very similar to the task of representing binary trees considered in section 2 above. Code for UCSD Pascal for all three operations is given in [Fielding 80a]. Possible further extensions include:

The implementation of the *NEXT* operation, for which provision has already been made in the record layout.

The implementation of Bplus-trees using disk files and disk file addresses rather than storage and *pointer* variables and the extension of this to provide a separate file access package for general use (the difficulties of the strong typing of Pascal have to be overcome to achieve this extension).

After the above two extensions the implementation of recovery procedures becomes possible.

Finally, allowing features such as key compression and multi-user access are also possible future developments.

CHAPTER 11

STEPWISE TRANSFORMATION OF SOFTWARE ARCHITECTURES

This chapter provides a further example of the use of a formal specification as the basis of architecture and design. The problem chosen is that of a file-handler and is thus close to the topic of database systems. The stepwise development given here starts with a simple specification; the development considers a realization on disk storage. The techniques (e.g. data type invariants, object transformation) of chapter 10 are illustrated. One new aspect of VDM which is illuminated here is the use of a formal specification in evolving the architecture of a system.

Thus the techniques of object and operation transformation are employed as a means of conquering architectual specification complexities, and the techniques of data structure invariance and object abstraction functions are employed as a means of studying the evolving architecture, as well as a means for proving correctness of transformation. The transformation stages can as well be seen as exemplifying realization stages of development, such as proven correct in chapter 10.

(The present chapter is based on [Bjørner 81a].)

CONTENTS

11.0 INTRODUCTION

Background

Sometimes software systems contain unnecessarily many, seemingly independent concepts. Occasionally a large number of such concepts are, however, necessary. Their presence being required in order to cope with a variety of "more-or-less" related concepts. (We think, here, of such things as functionality, efficiency, reliability, adaptability and extensibility, etc..) In all cases it is rather hard to grasp all the concepts, sort them out and interrelate them properly. In many cases this ability to dissect a software architecture into its many constituent notions is seriously hampered by opaque presentations of their interdependencies.

Proposed Remedies

Three possibilities for "solving" the apparent problem exist. Two extremes and a "middle road". Either, not to design such multi-concept systems at all; or, go on designing them in the old "hacker" fashion. Sometimes we shall choose the first extreme, sometimes the "middleroad" approach outlined below, but never the second "compromise".

Stepwise Development

By stepwise development of a software architecture we shall understand the following: first a model is established which exhibits, "as abstractly as deemed reasonable", the intrinsic concepts and facilities for which the software was intended in the first place. Then this model is subjected to object and/or operation transformations. We shall only illustrate object transformations. A sequence of such may be needed. Each step introduces further properties and/or details; none, some or all of which are exploited in exposing them to an external world. The order of the steps and their nature is dictated for example by technological and/or product-strategic considerations.

Overview of Example

Our example is that of a file handler system.

1. At the top level of architecture we focus our attention on files, file names, pages and page names as objects; and the creation and erasure of files, and writing, updating, reading, and deletion of pages. At this level files are named and consist of named pages.

At the top level no concession is made to the possible storing of files and their pages in such diverse storage media as foreground (fast access, "core"), or background (slow access, "disk") storage. The decision, which is hence recorded, of eventually implementing the storing of files and pages on disk-like devices, then predicates a need to be able to "look-up", reasonably fast, where, on possibly several disks, files and pages are stored.

2'. At the second level we therefore introduce first the notions of catalogues and directories, subsequently, as a further step of development, abstractions of the notions of main storage and disks.

Catalogues eventually record disk addresses of file directories, one per file. Directories eventually record disk addresses of pages. Our file system, at this level has one catalogue. We think, at the level of main storage and disks, of the one catalogue as always residing in main storage, whereas all directories are normally only stored on disks. To speed up access to disk pages we operate on main storage copies of directories. The intention to operate on a file is then indicated by its opening, an "act" which brings a disk directory copy into main storage. The intention to not operate further on a file is then indicated by its closing, an "act" which reverts the above copying.

2". Hence open and close operations are introduced.

They are file-related concepts primarily brought upon us by efficiency considerations. These efficiency concerns are rooted in insufficient technologies.

Neither at the top, nor at the second level of file handler architecting did we bother about the issue of reliability. We here define the reliability of our file handler as its ability to survive crashes. By a "crash" we restrictively mean anything which renders main storage information (catalogue and opened directories) useless. By total "survival" we mean the ability to continue (some time) after a "crash" as if no "crash" had occurred. (By "partial survival" we mean the ability to continue with at least a nonvoid sub-set of the files after a "crash" -- with the complement set of files being clearly identified.)

3. At the third level, building upon redundancies in catalogue-, directory and page recordings, we therefore introduce notions of checkpointing files and automatic recovery from "crashes".

11.1 TOP-LEVEL (File Handler) ARCHITECTURE (Stage 0)

Semantic Domains

Based on the immediately following English wording of what the 'state' Domain of our top-level file handler is we "derive" informally the formal Domain definitions.

The sole data structure of our file handler consists of a set of uniquely named files. Each file consists of a set of uniquely named pages. Let *Fn*, *Pn* and *PG* denote the further unspecified Domains of respectively file names, page names, pages. Then:

1. $FS \quad = Fn \underset{m}{\rightarrow} FILE$
2. $FILE = Pn \underset{m}{\rightarrow} PG$

We have completed our first task: that of specifying the most important aspects first, namely the semantic Domains. No specific invariants need be expressed, that is:

3. $inv\text{-}FS(fs) \triangleq \underline{true}$

Syntactic Domains

Five kinds of operations are applicable to our top-level file handler data: creation of new and erasure of old files, the write/update of new/old-, and the reading and deletion of existing, pages. Each of these operations can be thought of as being denoted by corresponding commands (or interface calls):

4. $Cmd = Crea \mid Eras \mid Put \mid Get \mid Del$

To create an initially empty file (of no pages) we need specify a new, hitherto unused file name. To erase an existing file we need specify the name of a file already in the system. To put a page into a file we need specify the names of the file and page, and the page itself. To get a page from a file we need specify the names of the file and page. Finally to delete a page we need specify the same:

5. $Crea :: Fn$
6. $Eras :: Fn$
7. $Put :: Fn\ Pn\ PG$
8. $Get :: Fn\ Pn$
9. $Del :: Fn\ Pn$

No well-formedness constraints need be specified for commands, that is: $is\text{-}wf\text{-}Cmd[e] \triangleq \underline{true}$.

Semantic Functions

We believe the above informal syntactic outline plus the following formal semantics to be sufficiently self-explanatory not to warrant the kind of detailed annotations that we would otherwise provide:

10. $\underline{type}\ Elab\text{-}Cmd: Cmd \to (FS \xrightarrow{\sim} (FS \mid PG))$
10.0 $Elab\text{-}Cmd[c](fs) \triangleq$
.1 $\underline{cases}\ c:$
.2 $(mk\text{-}Crea(f) \to fs \cup [f \mapsto [\,]],$
.3 $mk\text{-}Eras(f) \to fs \setminus \{f\},$
.4 $mk\text{-}Put(f,p,pg) \to fs + [f \mapsto fs(f) + [p \mapsto pg]],$
.5 $mk\text{-}Get(f,p) \to (fs(f))(p),$
.6 $mk\text{-}Del(f,p) \to fs + [f \mapsto (fs(f)) \setminus \{p\}])$
10.7 $\underline{pre}: pre\text{-}Elab\text{-}Cmd[c](fs)$

11.0 $pre\text{-}Elab\text{-}Cmd[c](fs) \triangleq$
.1 $\underline{cases}\ c:$
.2 $(mk\text{-}Crea(f) \to f \neg\in \underline{dom}\ fs,$
.3 $mk\text{-}Eras(f) \to f \in \underline{dom}\ fs,$
.4 $mk\text{-}Put(f,p,pg) \to f \in \underline{dom}\ fs,$
.5 $mk\text{-}Get(f,p) \to ((f \in \underline{dom}\ fs) \wedge (p \in \underline{dom}(fs(f)))),$
.6 $mk\text{-}Del(f,p) \to ((f \in \underline{dom}\ fs) \wedge (p \in \underline{dom}(fs(f)))))$

The type of $pre\text{-}Elab\text{-}Cmd$ follows from the type of $Elab\text{-}Cmd$:

11. *type*: *pre-Elab-Cmd*: *Cmd* $\rightarrow$ (*FS* $\rightarrow$ *BOOL*)

Conclusion of Top-Level Definition

We have completely specified the basic, major functions of a simple file handler system. The abstraction is just that: we have abstracted from any concern with how actual input of commands, including input of pages, and of how output of pages take place. We have also abstracted "away" considerations of what kind of diagnostics to use in case of erroneous input -- we have only defined, in *pre-Int-Cmd* what we mean by erroneous input. We have abstracted from any representation of files, and, in fact, the entire file system. Finally, we have not been, and shall not, in this entire example, be concerned with what pages are.

11.2 SECOND-LEVEL (File Handler) ARCHITECTURE (Stages 1-2-3)

We divide this, the second level specification, into three stages. First we introduce the object notions of catalogue and directories, then the notion of disk, and finally the object notions of storage and disk. The single aim of this level is to introduce the operation notions of open and close.

11.2.1 File Catalogue and Page Directories (Stage 1)

Semantic Domains

We subscript now our Domain names according to the number of stage of development. The 0'th stage (which was the top-level) gave us:

1-2. $FS_0 \;=\; Fn \overrightarrow{m} (Pn \overrightarrow{m} PG)$

To each file we now associate a page directory. Each directory records where pages are stored. Directories are named, and these names are recorded in a catalogue.

12. $FS_1 \;::\; CTLG_1 \;\; DIRS_1 \;\; PGS_1$
13. $CTLG \;=\; Fn \overleftrightarrow{m} Dn$
14. $DIRS_1 \;=\; Dn \overleftrightarrow{m} DIR_1$
15. $PGS_1 \;=\; Pa \overrightarrow{m} PG$
16. $DIR_1 \;=\; Pn \overleftrightarrow{m} Pa$

You may (justifiably) think of directories "translating" user-oriented page names into system-oriented page addresses, and PGS_1 to be a disk-like space within which all pages of all files are allocated. Let:

$$[f_1 \mapsto [p_{11} \mapsto g_{11}, p_{12} \mapsto g_{12}],$$
$$f_2 \mapsto [p_{21} \mapsto g_{21}],$$
$$f_3 \mapsto [\,]]$$

be an abstract, FS_0, file system. Its counterpart in FS_1 is for example:

$$mk\text{-}FS_1([f_1 \mapsto d_1, f_2 \mapsto d_2, f_3 \mapsto d_3],$$
$$[d_1 \mapsto [p_{11} \mapsto a_{11}, p_{12} \mapsto a_{12}],$$
$$d_2 \mapsto [P_{21} \mapsto a_{21}],$$
$$d_3 \mapsto [\,]],$$
$$[a_{11} \mapsto g_{11}, a_{12} \mapsto g_{12}, a_{21} \mapsto g_{21}])$$

Domain Invariant

Domain definitions (12.-16.) define too much. Not all combinations of catalogues, directories and pages go together. We must require (17.1) that there is a distinct directory in $DIRS_1$ for each file catalogued in $CTLG_1$; that (17.2) pages addressed in PGS_1 are actually recorded in directories; and that (17.3) every page, understood as page-address, is described in exactly one directory (that is belongs to exactly one file):

17.0 $inv\text{-}FS_1(mk\text{-}FS_1(c,ds,ps)) \triangleq$

.1 $(\underline{rng}\ c = \underline{dom}\ ds)$

.2 $\wedge(\underline{union}\{\underline{rng}\ d \mid d \in \underline{rng}\ ds\} = \underline{dom}\ ps)$

.3 $\wedge(\forall a \in \underline{dom}\ ps)(\exists! d \in \underline{dom}\ ds)(a \in \underline{rng}\ ds(d))$

The bijections of (13.), (14.) and (16.) already express that no two files have the same directory, that no two directories are identical, and that no two page names map to the same ("physical") page (-- by its address).

Abstraction: from FS_1 to FS_0

Given an FS_1 file system we can abstract a "corresponding" FS_0 from it. Abstraction (here called "retrieval") is a function:

18. *type:* $retr\text{-}FS_0: FS_1 \to FS_0$

18.0 $retr\text{-}FS_0(mk\text{-}FS_1(c,ds,ps))\underline{\Delta}$

.1 $[\, f \mapsto [\, p \mapsto ps((ds(c(f)))(p)) \mid p \in \underline{dom}\ ds(c(f)) \,] \mid f \in \underline{dom}\ c \,]$

We can only retrieve well-formed file systems:

18.2 *pre:* $inv\text{-}FS_1(mk\text{-}FS_1(c,ds,ps))$

We always assume our functions to apply only to well-formed objects, that is (18.2) is superfluous.

Injection: from FS_0 to FS_1

Given an abstract system we can inject it into any number of "corresponding systems". Injection is a relation.

Adequacy

We must ensure that to each abstract system there corresponds a non-trivial concrete which abstracts to it:

19. $(\forall s_0 \in FS_0)(\exists s_1 \in FS_1)(inv\text{-}FS_1(s_1) \supset (s_0 = retr\text{-}FS_0(s_1)))$

Syntactic Domains

No change to existing Domains, that is no refinements or transformations are necessary; and no new commands, that is no extension of the Command Domain.

Semantic Functions

We rewrite the $Elab\text{-}Cmd_0$ of section 11.1. That is: for fixed syntactic Domains but changed semantic Domains we need re-express the semantics, now in terms of the new semantic Domains:

20. *type:* $Elab\text{-}Cmd_1: Cmd \to (FS_1 \xrightarrow{\sim} (FS_1 \xrightarrow{\sim} (FS_1 \mid PG)))$

Instead of expressing $Int\text{-}Cmd_1$ as one "monolithic" function we express it in terms of 5 sub-functions, one for each command category:

21. *type*: $Int\text{-}Crea_1$: $Crea \rightarrow (FS_1 \xrightarrow{\sim} FS_1)$

22. *type*: $Int\text{-}Eras_1$: $Eras \rightarrow (FS_1 \xrightarrow{\sim} FS_1)$

23. *type*: $Int\text{-}Put_1$: $Put \rightarrow (FS_1 \xrightarrow{\sim} FS_1)$

24. *type*: $Val\text{-}Get_1$: $Get \rightarrow (FS_2 \xrightarrow{\sim} PG)$

25. *type*: $Int\text{-}Del_1$: $Del \rightarrow (FS_2 \xrightarrow{\sim} FS_1)$

We choose to "merge" the pre-condition checking into each function:

21.0 $Int\text{-}Crea_1[mk\text{-}Crea(f)](mk\text{-}FS_2(c,ds,ps))\underline{\triangle}$

.1   *if* $f \in \underline{dom}\ c$

.2   *then undefined*

.3   *else* ($\underline{let}\ d \in Dn - \underline{dom}\ ds\ \underline{in}$

.4 $mk\text{-}FS_1(c \cup [f \mapsto d], ds \cup [d \mapsto [\ ]], ps))$

22. $Int\text{-}Eras_1[mk\text{-}Eras(f)](mk\text{-}FS_2(c,ds,ps))\underline{\triangle}$

.1   *if* $f \in \underline{dom}\ c$

.2   *then* $mk\text{-}FS_1(c \backslash \{f\}, ds \backslash \{ct(f)\}, ps \backslash \underline{rng}(ds(c(f))))$

.3   *else undefined*

23.0 $Int\text{-}Put_1[mk\text{-}Put(f,p,pg)](mk\text{-}FS_2(c,ds,ps))\underline{\triangle}$

.1   *if* $f \in \underline{dom}\ c$

.2   *then if* $p \in \underline{dom}(ds(c(f)))$

.3   *then* $mk\text{-}FS_1(c,ds,ps + [(ds(c(f)))(p) \mapsto pg])$

.4   *else* ($\underline{let}\ a \in Pa - \underline{dom}\ ps\ \underline{in}$

.5 $\underline{let}\ ds' = ds + [c(f) \mapsto ds(c(f)) \cup p \mapsto a],$

.6 $ps' = ps \cup [a \mapsto pg]\ \underline{in}$

.7 $mk\text{-}FS_1(c,ds',ps'))$

.8   *else undefined*

24.0 $Val\text{-}Get_1[mk\text{-}Get(f,p)](mk\text{-}FS_1(c,ds,ps))\underline{\triangle}$

.1   *if* $(f \in \underline{dom}\ c) \wedge (p \in \underline{dom}(ds(c(f))))$

.2   *then* $ps(ds(c(f)))(p))$

.3   *else undefined*

25.0 $Int\text{-}Del[mk\text{-}Del(f,p)](mk\text{-}FS_2(c,ds,ps))\underline{\triangle}$

.1   *if* $(f \in \underline{dom}\ c) \wedge (p \in \underline{dom}\ (ds(c(f))))$

.2   *then* $mk\text{-}FS_1(c, ds + [c(f) \mapsto (ds(c(f))) \backslash \{p\}],$

.3 $ps \backslash \{(ds(c(f)))(p)\})$

.4   *else undefined*

And finally:

```
20.0   Elab-Cmd1[c](fs1) ≜
  .1     (is-Create) → Int-Crea[c](fs1),
  .2      is-Eras(c) → Int-Eras1[c](fs1),
  .3      is-Put(c)  → Int-Put1[c](fs1),
  .4      is-Get(c)  → Val-Get1[c](fs1),
  .5      is-Del(c)  → Int-Del[c](fs1))
```

Correctness

Correctness of the above realization of $Elab\text{-}Cmd_0$ in terms of $Elab\text{-}Cmd$ with respect to the realization of FS_0 in terms of FS_1 is expressed by means of the abstraction function:

```
26.    type: retr-RES1: (FS1 | PG) → (FS0 | PG)
26.0   retr-RES1(r) ≜
  .1      (is-FS1(r) → retr-FS0(r),T→r)
```

and is:

```
27.0   thm1(∀c∈ Cmd)
  .1          (∀fs0∈FS0)
  .2            (∀fs1 ∈ FS1)
  .3            (((inv-FS1(fs1)∧ retr-FS0(fs1)=fs0)
  .4             ∧ pre-Elab-Cmd[c](fs0))
  .5             ⊃
  .6         (retr-RES1(Elab-Cmd2[c](fs2)) = Elab-Cmd1[c](fs0)))
```

We do not prove that the above theorem holds for our first stage realization.

Automatic Operation Transformation

In fact, we claim, without demonstrating it in this book, that given the following "input": FS_i, $inv\text{-}FS_i$, $Elab\text{-}Cmd_i$, FS_{i+1} $inv\text{-}FS_{i+1}$, $retr\text{-}FS_i$, and thm_i (see above), one can devise automatic means for transforming semantic functions $Elab\text{-}Cmd_i$ into $Elab\text{-}Cmd_{i+1}$. Since the transformed result has to satisfy rather "narrow" constraints, there are not very many choices of implementations left free.

11.2.2 Disks (Stage 2)

Semantic Domains

We are given:

12. $FS_1 \quad :: \ CTLG_1 \quad DIRS_1 \quad PGS_1$
13. $CTLG_1 = Fn \overrightarrow{m} Dn$
14. $DIRS_1 = Dn \overrightarrow{m} DIR_1$
15. $PGS_1 = Pa \overrightarrow{m} PG$
16. $DIR_1 = Pn \overrightarrow{m} Pa$

The object transformation of this stage involves the "gathering" of directories and pages, that is of the above $DIRS_1$ and PGS_1 components of FS_1 into one component, called DSK_2 of FS_2. $DIRS_1$ and PGS_1 are modelled as maps, and DSK_2 will hence be a "merged" Domain of simiilar maps. Where before map domains were directory names, respectively page addresses, the "merged" (or "gathered") Domain will only have addresses in its map domain. We think of DSK_2 as modelling "actual" disks:

28. $FS_2 \quad :: \ CTLG_2 \ DSK_2$
29. $CTLG_2 = Fn \overrightarrow{m} Adr$
30. $DSK_2 = Adr \overrightarrow{m} (DIR_2 \mid PG)$
31. $DIR_2 = Pn \overrightarrow{m} Adr$

Here addresses *Adr* (like file names, *Fn*, and page names, *Pn*, and pages, *PG*) are further undefined.

Domain Invariant

Again the Domain definitions (28.-31.) define too much. In addition to the invariants ["carried over" from the very similar definitions of FS_1], we must (first) make sure that directory addresses (listed in the catalogue) really denote directories on the disk, respectively that page addresses listed in directories really denote pages on the disk. Once this is established we can retrieve an FS_1 object from such a "tentatively well-formed" FS_2 object, and this abstracted object must satisfy the earlier stated constraint:

32.0 $inv\text{-}FS_2(fs_2) \triangleq (wf\text{-}AdrDen(fs_2) \wedge inv\text{-}FS_1(retr\text{-}FS_1(fs_2)))$

33. <u>type</u>: *wf-AdrDen*: $FS_2 \to BOOL$
33.0 $wf\text{-}AdrDen(mk\text{-}FS_2(2,d)) \triangleq$
.1 $(\forall a \in \underline{rng}\ c)(is\text{-}DIR_2(d(a)) \wedge (\forall a' \in \underline{rng}(d(a)))(is\text{-}PG(d(a'))))$

<u>Abstraction from</u> FS_2 <u>to</u> FS_1

34.0 $retr\text{-}FS_1(mk\text{-}FS_2(c,d)) \triangleq$
.1 $mk\text{-}FS_1(c, [\ a \mapsto d(a)\ |\ a \in \underline{rng}\ c\ ], d \setminus \underline{rng}\ c)$

Here we now have assumed $Adr = Dn \mid Pa$, that is that:

33.0 $wf\text{-}AdrDen(mk\text{-}FS_2(c,d)) \triangleq$
.1 $(\forall a \in \underline{rng}\ c)$
.2 $((is\text{-}Dn(a) \wedge is\text{-}DIR_2(d(a))).$
.3 $\wedge (\forall a' \in \underline{rng}(d(a)))$
.4 $(is\text{-}Pa(a') \wedge is\text{-}PG(d(a'))))$

and:

34.2 $pre\text{-}retr\text{-}FS_1(fs_2) \triangleq wf\text{-}AdrDen(fs_2)$

We leave to the reader the rather straightforward transcription of <u>adequacy</u>, semantic functions and correctness theorem.

<u>11.2.3 Storage and Disk (Stage 3)</u>

We are given (28.-31.). We now face the reality of storages and disks. By a storage we shall understand a memory medium access to whose information is orders of magnitude faster than to information on what we shall then call disks! As was evident from e.g. lines 23.3 and 24.2 access to pages (on disk) goes via catalogue and directories, the latter also on disk. Thus two disk accesses per page access. [In this discussion we think of the catalogue as residing in storage.] To cut down on disk accesses we therefore decide to copy into storage the directories of those files whose pages we wish to access. In the resulting model all pages will still be thought of as stored only on the disk.

<u>Syntactic Domains</u>

In order to advise the system of an intent to begin and end operations on pages we introduce two new commands: <u>open</u> and <u>close</u>:

35. $Cmd_3 \;=\; Cmd_0 \mid Open \mid Close$

36. $Open :: Fn$

37. $Close :: Fn$

(The informal semantics of those are basically to bring a directory copy into storage, respectively to over-write the disk copy with the storage copy, subsequently deleting this latter copy.)

Semantic Domains

Now both storage and disk have directories:

38. $FS_3 :: STG_3 \; DSK_3$

39. $STG_3 :: CTLG_2 \; (Fn \underset{m}{\rightarrow} DIR_2)$

40. $DSK_3 = DSK_2$

which together with (29.,30.,32.) completely specifies the 3rd stage (of the 2nd development level). Observe our decision to let all, so-called opened files be represented in storage by directories identified by file names whereas directories on disk are identified by directory names, such as listed in the catalogue. Now we access directories directly, by-passing the catalogue. New directory entries (23.5) etc. are only to be recorded in the opened, that is storage, directories -- hence the copying-back upon closing!

Domain Invariants

As in the previous stage we express invariance in terms of an auxiliary function and the invariance of the abstraction of this stage of concretization retrieved back to the previous stage. The auxiliary function guarantees that retrieval is meaningful.

41.0 $inv\text{-}FS_3(fs_3) \triangleq (wf\text{-}StgDskOverlap(fs_3) \wedge inv\text{-}FS_2(retr\text{-}FS_2(fs_3)))$

The *wf-StgDskOverlap* checks that only catalogued files are opened (42.1) and that identical page names of opened files of storage and disk directory copies map to identical addresses (42.3):

42.0 $wf\text{-}StgDskOverlap(mk\text{-}FS_3(mk\text{-}STG_3(c,ods),dsk)) \triangleq$

.1 $((\underline{dom}\,ods \subseteq \underline{dom}\,c)$

.2 $\wedge(\forall f \in \underline{dom}\,c)((ods(f) \mid \underline{dom}(dsk(c(f))) = dsk(c(f)) \mid \underline{dom}(ods(f))))$

where the last line expresses the mutual restriction of file directories in storage (to the left) and on disk (to the right) to common domains.

Abstraction: from FS_3 to FS_2:

43.0 *retr-FS*$_2$*(mk-FS*$_3$*(mk-STG*$_3$*(c,ods),dsk))* $\triangleq$
.1 *mk-FS*$_2$*(c,dsk + [c(f) ↦ ods(f) | f ∈ ods])*

Semantic Functions

In general:

44. type: *Elab-Cmd*$_3$*: Cmd*$_3$ → *(FS*$_3$ ⥲ *FS*$_3$*)*

and in specific:

45. type: *Int-Open: Open* → *(FS*$_3$ ⥲ *FS*$_3$*)*
46. type: *Int-Close: Close* → *(FS*$_3$ ⥲ *FS*$_3$*)*

45.0 *Int-Open*$_3$*[mk-Open(f)](mk-FS*$_3$*(mk-STG*$_3$*(c,ds),dsk))* $\triangleq$
.1 if *(f ∈* dom *c) ∧ (f ¬ ∈* dom *ds)*
.2 then *mk-FS*$_3$*(mk-STG*$_3$*(c,ds ∪ [f ↦ dsk(c(f))]),dsk)*
.3 else undefined

46.0 *Int-Close*$_3$*[mk-Close(f)](mk-FS*$_3$*(mk-STG*$_3$*(c,ds),dsk))* $\triangleq$
.1 if *(f ∈* dom *c) ∧ (f ∈* dom *ds)*
.2 then *mk-FS*$_3$*(mk-STG*$_3$*(c,ds\{f}),dsk + [c(f) ↦ ds(f)])*
.3 else undefined

47.0 *Int-Crea*$_3$*[mk-Crea(f)](mk-FS*$_3$*(mk-STG*$_3$*(c,ds),dsk))* $\triangleq$
.1 if *f ∈* dom *c*
.2 then undefined
.3 else (let *a∈Adr -* dom *dsk* in
.4 *mk-FS*$_3$*(mk-STG*$_3$*(c ∪ [f ↦ a],ds),dsk ∪ [a ↦ []]))*

Creating a file does not "automatically" open it. If it did then line (47.4) should read: *mk-FS*$_3$*(mk-STG*$_3$*(c ∪ [f ↦ []]),dsk ∪ [a ↦ []])*

48.0 *Int-Eras*$_3$*[mk-Crea(f)](mk-FS*$_3$*(mk-STG*$_3$*(c,ds),dsk))* $\triangleq$
.1 if *(f ∈* dom *c) ∧ (f ¬ ∈* dom *ds)*
.2 then *mk-FS*$_3$*(mk-STG*$_3$*(c\{f},ds),dsk \ {c(f)} ∪* rng*(dsk(c(f))))*
.3 else undefined

We are permitted only to erase closed files.

```
49.0 Int-Put3[mk-Put(f,g,pg)](mk-FS3(mk-STG3(c,ds),dsk)) ≜
  .1     if (f ∈ dom c) ∧ (f ∈ dom ds)
  .2        then if p ∈ dom(ds(f))
  .3                then mk-FS3(mk-STG3(c,ds),dsk+[(ds(f))(p) ↦ pg])
  .4                else (let a∈Adr - dom dsk in
  .5                      let ds'  = ds+[f ↦ ds(f) ∪ [p ↦ s]],
  .6                          dsk' = dsk ∪ [a ↦ pg]] in
  .7                      mk-FS3(mk-STG3(c,ds'),dsk'))
  .8        else undefined

50.0 Val-Get3[mk-Get(f,p)](mk-FS3(mk-STG3(c,ds),dsk)) ≜
  .1     if (f ∈ dom c) ∧ (f ∈ dom ds) ∧ (p ∈ dom (ds(f)))
  .2        then dsk((ds(f))(p))
  .3        else undefined

51.0 Int-Del3[mk-Del(f,p)](mk-FS3(mk-STG3(c,ds),dsk)) ≜
  .1     if (f ∈ dom c) ∧ (f ∈ dom ds) ∧ (p ∈ dom (ds(f)))
  .2        then mk-FS3(mk-STG3(c,ds+[f↦ds(f)\{p}]),dsk\{(ds(f))(p)})
  .3        else undefined
```

Conclusion to Second-Level Definition

Only after a number of stages of development, in which an abstract, implementation unbiased architecture has been gradually biased towards a particular realization, did we introduce the (user) interface notions of open and close. We see these more as concessions to current technological constraints than as representing user-meaningful intrinsic notions. No decision has yet been made, by the models up to now, whether open and close are user- or system-specified commands. It is perfectly possible for a system to automatically issue the operations in response to some analysis of user processes.

11.3 THIRD-LEVEL (File-Handler) ARCHITECTURE (Stages 4-5-6)

The major aim of this level is to render the file handler architecture more robust to crashes. [Robustness is a measure of the reliability notion introduced in section 11.0.] Our solution to the problem of increased recoverability is to introduce two means, that is two notions, of accessing pages (on disk). One access 'path' goes from the storage catalogue via the storage directory -- as before -- to the disk pages. Another, "redundant", access 'path' is then introduced. It goes from a disk copy of the storage catalogue via directories also residing on disk to disk pages. Thus we shall "maintain" two kinds of file subsystems, but, as a new idea, not necessarily each others images. At any one time the two file sub-systems are to be well-formed, but not necessarily retrievable to the same abstract file system. We shall generally permit for example writes, updates and deletes only to be recorded in storage directories. We shall furthermore require that updates are treated as writes. Given now a situation where the storage and the disk file sub-systems are "equivalent", a sequence of writes, updates and deletes will then render the two different -- but with the ability that should a crash occur, then the disk sub-system can be used to replace the storage sub-system. Since we do not wish to backup too far into the past we introduce an operation which applies to files and renders the copies of directory and all pages for that file in storage and on disk the same, that is "equivalent". It does so by copying the storage copies onto the disk, overriding its information.

This level will consist of three stages (4-5-6) of transformation. Stage 4 introduces all the above-hinted and user-oriented notions. Stages 5 and 6 transform the model of stage 4 into successively more implementation-oriented models.

11.3.1 Storage and Disk File Sub-Systems (Stage 4)

Our departure point is (29.-31., 35.-51).

Semantic Domains

We repeat (29.-31., 38.-40.)

52. $FS_3 \quad :: \quad STG_3 \;\; DSK_2$ (38.)
53. $STG_3 \quad :: \quad CTLG_2 \; (Fn \overrightarrow{m} DIR_2)$ (39.)
54. $CTLG_2 \quad = \quad Fn \overrightarrow{m} Adr$ (29.)
55. $DIR_2 \quad = \quad Pn \overrightarrow{m} Adr$ (31.)
56. $DSK_2 \quad = \quad Adr \overrightarrow{m} (DIR_2 \mid PG)$ (40.,30.)

The "only" change (to the Domain equations) is in (56.)

57. $FS_4 \quad :: \quad STG_3 \quad DSK_4$
58. $DSK_4 \quad :: \quad CTLG_2 \quad DSK_2$

<u>Domain Invariant</u>

Storage directories may denote pages not denoted by disk directories. Not all disk pages need be denoted. Deletion of pages are only recorded in storage directories, that is no deletion of disk pages take place. There are two 'consistent' file sub-system notions:

59.0 $inv\text{-}FS_4(mk\text{-}FS_4(s,d)) \triangleq$
.1 $\quad (consistent\text{-}StgSS(s,d) \wedge consistent\text{-}DskSS(d))$

Storage sub-system 'consistency' speaks of invariance of the file-system "rooted" in storage catalogue and directories. Disk sub-system 'consistency' speaks of invariance of the file-system "rooted" in disk catalogue and disk directories. We express both in terms of the invariance of FS_2 abstractions of the file-subsystems. We can only abstract the storage sub-system if opened files are all catalogued (60.1).

60. $\underline{type}: \; consistent\text{-}StgSS: \; STG_3 \; DSK \to BOOL$
61. $\underline{type}: \; consistent\text{-}DskSS: \; DSK \to BOOL$

60.0 $consistent\text{-}StgSS(mk\text{-}STG_3(c,d),mk\text{-}DSK_4(,dsk)) \triangleq$
.1 $\quad (\underline{dom}\; d \subseteq \underline{dom}\; c) \wedge inv\text{-}FS_2(mk\text{-}FS_2(c,SabsDSK_2(c,d,dsk)))$

We abstract to FS_2 file systems since all we are interested in is access paths from catalogue via directories to pages irrespective of the notions of opened/closed.

62. $\underline{type}: \; SabsDSK_2: \; CTLG_2 \; (Fn \overrightarrow{m} DIR_2) \; DSK_2 \tilde{\to} DSK_2$
62.0 $SabsDSK_2(c,d,dsk) \triangleq$
.1 $\quad (\underline{let}\; as_s = Saddrs(c,d,dsk) \;\underline{in}$
.2 $\quad (dsk \mid as_s + [c(f) \mapsto d(f) \mid f \in \underline{dom}\; d])$

63.0 $Saddrs(c,d,dsk) \triangleq$
.1 $\quad (\underline{let}\; das = \underline{rng}\; c,$
.2 $\qquad opas = \underline{union}\{\underline{rng}\; dir \mid dir \in \underline{rng}\; d\},$
.3 $\qquad cpas = \underline{union}\{\underline{rng}(dsk(a)) \mid a \in \{c(f) \mid f \in \underline{dom}\, c \setminus \underline{dom}\, d\}\} \;\underline{in}$
.4 $\quad das \cup opas \cup cpas)$
63. $\underline{type}: \; CTLG_2 \; (Fn \overrightarrow{m} DIR_2) \; DSK_2 \tilde{\to} Addr\text{-}set$

The idea of $SabsDSK_2$ is to retrieve only those closed directories on disk which are accessible from the storage catalogue, and only those pages which are accessible via those closed directories and via the opened (storage) directories, and to extend the resulting DSK_2 object with the opened storage directories. Where these before were denoted by file names, they are now, on disk, denoted by the directory name recorded in the storage catalogue. *das* stand for directory addresses of all storage-accessible opened and closed directories, *opas* (*cpas*) for addresses of all most recently written and updated pages of all such opened (such closed) files. Since we shall extract these addresses repeatedly we have "invented" an auxiliary function, *Saddrs*. for that purpose.

64.0 $DabsDSK_2(c,dsk)$ $\underline{\underline{\Delta}}$
  .1 ($\underline{let}$ as_d = $Daddrs(c,dsk)$ $\underline{in}$
  .2 ($dsk \mid as_d$))

65.0 $Daddrs(c,dsk)$ $\underline{\underline{\Delta}}$
  .1 ($\underline{let}$ das = $\underline{rng}$ c $\underline{in}$
  .2 $\underline{let}$ pas = $\underline{union}\{\underline{rng}(dsk(a)) \mid a \in das\}$ $\underline{in}$
  .3 $das \cup pas$)

<u>Abstraction:</u> <u>from</u> FS_4 <u>to</u> FS_3

Two kinds of abstractions are possible: one from the storage "rooted" file sub-system, and another based on three disk "rooted" file sub-system:

66.0 $retr\text{-}FS_3(mk\text{-}FS_4(mk\text{-}STG_3(c,d),mk\text{-}DSK_4(,dsk)))$ $\underline{\underline{\Delta}}$
  .1 $mk\text{-}FS_3(mk\text{-}STG_3(c,d),dsk \mid Saddrs(c,d,dsk))$

67.0 $retr\text{-}FS_{3D}(mk\text{-}FS_4(,mk\text{-}DSK_4(c,dsk)))$ $\underline{\underline{\Delta}}$
  .1 $mk\text{-}FS_3(mk\text{-}STG_3(c,[\,]),dsk \mid Daddr(c,dsk))$

<u>Garbage Collection</u>

As is evident from the informal and (subsequent) formal description of write, update and delete commands we shall witness file systems with both disk directories and pages which are denoted by no catalogue, respectively no or only such inaccessible ("dead") directories. Garbage-collection then is an operation which removes all such "dead" directories and all such pages:

68. $\underline{type}$: $Garb\text{-}Coll: FS_4 \xrightarrow{\sim} FS_4$

68.0 $Garb\text{-}Coll(mk\text{-}FS_4(mk\text{-}STG_3(sc,d),mk\text{-}DSK_4(dc,dsk)))\ \underline{\underline{\Delta}}$
  .1 $(\underline{let}\ as_s = Saddrs(sc,d,dsk),$
  .2 $\qquad as_d = Daddrs(dc,dsk)\ \underline{in}$
  .3 $mk\text{-}FS_4(mk\text{-}STG_3(sc,d),mk\text{-}DSK_4(dc,dsk \mid (as_s \cup as_d))))$

Syntactic Domains -- and Informal Semantics

When a crash occurs one needs, in order to recover, to "roll-back" to a not too far distant past consistent state -- namely the disk sub-system current at the time of the crash. To avoid the "distance" between the time of the crash and the previous time when the subsystems retreived to the same abstract FS_3 system being "too big", one needs, "now and then", to bring the disk sub-system to reflect the state of the storage sub-system. For that purpose a so-called check-point command is introduced. It applies to individual, opened, file and bring the storage and disk catalogue entries for that file to both denote the same disk directory which is to be that of the opened file. A crash can be thought of as a command (issued by some Demon nice enough only to issue it properly in-between the "execution" of other commands). Its first effect is to "blank-out" all storage information. Its second effect is then to restore the storage sub-system to that of the disk sub-system.

69. $Cmd_4 \;=\; Cmd_3 \mid Check \mid Crash$
70. $Check \;::\; Fn$
71. $Crash \;::\; ()$

Semantic Functions

72. $\underline{type}$: $Elab\text{-}Cmd_4: Cmd_4 \rightarrow (FS_4 \xrightarrow{\sim} (FS_4 \mid PG))$

73.0 $Int\text{-}Crea_4[mk\text{-}Crea(f)](mk\text{-}FS_4(mk\text{-}STG_3(sc,d),mk\text{-}DSK_4(dc,dsk)))\ \underline{\underline{\Delta}}$
  .1 $\underline{if}\ f \in \underline{dom}\ sc$
  .2 $\quad \underline{then}\ \underline{undefined}$
  .3 $\quad \underline{else}\ (\underline{let}\ a \in Adr - \underline{dom}\ dsk\ \underline{in}$
  .4 $\qquad mk\text{-}FS_4(mk\text{-}STG_3(sc \cup [f \mapsto a],d),mk\text{-}DSK_4(dc,dsk \cup [\ \mapsto [\,]])))$

74.0 $Int\text{-}Eras[mk\text{-}Eras(f)](mk\text{-}FS_4(mk\text{-}STG_3(sc,d),dsk_4))\ \underline{\underline{\Delta}}$
  .1 $\underline{if}\ (f \in \underline{dom}\ sc) \wedge (f \neg\in \underline{dom}\ d)$
  .2 $\quad \underline{then}\ mk\text{-}FS_4(mk\text{-}STG_3(sc \setminus \{f\},d),dsk_4)$
  .3 $\quad \underline{else}\ \underline{undefined}$

```
75.0 Int-Open_4[mk-Open(f)](mk-FS_4(mk-STG_3(sc,d),mk-DSK_4(dc,dsk))) ≜
  .1     if (f∈dom sc) ∧ (f¬∈dom d)
  .2        then mk-FS_4(mk-STG_3(sc,d∪[f↦dsk(sc(f))]),
  .3                     mk-DSK_4(dc,dsk))
  .4        else undefined
```

```
76.0 Int-Close[mk-Close(f)](mk-FS_4(mk-STG_3(sc,d),mk-DSK_4(dc,dsk))) ≜
  .1     if (f∈dom sc) ∧ (f∈dom d)
  .2        then (let a∈Adr - dom dsk in
  .3              mk-FS_4(mk-STG_3(sc+[f↦a],d\{f}),
  .4                      mk-DSK_4(dc,dsk∪[a↦d(f)])))
  .5        else undefined
```

```
77.0 Int-Put_4[mk-Put(f,p,pg)](mk-FS_4(mk-STG_3(sc,d),mk-DSK_4(dc,dsk))) ≜
  .1     if (f∈dom sc) ∧ (f∈dom d)
  .2        then (let a∈Adr - dom dsk in
  .3              mk-FS_4(mk-STG_3(sc,d+[f↦d(f)+[p↦a]]),
  .4                      mk-DSK_4(dc,dsk∪[a↦pg])))
  .5        else undefined
```

```
78.0 Int-Del_4[mk-Del(f,p)](mk-FS_4(mk-STG_3(sc,d),dsk_4)) ≜
  .1     if f∈dom sc ∧ f∈dom d ∧ p∈dom(d(f))
  .2        then mk-FS_4(mk-STG_3(sc,d+[f↦d(f)\{p}]),dsk_4)
  .3        else undefined
```

```
79.0 Int-Check_4[mk-Check(f)](mk-FS_4(mk-STG_3(sc,d),mk-DSK_4(dc,dsk))) ≜
  .1     if (f∈dom sc) ∧ (f∈dom d)
  .2        then (let a∈Adr - dom dsk in
  .3              mk-FS_4(mk-STG_3(sc+[f↦a],d),
  .4                      mk-DSK_4(dc+[f↦a],dsk∪[a↦d(f)])))
  .5        else undefined
```

```
80.0 Int-Crash_4[mk-Crash()](mk-FS_4(,mk-DSK_4(dc,dsk))) ≜
  .1     mk-FS_4(mk-STG_3(dc,[]),mk-DSK_4(dc,dsk))
```

If necessary one can garbage collect after crashes:

```
81.0 Int-Crash'_4[crash](fs_4) ≜
  .1     Garb-Coll(Int-Crash_4[crash](fs_4))
```

11.3.2 "Flat" Storage and Disk (Stage 5)

Semantic Domains

Usually there is no "cell-space" distinction in storage between the catalogue and the collection of opened directories; and similarly: there is usually no "sector-space" distinction on disk(s) between the disk catalogue, on one hand, and disk directories and pages, on the other hand -- such as seemingly implied by Domain equations (53.), respectively (58.). We assume storage to be addressed say in "chunks" comparable to catalogues and directories; and disks addressed in "chunks" comparable to catalogues, directories and pages. We let the address space, *REF*, of storage have MASTER as a distinguished element, and address space, *REF*, of disk have COPY as a distinguished element. MASTER denotes the former $CTLG_2$ component of STG_3 and COPY the former $CTLG_2$ component of DSK_4. The storage catalogue record disk and storage addresses of opened files directories, but only disk addresses of closed files directories. The disk catalogue "copy" record only disk addresses of file directories. The storage catalogue records the disk address of its counterpart, the disk catalogue.

82. $REF = \underline{MASTER} \mid Ref$

83. $ADR = \underline{COPY} \mid Adr$

84. $FS_5 :: STG_5 \;\; DSK_5$

85. $STG_5 = (\underline{MASTER} \overrightarrow{m} SCTLG_5) \;\underline{\cup}\; (Ref \overrightarrow{m} DIR_5)$

86. $DSK_5 = (\underline{COPY} \overrightarrow{m} DCTLG_5) \;\underline{\cup}\; (Adr \overrightarrow{m} DIR_5 \mid PG))$

87. $SCTLG_5 = (\underline{MASTER} \overrightarrow{m} \underline{COPY}) \;\underline{\cup}\; (Fn \overrightarrow{m} Dadr)$

88. $DCTLG_5 = (\underline{CTLG} \overrightarrow{m} (\underline{MASTER} \mid \underline{COPY})) \;\underline{\cup}\; (Fn \overrightarrow{m} Adr)$

89. $Dadr = (Adr\ [Ref])$

Etcetera

We leave it to the reader to complete this stages' invariant, abstraction and semantic functions.

11.3.3 Storage and Disk Space Management (Stage 6)

Semantic Domains

Usually both storage and disk(s) represent limited resources in the sense of not permitting an infinite, but only a finite, amount of "space" for keeping catalogues, directories and pages. Our (map-based) models so far have assumed indefinitely sized such spaces. The aim of this last stage of object transformation is to introduce the notion of <u>storage</u> and <u>disk space management</u>. We assume therefore a limited amount of space both in storage and on disk(s). Instead of always being able to fetch new disk addresses (see for example (73.3), (76.2) and (77.2)) so-called <u>free lists</u> of allocatable sub-spaces is maintained, both for storage and for disk(s). We also assume that each such subspace is adequate and reasonably sized for both directories and pages -- these are the only quantities to be allocated and freed. The free lists are therefore modelled as sets of storage references respectively disk addresses not allocated. The quotation <u>FREE</u> denotes these lists:

90. $FS_6 \;::\; STG_6\ DSK_6$
91. $STG_6 \;=\; STG_5 \;\underline{\cup}\; (\underline{\text{FREE}} \;\overrightarrow{m}\; Ref\text{-}set)$
92. $DSK_6 \;=\; DSK_5 \;\underline{\cup}\; (\underline{\text{FREE}} \;\overrightarrow{m}\; Adr\text{-}set)$

<u>Domain Invariant</u>

93.0 $inv\text{-}FS_6(mk\text{-}FS_6(stg,disk)) \;\underline{\Delta}$
.1 $\quad(\underline{\text{FREE}} \in \underline{dom}\ stg) \wedge (stg(\underline{\text{FREE}}) \cap \underline{dom}\ stg = \{\})$
.2 $\quad\wedge(\underline{\text{FREE}} \in \underline{dom}\ dsk) \wedge (dsk(\underline{\text{FREE}}) \cap \underline{dom}\ dsk = \{\})$
.3 $\quad\wedge\ inv\text{-}FS_5(mk\text{-}FS_5(stg\backslash\{\underline{\text{FREE}}\},dsk\backslash\{\underline{\text{FREE}}\}))$

<u>Semantic Functions</u>

One illustration is sufficient to illuminate the idea:

94.0 $Int\text{-}Crea_6[mk\text{-}Crea(f)](mk\text{-}FS_6(stg,dsk)) \;\underline{\Delta}$
.1 $\quad\underline{if}\ f \in \underline{dom}(stg(\underline{\text{MASTER}}))$
.2 $\qquad\underline{then}\ \underline{undefined}$
.3 $\qquad\underline{else}\ \underline{if}\ dsk(\underline{\text{FREE}}) = \{\}$
.4 $\qquad\qquad\underline{then}\ \underline{undefined}$
.5 $\qquad\qquad\underline{else}\ (\underline{let}\ a \in dsk(\underline{\text{FREE}})\ \underline{in}$
.6 $\qquad\qquad\qquad mk\text{-}FS_6(stg+[\underline{\text{MASTER}} \mapsto stg(\underline{\text{MASTER}})+[f \mapsto (a,\underline{nil})]],$
.7 $\qquad\qquad\qquad\qquad dsk\cup[a \mapsto [\,]]+[\underline{\text{FREE}} \mapsto dsk(\underline{\text{FREE}})\backslash\{a\}]))$

<u>Conclusion to Third-Level Definition</u>

It turned out, perhaps somewhat surprisingly, that it was not too cumbersome to enrich our architecture to first embody the user-oriented aspects of reliability, recoverability, checkpointing and garbage collection; and then to turn it, some would think, radically, in the direction of a rather straightforward implementation.

11.4 SUMMARY

There remains to implement the resulting architecture. But since those (many) stages are not the concern of this chapter we shall leave it out! The concern, instead, of this chapter was to advocate, and show through a reasonably realistic example, the idea, respectively feasibility, of stepwise transformation of software architectures. We remind the reader of our remarks of the first three subsections of section 11.0. The conclusions we draw from the example are the following:

(1) It is desirable to study the architecture of what one is about to implement. Once implemented the product, whatever it is, will have great impact on users and/or systems. Considering the enormity of most such impacts, the intellectual, human and economic expenditures to be distributed over the "life-time" of the product, it is quite reasonable to spend far more time on studying the architecture.

(2) We say that "we study the architecture". By that we mean that the techniques of writing down, or formulating, Domain invariants and Domain abstractions (retrievals), besides being required in correctness proofs, also play an indispensable rôle in clarifying and adjusting the architecture proposal.

(3) We can demonstrate that spending increased resources on "paperwork", that is on architecture proposals formulated as exemplified is more advantageous than binding oneself to prototype implementations being disturbed by realization aspects, most often of the kind: "How do I program my way around 'this or that' host system peculiarity which I know will not be present in the actual system". We are all too often rushing into implementation before having properly understood our objectives.

(4) It is possible, as demonstrated, to conquer complexity through decomposition. But it is a developmental decomposition represented by "approximation". First we approximate what we consider most

important. In other examples than the one shown, reliability could be considered most important, and probably should have lead to a rather different sequence of architecture transformations. What we have shown is the kind of techniques used in stepwise architecture transformation.

11.5 BIBLIOGRAPHY

The incentive to provide a formal model of specifically the file handler illustrated in this chapter came from J.R.Abrial [Abrial 80*(4)]. Abrial acknowledges C.A.R.Hoare. The system modelled is believed to be that of OS6 [Stoy 72ab]. The model in [Abrial 80*(4)] introduces almost all notions in a first stage.

CHAPTER 12

FORMALIZATION OF DATA MODELS

This chapter illustrates the use of VDM on database applications. Database architectures can be likened to programming languages; implementations can be likened to interpreters and compilers and are discussed in chapter 13. Although not the main purpose, this chapter introduces the reader to many of the current concepts in the database world (relational, hierarchical, and network approaches). The material comprises a careful demonstration of how models are constructed; their components; the interrelation of the components; and the choice of abstraction principles.

This chapter is based on [Bjørner 80c], but is extensively revised and enlarged. Other papers which apply VDM specification techniques to database problems include [Hansal 76a, Nilsson 76a, Owlett 77a, Owlett 79a, Bjørner 80e, Lamersdorf 80ab, Neuhold 80a, Lindenau 81a, Olnhoff 81a, Neuhold 81a, Bjørner 82c].

CONTENTS

12.0 INTRODUCTORY CHARACTERIZATIONS

By a Data Model (DM) we shall simply understand a data type; that is: a set of objects and operations.

By a Database Management System (DBMS) we shall (corresponding simply) understand a system which supports the storing of the DM objects and the execution of the DM operations.

By a Database (DB) we shall understand a particular such collection of data being administered by a particular such DBMS.

Thus a DM is to us like a programming language. A DBMS, then, is like a processor (for example interpreter) for the DM. Finally a DB is like a specific program formulated in the DM language and interpreted on the DBMS processor for that language.

Like we can distinguish, in the area of "ordinary" programming languages, among "equivalence classes" of so-called ALGOL-like, LISP-like, SNOBOL-like, etc. languages (that is languages built up around rather distint data type and programming construct ideas), so we will, at the moment distinguish between three kinds of Data Models.

Our treatment, in this chapter, will therefore focus on abstract specifications of these three Data Models. They are the so-called Relational, the Hierarchical and the Network Data Models. Chapter 13 will then sketch stages of developments towards Database Management Systems for the latter two of the Data Models, namely an IBM IMS-like DBMS for the hierarchical DM and a CODASYL/DBTG-like DBMS for the network DM.

Common to all three DMs is the ability to speak of their objects in isolation from the operations applicable to them. Our presentation will therefore, within each of the three models, be subdivided into a first part dealing with representional abstractions of data objects, followed by a second part dealing with operational abstractions of operations on data.

Operations on data, that is on the entire aggregate of the usually composite data object of a database, fall in two classes: meta-functions and functions. Meta-functions are operations concerned with manipulating a description of the data of the database; functions are operations concerned with operating upon the data "itself", that is the non-descriptive parts. Some Data Models do not elaborate on this (so-called Schema-based) distinction. Our treatment will mostly focus on ordinary data functions. Such functions fall in two groups: data querying- and data manipulation commands. Data querying commands denote the evaluation, or extraction of data, $d \in D$, from, but no change to, the database data aggregate, $db \in DB$. Data manipulation commands denote that is interpret to a change of the database aggregate (from db to db').

type: *Val-Query*: $DB \rightarrow D$
type: *Int-Manip*: $DB \rightarrow DB$

Given a definition of the Domain of database objects one can, in general, define a variety of classes of for example query operations. This variety can be characterized by two extremes. These are sometimes referred to as procedural versus non-procedural operations. We shall term them algebraic, respectively logic operations. An algebraic operator basically speaking specifies how to extract data -- based on its its form. A logic operator roughly speaking specifies what to extract -- based on its content, that is on properties. (We could as well call the operation classes: syntactic, respectively semantic.)

In our treatment we shall exemplify both kinds of operations in the relational DM. The sections on the two other DMs will only exemplify algebraic operations. We invite the reader to propose and properly formalize for example predicate calculus based query operations on the hierarchical and/or network DMs. There is nothing intrinsic in these latter DMs which prevent such a set of operations.

12.1 THE RELATIONAL DATA MODEL

12.1.1 The Data Aggregates

The major, or main, data (structure or) aggregate of the RDM is that of a set of uniquely named relations:

1. $RDS = Rnm \underset{m}{\rightarrow} REL$

Each relation consists of an unordered collection of rows:

2. $REL \; = \; ROW\text{-}set$

(Rows are often referred to as 'tuples' -- not to be confused with the VDM specification language data type tuples.) Each row consists of a fixed number of distinctly attributed, that is 'named' element values. Two ways of modelling rows are possible:

3'. $ROW' \; = \; VAL^{+}$

models rows as tuples of values with these being individually 'named' by their index position. Since ordering among row elements is of no importance and since, moreover, one mostly prefers to refer to individual row elements by a more freely chosen attribute name we usually prefer the model rows by:

3". $ROW'' \; = \; Anm \underset{m}{\rightarrow} VAL$

All rows of any relation have the same number of similarly named elements:

4.' $is\text{-}wf\text{-}REL'(rel) \triangleq (\forall r_1, r_2 \in rel)((\underline{len}\ r_1 = \underline{len}\ r_2) \wedge (\ldots)')$

respectively:

4." $is\text{-}wf\text{-}REL''(rel) \triangleq (\forall r_1, r_2 \in rel)((\underline{dom}\ r_1 = \underline{dom}\ r_2) \wedge (\ldots)'')$

We also illuatrate, but do not detail, the well-formedness constraints which express, $(\ldots)$, that values from corresponding fields of any two rows must be of the same primitive ("scalar") type:

$$(\ldots)'' \; : (\forall n \in \underline{dom}\ r_1)(type(r_1(n)) = (type(r_2(n)))$$

The issues at stake when choosing between ROW' and ROW'' will be illustrated as we turn to an explication of algebraic operations on and between relations.

12.1.2 The Operations

We shall illustrate two kinds of operations: algebraic and logic. The latter are embedded in a rather general form of a predicate calculus.

AN ALGEBRAIC QUERY LANGUAGE

The relational algebra consists, besides relations, of the following operations: select, project, θ-join and divide. We consider these to be denoted by objects of the like-named command Domains:

5. *Cmd* = *Sel* | *Proj* | *Join* | *Div*

We can now either base our further description on the tuple, that is *ROW'*, explication of rows, or on the map, that is *ROW"*, or attribute named explication of rows. To illustrate the consequences of choosing one over the other we exemplify both alternatives, thus illuminating their consequences.

Before, however, detailing the formal definition of each of the individual vidual command Domains we informally define their semantics.

Informal Semantics and Formal Syntax

Selection operates on a single relation, *rel*, and delivers the relation of all those rows, in *rel*, whose elements in given attribute positions equals correspondingly given values:

6.' *Sel'* :: *Rnm* $(Nat1 \underset{m}{\rightarrow} VAL)$
6." *Sel"* :: *Rnm* $(Anm \underset{m}{\rightarrow} VAL)$

Projection operates on a single relation, *rel*, and delivers the relation of rows each of which is a sub-segment of the rows of *rel*:

7.' *Proj'* :: *Rnm* $Nat1^+$
7." *Proj"* :: *Rnm* *Anm-set*

Join operates on two, not necessarily distinct relations, rel_1 and rel_2. It forms the "composition" of exactly those rows, $r_1 @ r_2$, from rel_1 and rel_2, which in pairwise given positions have equal values:

8.' *Join'* :: $(Rnm \times Nat1^+)$ $(Nat1^+ \times Rnm)$
8." *Join"* :: $(Rnm \times Anm^+)$ $(Anm^+ \times Rnm)$

(The @ operation is meta-linguistic. Its particular meaning will be defined, below, relative to each of the two row-variants.)

Division operates on two relations: the dividend, rel_a, and the divisor, rel_b. The quotient is a relation. It is a projection of rel_a with respect to the complement of dividend fields, il_a, with only those rows, symbolically: $x \oplus y$ in rel_a, contributing a sub-segment x all of whose corresponding (il_a-projected) y components form a relation which includes the il_b projected divisor. Thus to specify a divide command we require, besides the names of the dividend and divisor relations, the respective (complementing) row element positions (field selectors):

9.' $Div' \ :: \ (Rnm \times Nat1^+) \quad (Nat1^+ \times Rnm)$

9." $Div'' \ :: \ (Rnm \times Anm^+) \quad (Anm^+ \times Rnm)$

Syntactic Well-formedness

Given just the syntactic command objects certain obvious constraints must be safisfied:

10. $is\text{-}wf\text{-}Proj'[mk\text{-}Proj'(,il)] \ \underline{\Delta} \ unique(il)$

where *unique* is a function which checks that the elements of its argument list, *al*, are all unique, for example:

11. $unique(al) \ \underline{\Delta} \ (\forall i,j \in \underline{inds}\ al)(al[i]=al[j] \supset i=j)$

12.0 $is\text{-}wf\text{-}Join[mk\text{-}Join((,al_1),(al_2,))] \ \underline{\Delta}$

.1 $(\underline{len}\ al_1 = \underline{len}\ al_2)$

[.2 $\wedge \ (unique(al_1) \wedge unique(al_2))$]

Where, optionally ([...] around line 12.2), we have expressed uniqueness of individual join fields.

13.0 $is\text{-}wf\text{-}Div[mk\text{-}Div((,al_1),(al_2,))] \ \underline{\Delta}$

.1 -- same as for *Proj*!

Types of *is-wf-...* and *unique* functions are:

14. <u>type:</u> $is\text{-}wf\text{-}... \ Cmd \rightarrow BOOL$

15. <u>type:</u> $unique: (Nat1^+ \mid Anm^+) \rightarrow BOOL$

Semantic Constraints

Given commands in the context of a relational data system, $rds \in RDS$, additional constraints must be satisfied:

```
16.0  pre-E_cmd[c](rds) ≜
  .1     cases c:
  .2       mk-Sel'(r,ivm)                 → ((r ∈ dom rds) ∧ (rds(r) ≠ {})
  .3                                         ∧(let row ∈ rds(r) in
  .4                                           dom ivm ⊆ inds row)),
  .5       mk-Proj"(r,ans)                → ((r ∈ dom rds) ∧ (rds(r) ≠ {})
  .6                                         ∧(let row ∈ rds(r) in
  .7                                           ans ⊆ dom row)),
  .8       mk-Join'((r1,l1),(l2,r2))      → ((r1 ∈ dom rds) ∧ (r2 ∈ dom rds)
  .9                                         ∧(rds(r1) ≠ {}) ∧ (rds(r2) ≠ {})
  .10                                        ∧(let rw1 ∈ rds(r1),
  .11                                              rw2 ∈ rds(r2) in
  .12                                          (elems l1 ⊆ inds rw1)∧
  .13                                          (elems l2 ⊆ inds rw2))),
  .14      mk-Div"((r1,l1),(l2,r2))       → ((r1 ∈ dom rds) ∧ (r2 ∈ dom rds)
  .15                                        ∧(rds(r1) ≠ {}) ∧ (rds(r2) ≠ {})
  .16                                        ∧(let rw1 ∈ rds(r1),
  .17                                              rw2 ∈ rds(r2) in
  .18                                          (elems l1 ⊆ dom rw1)
  .19                                         ∧(elems l2 ⊆ dom rw2)))
16.20  type:  pre-E_cmd: Cmd → (RDS → BOOL)
```

The constraint $r \in$ *dom* *rds* expresses that the relation name names a relation in the actual system (*rds*), and $rds(r) \neq \{\}$ that this relation is non-empty. The latter requirements are strictly speaking not necessary, but are included here to be able to test syntactic correctness of remaining command components. Normally the *pre-* checking could be, or is, done "against" (not the proper data part, but) a 'catalogue' describing all relations. We have not modelled such a 'schema' facility, one which could itself be a (specifically designated) relation. But we could easily do so.

Semantic Functions

Given the informal description semantics descriptions of the meaning of individual command categories it should now be easy to decipher:

17.0' $E\text{-}Sel'[mk\text{-}Sel'(r,ivm)](rds) \triangleq$
.1' $\{ row \mid row \in rds(r) \wedge (\forall i \in \underline{dom}\ ivm)(row[i] = ivm(i)) \}$

17.0" $E\text{-}Sel''[mk\text{-}Sel''(r,avm)](rds) \triangleq$
.1" $\{ row \mid row \in rds(r) \wedge (\forall a \in \underline{dom}\ avm)(row(a) = ivm(a)) \}$

Here the distinction between the two (the row-tuple and the row-map) models was almost invisible ($row[i]$ versus $row(a)$).

18.0' $E\text{-}Proj'[mk\text{-}Proj'(r,il)](rds) \triangleq$
.1' $\{ \langle row[il[j]] \mid 1 \leq j \leq \underline{len}\ il \rangle \mid row \in rds(r) \}$

in contrast to:

18.0" $E\text{-}Proj''[mk\text{-}Proj''(r,as)](rds) \triangleq$
.1" $\{ [\ a \mapsto row(a) \mid a \in as\ ] \mid row \in rds(r) \}$

Next:

19.0' $E\text{-}Join'[mk\text{-}Join'((r_1,l_1),(l_2,r_2))](rds) \triangleq$
.1' $\{ rw_1 \frown rw_2 \mid (rw_1 \in rds(r_1)) \wedge (rw_2 \in rds(r_2))$
.2' $\wedge (\forall i \in \underline{inds}\ l_1)(rw_1[l_1[i]] = rw_2[l_2[i]])) \}$

in sharper contrast to:

19.0a $E\text{-}Join''[mk\text{-}Join''(r_1,l_1),(l_2,r_2))](rds) \triangleq$
.1a $\{ rw_1 \cup rw_2 \mid (rw_1 \in rds(r_1)) \wedge (rw_2 \in rds(r_2))$
.2a $\wedge (\forall i \in \underline{inds}\ l_1)(rw_1(l_1[i] = rw_2(l_2[i])) \}$

This latter (specifically: $rw_1 \cup rw_2$) only works, that is is only well-defined provided line 20.4:

20.0 $pre\text{-}E\text{-}Join''[mk\text{-}Join''((r_1,l_1),(l_2,r_2))](rds) \triangleq$
.1 (... repetition of 16.8-9 ...)
.2 $\wedge(\underline{let}\ rw_1 \in rds(r_1),$
.3 $rw_2 \in rds(r_2)\quad \underline{in}$
.4 $((\underline{dom}\ rw_1 \cap \underline{dom}\ rw_2 = \{\})$
.5 $\wedge(\underline{elems}\ l_1 \in \underline{dom}\ rw_1) \wedge (\underline{elems}\ l_2 \subseteq \underline{dom}\ rw_2))$

If we permit attribute (that is column) names of joined relations to be common then we must "invent" some "renaming" scheme, for example:

```
19.1b   { [(r1,a1) ↦ rw1(a1) | a1 ∈ dom rw1]
   .2b  ∪ [(r2,a2) ↦ rw2(a2) | a2 ∈ dom rw2]
   .3b       | (rw1 ∈ rds(r1)) ∧ (rw2 ∈ rds(r2))
   .4b       ∧ (∀i ∈ inds l1)(rw1(l2[i])) = rw2(l2[i])) }
```

which then replaces 19.1a"-2a". The map merge, ∪, in 19.1a" and the relation-attribute name pairing and merge, $(..,..)$ and ∪, in 19.1b-2b, then "explains" the previously unexplained ⊗ meta-operator.

Finally we formalize division. Without proof (of equivalence) we rephrase the earlier stated description of the division operator. Let $mk\text{-}Div((r_1,l_1),(l_2,r_2))$ be the divided command in question. First we construct an auxiliary relation *rel* from the dividend relation $rds(r_1)$ by projecting on the positions complementary to those listed in l_1. Then we select only those rows, *row*, from *rel*, for which the following condition is satisfied. Namely the relation, *rel'*, formed from the divisor relation, $rds(r_2)$, by projections on l_2, must be wholly contained in, that is a subset of, the relation formed by projections on l_1 of those rows *row'* in the dividend, $rds(r_1)$, whose complementing positions equal *row*.

```
21.0   E-Div'[mk-Div'((r1,l1),(l2,r2))](rds) ≜
  .1      (let (dvd,dsr)  = (rds(r1),rds(r2)) in
  .2           cl         = complement(l1,dvd)  in
  .3       let (rel,rel') = (project(dvd,cl),project(dsr,l2) in
  .4       {row | (row∈rel)
  .5              ∧rel'⊂{p(row',l1)|row'∈dvd∧row=p(row',cl)}})

22.0   complement(rel,l,rel) ≜ (let rw ∈ rel in
                                 <i | 1≤i≤len rw ∧ i¬∈elems l>)

23.0   project(rel,l)          ≜  {p(row,l) | row ∈ rel}

24.0   p(row,l)                ≜ <row[l[i]] | 1 ≤ i ≤ len l>
where:
22.    type:  complement:  Nat1+   × REL'  → Nat1+
23.    type:  project:     REL'    × Nat1+ → REL'
24.    type:  p:           ROW'    × Nat1+ → ROW'
```

and, in general:

17-19. <u>type</u>: *E-Cmd: Cmd* $\overset{\sim}{\to}$ *(RDS* $\overset{\sim}{\to}$ *REL)*

Other ways of specifying the semantic functions could be given. We next illustrate function definition by so-called <u>pre-/post-</u> conditions. If:

25. <u>type</u>: $F:\ A \to B$

then:

26. <u>type</u>: $pre\text{-}F:\ A \to BOOL$

27. <u>type</u>: $post\text{-}F:\ A \times B \to BOOL$

are the types of functions which determine the applicability of an A argument to F, that is specifies Fs domain, respectively give the property that any result, $b \in B$, must satisfy relative to an applicable argument $a \in A$:

28. $pre\text{-}F(a) \supset (\exists! b \in B)(F(a) = b)$

29. $pre\text{-}F(a) \wedge post\text{-}F(a,b) \supset (F(a) = b))$

```
30.0  pre-E-Sel'([mk-Sel'(r,ivm)],rds)) ≜
  .1     ((r ∈ dom rds)
  .2     ∧((rds(r) ≠ {}) ⊃ (let row ∈ rds(r) in (dom ivm ⊆ inds row))))
```

-- which we already specified in 16.2-4.

```
31.0  post-E-Sel'(([mk-Sel'(r,ivm)],rds),rel) ≜
  .1     ((rel ⊆ rds(r))
  .2     ∧(∀row ∈ rel)(∀i ∈ dom ivm)(row[i]=ivm(i)))

32.0  post-E-Proj'(([mk-Proj'(r,il),rds)],rel) ≜
  .1     (∀row ∈ rel)
  .2        (∃rw ∈ rds(r))
  .3           ((len row = len il)
  .4           ∧(∀i ∈ inds row)(row[i] = rw[il[i]]))

33.0  post-E-Join'(([mk-Join'((r1,l1),(l2,r2))],rds),rel) ≜
  .1     (∀rw1 ∈ rds(r1),rw2 ∈ rds(r2))
  .2        ((rw1^rw2 ∈ rel)
  .3        ≡ (∀i ∈ inds l1)(rw1[l1[i]]=rw2[l2[i]]))
```

etc.

A PREDICATE CALCULUS QUERY LANGUAGE

The predicate calculus based query language now to be illustrated is the basis for the SQL query language of IBMs System/R relational DBMS, but is otherwise based on DSL-alpha.

Syntax and Informal Semantics

A program in this language is a query. A query consists of three parts. The first part is a specification of the names of relations, possibly projected to individual columns, that is attributes, to be delivered as the result. This part is called a target specification list. The second part is a specification of which properties rows of these, possibly projected, relations must satisfy. This part is a predicate expression in which arbitrary identifiers may be used to stand for virtual relations. Which relations they stand for is specified in the thirds part, the virtual relation identifier to virtual relation expression. A virtual relation expression is a possibly operator/ operand expression which evaluates to a relation:

1. *Query* :: $Targ^+$ (*Vid* $\underset{m}{\rightarrow}$ *Range*) *Pred*
2. *Targ* :: *Vid* [*Nat1*]

Range expressions either denote existing relations directly or relations which are the set theoretic union, intersection or non-symmetric complement of two, possibly virtual relations:

3. *Range* = *Rnm* | *InfixR*
4. *InfixR* :: *Range* *SOp* *Range*
5. *SOp* = <u>UNION</u> | <u>INTERSECTION</u> | <u>COMPLEMENT</u>

Finally we analyze the syntax of predicates. Four kinds are provided: quantified, infix and negated propositional and atomic:

6. *Pred* = *QPred* | *IPred* | *NPred* | *APred*
7. *QPred* :: ((<u>ALL</u>|<u>EXIST</u>) *Tid* *Rnm*) *Pred*
8. *IPred* :: *Pred* (<u>AND</u>|<u>OR</u>) *Pred*
9. *NPred* :: *Pred*
10. *APred* :: *Term* *ROp* *Term*
11. *ROp* = <u>LESEQ</u> | <u>LESS</u> | <u>EQ</u> | <u>NEQ</u> | <u>LAREQ</u> | <u>LARG</u>

Quantified predicates *mk-QPred((q,t,r),p)* representationally abstract $(\forall t \epsilon r)(p)$ or $(\exists t \epsilon r)(p)$ where q=ALL, respectively q = EXIST. Semantically they express whether p is true for all rows, respectively at least one, row, t, in the relation named r. Infix predicates express the conjunction or disjunction of two predicates. Negate predicates the negation of a predicate. Finally an Atomic predicate expresses relations between row elements and/or constant values, that is:

12. *Term* = *Elem* | *VAL*
13. *Elem* :: (*Vid* | *Tid*) × *Nat1*

Well-formedness, or Context Constraints

It is clear that certain constraints on queries must be satisfied. These constraints are of two kinds referred to as internal and external constraints. Internal constraints express well-formedness of one query part with respect to another query part. External constraints express well-formedness with respect to existing relations of the database.

Examples of constraints are: [internal:] only virtual relation identifiers defined in the range part of a query can be referred to in the target specifications, [external:] and the row position used there must be in the interval of positions for tuples, that is rows, of the identified virtual relation. Similar for virtual relations mentioned in atomic predicates. In these latter, if a term refers to a row identifier, in *Tid*, [internal:] then the term must be in the scope of a quantification defining that row identifier, and [external:] the row element position of the term must likewise be in the internal of positions for tuples, that is rows, of the 'range' relation correspondingly named in the quantification, that is of r in *mk-QPred((q,t,r),p)*.

We therefore define a function, *Interval*, which when applied to an actual relation name, *Rnm*, and a relational data system, *RDS*, yields the index set of row tuples of the named relation:

13. type: *Interval*: *Rnm* → (*RDS* → *Nat1-set*)

13.0 *Interval(r)(rds)* $\triangleq$
  .1 (let *row* ϵ *rds(r)* in inds *row*)
  .2 pre: *rds(r)* $\neq$ {}

We express both internal and external constraints in one function:

```
14.0   pre-E-Query[mk-Query(tl,rm,p)](rds) ≜
  .1        wfRanges[rm](rds)
  .2      ∧ wfTargl[tl](D(rm,rds))
  .3      ∧ is-wf-Pred[p](rds)(D(rm,rds))

15.0   WfRanges[rm](rds) ≜
  .1      (∀r ∈ rng rm)(is-wf-Range[r](rds))

16.0   is-wf-Range[rng](rds) ≜
  .1      cases rng:
  .2        (mk-InfixR(r1,,r2) → (is-wf-Range[r1](rds)
  .3                              ∧is-wf-Range[r2](rds)
  .4                              ∧I(r1,rds) = I(r2,rds))
  .5          T                 →  rng ∈ dom rds)

17.    type:  I: Range  RDS → Nat1-set

17.0   I(rng,rds) ≜
  .1      cases rng: (mk-InfixR(r1,,) → I(r1,rds),
  .2                  T               → Interval(rds(rng)))
```

In expressing well-formedness of target specification list and predicate we make use of a dictionary-like construction built from the range specification and recording the row tuple intervals of pertinent (virtual) relations:

```
18.    DICT   = ((Vid | Tid) →m Nat1-set)

19.    type: D: (Vid →m Range)  RDS → DICT

19.0   D(rm,rds) ≜ [r ↦ I(rm(r),rds) | r ∈ dom rm]

20.0   WfTargl[tl](δ) ≜
  .1      (∀t ∈ elems tl)(is-wf-Targ[t](δ))

21.0   is-wf-Targ[mk-Targ(v,i)](δ)
  .1      (v ∈ dom dict) ∧ (i ∈ δ(v))
```

```
22.0  is-wf-Pred[p](rds)(δ) ≜
  .1     cases p:
  .2       (mk-QPred((,t,r),p') → (r ∈ dom rds)
  .3                               ∧(let δ' = δ + [t ↦ I(r,rds)] in
  .4                                 is-wf-Pred[p'](rds)(δ'))),
  .5        mk-IPred(p1,,p2)    → (is-wf-Pred[p1](rds)(δ)
  .6                               ∧is-wf-Pred[p2](rds)(δ)),
  .7        mk-NPred(p')        → is-wf-Pred[p'](rds)(δ),
  .8        mk-APred(t1,,t2)    → (is-wf-Term[t1](δ)
  .9                               ∧is-wf-Term[t2](δ)))

23.0  is-wf-Term[t](δ) ≜
  .1     cases t: (mk-Elem(id,i) → (id ∈ dom δ)
  .2                               ∧(id ∈ δ(id)),
  .3               T              → true)

14.  type: pre-E-Query:  Query            → (RDS         → BOOL)
15.        WfRanges:     (Vid ⇸ Range)    → (RDS         → BOOL)
16.        is-wf-Range:  Range            → (RDS         → BOOL)
20.        WfTargl:      Targ+            →       (DICT  → BOOL)
21.        is-wf-Targ:   Targ             →       (DICT  → BOOL)
22.        is-wf-Pred:   Pred             → (RDS → (DICT → BOOL))
23.        is-wf-Term:   Term             →       (DICT  → BOOL)
```

We have highlighted some, but not all aspects of checking the consistency of queries of a predicate-based language. We next turn to their semantics.

Formal Semantics

The general form of a query can be given schematically:

```
24.   mk-Query(<mk-Targ(vi,ini),mk-Targ(vj,inj),...,mk-Targ(vk,ink)>,
               [v1 ↦ rng1,v2 ↦ rng2,...,vn ↦ rngn]
               predicate)
```

We refer to the informal semantics subsection of this section for an informal wording of the semantics of such a query. We "translate" that (incomplete) specification into the complete formalization below. This formal definition is based on the following auxiliary constructs: For each of the virtual relation names, v, we construct the relation denoted by its corresponding range expression, *rng*. We collect these in a table *rm* (25.1). This table, or map, thus pairs names to sets of rows. For each combination, *m*, of rows, one from each named virtual relation, we check (*E-Pred*) whether the *predicate* is satisfied. If so, we construct (*C*), from *m*, a projection based on the target list specification *tl*. And we do so for all combinations. Applicable such *m* contribute to the final answer which itself is a relation:

```
25.0   E-Query[mk-Query(tl,irm,p)](rds) ≜
  .1       (let rm = [v ↦ E-Range[irm(v)](rds) | v ∈ dom irm] in
  .2        {conc(C(tl,m)) | m ∈ G(rm) ∧ E-Pred[p](m)(rds)})

25.    type: Query ⥲ (RDS ⥲ REL')

26.0   E-Range[r](rds) ≜
  .1       cases r:
  .2         (mk-InfixR(r1,o,r2)
  .3             → (let rel1 = E-Range[r1](rds),
  .4                    rel2 = E-Range[r2](rds)  in
  .5                cases o: (UNION          → rel1 ∪ rel2,
  .6                          INTERSECTION   → rel1 ∩ rel2,
  .7                          COMPLEMENT     → rel1 \ rel2)),
  .8          T  → rds(r))

26.    type:  Rang ⥲ (RDS → REL')

27.    type: E-Pred: Pred → (TABLE → (RDS → BOOL))

27.0   E-Pred[p](map)(rds) ≜
  .1       cases p:
  .2         (mk-QPred((q,t,r),p')
  .3            → (let rel = rds(r)  in
  .4               cases q:
  .5                 (ALL     → (∀row ∈ rel)
  .6                                   (E-Pred[p'](map + [t ↦ row])(rds),
  .7                  EXISTS → (∃row ∈ rel)
  .8                                   (E-Pred[p'](map + [t ↦ row])(rds))),
  .9          mk-IPred(p1,o,p2)
  .10            → (let b1 = E-Pred[p1](map)(rds),
  .11                   b2 = E-Pred[p2](map)(rds)  in
  .12              cases o: (AND → b1∧b2, OR → b1∨b2)),
```

```
  .13        mk-NPred(p')
  .14          → ¬E-Pred[p'](map)(rds),
  .15        mk-APred(t1,o,t2)
  .16          → (let e1 = E-Term[t1](map),
  .17                 e2 = E-Term[t2](map)  in
  .18            cases o: (LESEQ → e1 ≤ e2, LESS → e1 < e2
  .19                      EQ    → e1 = e2, NEQ  → e1 ≠ e2
  .20                      LAREQ → e1 ≥ e2, LARG → e1 > e2)))
```

where:

```
28.    TABLE  =  ((Vid | Tid) ⇸m ROW')

29.0   E-Term[t](tbl) ≜
  .1     cases t:
  .2       (mk-Elem(id,i) → (tbl(id))[i],
  .3        T              → t)
29.    type:  Term ⥲ (TABLE ⥲ VAL)
```

The two auxiliary functions *G* and *C* are finally defined. *G* takes an object in $(A \xrightarrow{m} B\text{-}set)$ and delivers an object in $(A \xrightarrow{m} B)\text{-}set$. For each combination of (a_1,b_{1k}), ..., (a_m,b_{mj}) in:

$$[a_1 \mapsto \{b_{11},\ldots,b_{1n1}\},\ldots,b\ a_m \mapsto \{b_{m1},\ldots,b_{mnm}\}]$$

G delivers an element map:

$$[a_1 \mapsto b_{1k},\ldots,a_m \mapsto b_{mj}]$$

in the set $G(rm)$ of such maps:

```
30.    type:  G:  (Vid ⇸m ROW-set) → (Vid ⇸m ROW)-set
30.0   G(rm) ≜
  .1     if rm = []
  .2       then {[]}
  .3       else {[v ↦ row] ∪ m | v ∈ dom rm ∧ row ∈ rm(v)
  .4                              ∧ m ∈ G(rm\{v})}
```

and:

```
31.    type: C: Targ+ TABLE  ⥲  ROW+
31.0   C(tl,map) ≜
  .1     <cases tl[i]:
  .2       mk-Targ(v,nil) → map(v),
  .3       mk-Targ(v,j)   → <(map(v))[i]>   | 1 ≤ i ≤ len tl>
```

This concludes our treatment of the semantics of the [SQL-] (or DSL-alpha) predicate-based query language as basically used in the IBM System/R DBMS.

12.2 THE HIERARCHICAL DATA MODEL

In this section we describe the development of various models of database systems using the hierarchical model.

First, we introduce the hierarchical model and set up a data model of a very simple hierarchical database. Using this model, the semantics is defined for two simple query languages corresponding to the languages of the Information Management system (IMS) of IBM, and the SYSTEM 2000 of MRI.

12.2.1 Concepts of the Hierarchical Model

The aim of this section is to explain the concepts of the hierarchical data model, and to show how these may be formalized. We shall do this on basis of a traditional example from which we isolate the main concepts: the schema and the data hierarchy.

A Traditional Presentation

Hierarchical Database concepts are very often explained on the basis of a sample or "snapshot" database like the one in the figure below:

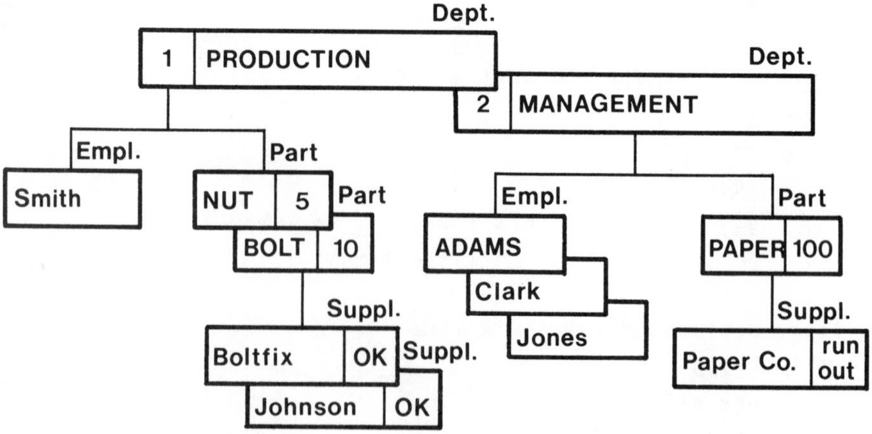

Fig. 1

Usually, one is told that the example is simple and unrealistic. But one can deduct the following laws from the diagram:

(1) Data are grouped into "boxes" called records.
(2) The records are arranged in a tree structure.
(3) Some records share the same structure, called record type.
(4) Records having the same type occur at the same level of the database.
(5) Records of one type have children out of a certain set of other types. No record of another type has children of this type.
(6) For all records of the same type, the parents of these share a type too.

(4) and (5) are consequences of (6). To summarize the specific relationships among types, a Hierarchical Definition tree, Hierarchy Chart, or Hierarchy Diagram is often given:

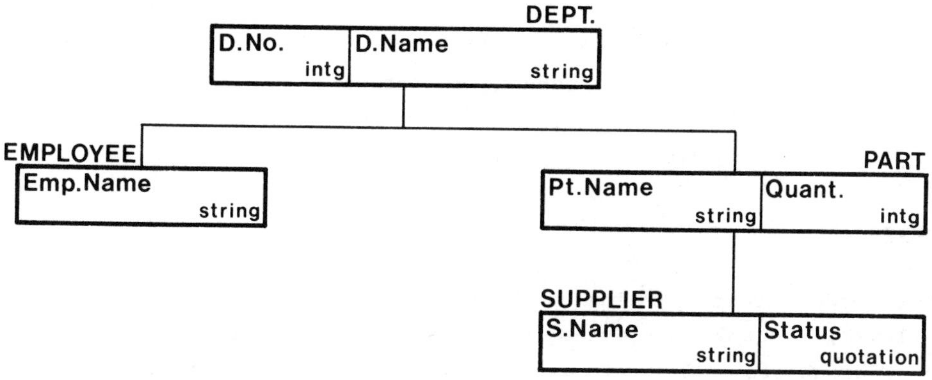

Fig. 2

The diagram shows the "pattern" of data in the database, and is sometimes called the schema of the database.

MODELLING THE SCHEMA

We start our modelling by considering a simplified Hierarchy Diagram like the left one on the next page:

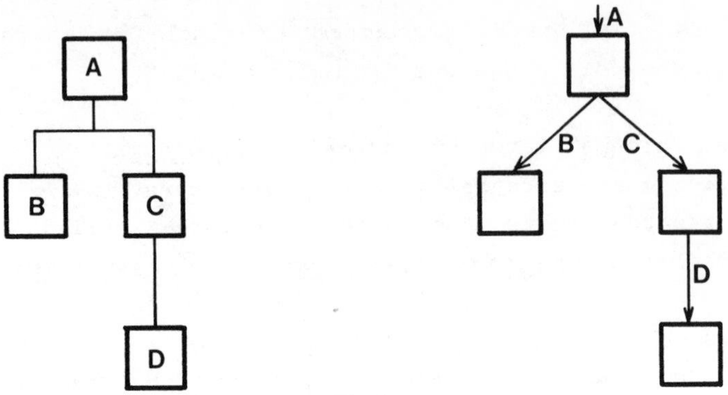

Fig. 3

We see that it is made up of record type names arranged in a tree structure. How do we model this? From the right hand diagram, which is just another way of picturing the one on the left, we more readily see that a Hierarchy Diagram *(HD)* can be modelled by:

1. $HD = RTId \underset{m}{\rightarrow} HD$

where *RTId* are Record Type Identifiers which may be considered to be *Token*'s. An *HD*-object corresponding to the diagram above is thus:

2. $[\ A \mapsto [\ B \mapsto [\,], C \mapsto [\ D \mapsto [\,]]]]$

-- Extension

In this model it is possible to have several record types at the uppermost level, thereby introducing a forest of hierarchies corresponding to several databases. The tree wiew may be retained by introducing an imaginative anonymous "system" type being the parent of all upper level types:

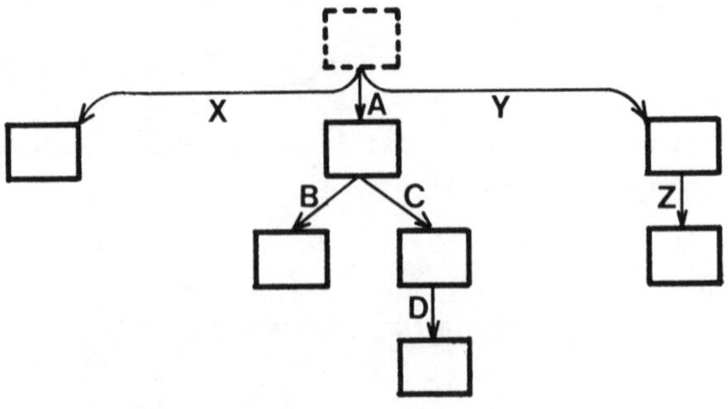

Fig. 4

The *HD* model thus shows the tree below the "system" type.

Inclusion of Record Types

The schema should also record the various record structures, the record types. How these may be included in the model depends on the constraints on the type names. Three policies arise:

(a) Duplicate names allowed; they denote the same type.
(b) Duplicate names allowed; they may denote different types.
(c) Duplicate names not allowed.

In actual systems, case (c) is usually dominant.

Now, turning to the problem of including Record Types two alternatives seem to emerge. Either we can give the association of Record Types to Record Type Names in conjunction with the hierarchy, or the Record Types can be inserted in the hierarchy (at the place of the "boxes"). Introducing the term catalogue for the data structure that describes the "shape" of a database or the "pattern" of its data, we get:

3. $CTLG' \;::\; HD \quad (RTId \underset{m}{\rightarrow} RecTp)$
4. $CTLG \;=\; RTId \underset{m}{\rightarrow} (RecTp \times CTLG)$

We see that *CTLG'* is able to handle cases (a) and (c), but that *CTLG* can handle all three cases. We therefore choose *CTLG* being the most general model.

-- The Record Type

The Record Type should describe the structure of all records of a record class. Since a record is a collection of named data values, the Record Type must include the names of the data items, and the type of values allowed for each named item. We shall call the names for field identifiers (*FieldId*'s). The Types may be INTEGER, STRING, etc.:

5. $RecTp \;=\; FieldId \underset{m}{\rightarrow} TYPE$
6. $FieldId \;=\; Token$
7. $TYPE \;=\; \ldots \mid \underline{\mathrm{INTEGER}} \mid \ldots$

Well-formedness

Having defined the whole catalogue we must decide whether to allow all such catalogues. Although not necessary for the model, we choose to apply name-constraint (c) since this is typical for actual systems and seems to be part of the hierarchical data model.

Thus, we do not allow any two type names in the whole catalogue to be identical. Using an auxiliary function which collects all names of a (sub) catalogue this can be formalized by:

8.1 $inv\text{-}CTLG(ctlg) \triangleq$
.2 $(\forall id \in \underline{dom}\ ctlg)$
.3 $(\underline{let}\ (rectp, ctlg') = ctlg(id)\ \underline{in}$
.4 $inv\text{-}RecTp(rectp) \wedge inv\text{-}CTLG(ctlg'))$
.5 $\wedge\ (\forall id_1, id_2 \in \underline{dom}\ ctlg)$
.6 $(\underline{let}\ ids_1 = collect\text{-}names(s\text{-}CTLG(ctlf(id_1))),$
.7 $ids_2 = collect\text{-}names(s\text{-}CTLG(ctlg(id_2))\ \underline{in}$
.8 $(ids_1 \cap \underline{dom}\ ctlg = \{\}) \wedge (id_1 \neq id_2 \supset ids_1 \cap ids_2 = \{\}))$
.9 $\underline{type}:\ CTLG \rightarrow Bool$

9.1 $collect\text{-}names(ctlg) \triangleq$
.2 $\underline{dom}\ ctlg \cup \underline{union}\ \{collect\text{-}names(s\text{-}CTLG(ctlg(id))) \mid id \in \underline{dom}\ ctlg\}$
.3 $\underline{type}:\ CTLG \rightarrow RTId\text{-}set$

inv-RecTp will be only partially specified. Here we require at least one field to be present:

10.1 $inv\text{-}RecTp(rectp) \triangleq ((rectp \neq [\,]) \wedge \ldots)$

The Hierarchical Path Concept

A hierarchical path *(HP)* is a useful notion by which we shall understand a sequence of record type names which starts at (one of) the root(s) of the hierarchical diagram, and follows the branches of the tree. Thus:

11. $HP = RTId^{+}$

The validity of such a path must be checked against a given catalogue:

```
12.1  pre-HP(hp)(ctlg) ≜
  .2      cases hp:
  .3          <>           → true,
  .4          <id>^hp'     → id∈dom ctlg ∧ pre-HP(hp')(s-CTLG(ctlg(id)))
  .5  type: HP  →  (CTLG  ⇸  Bool)
```

-- Some Hierarchical Path Operations

A Hierarchical Path may be used to select the corresponding sub-catalogue and record type:

```
13.1  sub-catalogue(hp,ctlg) ≜
  .2      cases hp: <>          → ctlg,
  .3                <id>^hp'    → sub-catalogue(hp',s-CTLG(ctlg(id)))
  .4  type:  RTId* × CTLG ⇸ CTLG
```

```
14.1  lookup-rectp(hp,ctlg) ≜
  .2      (let hp'^<id> = hp in  s-RecTp(sub-catalogue(hp',ctlg)(id)))
  .3  type:  HP × CTLG ⇸ RecTp
```

Finally, we will utilize our unique record type names to find the complete Hierarchical Path corresponding to such a name.

```
15.1  find-hp(id,ctlg) ≜
  .2      (id∈dom ctlg → <id>,
  .3       T      → (let id'' = (Δid'∈dom ctlg)
  .4                              (id∈collect-names(s-CTLG(ctlg(id'))) in
  .5                 <id'>^find-hp(id,s-CTLG(ctlg(id'))) )
  .6  type:  RTId × CTLG ⇸ HP
  .7  pre:   id∈collect-names(ctlg)
```

THE HIERARCHICAL MODEL

Record Instances

A record is a collection of named data values:

```
16.   Rec  =  FieldId →m VAL
17.   VAL  =  ... | Int | ...
```

A record is said to be an instance or occurrence of a record type if it has the "structure" prescribed by the record type, that is, it has exactly the same field-names as present in the type, and the value of each named field belongs to the type associated with the name in the record type. Assuming a function *type-of* that returns the type of a value, we can formalize the above statement:

18.1 *inv-Rec(rec)rectp* $\triangleq$

.2 *(<u>dom</u> rec = <u>dom</u> rectp)* $\wedge$

.3 *($\forall$fid$\in$<u>dom</u> rec) (type-of(rec(fid)) = rectp(fid))*

.4 *<u>type</u>: Rec → (RecTp $\overset{\sim}{\to}$ Bool)*

19. *<u>type</u>: type-of: VAL → TYPE*

Observe that the name-set is fixed (18.2) thereby prohibiting varying records etc.

<u>Hierarchy Model</u>

Consider part of the hierarchy diagram above:

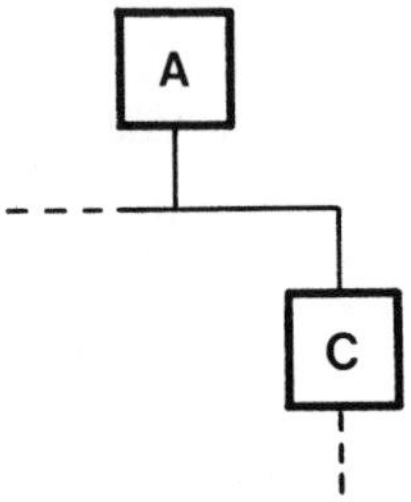

Fig. 5

The branch from *A* down to *C* is indicates a *1:n* relationship between *A*-records and *C*-records, that is to say:

- With each *A* record is associated a number (possibly zero) of *C* records called the *A* record's <u>children</u> of type *C* .

- With each *C*-record is associated exactly one *A* record called the <u>parent</u> of the *C*-record.

To illustrate these relations, a sample or "snapshot" database is often drawn:

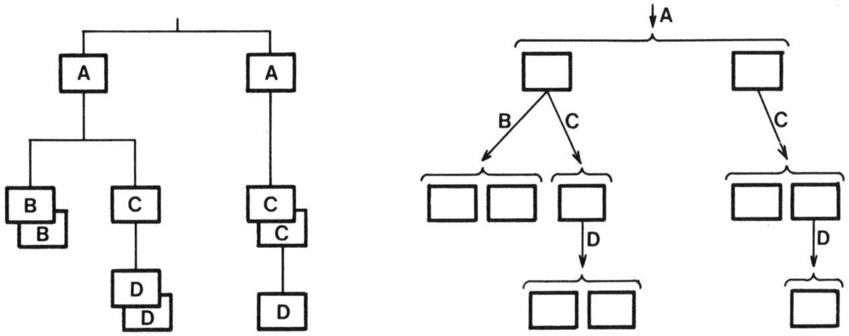

Fig. 6

The right side refiguring shows that we may model the database by:

20. *DB* = *RTId* $\underset{m}{\rightarrow}$ *(Rec* × *DB)-set*

21. *HDBS* :: *CTLG* *DB*

In fact, the model covers several databases under the imaginary system-record. Finally, a Hierarchical Database System *(HDBS)* is defined as consisting of a Catalogue and a Database.

<u>Well-formedness</u>

Of course we will not accept all *DB*-objects as databases; only database s corresponding to some catalogue are allowed. We may try to exploit the database structure to see that sub, and sub-sub-records have the same structure etc. However it is much more convenient only to consider databases in connection with a catalogue. We therefore define a function to check that a database has the structure given by a catalogue, that is we define the <u>invariant</u> over the *HDBS* Domain:

```
22.1   inv-HDBS(mk-HDBS(ctlg,db)) ≜
  .2      dom db = dom ctlg ∧
  .3      (∀id∈dom db)
  .4         (let (rectp,ctlg') = ctlg(id) in
  .5          (∀(rec,db')∈db(id))
  .6            (inv-Rec(rec)rectp ∧
  .7             inv-HDBS(mk-HDBS(ctlg',db')))))
  .8   type: HDBS → Bool
```

Note in 22.2 that we demand all Record Type names to be present in the database. As a result, the database part [*id* ↦ {}, ...] is not equivalent to [...] .

Unique Identification

When defining the data manipulation languages, it is convenient to be able to uniquely identify each record occurrence. Since our model is a top-down model of the tree, such an identification must reflect this. That is, the identification should indicate how to reach the record starting at the database root. Therefore, to identify a record *R* we must at the top-level indicate which record occurrence contains *R* in its associated sub-database. For this sub-database, we must again identify the record of which *R* is a descendant.

At each level, the record occurrence is given by a record type *t* and an indication of which record of the record set of type *t* is chosen. To uniquely identify records within a record set we may either choose to require unique key fields of the records, or we may choose to assign a unique name or label to each record in the set. To lead up to the retrieval languages defined later in which no key fields are required, we choose the latter technique.

When Record labels are introduced, the database domain is redefined to:

23. *DB* = *RTId* $\underset{m}{\rightarrow}$ *(RecLab* $\underset{m}{\rightarrow}$ *(Rec × DB))*
24. *RecLab* = *Token*

We shall call the unique record identification a path:

25. *Path* = *(RTId × RecLab)**

The record identifications from the upper level to the record level are given from left to right. The empty path identifies the imaginary "system record". Thus, the set of all records in a database can be represented by the set of all possible paths in the database:

26.0 *all-paths(db)* $\triangleq$
.1 {<>} ∪ { *<(id,l>^p* | *id*∈dom *db* ∧ *l*∈dom *db(id)* ∧
.2 *p*∈*all-paths(s-DB(db(id)(l)))* }
.3 type: *DB* → *Path-set*

Given a path, it is often convenient to look up the record it designates and its associated sub-database:

```
27.0  sub-database(p,db) ≜
  .1    cases p: <>                → db
  .2             <(id,lab)>^p'     → sub-database(p',s-DB(db(id)(lab)))
  .3  type: Path  DB  ⥲  DB
  .4  pre:  p∈all-paths(db)
```

```
28.0  lookup-rec(p,db) ≜
  .1    (let p'^<(id,lab)> = p  in
  .2     s-Rec(subdatabase(p',db(id)(lab)))
  .3  type: Path  →  (DB  ⥲  Rec)
  .4  pre:  p∈all-paths(db)\{<>}
```

Note that the "system" record cannot be retrieved.

With the path identification of records, we see that one record is an ancestor of another if its path is an prefix of the other path. We shall say that two records are <u>independent</u> if none of them is an ancestor of the other. This may be formalized by:

29.1 is-prefix(p_1,p_2) ≜ ($\exists p_3 \in$Path) ($p_2 = p_1$^p_3)

.2 type: Path × Path → Bool

30.1 indep(p_1,p_2) ≜ ¬is-prefix(p_1,p_2) ∧ ¬is-prefix(p_2,p_1)

.2 type: Path × Path → Bool

SUMMARY OF A SIMPLE HIERARCHICAL DATABASE SYSTEM

These semantic domains form the basis for the languages defined in section 12.2.2 and 12.2.3.

```
31.   HDBS      ::  CTLG   DB
32.   CTLG      =   RTId ⇸ (RecTp × CTLG)
33.   DB        =   RTId ⇸ (RecLab ⇸ (Rec × DB))
34.   RecTp     =   FieldId ⇸ TYPE
35.   Rec       =   FieldId ⇸ VAL
36.   TYPE      =   INTEGER | ...
37.   VAL       =   Intg | ...
38.   RTId      =   Token
39.   RecLab    =   Token
40.   FieldId   =   Token
```

12.2.2 A Hierarchy Oriented Query Language

In this section, we define a simple language that uses hierarchical paths as a basic concept. The DL/1 language of IMS does so. However, our language will be less procedural than DL/1.

Search String

The main idea in the hierarchy-oriented languages is that the records to be considered are denoted by essentially a hierarchical path augmented with qualifications at each level. The records selected are those of the last type of the path for which the qualifications for themselves and all their anchestors are satisfied. The syntactical construct whose purpose is to select records in the database for further actions is here called a Search String. We here assume that either the qualification is omitted, or it demands a given field to have a certain value.

```
44.    SearchStr   =   (RTId × [Qual])*
45.    Qual        =   (FieldId × VAL)
```

(The empty search string can (as usual) be considered to select the imaginary "system record".)

For a search string to be valid, the record types must follow a hierarchical path from the root and the last record type. Furthermore, at each level, the qualification must, if present, use a field of the corresponding record type and the value must be of the right type:

```
43.1   pre-SearchStr[ss]ctlg ≜
  .2      cases ss:
  .3      (<>                 → true,
  .4       <(id,qual)>^ss'    → id ∈ dom ctlg ∧
  .5                            (let (rectp,ctlg') = ctlg(id)  in
  .6                             (qual=nil ∨ pre-Qual[qual]rectp) ∧
  .7                             pre-SearchStr[ss']ctlg'))
  .8   type:  SearchStr → (CTLG ⥲ Bool)

44.1   pre-Qual[qual]rtp ≜
  .2     (let (fid,v)=qual in  fid∈dom rtp ∧ type-of(v)=rtp(fid))
  .3   type: Qual → (RecTp → Bool)
```

-- Selection

As all the ancestors have to fulfil their qualification for an "end" record to be selected, we may start our search at the root of the database. Since the selected set is given by the set of paths identifying the records, the meaning of evaluating a search string may then be formally defined by:

```
45.1   eval-SearchStr[ss]db ≜
  .2     cases ss:
  .3      (<>      → {<>},
  .4      <(id,q)> ^ ss'
  .5               → (let rs  = db(id)                              in
  .6                  let rs' = rs|{ l | l∈dom rs ∧
  .7                                      satisfy(s-Rec(rs(l),q)} in
  .8                  {<(id,l)>^p|l∈dom rs' ∧
  .9                            p∈eval-SearchStr[ss']s-DB(rs'(l))}))
  .10  type: SearchStr ⥲ (DB ⥲ Path-set)
  .11  pre:  (∃ctlg ∈ CTLG)(inv-HDBS(mk-HDBS(ctlg,db))

46.1   satisfy(r,q) ≜ ((q=nil) ∨ (let (fid,v)=q in r(fid)=v))
  .2   type: Rec × [Qual] ⥲ Bool
  .3   pre:  (∃rtp∈RecTp)(inv-Rec(r)rtp) ∧ pre-Qual[q]rtp)
```

A HIERARCHICY ORIENTED LANGUAGE

Now, having defined the basic concept of our language, we are ready to set up a full set of commands covering retrieval, insertion, deletion, and updating.

```
47.   Cmd     =  Search | Insert | Delete | Update
48.   Search  :: SearchStr
49.   Insert  :: SearchStr   RTId     Rec
50.   Delete  :: SearchStr
51.   Update  :: SearchStr   FieldId    Op
52.   Op      =  ...
```

All of these commands are data functions, that is they do not modify, or directly list catalogue information although they use it for accessing the database properly. Informally we wish the semantics of the commands to be as follows:

Search: The result is the set of records identified by the search string.

Insert: The record, which must be of the given type, is inserted directly below each record denoted by the search string.

Delete: Each record denoted by the search string is deleted, and with it all of its descendants.

Update: The given field of each record denoted by the search string is modified by the given operation. *Op* is a syntactical expression which denotes a value modifying function (for example "+5" denoting $\lambda x.x+5$). However, we are not interested in the abstract syntax of this function, and will assume functions to check and evaluate such an object.

Well-formedness, Pre-Conditions

The commands must satisfy certain constraints as indicated above. The precondition predicate is defined by cases below. It uses only catalogue information:

53. *type: pre-Cmd: Cmd → (CTLG ⥲ Bool)*

Of course, for all commands the search string must be well-formed. For the *Search* command, this is the only condition to be checked:

54.1 *pre-Cmd[mk-Search(ss)]ctlg* $\triangleq$ *pre-SearchStr[ss]ctlg*

For an *Insert* command it must be checked that the given record type is in continuation of the search string, that is that the type is immediately below the type designated by the hierarchical path of the search string (55.5). Also, the given record must belong to this type:

```
55.1  pre-Cmd[mk-Insert(ss,rtpid,rec)]ctlg ≜
  .2    pre-SearchStr[ss]ctlg ∧
  .3    (let hp     = extract-hp[ss]             in
  .4     let ctlg' = sub-catalogue(hp,ctlg)   in
  .5     rtpid ∈ dom ctlg' ∧
  .6       (let (rectp,) = ctlg'(rtpid)       in
  .7        inv-Rec(rec)rectp ))
```

56.1 $extract\text{-}hp[ss] \triangleq <\ id \mid 1 \leq i \leq \underline{len}\ ss \wedge ss[i]=(id,)\ >$

.2 $\underline{type}:\ SearchStr \rightarrow HP$

With the *Delete* command, one is not allowed to delete the "system record":

57.1 $pre\text{-}Cmd[mk\text{-}Delete(ss)]ctlg \triangleq ss \neq <> \wedge pre\text{-}SearchStr[ss]ctlg$

For an *Update* command it must be checked that the search string does not designate the system record, that is is empty. Furthermore, the field must belong to the record type of the search string, and the type of the operator must be applicable to the field. Given:

58. $\underline{type}:\ is\text{-}wf\text{-}Op:\quad Op \rightarrow Bool$ left unspecified

and

59. $\underline{type}:\ operatortype:\quad Op \xrightarrow{\sim} Type$ left unspecified

we get:

60.1 $pre\text{-}Cmd[mk\text{-}Update(ss,fid,op)]ctlg \triangleq$

.2 $ss \neq <> \wedge pre\text{-}SearchStr[ss]ctlg \wedge$

.3 $(\underline{let}\ hp = extrtact\text{-}hp[ss]\ \underline{in}$

.4 $\underline{let}\ rectp = lookup\text{-}rectp(hp,ctlg)\ \underline{in}$

.5 $fid \in \underline{dom}\ rectp \wedge rectp(fid)=operatortype[op]) \wedge pre\text{-}Op[op]$

<u>Semantic Functions</u>

The meaning of a command depends on its kind:

61.1 $elab\text{-}Cmd[cmd]hdbs \triangleq$

.2 $(is\text{-}Search(cmd) \rightarrow eval\text{-}Search[cmd]hdbs$

.3 $is\text{-}Insert(cmd) \rightarrow int\text{-}Insert[cmd]hdbs$

.4 $is\text{-}Delete(cmd) \rightarrow int\text{-}Delete[cmd]hdbs$

.5 $is\text{-}Update(cmd) \rightarrow int\text{-}Update[cmd]hdbs)$

.6 $\underline{type}:\ Cmd \rightarrow (HDBS \xrightarrow{\sim} (Rec\text{-}set \mid HDBS)$

.7 $\underline{pre}:\ pre\text{-}Cmd[cmd]hdbs$

The commands are divided into two groups: the retrieval command and the modifying commands, respectively *Search* and *Insert, Delete* & *Update*. The retrieval command only extracts information from the database:

62. $\underline{type}:\ eval\text{-}Search:\ Search \rightarrow (HDBS \xrightarrow{\sim} Rec\text{-}set)$

whereas the modifying commands only alters the data of the *HDBS*:

```
63.    type:  int-Insert: Insert → (HDBS ⥲ HDBS)
64.    type:  int-Update: Update → (HDBS ⥲ HDBS)
65.    type:  int-Delete: Delete → (HDBS ⥲ HDBS)
```

-- Retrieval

The result of the *Search* command is the set of records identified by the search string. Since the search string does not specify any order among the selected records, the result is likewise unordered, that is a set:

```
66.1   eval-Search[mk-Search(ss)] mk-HDBS(ctlg,db) ≜
  .2      (let paths = eval-SearchStr[ss]db in
  .3       {lookup-rec(p,db) | p ∈ paths\{<>}})
```

Note that the "system record" cannot be yielded.

-- Modification Functions

The modification commands usually change some sub-database, but since our model is top down, this has to be reflected all the way up to the root. Therefore, it seems convenient to have one function which, given a "reference" to a sub-database (that is a path) and a change-function for this subdatabase, propagates the change all the way up to the root. Suppose only one sub-database is to be changed. Then the required function could be:

```
67.1   modify1(p,mod,db) ≜
  .2     cases p:
  .3       (<>              → mod(db),
  .4        <(id,lab)>^p'  → (let (rec,db') = (db(id))(lab)           in
  .5                          let db"       = modify1(p',mod,db')    in
  .6                          db + [id ↦ db(id) + [lab ↦ (rec,db")]]))
  .7   type: Path × (DB → DB) × DB  ⥲  DB
  .8   pre:  p∈all-paths(db)
```

This function may also be specified indirectly, using:

```
69.1   indep-paths(p,db) ≜   {p' | p'∈all-paths(db) ∧ indep(p,p')}
  .2   type: Path × DB ⥲ Path-set
  .3   pre:  p∈all-paths(db)
```

```
68.1  type:  modify1': Path × (DB → DB) × DB  ⥲  DB
  .2  pre-modify1'(p,mod,db) ≜ p∈all-paths(db)
  .3  post-modify1'(p,mod,db)(db') ≜
  .4     (p∈all-paths(db')
  .5      ∧indep-paths(p,db)=indep-paths(p,db')
  .6      ∧(∀p'∈indep-paths(p,db))
  .7           (lookup-rec(p',db)=lookup-rec(p',db'))
  .8      ∧sub-database(p,db') = mod(sub-database(p,db)))
```

Here, the case will be that many sub-databases should be changed using the same change function. The sub-databases should be independent to get a deterministic effect. Such a modification function may be written in many ways. We could do the changes one at a time, but in unspecified order:

```
70.1  modify(ps,mod,db) ≜
  .2     if ps = {}
  .3        then db
  .4        else (let p ∈ ps in
  .5               let db' = modify1(p,mod,db)  in
  .6               modify(ps\{p},mod,db'))
  .7  type:   Path-set × (DB → DB) × DB  ⥲  DB
  .8  pre:    ps⊆all-paths(db) ∧ (∀p,p'∈ps) (p≠p' ⊃ indep(p,p'))
```

A rather mechanic solution. An implicit specification may easily be given changing (in 68.) *p* to *ps*, (in 68.2,4) ∈ to ⊆, extending *indep-paths* to handle sets, and finally changing (68.8) to:

```
68.8'  ∧ (∀p∈ps) (sub-database(p,db') = mod(sub-database(p,db))
```

-- Modification Commands

Having defined the modification function we are now able to give the semantics of the modifying commands. For the *Insert* command, the change is to add a new record associated with an empty subdatabase:

```
71.1   int-Insert[mk-Insert(ss,rtpid,rec)] mk-HDBS(ctlg,db) ≜
  .2     (let hp = extract-hp[ss]^<rtpid>                                in
  .3      let ps = eval-SearchStr[ss]db                                  in
  .4      let empty = [id → [] | id∈dom sub-catalogue(hp,ctlg)]         in
  .5      let mod(subdb) =
  .6          (let lab∈Reclab \ dom subdb(rtpid) in
  .7           subdb + [rtpid ↦ subdb(rtpid)∪[lab ↦ (rec,empty)]]) in
  .8      mk-HDBS(ctlg,modify(ps,mod,db)))
```

For the *Delete* command we have to view the search string as consisting of two parts. The first *lenss-1* elements which identify the records which are to stay and which records in their sub-database are to be deleted, and the last element which selects the records of the sub-database to be deleted. Using:

```
72.1   satisfying-labels(rs,q) ≜ { l | l∈dom rs ∧ satisfy(rs(l),q) }
  .2   type: (RecLab m→ (Rec × HDB)) ×[Qual] → RecLab-set
```

we get:

```
73.1   int-Delete[mk-Delete(ss)] mk-HDBS(ctlg,db) ≜
  .2     (let ss'^<(id,qual)> = ss                                      in
  .3      let ps = eval-SearchStr[ss']db                                 in
  .4      let mod(subdb) =
  .5         (let rs = subdb(id)                                         in
  .6          let rs' = rs \ satisfying-labels(rs,qual)                  in
  .7          subdb + [id ↦ rs'])                                        in
  .8      mk-HDBS(ctlg,modify(ps,mod,db)))
```

The *Update* command goes almost the same way:

```
74.1   int-Update[mk-Update(ss,fid,op)] mk-HDBS(ctlg,db) ≜
  .2     (let ss'^<(id,qual)> = ss                                      in
  .3      let ps = eval-SearchStr[ss']db                                 in
  .4      let f(r) = r + [fid ↦ eval-Op[op](r(fid))]                     in
  .5      let mod(subdb) =
  .6          (let rs = subdb(id)                                        in
  .7           let ls = satisfying-labels(rs,qual)                       in
  .8           let rs'= rc + [l ↦ (f(r),db) | l∈ls ∧(r,db)=rs(l)]        in
  .9           subdb + [id ↦ rs'])                                       in
  .10     mk-HDBS(ctlg,modify(ps,mod,db)))
```

TOWARDS IMS

We shall, as the final subject of our treatment of hierarchical search languages, indicate how the principles given here may be extended to the so-called traversal languages like DL/1 of IMS. An IMS based model on these ideas can be found in [Bjørner 82c]. Here too, we shall use IMS as a reference for our discussion of traversal languages.

The main differences between the language given so far and IMS is that in IMS, the records are accessed one at a time, and in a certain order called the hierarchical order or sequence. Here we shall show how this will influence our model. For brevity, we will consider only record retrieval.

Hierarchical Order

The hierarchical ordering of the records corresponds to a parent-first, left-to-right traversal of the database tree when drawn as a diagram. The parent-first part of the ordering is given by the top-down structure, but the left-to-right ordering must be established explicitly at each level, that is in each sub-database. The records of a sub-database are first of all ordered by their record types, in the same way as the record types in each sub-catalogue are ordered as from left to right in the hierarchical diagram. Within each record type of a sub-database, the records must be ordered by some means, for example by the value of a key field.

There are various ways to incorporate the hierarchical ordering into our data model. To determine the ordering among record types in each sub-catalogue, we could add an extra component to the catalogue:

75. $CTLG :: (RTId \underset{m}{\rightarrow} RecTp) \quad Ord$

The order component should impose some ordering on the record types of the catalogue, for example by associating an ordinal number to each type, or by establishing a "chain":

76. $Ord = RTId \underset{m}{\rightarrow} Nat$ or

77. $Ord = RTId \underset{m}{\rightarrow} [RTId]$

The ordering of records within each record type could be done through a key field, but since IMS does not require unique keys this is not applicable here. The ordering could also be given by an ordering component as above, where the ordinal number case would be equivalent to arranging the records in a list:

78. $DB \quad = \quad RTId \underset{m}{\rightarrow} (Rec \times DB)^{*}$

However, since we do not wish to change our established data model and associated operations here, we shall simply assume that we implicitly, at each level, have access to a total, irreflexive, assymetric, and transitive ordering operation among record types $<<_{tp}$, and to one among record labels $<<_{lab}$, where $x << y$ models that x is to the left of y in the diagram.

It is easily seen that the hierarchical ordering among the records corresponds to a lexicographical ordering on the paths identifying the records. Therefore, we can define that one record given by the path p_1 precedes a record with path p_2 in the hierarchical sequence by:

79.1 $precedes(p_1,p_2) \ \underline{\underline{\Delta}}$

.2 $\quad (p_2 = \langle\rangle \rightarrow \underline{false},$

.3 $\quad\; p_1 = \langle\rangle \rightarrow \underline{true},$

.4 $\quad\; T \rightarrow (\underline{let}\ \langle(id_1,lab_1)\rangle \frown p_1' = p_1\ \underline{in}$

.5 $\qquad\qquad \underline{let}\ \langle(id_2,lab_2)\rangle \frown p_2' = p_2\ \underline{in}$

.6 $\qquad\qquad (id_1 \neq id_2 \rightarrow id_1 <<_{tp} id_2,$

.7 $\qquad\qquad\; lab_1 \neq lab_2 \rightarrow lab_1 <<_{lab} lab_2,$

.8 $\qquad\qquad\; T \rightarrow precedes(p_1',p_2'))))$

.9 $\underline{type}:\ Path \times Path \xrightarrow{\sim} Bool$

We shall also need a function that given a non-empty set of paths returns the first of these according to the hierarchical ordering:

80.1 $first(paths) \ \underline{\underline{\Delta}}\ (\Delta p \in paths)(\forall p' \in paths)(p \neq p' \supset precedes(p,p'))$

.2 $\underline{type}:\ Path\text{-}set \xrightarrow{\sim} Path$

<u>Record retrieval</u>

In IMS, only one record is retrieved at a time. Therefore, in order to achieve the effect of our Search command, that is to get all records satisfying the search string, two commands are provided:

```
81.     GetUnique  ::  SearchStr
82.     GetNext    ::  [SearchStr]
```

Get Unique will return the first record in the hierarchical sequence satisfying the search string. It will furthermore establish what is called current position of this record. This position is used in Get Next commands which will return the first record following the current position and satisfying the search string, and will set 'current position' to this record. If no search string is given, Get Next will return the record immediately after 'current position' thereby allowing a complete traversal of the database in hierarchical order. The 'current position' is held as a separate component of the database system:

```
83.     HDBS'      ::  CTLG   DB   POS
84.     POS        =   Path
```

If no record can be found, we indicate this by returning the *nil* object. Since 'current position' is changed by the retrieval, the type of the interpretations functions for these commands become:

```
85.     type:  int-GetUnique:  GetUnique ⥲ (HDBS' ⥲ HDBS' × [Rec])
86.     type:  int-GetNext:    GetNext   ⥲ (HDBS' ⥲ HDBS' × [Rec])

87.1    int-GetUnique[mk-GetUnique(ss)]hdbs ≜
  .2      (let mk-hdbs'(ctlg,db,pos) = hdbs    in
  .3       let paths = eval-SearchStr[ss]db    in
  .4       paths={}  → (hdbs,nil),
  .5       T         → (let path = first(paths) in
  .6                     (mk-HDBS'(ctlg,db,path),lookup-rec(path,db))

88.1    int-GetNext[mk-GetNext(ss)]hdbs ≜
  .2      (let mk-HDBS'(ctlg,db,pos) = hdbs                    in
  .3       let paths = (ss=nil  → all-paths(db),
  .4                    T        → eval-SearchStr[ss]db        in
  .5       let paths' = { p | p∈paths ∧ precedes(pos,p) } in
  .6       paths'={} → (hdbs,nil),
  .7       T         → (let path = first(paths) in
  .8                     (mk-HDBS'(ctlg,db,path),lookup-rec(path,db))
```

IMS also maintains a position called Parent Position which is used by a so-called Get Next Within Parent command. Furthermore, parts of the search string (which is called Search Argument List in IMS) may be left out. The detailled modelling of these facilities can be found in [Bjørner 82c].

12.2.3 Selection Languages

In this section we describe and model the characteristics of languages used in hierarchical database systems as for example SYSTEM 2000 of MRI. Due to their nature, such languages are often called "selection languages". They are high-level languages and given a proper syntax the semantics may be quite close to the intuitive meaning of the construct interpreted as a sentence. In SYSTEM 2000 the language is even called the "Natural Language Feature".

First, we give some examples of selective queries to introduce the idea behind these languages. On the basis of these we then introduce some basic views on the database and give some basic operations including the important *broom* concept. These are used in the following definition of a small language including only single selection. We then show how single selections may be combined in two different ways using boolean operators, and finally we discuss some disadvantages of the so-called tree and how they can be remedied by a special selection construct.

Note, that since selection languages are characterized by the way they select records for operation and not by the operations themselves, only retrieval expressions are covered here.

A Selection Example

In order to let you have an idea of how selective languages work, we shall show a few selection queries based on the following hierarchical diagram:

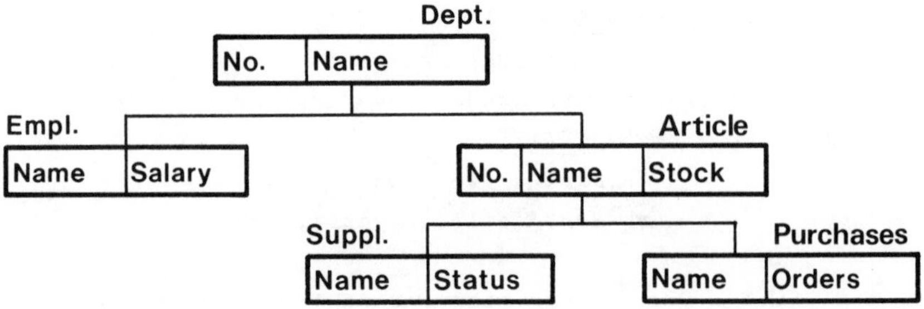

Fig. 7

The diagram describes the database structure of a larger trading firm divided into departments which each deals with certain articles.

In general, a selection language request or command has the form:

<action part> <u>where</u> <selection part>

The intended semantics is that the action in the action part is applied to the set of nodes designated by the selection part.

We start with one of the most simple kinds of query, for example "print the names of articles for which there are more than 1000 items in stock". This may be achieved by the command:

<u>print</u> Article.Name <u>where</u> Article.Stock >= 1000

All the employees in a certain department, for example the Food Department, may be found by:

<u>print</u> Empl.Name <u>where</u> Dept.Name = "Food"

Note that we select on the basis of a Department field, but actually use an Employee field. Thus, the selection of Department records automatically gives access to all descendants of the selected records. This is often called "downward normalization". In the same way all suppliers that supply a certain department can be found. Another query could be:

<u>print</u> Dept.Name <u>where</u> Article.No = 123

which will be interpreted as "all departments which deal with article no. 123". Thus, in this case we see that the selection of an article on the basis of its number automatically includes its parent (in general: ancestors). This may be called "upward normalization". Changing the command to:

<u>print</u> Suppl.Name <u>where</u> Article.No = 123

will give us all suppliers which supply the specific article to one or more departments. If we are interested in only those which supply a specific department, we can use:

<u>print</u> Suppl.Name <u>where</u> Article.No = 123 <u>and</u> Dept.Name = "Food"

As we see, selections may in general be combined by boolean operators. Another example is to "find the departments which trade with the firm 'Smith'".

<u>print</u> Dept.Name <u>where</u> Suppl.Name = "Smith"
<u>and</u> Purchases.Name = "Smith"

The semantics of boolean combinators, which seems rather natural, is discussed later. Finally, suppose we are interested in those articles which may be supplied by "Jones & Co." and may be sold to "Printall". We may try:

<u>print</u> Article.Name <u>where</u> Suppl.Name = "Jones & Co."
<u>and</u> Purchaser.Name = "Printall"

Unfortunately, this command will return the desired article names in some systems, whereas other systems will tell us that there are no such articles. This problem is further treated in the section named "The Has Clause".

<u>Regarding the Database as a Tree</u>

The readers who are familiar with the IMS System may have wondered why we have chosen such an abstract view on the hierarchical tree in the model presented (31.-40.), knowing that, in IMS it suffices to make a pointer structure imposing both a hierarchical structure on the records, and a sequential order in which they are to be retrieved. The reason is that such a model (which is really one kind of IMS implementation, see Chapter 13) is not a good starting point for explaining and modelling selection languages. The main view of the database in these languages is that of a <u>tree</u> of nodes where each node has an associated record. Now, as stated above, a selection command first qualifies a set of nodes (and thereby records) which are then considered (but not necessarily used) by some action. Therefore, a good data model should easily adapt to the tree view.

-- <u>The Database as a Tree of Records</u>

Recalling the model of the database part (33.):

89. $DB \quad = \quad RTId \underset{m}{\to} (RecLab \underset{m}{\to} (Rec \times DB))$

we see that it does not immediately regard the database as a tree of records. However, changing the model to:

90. $TDB \quad = \quad (RTId \times RecLab) \underset{m}{\to} (Rec \times TDB)$

we get a model where each record is directly connected to its children by branches labelled by *(id,lab)* pairs. A given *DB* may easily be transformed into a "pure" tree *TDB* by:

91.1 $tree\text{-}view(db) \;\underline{\underline{\Delta}}$

.2 $\quad [(id,lab) \mapsto (rec,tree\text{-}view(db')) \mid id \in \underline{dom}\; db \wedge lab \in \underline{dom}\; db(id) \wedge$

.3 $\quad\quad (rec,db') = db(id)(lab) \quad]$

.4 $\underline{type}: \; DB \to TDB$

Being aware of this relationship we retain the original model, but speak in terms of the tree view!

-- <u>Interpreting a Path</u>

The path concept was introduced to enable unique identification of the records in the database thereby making it possible to speak of a record from the "outside" of the database in spite of its top-down structure. Speaking in tree terms, a Path (28.) is the sequence of branch-labels on the way from the root record ("system record") to a certain record occurrence. Therefore, a path may have two immediate interpretations:

A. The path designates one record: the record at the end of the path. This is the view which motivated the path concept.

B. The path designates a set of records: all the records along the path, including the "system" record and the record at the end of the path. It may also be considered as a subtree; one without branches.

As both interpretations will be used in this section, we rename the Path domain to emphasize this differentiation. Thus, when speaking of single records or nodes we use the domain *Node*. The second interpretation will be used only for paths ending in leaf nodes of the database tree. In this case, the path will be called a <u>stem</u>:

92. *Node = Stem = Path = (RTId × RecLab)**

-- Node and Stem Operations

Stems are important since they form the basis for regular trees defined below. We therefore introduce a few node and stem operations here. The first one is for pragmatic reasons only.

93.1 *all-nodes(db)* $\triangleq$ *all-paths(db)*

94.1 *node-type(n)* $\triangleq$ *cases n: (<> → SYSTEM, n'^(id,) → id)*
 .2 *type: Node → (SYSTEM | TYPE)*

A stem must end in a leaf node of the database (see figure below). In terms of our model this requirement can be expressed by:

95.1 *inv-Stem(st)db* $\triangleq$ *st∈all-paths(db) ∧ sub-database(st,db)=[]*
 .2 *type: Stem → (DB* $\tilde{\rightarrow}$ *Bool)*

All the stems of a database can be determined in the same way:

 .1 *all-stems(db)* $\triangleq$ *{st | st∈all-paths(db)∧sub-database(st,db)=[]}*
 .2 *type: DB* $\tilde{\rightarrow}$ *Stem-set*

We shall also be interested in the nodes represented in a stem:

95.1 *nodes-of-stem(st)* $\triangleq$ *{ p | p∈Node ∧ is-prefix(p,st) }*
 .2 *type: Stem → Node-set*

(Note that the type: *Path → Path-set* might have been confusing.)

-- Brooms

A broom is a general tree concept which turns out to be very important in many selection languages. Given a node in a tree, the broom of this node is generally defined by:

broom(n) $\triangleq$ *{n}* ∪ { *n'* | *n'* is a descendant of *n* }
∪ { *n'* | *n'* is an ancestor of *n* }

See illustration below. In our model we may use the dependency concept:

96.1 *broom(n) db* $\triangleq$ { *n'* | *n'∈all-nodes(db)* ∧ ¬ *indep(n,n')* }
 .2 type: *Node* $\rightsquigarrow$ *(DB* $\rightsquigarrow$ *Node-set)*
 .3 pre: *n∈all-paths(db)*

-- Regular Trees

The notion of regular trees given here is a slightly modified version of the one given in [Hardgrave 72a] upon which much of the following material based. A regular tree with respect to a database tree is a sub-tree whose leaf nodes are also leaf nodes in the database. See illustration below. As it can be seen, the nodes of a regular tree is the union of the stems leading to the leaves. A regular tree may therefore be represented by the stems of its leaves:

97. *RegTree* = *Stem-set*

We also see that a broom of some node is a regular tree. In this representation the broom is given by:

98.1 $broom_T(n)db$ $\triangleq$ { *n^stem* | *stem∈all-stems(sub-database(n,db))* }
 .2 type: *Node* $\rightsquigarrow$ *(DB* $\rightsquigarrow$ *RegTree)*

99.1 *nodes-of-tree(rt)* $\triangleq$ union { *nodes-of-stem(st)* | *st∈rt* }
 .2 type: *RegTree* → *Node-set*

We now define the regular tree operations intersection, union, and negation as the corresponding set operations on the *Stem-sets* representing the trees. In this way the operations always results in regular trees.

-- Illustration of Tree Concepts

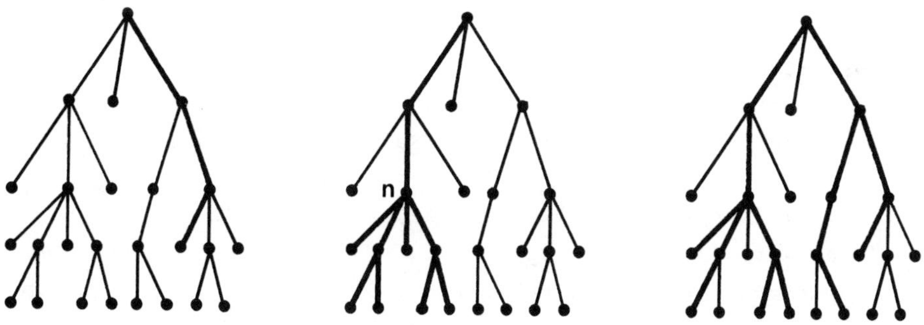

A stem *broom(n)* A regular tree

Fig. 8

A SMALL SELECTION LANGUAGE

We are now ready to define and model a small language involving only selection on the basis of one field.

Abstract Syntax

```
100.  Cmd          :: Action   Where
101.  Where        :: SelExp
102.  SelExp       =  FieldSel | ...
103.  FieldSel     :: FieldDesig   Qual
104.  Action       =  Print | ...
105.  Print        :: FieldDesig-set
106.  FieldDesig   :: RTId   FieldId
107.  Qual         =  Eq | ...
108.  Eq           :: Val
```

(The purpose of the extra Where-level will become apparent later.)

Well-formedness

The only constraints which we shall impose on the constructs are that Field-designators must exist in the catalogue, and that the qualification is of the right type.

```
109.1 pre-Cmd[mk-Cmd(act,mk-Where(se))]ctlg ≜
   .2     pre-Action[act]ctlg ∧ pre-SelExp[se]ctlg

110.1 pre-Action[act]ctlg ≜
   .2     cases act:
   .3       (mk-Print(fds) → (∀fd∈fds) pre-FieldDesig[fd]ctlg, ... )

111.1 pre-SelExp[se]ctlg ≜
   .2     cases se:
   .3       (mk-FieldSel(,) → pre-FieldSel[se]ctlg, ... )

112.1 pre-FieldSel[mk-FieldSel(fd,qual)]ctlg ≜
   .2     pre-FieldDesig[fd]ctlg ∧
   .3       (let hp = find-hp(s-RTId(fd),ctlg)                    in
   .4        let fieldtp = sub-catalogue(hp,ctlg)(s-FieldId(fd)) in
   .5        pre-Qual[qual]fieldtp )
```

```
113.1  pre-Qual[qual]fieldtp ≜
  .2      cases qual: (mk-Eq(val) → type-of(val)=fieldtp, ... )

114.1  pre-FieldDesig[mk-FieldDesig(id,fid)]ctlg ≜
  .2      id∈collect-names(ctlg)
  .3    ∧ fid∈sub-catalogue(find-hp(id,ctlg),ctlg)

115.   type: pre-X:  X → (CTLG ⇸ Bool)       where X is Action,SelExp,
                                             FieldSel, resp. FieldDesig
116.   type: pre-Qual: Qual → (TYPE → Bool)
```

Action interpretation

The semantics of a command is to select a set of records by the Where-clause, and then impose the specified action on these.

```
117.1  int-Cmd[mk-Cmd(act,wh)]hdbs ≜
  .2     (let nodes = eval-Where[wh]hdbs in
  .3      int-Action[act](nodes)hdbs)
  .4   type:  Cmd ⇸ (HDBS ⇸ (HDBS | Table | ... )
```

The type of the result depends on the specific action. For example, the result of a Print command may be a Table giving the different values occurring in the specified fields of the selected records.

```
118.   Table  =  FieldDesig →m Val-set

119.1  int-Action[mk-Print(fds)](nodes) mk-HDBS(ctlg,db) ≜
  .2      [ fd ↦ select-field-vals(nodes,fd,db) | fd∈fds ]
  .3   type:  Action ⇸ (Node-set → (HDBS ⇸ Table)))

120.1  select-field-vals(nodes,mk-FieldDesig(id,fid),db) ≜
  .2      { lookup-rec(n)(fid) | n ∈ nodes ∧
  .3                             n ≠ <> ∧ n[len n] = (id, ) }
  .4   type:  Node-set × FieldDesig × DB  ⇸  Val-set
```

Where evaluation

The Where-clause is evaluated in two steps. First, a number of nodes are directly selected according to the Field Selector. To achieve the effect of upward and downward "normalization" mentioned in the introduction these nodes are then qualified to give an extended set of nodes.

```
121.1  eval-Where[mk-Where(se)] mk-HDBS(,db) ≜ eval-SelExp[se]db
   .2  type:  Where ⥲ (HDBS ⥲ Node-set)

122.1  eval-SelExp[se]db ≜
   .2     cases se:
   .3       (mk-FieldSel(fd,qual) →  (let nodes = select(fd,qual)db in
   .4                                   qualify(nodes)db),
   .5         ...   )
   .6   type:  SelExp ⥲ (DB ⥲ Node-set)

123.1  select(mk-FieldDesig(id,fid),qual) db ≜
   .2     { n | n∈all-nodes(db) ∧ node-type(n)=id ∧
   .3            match((lookup-rec(n,db)(fid),qual) }
   .4  type:  FieldDesig × Qual ⥲ (DB ⥲ Node-set)

124.1  match(val,qual) ≜  cases qual: (mk-Eq(val') → val=val', ... )
   .2  type:  VAL × Qual → Bool
```

-- Qualification

The purpose of qualification is to extend the set of selected notes by including nodes which are in a certain relationship to those directly selected. These nodes are called indirectly selected. In almost all systems, the relation is given by:

> A node is indirectly selected if at least one of its ancestors or descendants is directly selected.

This notion of qualification corresponds well to an intuitive interpretation of upward and downward normalization. Furthermore, it is easily seen that the nodes qualified by a directly selected node are those of the broom of the node. Thus, the total set of qualified nodes may be found by

```
125.1  qualify(nodes)db ≜  union { broom(n)db | n∈nodes }
   .2  type:  Node-set ⥲ (DB ⥲ Node-set)
```

A BOOLEAN SELECTION LANGUAGE

We now extend our language by constructs which will allow us to select on the basis of more than one field as indicated in the introduction. The new select constructs are:

```
126.  SelExp   = FieldSel | And | Or | Not | ...
127.  And      :: SelExp   SelExp
128.  Or       :: SelExp   SelExp
129.  Not      :: SelExp
```

These constructs are well-defined if their components are.

In order to achieve the "natural" interpretation effect on these constructs, all systems combine the nodes of their components. Also, the systems agree that directly selected nodes should still be qualified before they are combined. However, there are two essentially different ways to do these combinations: the set-theoretic and the tree-theoretic which we shall deal with in turn.

Set-Theoretic Combination

According to this principle, the nodes designated by the component expressions are simply combined using the usual set operations. Therefore we simply get the following new cases of the *eval-SelExp* function:

```
130.1  eval-SelExp[mk-And(se1,se2)]db ≜
   .2    (let nodes1 = eval-SelExp[se1]db,
   .3         nodes2 = eval-SelExp[se2]db in
   .4     nodes1 ∩ nodes2)
```

The *Or* case is of course similar.

```
131.1  eval-SelExp[mk-Not(se)]db ≜
   .2    (let nodes = eval-SelExp[se]db in
   .3     all-nodes(db)\nodes)
```

Tree-Theoretic Combination

It is easily seen that the set combinations may result in node-sets which are not sub-trees of the database, and upward and downward normalization may therefore become difficult to define properly. To avoid this, some systems (including SYSTEM 2000) apply another combination principle based on regular trees and the associated tree operations.

In this approach, the denotation of a Select Expression is no longer a set of nodes, but instead (more restrictively) a regular tree. The semantics of the select operators may then defined by (or as) the corresponding tree operations. In order to incorporate this in our model, a few functions and types need to be redefined:

132.1 $qualify_T(ns)db \triangleq \underline{union}\ \{\ broom_T(n)db \mid n \in ns\ \}$
   .2 $\underline{type}$: $Node\text{-}set \xrightarrow{\sim} (DB \xrightarrow{\sim} RegTree)$

The type of *eval-SelExp* changes to:

133. $\underline{type}$: $eval\text{-}SelExp_T$: $SelExp \xrightarrow{\sim} (DB \xrightarrow{\sim} RegTree)$

However, the function definition remains the same, except that "nodes" for pragmatic reasons should be renamed "stems" everywhere except in 122. Finally we are now ready to use the extra Where-level in the syntax since the result of evaluating a Where-clause should still be a Node-set.

134.1 $eval\text{-}Where_T[mk\text{-}Where(se)]\ mk\text{-}HDBS(,db) \triangleq$
   .2 $nodes\text{-}of\text{-}tree(eval\text{-}SelExp[se]db)$

Differences Between Set and Tree Combination

Here we shall look at the semantics and pragmatics of the two kinds of boolean combination. As already stated, the set operations work on node sets whereas the tree operations work on regular trees. We shall say that a node set is similar to a regular tree if it equals the nodes of the tree. We see immediately that the result of a Field Selection is similar in the two systems. It is also seen that the or operator yields similar results provided the operands are similar. Thus, the origin of any differences must be the and and the not operators which are discussed below.

-- The And Operator

Analyzing the and operation we find that as long as the fields combined are different and on the same hierarchical path, the results will be similar. This was the case in the introductory example (now a little less concrete):

print Suppl.Name where Dept.Name = *D* and Article.No = *n*

where the semantics in both cases corresponds to "those suppliers which supply article *n* to department *D*". However, in the last example of the introduction:

print Article.No where Suppl.Name = *S* and Purchaser.Name = *P*

the field selectors are no longer on the same hierarchical path. In the tree combination case, this implies that they cannot have any stems in common and therefore the result is an empty regular tree. Using set combination, we see that the result is those records on the common path which have descendants satisfying the qualifications. Thus, the command above will result in exactly the articles we want. However, consider:

print Dept.Name where Suppl.Name = *S* and Purchaser.Name = *P*

This command will give the "departments which are supplied by *S* and sell to *P*", but there need not be a single article in the department for which this is the case. Thus, the latter command may give results even though the first does not, that is the effect of upward normalization has been lost, and it is not possible to get those departments where the condition is satisfied by at least one single article. We may also try to get "those suppliers that supply articles also supplied by *S* and sold to *P*" using:

print Suppl.Name where Suppl.Name = *S* and Purchaser.Name = *P*

However, this command will not give any results even using set combination since we have lost the descendants of the selected articles. Finally we try to conjoin two selections on the same field:

print Dept.Name where Suppl.Name = S_1 and Suppl.Name = S_2

($S_1 \neq S_2$). Using tree combination we get no result, justified by the fact that no supplier can have two names. In the set approach we get "those departments which are supplied by both S_1 and s_2". Again we cannot get the departments which deal with an article supplied by both suppliers.

-- The Not Operator

Since the not operator in both approaches may be distributed according to De Morgans Laws, we need only consider negation of single Field Selectors. A command like:

print Dept.Name where Article.No = *n*

is generally interpreted as "those departments under which there exists an article with number *n*". Now consider:

print Dept.Name where not Article.No = *n*

Using set combination this will result in "those departments which do not deal with article *n*", whereas the tree principle will give "those departments under which there is anything different from article number *n*". Note the difference, and that none of them makes "not Article.No = *n*" equivalent to "Article.No ≠ *n* "! Another problem is that:

print Empl.Name where not Article.No = *n*

will in both cases give all employees although they have nothing to do with article numbers. This problem may be solved by using type constrained negation, where the negation returns only nodes with types such as those negated. Here we consider only the tree combination case:

135.1 *eval-SelExp[mk-Not(se)]hdbs* $\underline{\Delta}$
.2 *(let stems = eval-SelExp[se]db in*
.3 *let types = { node-type(st) | st∈stems } in*
.4 *{ st' | st'∈all-stems(db)\stems ∧ node-type(st')∈types })*

Now "not Article.No = *n*" becomes equivalent to "Article.No ≠ *n*"!

The Has-Clause

To sum up, both combination principles have some advantages:

Set: Useful, although restricted and operation. Negation corresponds to universal quantification.

Tree: Always regular trees as result, that is no normalization lost.

Not operation negates select condition.

In practice, many systems use the tree combination principle (among others SYSTEM 2000). The main disadvantage is the restricted and operation. To compensate for this, these systems also offer a so-called Has-clause which enables re-selection/qualification at any level:

```
136.   SelExp    =  ... | Has
137.   Has       :: RTId   SelExp

138.1  eval-SelExp[mk-Has(id,se)]db ≜
   .2    (let nodes  = nodes-of-tree(eval-SelExp[se]db)   in
   .3     let nodes' = { n | n∈nodes ∧ node-type(n)=id }  in
   .4     qualify(nodes')db )
```

The Has-clause gives us many new possibilities. For example we can get "the employees in the departments where at least one single article is supplied by *S* and sold to *P*", and we may achieve the universal quantification effect:

```
print Empl.Name where Dept has Article has (Suppl.Name = S  and
                                             Purchaser.Name = P )

print Dept.Name where not Dept has Article.No = n
```

12.2.4 Concluding Remarks on the Hierarchical Data Model

We have in 12.2.1 build up a top-down model of a hierarchical database. This model was used directly for the hierarchy-oriented language defined in 12.2.2. Although a little more abstract than needed, the model could also be used for the more procedural traversal languages like IMS. In 12.2.3 we formalized a number of concepts (brooms, etc.) on top of our top-down model in order to enable a more global tree-view of the database. Using these, we could easily give the semantics of the most important selection language constructs. All this seems to indicate that our model is a reasonable starting point for hierarchical database modelling -- as also evidenced by [Bjørner 82c]. However, for use in connection with selection languages only, a more global tree-like model may turn out to be more suitable.

We shall finally stress that a primary concern of this section has been to illustrate a model development process. This has been tried through many concrete examples and careful model description. The length of this section, compared to those on the relational model and on the network model, is thus not an indication of a special interest in, or support of the hierarchical model, but rather of a general emphasis on modelling pragmatics.

12.3 THE NETWORK DATA MODEL

The network data model to be formalized in this section is based on Bachmanns 'Data Structure Diagrams'. We present abstractions of the data model behind the CODASYL/DBTG proposal and, hence of the data model underlying such DBMSs as IDS/2, IDMS, DMS1100, etc.

By a network we understand a directed graph. By a network data model we understand an interpretation and utilization of the nodes and edges as follows: nodes denotes aggregates of records; edges denotes relations between the records denoted by the connected nodes; and the paths of the graph enable operations to extract collections of records of the "end" node of a path based on properties satisfied by records of all nodes of the path. Exactly what is meant by aggregates, relations and extraction is then the purpose of our formalization.

12.3.1 The Data Aggregate

Our presentation of the relational data model data aggregate was 'matter-of-factly': we merely stated the model. The hierarchical data aggregate model was arrived at as the result of an analysis of given example pictures. In presenting the network data aggregate model we shall proceed in yet a third way. Whereas our analysis of hierarchical database "snapshots" lead to a top-down presentation, we shall now start with the primitives and end up with their synthesis into networks. As was the case in our presentation of the hierarchical model we shall also use pictures, but now in an a-posteriori supporting rôle.

Our objective is to describe the syntax and semantics of so-called data structure diagrams. These consists, picturially of boxes (nodes) and arrows (directed edges). We next explain the meaning of boxes, the meaning of arrows, and finally the syntactic rules for well-formed data structure diagrams.

A box denotes, ~, a set of Records. We take records as our first primitive:

1.  ~ $R\text{-}set$

Fig. 9

Arrows will (come to) play the rôle of operators infixed between two, not necessarily distinct boxes:

2. 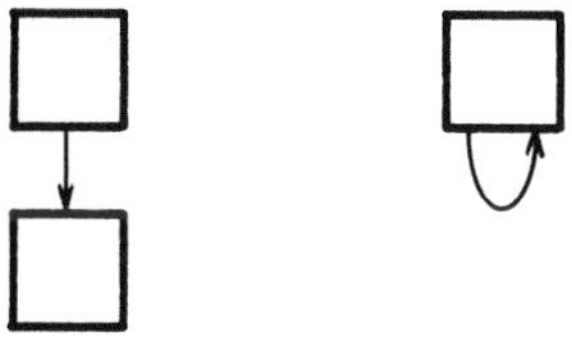

Fig. 10

The meaning of arrows, in general, is that of a map from records to sets of records:

3.  ~ $(R \underset{m}{\to} R\text{-}set)$

Fig. 11

The meaning of an arrow, in particular from a box denoting the record set rs_f to a box denoting the record set rt_t, is a map, m, whose domain is, in general, a subset of rs_f, and whose range is a set of sets of records whose union is, in general, a subset of rs_t:

4. $m \in (R \underset{m}{\to} R\text{-}set);$
5. $\underline{dom}\ m \subseteq rs_f,\ \underline{union}\ \underline{rng}\ m \subseteq rs_t$

A data structure diagram is a collection of uniquely named boxes and uniquely named arrows, the latter infixed between existing boxes. Box and arrow names are then our remaining primitives. The records of the Box from which an arrow emanates and which are in the domain of the map denoted by the arrow are called <u>owner</u> records, while the records of the file to which an arrow is incident and which are in some set(s) of records of the range of the arrow denoted map are called <u>member</u> records. The arrow denotation is, in CODASYL/DBTG rather confusingly, called a 'settype'; we shall call it a relation.

The Domain of data structure diagrams can syntactically then be formalized as:

6. DSD_{syn} :: $Fid\text{-}set \times (Sid \underset{m}{\rightarrow} (Fid \times Fid))$

The set of file names represent the boxes, and the map from arrow names to the pairs of <u>from</u> box and <u>to</u> box names represent the arrows and where they are infixed. The diagram:

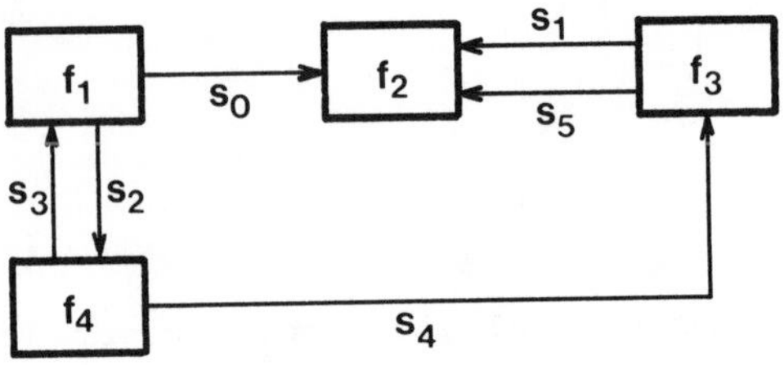

Fig. 12

then corresponds to the abstract object denoted by the following expression:

7.0 $mk\text{-}DSD_{syn}(\{f_1,f_2,f_3,f_4\},$
.1 $[s_0 \mapsto (f_1,f_2), s_1 \mapsto (f_3,f_2), s_2 \mapsto (f_1,f_4),$
.2 $s_3 \mapsto (f_4,f_1), s_4 \mapsto (f_4,f_3), s_5 \mapsto (f_3,f_2)])$

We observe the constraint that "to each arrow there corresponds two boxes in the data structure diagram":

8.0 $inv\text{-}DSD_{syn}(mk\text{-}DSD_{syn}(fs,sffm)) \triangleq$
.1 $(\forall s \in \underline{dom}\ sffm)$
.2 $(\underline{let}\ (f_f,f_t) = sffm(s)\ \underline{in}\ \{f_f,f_t\} \subseteq fs)$

Semantically the data structure diagrams can be formalized, using (1.) and (3.):

```
9.      DSD_sem :: (Fid m→ R-set)   (Sid m→ (R m→ R-set))
```

which we annotate: to file names, in *Fid*, correspond sets of records; and to arrow names, in *Sid*, maps from records to (sub)sets of records. Combining the syntactic and semantic abstractions we get:

```
10.     DSD     :: (Fid m→ R-set)   (Sid m→ ((Fid × Fid) × (R m→ R-set))
```

which we annotate: to file names correspond, as in the semantic "view", sets of records; and to arrow names correspond two things: (syntactically) the pair of from/to identification, and (semantically) the map from 'from' records to sets of 'to' records.

Combining the two constraints: (8.) and (5.) we get:

```
11.0 inv-DSD(mk-DSD(fm,sm)) ≜
  .1      (∀s ∈ dom sm)
  .2         (let ((f,t),m) = sm(s)  in
  .3         ({f,t} ⊆ dom fm)
  .4      ∧  ((dom m ⊆ fm(f) ∧ (union rng m ⊆ fm(t))))
```

Given the holding of these constraints we can express the following relations between *DSD*, on one side, and DSD_{syn} and DSD_{sem}, on the other side:

```
12.0    retr-DSD_syn(mk-DSD(fm,sm)) ≜
  .1       mk-DSD_syn(dom fm,[s ↦ (f,t) | s∈dom sm ∧ ((f,t),)=sm(s)])
12.     type:  DSD ⥲ DSD_syn

13.0    retr-DSD_sem(mk-DSD(fm,sm)) ≜
  .1       mk-DSD_sem(fm,[s ↦ m | s∈dom sm ∧ (,m)=sm(s)])
13.     type:  DSD ⥲ DSD_sem

14.0    inj-DSD(mk-DSD_syn(fs,ss),mk-DSD_sem(fm,sm')) ≜
  .1       mk-DSD(fm,[s ↦ (ss(s),sm')) | s∈dom ss])
  .2       pre: (fs = dom fm) ∧ (dom ss = dom sm')
  .3            ∧ inv-DSD_syn(mk-DSD_syn(fs,ss))
  .4            ∧ (∀s ∈ dom ss)(let (f,t) = ss(s)  in
  .5                               (dom sm'(s) ⊆ fm(f))
  .6                               ∧(union rng sm'(s) ⊆ fm(t)))
14.     type:  DSD_syn × DSD_sem  →  DSD
```

where:

15.0 $(\forall dsd \in DSD)(inv\text{-}DSD(dsd) \supset$

.1 $(inj\text{-}DSD(retr\text{-}DSD_{syn}(dsd), retr\text{-}DSD_{sem}(dsd)) = dsd))$

Restrictions and Extensions to the Data Aggregate Model

First we deal with a restriction. Historically the following constraint had been imposed: under any arrow denoted map, two distinct records of its domain map into disjoint sets of records. We express this (further) constraint by joining an additional line (11.5) to formula (11.):

11.5 $(\forall r_1, r_2 \in \underline{dom}\ m)((r_1 \neq r_2) \supset (m(r_1) \cap m(r_2) = \{\}))$

One (logical) reason for this restriction is that it allows a network database user to model (tree-like) hierarchies. We shall attempt in chapter 13, section 2 to give another (physical) reason for this restriction.

Then we turn to generalizations on the theme of variations on the syntax of arrows and correspondingly denoted meanings. Up tp now we have dealt with arrows (i) emanating from exactly one box and being incident upon exactly one box. We now formalize the syntax and semantics of arrows which (ii and iii) emanate from one but are incident upon more than one box, or (iv, v and vi) emanate from several and are incident upon exactly one, respectively more than one box:

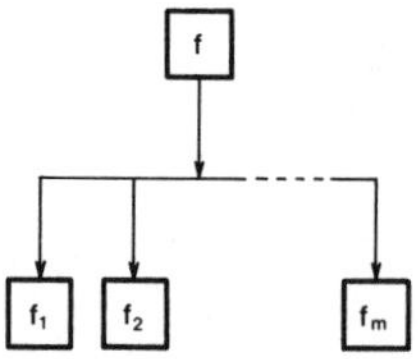

Fig. 13

$mk\text{-}FT_{ii}(f, \{f_1, f_2, \ldots, f_m\})$

$mk\text{-}FT_{iii}(f, \{f_1, f_2, \ldots, f_m\})$

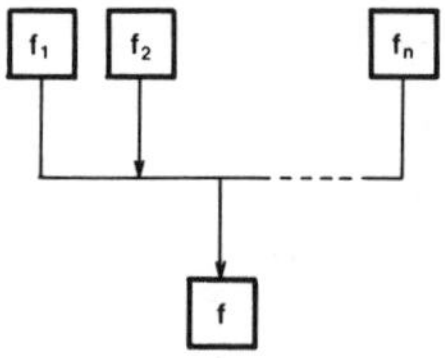

Fig. 14

$mk\text{-}FT_{iv}(\{f_1, f_2, \ldots, f_n\}, f)$

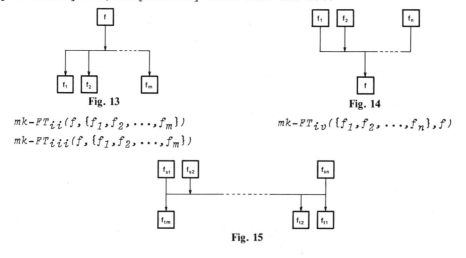

Fig. 15

$mk\text{-}FT_{v/vi}(\{f_{s1}, f_{s2}, \ldots, f_{sn}\}, \{f_{tm}, \ldots f_{t2}, f_{t1}\})$

In DSD_{syn} [DSD] we mapped *Sid* into *(Fid Fid)* [*((Fid Fid) (R $\underset{m}{\rightarrow}$ R-set))*] we now map *Sid* into *FT* (*SET*). The Domain *FT* has the six forms:

16. $FT = FT_{11} \mid FT_{1M1} \mid FT_{1MK} \mid FT_{N1} \mid FT_{NM1} \mid FT_{NMK}$

where:

17. $FT_{i} \equiv FT_{11}$ :: *Fid Fid*
18. $FT_{ii} \equiv FT_{1M1}$ :: *Fid Fid-set*
19. $FT_{iii} \equiv FT_{1MK}$ :: *Fid Fid-set*
20. $FT_{iv} \equiv FT_{N1}$ :: *Fid-set Fid*
21. $FT_{v} \equiv FT_{NM1}$ :: *Fid-set Fid-set*
22. $FT_{vi} \equiv FT_{NMK}$ :: *Fid-set Fid-set*

The associated meaning of arrows are given next. Basically their meaning is a map from records of the source box(es) to sets of records of the target box(es). [Having already disposed of (i) we "start" with (ii and iii).] Either of two meanings can be attached to the arrow which forks out to many boxes. One associates with a record of *F*, the set of records denoted by *f*, a non-empty set of records of some F_i; the other associates with a record of *F*, for each target box (file), F_i, a set of its records:

23.0 $SET = SET_{11} \mid SET_{1M1} \mid SET_{1MK} \mid SET_{N1} \mid SET_{NM1} \mid SET_{NMK}$

24. SET_{11} :: *(Fid × Fid) (R $\underset{m}{\rightarrow}$ R-set)*
25. SET_{1M1} :: *Fid (R $\underset{m}{\rightarrow}$ (Fid × R-set))*
26. SET_{1MK} :: *Fid (R $\underset{m}{\rightarrow}$ (Fid $\underset{m}{\rightarrow}$ R-set))*

Turning next to arrows which fork inwards (iv). To each record of each source box there corresponds a set of records of the same target box:

27. SET_{N1} :: *((Fid × R) $\underset{m}{\rightarrow}$ R-set) × Fid*

Finally consider the multiple-source/multiple-target arrows. Again two meanings are possible -- corresponding, for each record of some source box, to the situations (ii and iii).

28. SET_{NM1} :: *(Fid × R) $\underset{m}{\rightarrow}$ (Fid × R-set)*
29. SET_{NMK} :: *(Fid × R) $\underset{m}{\rightarrow}$ (Fid $\underset{m}{\rightarrow}$ R-set)*

For each of these 'new' arrows (ii-vi) we must express suitable constraints:

```
30.0  inv-DSD(mk-DSD(fm,sm)) ≜
  .1      (∀s ∈ dom sm)(inv-SET(sm(s))(fm))

31.0  inv-SET1M1(mk-SET1M1(f,m))(fm) ≜
  .1      ((f ∈ dom fm)
  .2      ∧ (∀r ∈ dom m)((r ∈ fm(f))
  .3                    ∧ (let (t,rs) = m(r) in (t ∈ dom fm)
  .4                    ∧ (rs ⊆ fm(t)))))

32.0  inv-SET1MK(mk-SET1MK(f,m))(fm) ≜
  .1      ((f ∈ dom fm)
  .2      ∧ (∀r ∈ dom m)((r ∈ fm(f))
  .3                    ∧ (let m' = m(r) in
  .4                        (∀t ∈ dom m')((t ∈ dom fm)
  .5                                      ∧ (m'(t) ⊆ fm(t))))))

33.0  inv-SETN1(mk-SETN1(m,t))(fm) ≜
  .1      ((t ∈ dom fm)
  .2      ∧ (∀(f,r) ∈ dom m)((f ∈ dom fm)
  .3                        ∧ (r ∈ fm(f))
  .4                        ∧ (m(f,r) ⊆ fm(t))))

34.0  inv-SETNM1(mk-SETNM1(m))(fm) ≜
  .1      (∀(f,r) ∈ dom m)((f ∈ dom fm)
  .2                      ∧ (r ∈ fm(r))
  .3                      ∧ (let (t,rs) = m(f,r)  in
  .4                         ((t ∈ dom fm)
  .5                      ∧ (rs ⊆ fm(t)))))

35.0  inv-SETNMK(mk-SETNMK(m))(fm) ≜
  .1      (∀(f,r) ∈ dom m)((f ∈ dom fm)
  .2                      ∧ (r ∈ fm(f))
  .3                      ∧ (let m' = m(f,r)  in
  .4                         (∀t ∈ dom m')((t ∈ dom fm)
  .5                                       ∧ (m'(t) ⊆ fm(t)))))
```

[Reviewing formulae (24.-29.) we observe how one could "almost" derive formulae by simple syntactic manipulations, or by manipulations, of an algebraic nature, which ascribe particular Domain operations (×, $\xrightarrow[m]{}$, |, *-set*, ..., including grouping *()*).]

12.3.2 The Operations

We shall illustrate operations only on the simplest form of data aggregates, that is involving only simple arrow relations (*SET11*) as defined by (10.).

Three kinds of operations will be investigated: operations on files, relations and entire data structure diagrams. To the first group, belong the operations of writing [, updating, reading] and deleting records; to the second, those of connecting and disconnecting records to, respectively from relations; and to the third group, the retrieve operation of finding desired records. We shall illustrate variations of the non-bracketed ([...]) operations.

File Operations

```
36.    FCmd    =  Write | Delete
37.    Write   :: Fid   R
38.    Delete  :: Fid   R
```

Writing a record to a file does not interfere with relations involving that file ("insertion manual"):

```
39.    type: Write: DSD ⥲ DSD
39.0   Int-Write[mk-Write(f,r)](mk-DSD(fm,sm)) ≜
  .1     if (f ∈ dom fm) ∧ (r ¬∈ fm(f))
  .2       then mk-DSD(fm + [f ↦ fm(f) ∪ {r}],sm)
  .3       else undefined
```

At least two kinds of semantics can be ascribed to the delete operation. Either we can only delete records which are not in any relation involving the file:

```
40.    type: Delete: DSD ⥲ DSD
40.0   Int-Delete[mk-Delete(f,r)](mk-DSD(fm,sm)) ≜
  .1     if ((f ∈ dom fm) ∧ (r ∈ fm(f))
  .2        ∧ (∀((f,),m) ∈ rng sm)(r ¬ ∈ dom m)
  .3        ∧ (∀((,f),m) ∈ rng sm)(r ¬ ∈ union rng m))
  .4       then mk-DSD(fm + [f ↦ fm(f)\{r}],sm)
  .5       else undefined
```

Or deletion propagates to all such relations, that is "triggers" corresponding "disconnect" operations:

```
41.0   Int-Delete[mk-Delete(f,r)](mk-DSD(fm,sm)) ≜
  .1      (let fm' = fm + [f ↦ fm(f)\{r}],
  .2           sm' = [s ↦ ftr
  .3                  | s ∈ dom sm
  .4                  ∧ ftr=(let ((fr,to),rel) = sm(f) in
  .5                         f∈{fr,to}
  .6                           → ((fr,to),[r' ↦ rs | r'∈dom rel\{r}
  .7                                                 ∧ rs=rel(r')\{r}]),
  .8                         T → sm(f))] in
  .9       mk-DSD(fm',sm'))
```

Lines (41.6-7.) express the disconnection of *r* from the domain (41.6) and range (41.7) of all those relations (*rel*) which involve the file *f* either as source (*f* = *fr*) or target (*f* = *to*), that is either as owner or member. All other relations are unaffected (41.8). Lines (41.6-7.) express disconnection rather "generously" in that no question is asked whether *r* actually is involved in *rel*!

'Set' Operations

```
42.    Connect  ::  Sid    (R × R-set)
43.    DisConn  ::  Sid    (R × R-set)
```

The *Connect* operation *mk-Connect(s,(r,rs))* intuitively inserts the 'relation': [*r* ↦ *rs*] as part of the denotation of *s*:

```
44.0   Int-Connect[mk-Connect(s,(r,rs))](mk-DSD(fm,sm)) ≜
  .1      if s ¬∈ dom sm
  .2         then undefined
  .3         else (let ((f,t),rel) = sm(s)  in
  .4               if r ¬∈ fm(f) ∧ rs ¬⊆ fm(t)
  .5                  then undefined
  .6                  else (let rel' = if r ∈ dom rel
  .7                                      then rel + [r ↦ rel(r) ∪ rs]
  .8                                      else rel ∪ [r ↦ rs]  in
  .9                        let sm' = sm + [s ↦ ((f,t),rel']   in
  .10                       mk-DSD(fm,sm')))
44.    type:  Connect → (DSD ⥲ DSD)
```

No check is made for records of *rs* already in the denotation of *s* under *r*. The *Disconnect* operation "undoes" what the connect operation is doing:

```
45.0   Int-DisConn[mk-DisConn(s,(r,rs))](mk-DSD(fm,sm)) ≜
  .1      if s ¬∈ dom sm
  .2         then undefined
  .3         else (let ((f,t),rel) = sm(s)  in
  .4               if r ¬∈ fm(f) ∧ rs ¬⊆ fm(t)
  .5                ∧ r ¬∈ dom rel ∧ rs ¬⊆ rel(r)
  .6                  then undefined
  .7                  else (let rel' = if rs = rel(r)
  .8                                      then rel \ {r}
  .9                                      else rel + [r ↦ rel(r)\rs] in
  .10                      let sm'  = sm + [s ↦ ((f,t),rel')]  in
  .11                      mk-DSD(fm,sm')))
45.    type:  DisConn → (DSD ⥲ DSD)
```

Data Structure Diagram "Navigations"

-- Paths

A sequence, $<s_1,s_2,\ldots,s_n>$, of arrow ('set' or relation) names may determine a 'path' through a data structure diagram *mk-DSD(fm,sm)*, as follows: each s_i, if actually the name of some arrow in *sm*, determines a triple: $sm(s_i)=((f_i,t_i),rel_i)$, thus the arrow name sequence above determines a sequence of from-to file names: $<(f_1,t_1),(f_2,t_2),\ldots,(f_{i-1},t_{i-1}),(f_i,t_i),(f_{i+1},t_{i+1}),\ldots,(f_n,t_n)>$. If for all appropriate i we have: $t_{i-1}=f_i$ then we say that $<s_1,s_2,\ldots,s_n>$ is forwardwell-formed. If for all appropriate i, either $t_i=t_{i+1}$ (that is $f_i=f_{i+1}$) or $t_{i-1}=f_i$, then we say that it is un-directed well-formed. A forward-well-formed path is an odinary path in the directed graph determined by any data structure diagram. A well-formed path is a path in the corresponding un-directed graph. Well-formed paths may thus embed arrows in opposing directions.

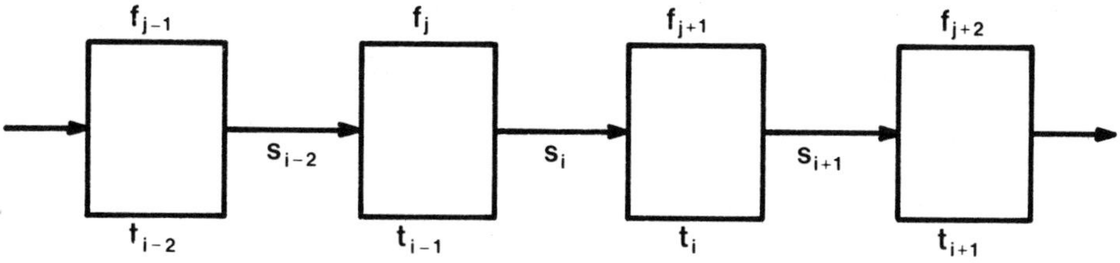

Fig. 16 Forward well-formed Path

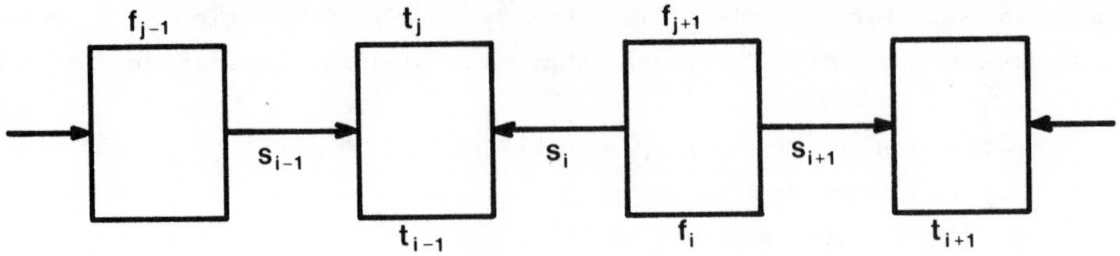

Fig. 17 Undirected well-formed Path

-- <u>Images</u> <u>and</u> <u>Inverse</u> <u>Images</u>

We are given an arrow, s, and a set of records, rs, of either the <u>from</u> f or the <u>to</u> t file of the arrow, and are asked to compute the <u>image</u>, respectively the <u>inverse</u> <u>image</u>, of rs "under the arrow". A figure and a formula for each of the two situations should suffice:

$$irs = \underline{union}\{rel(r) \mid r \in rs\}$$

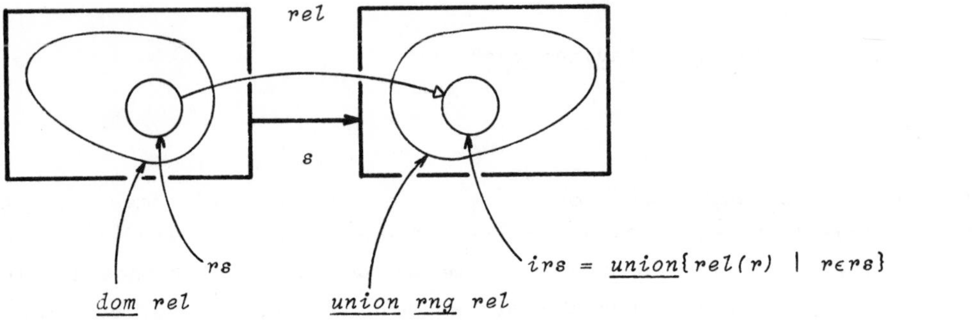

Fig. 18

The <u>inverse</u> <u>image</u> is the set of all those records of the domain of rel which, in rd, map into set of records properly overlapping with rs:

$$iirs = \{r \mid r \in \underline{dom}\ rel \wedge (rel(r) \cap rs \neq \{\})\}$$

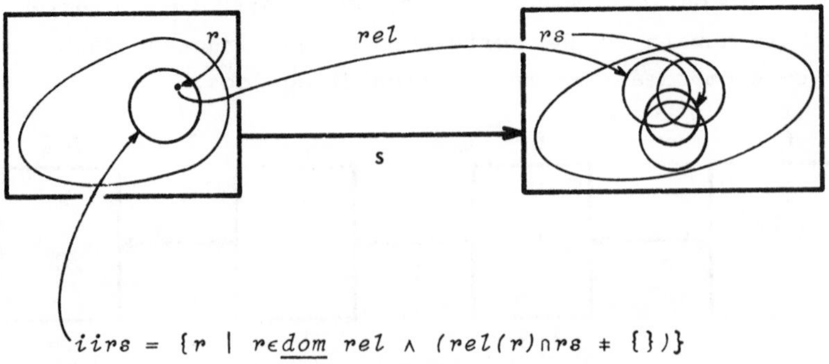

Fig. 19

-- Navigational Retrieval

Given a starting file, f, a set of records, rs, and a well-formed path $sl=<s_1,s_2,\ldots,s_n>$ we wish to find the set of records rs' which is the combined image/inverse-image of rs under sl:

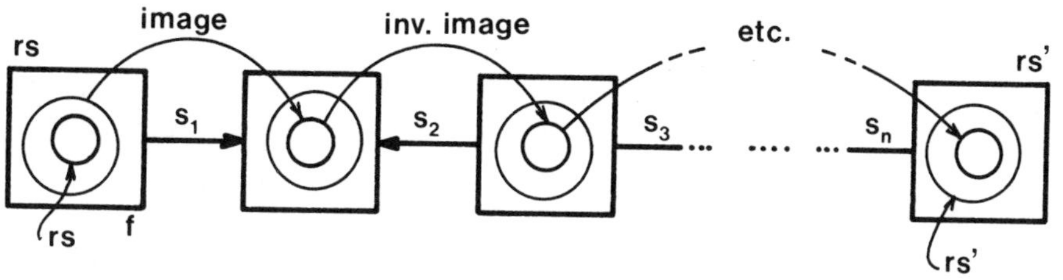

Fig. 20

To effect the retrieval of rs' we specify a command, its syntax and semantics:

46. $Find \;::\; Fid \quad Sid^{+} \quad R\text{-}set$

47.0 $Val\text{-}Find[mk\text{-}Find(f,sl,rs)](mk\text{-}DSD(fm,sm)) \triangleq$
 .1 $\quad V(f,sl,rs)(sm)$
47. $\underline{type}\text{:} \; Find \to (DSD \xrightarrow{\sim} DSD)$

48.0 $V[f,sl,rs](sm) \triangleq$
 .1 $\quad \underline{if}\; sl=<>$
 .2 $\quad\quad \underline{then}\; rs$
 .3 $\quad\quad \underline{else}\; (\underline{let}\; ((fr,to),rel) = sm(\underline{hd}\; sl) \;\; \underline{in}$
 .4 $\quad\quad\quad \underline{cases}\; f\text{:}$
 .5 $\quad\quad\quad\quad (fr \to V[to,\underline{tl}\; sl,\underline{union}\{rel(r) \mid r \in rs\}](sm),$
 .6 $\quad\quad\quad\quad\; to \to V[fr,\underline{tl}\; sl,\{r \mid r\in\underline{dom}\; rel \wedge rel(r) \cap rs \neq \{\}\}](sm),$
 .7 $\quad\quad\quad\quad\; T \;\to \underline{undefined}))$
48. $\underline{type}\text{:}\; Fid \times Sid^{*} \times R\text{-}set \to ((Sid \underset{m}{\to} SET_{11}) \to R\text{-}set))$

Other forms of navigational retrieval can be defined. One immediate variant on the above is to include, for each arrow specification, a predicate function which "filters" only such records in the image, or inverse image, which satisfy some property:

49. $p \in P \;=\; R \to Bool$
50. $Find \;::\; Fid \quad (Sid \times P)+ \quad R\text{-}set$

```
51.0 V[f,spl,rs](sm) ≜
  .1     if spl= <>
  .2       the rs
  .3       else (let (s,p) = hd spl in
  .4             if s∈dom sm
  .5               then (let ((fr,to),rel) = sm(s) in
  .6                     cases f:
  .7                      (fr → (let rs" = union{rel(r) | r∈rs} in
  .8                             let rs' = {r | rs" ∧ p(r)} in
  .9                             V[to,tl spl,rs'](sm)),
  .10                      to → (let rs" = {r|r∈dom rel∧rel(r)∩rs≠{}} in
  .11                            let rs' = {r | r∈rs" ∧ p(r)} in
  .12                            V[fr,tl spl,rs'](sm)),
  .13                      T  →  undefined))
  .14             else undefined)
```

51.   *type:* $Fid \times (Sid \times P)^* \times R\text{-}set \rightarrow ((Sid \underset{m}{\rightarrow} SET_{11}) \rightarrow R\text{-}set)$

This last definition, incidentally, checked for existence of arrows before checking for undirected path well-formedness -- something the previous definition assumed, but did not check!

CHAPTER 13

REALIZATION OF DATABASE MANAGEMENT SYSTEMS

This chapter continues the application of VDM to database applications. As explained above, the various architectures correspond to programming languages. The implementation of the architecture corresponds to an interpreter or, in cases, to a compiler. Just as VDM can be used to justify the design of an interpreter or compiler with respect to the definition of the language, this chapter briefly illustrates how a database management system implementation can be related to the specification of a data model. Implementations of both hierarchic and network architectures are discussed in this chapter; some of the standard (for example HDAM) IMS representations are discussed for the former. This chapter again illustrates the concepts of object transformations reviewed in chapters 10 and 11.

CONTENTS

13.0 INTRODUCTION

In this last chapter we shall briefly roundoff the ideas of chapters 10, 11 and 12. We illustrate the transition from some of the formal, architecturally abstract database data models of chapter 12 towards more concrete specifications of the database management systems (DBMS) which implement these models. We exemplify only the object transformations involved. Chapter 10 has amply exemplified the related operation transformations. And we display aspects of only hierarchical and network database systems.

13.1 HIERARCHICAL DATABASE MANAGEMENT SYSTEMS

We assume a slightly different data model than the one illustrated in section 12.2.1. And we focus attention only on the data part of the data model. (That is: we omit consideration of the catalogue part.) This subsection presents four models, one abstract and three concrete (HSAM, $HDAM_{ct}$, $HDAM_{fp}$). First we restate the abstract model. This model is considered an abstraction of an appropriate part of IBMs IMS DBMS. IBM does not deliver abstractions. IBM delivers concretizations. In fact IBM offers three variants of IMS. These are referred to as the hierarchical sequential access method (HSAM), the hierarchical direct access method (HDAM) with child-twin pointers $HDAM_{ct}$, and HDAM with file pointers $HDAM_{fp}$.

13.1.1 Abstract IMS Data Part

Informally an IMS data part, *DP*, is abstracted as follows: A *DP* consists of a number of uniquely named physical database records, *P*, with names in *F*. Each *P* consists of an ordered sequence of segments, *S*. Each segment, *S*, has three components: a sequence field which is an integer, a number of other uniquely named fields (of some type), and a data part. (The last component description refers to what is being defined. From this recursion, then, stems the 'hierarchy'.)

1. $DP = F \underset{m}{\vec{\ }} P$
2. $P = S^*$
3. $S :: Int \ (Sn \underset{m}{\vec{\ }} VAL) \ DP$

Within a given data part there is, according to the above informal and formal descriptions, no ordering among the uniquely (F) named physical database records.

13.1.2 Hierarchical Sequential Access Methods, HSAM

In IMS, not just in its HSAM version, but in general, there is an ordering among the Ps of any DP. It is straightforward to model such an ordering:

4. $DP_{hsam} = (F\ P_{hsam})^*$
5. $P_{hsam} = S_{hsam}{}^*$
6. $S_{hsam} :: Intg\ (Sn \underset{m}{\to} VAL)\ DP_{hsam}$

7.0 $is\text{-}wf\text{-}DP_{hsam}(dp) \triangleq$
.1 $\quad is\text{-}unique(<s\text{-}F(dp[i])\ |\ 1 \le i \le \underline{len}\ dp>)$
.2 $\quad \wedge\ (\forall(,pdbr) \in \underline{elems}\ dp)$
.3 $\qquad (\forall mk\text{-}S_{hsam}(,,dp') \in \underline{elems}\ pdbr)$
.4 $\qquad\quad is\text{-}wf\text{-}DP_{hsam}(dp')$

8.0 $retr\text{-}DP(dp) \triangleq [f \mapsto retr\text{-}P(pdbr)\ |\ (f,pdbr) \in \underline{elems}\ dp]$

9.0 $retr\text{-}PDBR(sl) \triangleq <retr\text{-}S(sl[i])\ |\ 1 \le i \le \underline{len}\ sl>$

10.0 $retr\text{-}S(mk\text{-}S_{hsam}(i,svm,dp)) \triangleq mk\text{-}S(i,svm,retr\text{-}DP(dp))$

There is almost an inverse to the retrieve, or abstraction, functions. That is there is an injection relation ($\nrightarrow$):

$inj\text{-}DP(mk\text{-}DP_{hsam}(dp)) \triangleq <(f,inj\text{-}SL(dp(f)))\ |\ f \in \underline{dom}\ dp>$
$\underline{type}$: $DP \nrightarrow DP_{hsam}$

$inj\text{-}P(sl) \triangleq <inj\text{-}S_{hsam}(sl[i])\ |\ 1 \le i \le \underline{len}\ sl>$
$\underline{type}$: $S^* \nrightarrow P$

$inj\text{-}S(mk\text{-}S(i,svm,dp) \triangleq mk\text{-}S_{hsam}(i,inj\text{-}FVAL(svm),inj\text{-}DP(dp))$
$\underline{type}$: $S \nrightarrow S_{hsam}$

$inj\text{-}FVAL(svm) \triangleq <(s,v)\ |\ s \in \underline{dom}\ svm \wedge v = svm(s)>$
$\underline{type}$: $(Sn \underset{m}{\to} VAL) \nrightarrow (Sn\ VAL)^*$

Tape Formatting

The HSAM organization is well-suited for, and conceived of in connection with, storing data parts on a magnetic tape. The hierarchical structure:

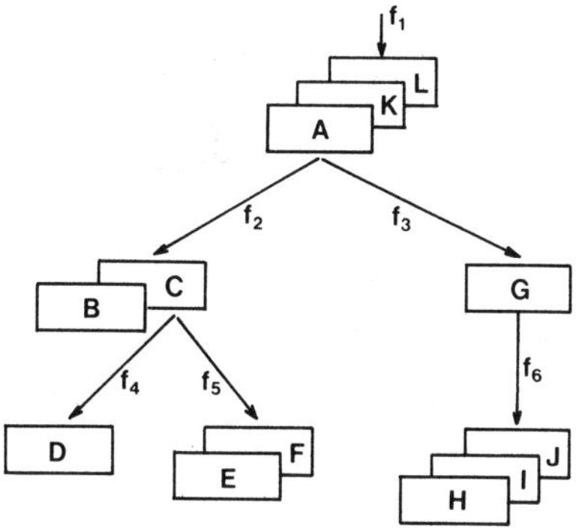

Fig. 1

-- omitting important details, thus is basically "stored" as:

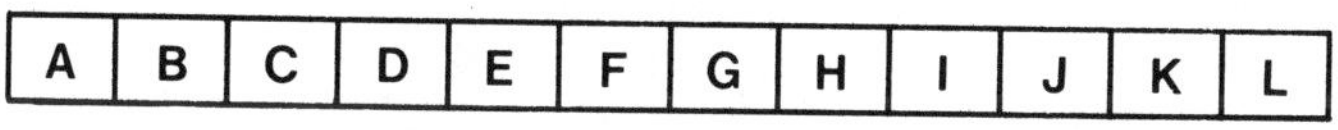

Fig. 2

That is as the concrete object:

```
<(f1,
  <mk-S(a,
         <(f2,
            <mk-S(...B...),
             mk-S(c,
                    <(f4,
                       <mk-S(...D...)>),
                     (f5,
                       <mk-S(...E...),
                        mk-S(...F...)>)>)>)>),
         (f3,
           <mk-S(q,
                   <(f6,
                      <mk-S(...H...),
                       mk-S(...I...),
                       mk-S(...J...)>)>)>)>),
  mk-S(...K...),
  mk-S(...L...)>)>
```

[Here we have abbreviated S_{hsam} into S, and the sequence field integer and other field values into one (lower case roman) component.] The problem we wish to briefly consider is that of designing a concrete <u>linear</u> representation of DP objects. Basically that problem is always one of representing the abstract syntax for DP_{hsam} by a concrete, e.g. BNF, grammer DP_{bnf}. Sequence (S_{hsam}*) of objects are usually BNF-"programmed" as left- or right-recursive structures; but we do not care whether it is left- or right-leaning. In this "exercise" we decide to design the linear representation as a fully "bracketed" structure using marked parantheses and marked comma delimiters:

```
DPbnf       ::= DP< Filebnf { DP, Filebnf }* >PD |
Filebnf     ::= F( Fname , PDBRbnf )F
PDBRbnf     ::= SL< SegListbnf >LS
SegListbnf  ::= Segm { SL, Segm }*                 |
Segmbnf     ::= S( IntgSVAL s, DPbnf )S
```

(Here we have lumped into one object, *IntgSVAL*, the sequence field integer and other segment field values.) The previously shown abstract object now can be given the linear representation below:

```
DP< F( f1 f,
      SL< S( a s,
            DP< F( f2 f,
                  SL< S(... B ...)S SL,
                     S( c s,
                        DP< F( f4 f,
                              SL< S(... D ...)S >LS )F DP,
                           F( f5 f,
                              SL< S(... E ...)S >LS )F >PD )S >LS DP,
               F( f3 f,
                  SL< S( g s,
                        DP< F( f6 f,
                              SL< S(... H ...)S SL,
                                 S(... I ...)S SL,
                                 S(... J ...)S >LS )F >PD )S >LS )F >PD )S SL,
         S(... K ...)S SL,
         S(... L ...)S >LS )F >PD
```

In un-indented, i.e. non-structured textual form the above becomes:

DP< F(f_1 f, SL< S(*a* s, DP< F(f_2 f, SL< S(... *B* ...)S SL, S(*c* s, DP< F(f_4 f, SL< S(... *D* ...)S >LS)F DP, F(f_5 f, SL< S(... *E* ...)S)LS)F >PD)S >LS DP, F(f_3 f, SL< S(*g* s, DP< F(f_6 f, SL< S(... *H* ...)S SL, S(... *I* ...)S SL, S(... *J* ...)S >LS)F >PD)S >LS)F >PD S(... *K* ...)S SL, S(... *L* ...)S >LS)F >PD

Using conventional syntax analysis tools one can easily generate a parser which reads such strings and, by means of suitable, simple actions connected to appropriate productions, effects the operations of *mk*- or *s*-function decomposition as used in our various elaboration functions of e.g. section 2.2 of chapter 12.

13.1.3 Hierarchical Direct Access Methods, HDAM

The ordering relation suggested by the physical juxtaposition relation of magnetic tape offsets, or addresses can, however, be achieved in other ways. The *DP* part of segments, in the abstract *S*, as well as in the sequential S_{hsam}, models, can be considered as being contained in segments. Containment will now be replaced by designation. That is: proper parts of segments will contain pointers to *DP* structures, and these together with "proper" components will be physically allocated to any storage fragment. "Proper" components of segments will be those not involving parts. The following figure should illustrate our point:

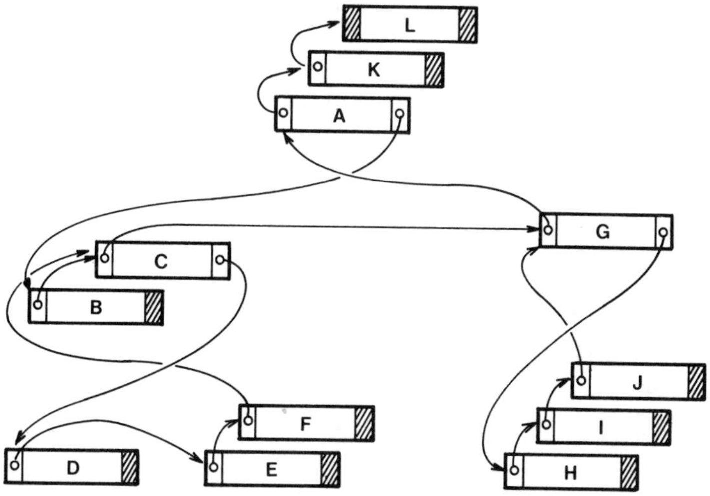

Fig. 3

Several pointer organizations are possible. The above embodies a notion of the "left" pointer designating (1) the "next segment" within a "segment list", (2) the "first segment of the next (twin) brother/sister segment list", or (3) the "parent segment". The "right" pointer of any segment designates a "first" child segment, if any.

Instead of having a pointer designating a child segment of some such first child file, we permit segments to individually designate the "first" segment of all children files:

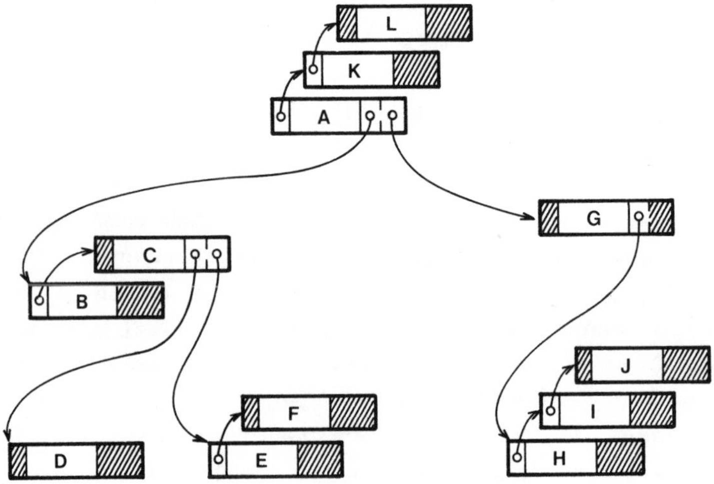

Fig. 4

These two organizations will now be formalized.

<u>The Child/Twin Pointer Scheme</u>, <u>$HDAM_{ct}$</u>

$$DP_{ct} \quad :: \quad [\ Ptr\ ] \quad (Ptr \underset{m}{\rightarrow} F) \quad STG_{ct}$$
$$STG_{ct} \quad = \quad Ptr \underset{m}{\rightarrow} S_{ct}$$
$$S_{ct} \quad :: \quad [\ PTR\ ] \quad (Intg(Sn \underset{m}{\rightarrow} VAL)) \quad [\ Ptr\ ]$$
$$PTR \quad = \quad NsPtr \mid TwPtr \mid PaPtr$$
$$NsPtr \quad :: \quad Ptr$$
$$TwPtr \quad :: \quad Ptr$$
$$PaPtr \quad :: \quad Ptr$$

The particular object shown earlier now has the following $HDAM_{ct}$ representation:

$$
\begin{array}{l}
mk\text{-}DP_{ct}(p_a, \\
\quad [pa \mapsto f_1,\ p_b \mapsto f_2,\ p_c \mapsto f_4,\ p_e \mapsto f_5,\ p_g \mapsto f_3,\ p_n \mapsto f_6], \\
\quad [p_a \mapsto mk\text{-}S_{ct}(mk\text{-}NsPtr(p_k),\ \mathrm{a}\ ,p_b), \\
\quad\ p_b \mapsto mk\text{-}S_{ct}(mk\text{-}NsPtr(p_c),\ \mathrm{b}\ ,\underline{nil}), \\
\quad\ p_c \mapsto mk\text{-}S_{ct}(mk\text{-}TwPtr(p_g),\ \mathrm{c}\ ,p_d), \\
\quad\ p_d \mapsto mk\text{-}S_{ct}(mk\text{-}TwPtr(p_e),\ \mathrm{d}\ ,\underline{nil}), \\
\quad\ p_e \mapsto mk\text{-}S_{ct}(mk\text{-}NsPtr(p_f),\ \mathrm{e}\ ,\underline{nil}), \\
\quad\ p_f \mapsto mk\text{-}S_{ct}(mk\text{-}PaPtr(p_c),\ \mathrm{f}\ ,\underline{nil}), \\
\quad\ p_g \mapsto mk\text{-}S_{ct}(mk\text{-}PaPtr(p_a),\ \mathrm{g}\ ,p_h), \\
\quad\ p_h \mapsto mk\text{-}S_{ct}(mk\text{-}NsPtr(p_i),\ \mathrm{h}\ ,\underline{nil}), \\
\quad\ p_i \mapsto mk\text{-}S_{ct}(mk\text{-}NsPtr(p_j),\ \mathrm{i}\ ,\underline{nil}), \\
\quad\ p_j \mapsto mk\text{-}S_{ct}(mk\text{-}PaPtr(p_g),\ \mathrm{j}\ ,\underline{nil}), \\
\quad\ p_k \mapsto mk\text{-}S_{ct}(mk\text{-}NsPtr(p_l),\ \mathrm{k}\ ,\underline{nil}), \\
\quad\ p_l \mapsto mk\text{-}S_{ct}(\underline{nil},\qquad \mathrm{l}\ ,\underline{nil})])
\end{array}
$$

Exercise: We leave it, as a non-trivial exercise, for the reader to define the $inv\text{-}DP_{ct}$ and $retr\text{-}DP$ functions.

The File Pointer Scheme, $HDAM_{fp}$

$$
\begin{array}{lll}
DP_{fp} & :: & (F \underset{m}{\to} Ptr)\quad STG_{fp} \\
STG_{fp} & = & Ptr \underset{m}{\to} S_{fp} \\
S_{fp} & :: & [Ptr]\quad (Intg(Sn \underset{m}{\to} VAL))\quad (F \underset{m}{\to} Ptr)
\end{array}
$$

-- and now the object representation is:

$$
\begin{array}{l}
mk\text{-}DP_{fp}([f_1 \mapsto p_a],[p_a \mapsto mk\text{-}S_{fp}(p_k,\ \mathrm{a}\ ,[f_2\mapsto p_b, f_3\mapsto p_g]), \\
\qquad p_b \mapsto mk\text{-}S_{fp}(p_c,\ \mathrm{b}\ ,\ [\,]\ ), \\
\qquad p_c \mapsto mk\text{-}S_{fp}(\underline{nil},\ \mathrm{c}\ ,[f_4\mapsto p_d, f_5\mapsto p_e]), \\
\qquad p_d \mapsto mk\text{-}S_{fp}(\underline{nil},\ \mathrm{d}\ ,\ [\,]\ ), \\
\qquad p_e \mapsto mk\text{-}S_{fp}(p_f,\ \mathrm{e}\ ,\ [\,]\ ), \\
\qquad p_f \mapsto mk\text{-}S_{fp}(\underline{nil},\ \mathrm{f}\ ,\ [\,]\ ), \\
\qquad p_g \mapsto mk\text{-}S_{fp}(\underline{nil},\ \mathrm{g}\ ,[f_6\mapsto p_h]), \\
\qquad p_h \mapsto mk\text{-}S_{fp}(p_i,\ \mathrm{h}\ ,\ [\,]\ ), \\
\qquad p_i \mapsto mk\text{-}S_{fp}(p_j,\ \mathrm{i}\ ,\ [\,]\ ), \\
\qquad p_j \mapsto mk\text{-}S_{fp}(\underline{nil},\ \mathrm{j}\ ,\ [\,]\ ), \\
\qquad p_k \mapsto mk\text{-}S_{fp}(p_l,\ \mathrm{k}\ ,\ [\,]\ ), \\
\qquad p_l \mapsto mk\text{-}S_{fp}(\underline{nil},\ \mathrm{l}\ ,\ [\,]\ )])
\end{array}
$$

Exercise: Formulate the $inv\text{-}DP_{fp}$ and $retr\text{-}DP$ functions.

The "inverse" of the *retr-DP* function, a so-called injection function, can be constructed. It is not "an exact" inverse. Its type is relational:

$$\underline{type}: \ inj\text{-}DP_{fp}: DP \nrightarrow DP_{fp}$$

It satisfies:

$$(\forall dp \in DP)(retr\text{-}DP(inj\text{-}DP_{fp}(dp)) = dp)$$

but not:

$$(\forall dp_{fp} \in DP_{fp})(inj\text{-}DP_{fp}(retr\text{-}DP(dp_{fp})) = dp_{fp})$$

We design our $inj\text{-}DP_{fp}$ in stages, bottom up. First we define:

```
type:  alloc:           → (Σ → Σ Ptr)
type:  Allocate F-set → (Σ → Σ (F ⇀m Ptr))

alloc() ≜ (def p ∈ Ptr dom c Stg;
               Stg := c Stg ∪ [p↦undefined];
               return(p))

Allocate(fs) ≜ if fs = {}
                    then []
                    else (let f ∈ fs in
                             def p: alloc();
                             def m: Allocate(fs - {f});
                             return([[f ↦ p] ∪ m]))
```

The model now is imperative:

```
dcl Stg := [] type STG_fp;
Σ       =  (Stg ⇀m STG_fp)

type:  inj-DP_fp: DP → (Σ → Σ (F ⇀m Ptr))

inj-DP_fp(dp) ≜
   (def m: Allocate(dom dp);
    for all f∈dom dp do inj-SL_fp(dp(f))(m(f),nil,nil);
    return(m))
```

```
inj-SLfp(sl)(cp,pp,s) ≜
   if sl=<>
      then  if pp=nil then I else Stg := c Stg + [pp ↦ s]
      else (if pp=nil
               then I
               else (let mk-Sfp(nil,r,m) = s in
                        Stg := c Stg + [pp ↦ mk-Sfp(cp,r,m)]);
            let mk-S(i,vm,dp) = hd sl in
            def m                : inj-DPfp(dp);
            def np               : if tl sl=<> then nil else alloc();
            inj-SLfp(tl sl)(np,cp,mk-Sfp(nil,(i,vm),m)))

type:  inj-SLfp: S* → ((Ptr × [ Ptr ] × [ Sfp ] ) → (Σ → Σ))
```

13.2 NETWORK DATABASE MANAGEMENT SYSTEMS

We no expand on section 12.3.1. The data model was:

$$DSD_0 \;::\; (Fid \underset{m}{\rightarrow} R_0\text{-}set)(Sid \underset{m}{\rightarrow} ((Fid \times Fid)(R_0 \underset{m}{\rightarrow} R_0\text{-}set)))$$

We focus on just one "arrow", i.e. "DBTG-set":

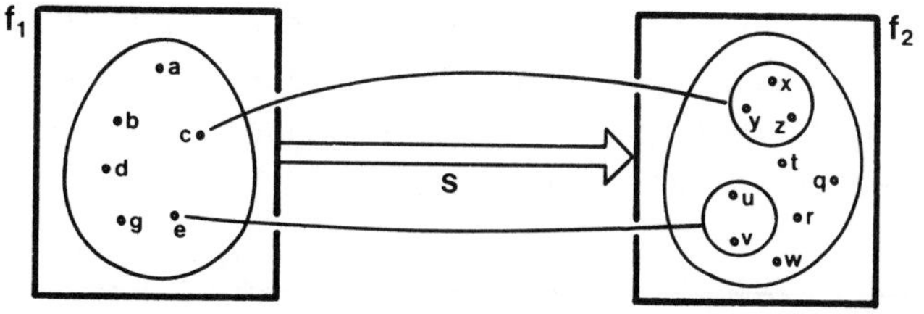

Fig. 5

As a *DSD* object it is represented by:

```
mk-DSD([f1 ↦ {a,b,c,d,e,g} ,
        f2 ↦ {x,y,z,u,v,w,q,r,t}],
       [s  ↦ ((f1,f2),[c↦{x,y,z},e ↦ {u,v}])])
```

We note a seeming duplication of objects: $x,y,z,y,v,c,$ and e, in both file objects and "DBTG-sets"s.

For the purposes of the development in this section we redraw the above example, ascribing a "box" to each record:

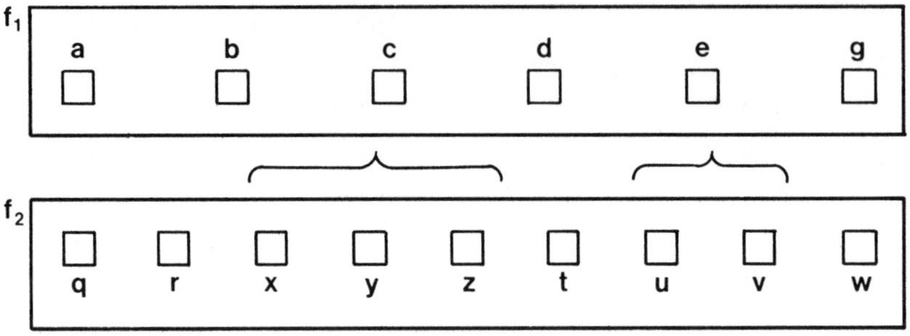

Fig. 6

We think, in a first step of development, of the "boxes" as allocated to disjoint storage cells. Each such record cell is uniquely designated by a pointer. Thus the R_0-*set* part of the files component, i.e. $(Fid \underset{m}{\rightarrow} R\text{-}set)$, is itself realized by a map: $(Ptr \underset{m}{\rightarrow} R)$. The $(R_0 \underset{m}{\rightarrow} R_0\text{-}set)$ component of the "DBTG-set" component, i.e. the braces of the above figure, is in this tentative, "trial" stage of development, realized as follows: with each owner record in the domain of $(R_0 \underset{m}{\rightarrow} R_0\text{-}set)$ is associated a pointer field to a potential arbitrary "first" member record (in the range of that map). And to each member record is associated a pointer field to a potential "next" member record:

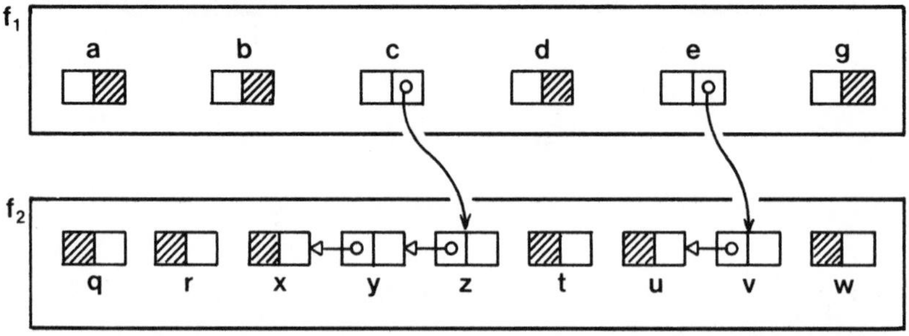

Fig. 7

This tentative implementation corresponds to a Domain definition of the realized DSD_0:

$$
\begin{array}{lll}
DSD_1 & :: & FILES_1 \quad SETS_1 \\
FILES_1 & = & (Fid \underset{m}{\rightarrow} (Ptr \underset{m}{\rightarrow} R_1)) \\
SETS_1 & = & (Sid \underset{m}{\rightarrow} (Fid \times Fid)) \\
R_1 & :: & R \;\; [\; Ptr \;]
\end{array}
$$

-- with the above illustrated DSD object being represented by:

$$
\begin{array}{lllll}
mk\text{-}DSD_1([\, f_1 & \mapsto [\; p_a \mapsto mk\text{-}R_1(\mathrm{a},\underline{nil}), & p_d \mapsto mk\text{-}R_1(\mathrm{d},\underline{nil}), \\
 & \quad\;\; p_b \mapsto mk\text{-}R_1(\mathrm{b},\underline{nil}), & p_e \mapsto mk\text{-}R_1(\mathrm{e},p_v), \\
 & \quad\;\; p_c \mapsto mk\text{-}R_1(\mathrm{c},p_z), & p_g \mapsto mk\text{-}R_1(\mathrm{g},\underline{nil})\,], \\
\quad f_2 & \mapsto [\; p_q \mapsto mk\text{-}R_1(\mathrm{q},\underline{nil}), & p_t \mapsto mk\text{-}R_1(\mathrm{t},\underline{nil}), \\
 & \quad\;\; p_r \mapsto mk\text{-}R_1(\mathrm{r},\underline{nil}), & p_n \mapsto mk\text{-}R_1(\mathrm{u},\underline{nil}), \\
 & \quad\;\; p_x \mapsto mk\text{-}R_1(\mathrm{x},\underline{nil}), & p_r \mapsto mk\text{-}R_1(\mathrm{v},p_n), \\
 & \quad\;\; p_y \mapsto mk\text{-}R_1(\mathrm{y},p_x), & p_w \mapsto mk\text{-}R_1(\mathrm{w},\underline{nil}), \\
 & \quad\;\; p_z \mapsto mk\text{-}R_1(\mathrm{z},p_y) \;]\;], & \\
\quad [s \mapsto (f_1,f_2) \;]) & &
\end{array}
$$

But there is a problem, in fact three, the above realization is constrained: (A) it only permits at most one "arrow" incident upon or emanating from a file, (B) it makes the representation of records of any file dependent on their possibly partaking in some "DBTG-set", and (C) it does not permit the overlapping, or sharing of member records.

To solve all three problems at once we propose another realization. We first show an example of what the realization results in:

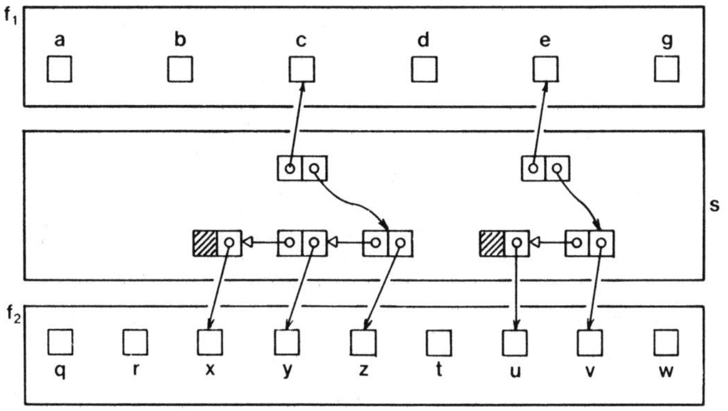

Fig. 8

We then explain the realization with respect to the previous "tentative" (but insufficient "realization") in terms of some surgical "operations": (i) we have cut away, from the owner and member records their pointer fields; (ii) we have then made these pointer parts into "records" themselves, (iii) joining to the new pointer fields containing pointers "back to" the owner, respectively the member records they were separated from. Now [(B)] owner- and member record representations are independent of the "DBTG-sets" they potentially partake of. Now [(A)] any file may take part in several "DBTG-sets". In fact [(C)]: to each such "DBTG-set" (or "arrow") there is exactly one pointer constellation as illustrated above, and shown "sandwiched" between the two files.

The Domain specification becomes:

$$
\begin{array}{lll}
DSD_2 & :: & FILES_2 \times SETS_2 \\
FILES_2 & = & (Fid \underset{m}{\vec{\ }} (Ptr \underset{m}{\vec{\ }} R)) \\
SETS_2 & = & (Sid \underset{m}{\vec{\ }} ((Fid \times Fid) \times OWN \times MBR)) \\
OWN & = & Ptr_o \underset{m}{\vec{\ }} OR \\
MBR & = & Ptr_m \underset{m}{\vec{\ }} MR \\
OR & :: & Ptr_r \times Ptr_m \\
MR & :: & [\ Ptr_m\ ] \times Ptr_r
\end{array}
$$

-- with the above illustrated *DSD* object being represented by:

$$
\begin{array}{l}
mk\text{-}DSD_2([\ f_1 \mapsto [\ p_a \mapsto \mathrm{a},\ p_b \mapsto \mathrm{b},\ p_c \mapsto \mathrm{c} \\
\qquad\qquad p_d \mapsto \mathrm{d},\ p_e \mapsto \mathrm{e},\ p_g \mapsto \mathrm{g}\ ], \\
\qquad f_2 \mapsto [\ p_q \mapsto \mathrm{q},\ \ p_r \mapsto \mathrm{r},\ p_x \mapsto \mathrm{x},\ p_y \mapsto \mathrm{y}, p_z \mapsto \mathrm{z}, \\
\qquad\qquad p_t \mapsto \mathrm{t},\ \ p_u \mapsto \mathrm{u},\ p_v \mapsto \mathrm{v},\ p_w \mapsto \mathrm{w}\ ]], \\
\quad [\ s\ \mapsto ((f_1,f_2), \\
\qquad [op_c \mapsto mk\text{-}OR(p_c,mp_z),op_e \mapsto mk\text{-}OR(p_e,nil)], \\
\qquad [mp_z \mapsto mk\text{-}MR(mp_y,p_z),mp_y \mapsto mk\text{-}MR(mp_x,p_y), \\
\qquad\ mp_x \mapsto mk\text{-}MR(\underline{nil},p_x),mp_v \mapsto mk\text{-}MR(mp_w,p_v), \\
\qquad\ mp_w \mapsto mk\text{-}MR(\underline{nil},p_w)])])
\end{array}
$$

We have illustrated a stage of development: from the abstract *DSD* to the pointer-based, more concrete DSD_2. Subsequent development steps could now allocate all records: file records and owner and member pointer records of all files and all "DBTG-sets/arrows" in one pointer-based storage medium. Models of the CODASYL/DBTG notions of "areas" and "current-of" can, and probably should, be entered into our development before doing such an ultimate concretization.

POSTSCRIPT

As a conclusion to many pages of formal material, we should like to offer some personal comment on what has been achieved and what remains to be done. VDM is one development method and it is clear that others exist and will be created. But, in our opinion, systematic development methods have been shown to be useful. Our aim is to be able to tackle the development of large computer systems with a disciplined engineering approach. For many classes of problems this is now possible and this book illustrates how specifications and design can be recorded systematically. There is no suggestion here that the creative aspects of design are being mechanized: it is the ability to record and justify designs which is being proposed. It is the availability of a generally recognized notation which will enable computer scientists to record their knowledge in a way which will be used by others.

A further advantage of an agreed semantic definition method should come in teaching. The approach taken in chapter 4 to an analysis of language concepts and in chapter 12 to database concepts indicates how we believe such material should be taught. Teachers can only focus on concepts if some form of model is discussed. It should be clear that the underlying concepts are far more basic than the detailed syntactic issues which are so often allowed to obscure them.

VDM has here been applied to a number of applications and is being applied by people in industry to a wide range of problems. What are the limitations (and thus the research challenges)? The problems involved with parallelism have been completely ignored in this book. Our research in this area is reported in [Bjørner 80f, Jones 81a] and our colleague of the IBM Vienna Laboratory, Hans Bekić is actually working on this topic. Our reasons for not discussing parallelism in this book are not a lack of ideas but rather the plethora of proposals for basically different approaches to this important topic. Clearly this is an area for experiments and research.

Another area where research is necessary is the decomposition of specifications. Here, the current book should provide a valuable source of problems. How, for instance could the common parts of the ALGOL 60 and Pascal definitions be factored out so that the commonality and differences are more apparent? Research in this area has been undertaken in the framework of "Z" [Abrial 80*] and "CLEAR" [Burstall 77a]; specific proposals relating to languages are being made by Peter Mosses ([Mosses 77a, Mosses 81a]).

A very pressing need is for the development of a support system which aids the control and modification of large definitions and designs. At its simplest, such a support system is a state-of-the-art undertaking. There is, however, ample scope for research projects aimed at mechanizing aspects of checking uses of VDM.

BIBLIOGRAPHY AND REFERENCES

Abbreviations

ACM	*A*ssociation for *C*omputing *M*achinery, New York, USA
Acta	*Acta* Informatics, Journal, S-V
ANSI	*A*merican *N*ational *S*tandards *I*nstitute, Standards on Computers and Information Processing
Ann.Rev.	*Ann*ual *Rev*iew in: 'Automatic Programming', Pergamon Press
BIT	Nordisk *T*idsskrift for *I*nformations *B*ehandling
CACM *X,Y*	*C*ommunications of the *ACM*, vol. *X*, No. *Y*
Comp.J. *X*	*Comp*uter *J*ournal, vol.*X*, British Computer Society
IBM RC*ZZ*	*IBM* Ths.J.Watson *R*esearch *C*enter, Yorktown Heights N.Y., Report No. RC*ZZ*
ICALP	*I*nternational *C*olloquium on *A*utomata, *L*anguages & *P*rogramming, European Association for Theoretical Computer Science
ICS'*ZZ*	*I*nternational *C*omputing *S*ymposium, ACM Europe, 19*ZZ*
IFIP'*ZZ*	*I*nternational *F*ederation for *I*nformation *P*rocessing, World Congress Proceedings, N-H, 19*ZZ*
IJCIS	*I*nternational *J*ournal of *C*omputer and *I*nformation Sciences
IPL *X*	*I*nformation *P*rocessing *L*etters, N-H, Vol. *X*
JACM *X,Y*	*J*ournal of the *ACM*, Vol. *X*, No. *Y*
LNCS *X*	*L*ecture *N*otes in *C*omputer *S*cience, S-V, Vol. *X*
MFCS'*XX*	*M*athematical *F*oundations of *C*omputer *S*cience, Proceedings, S-V, 19*XX*
MI-*X*	*M*achine *I*ntelligence, Vol. *X*, (ed.D.Michie et al.), Edinburgh University Press
MIT TR-*XX*	*MIT* Techn.Rept. *XX*, Lab.f.Comp.Sci., Mass.Inst. of Techn., Cambridge, Mass., USA.
N-H	*N*orth-*H*olland Publishing Co., Amsterdam, The Netherlands

POPL	*P*rinciples *o*f *P*rogramming *L*anguages, SIGPLAN/SIGACT Symposium, ACM Conference Record/Proceedings
PRG-*XX*	*P*rogramming *R*esearch *G*roup, Techn.Monograph PRG *XX* Oxford Univ., Computing Laboratory
San Jose RJ-*X*	IBM Research, *San Jose*, California, USA, Report RJ-*X*
SE-X	IEEE (Inst. of Electrical & Electronics Engineers) Transactions on *S*oftware *E*ngineering, vol. *X*, N.Y.
SIGACT SIGPLAN SIGOPS	ACM *S*pecial *I*nterest *G*roup on: *A*utomata & *C*omputability *T*heory, *P*rogramming *LAN*guages, *OP*erating *S*ystems, Notices
Stanford CS-*XXX*	*Stanford* University, Computer Science Department, Rept. CS-*XXX*
S-V	*S*pringer-*V*erlag, Heidelberg - New York - Berlin
SWAT	Symposium on *SW*itching & *A*utomata *T*heory, Inst. of Electrical & Electronics Engineers, N.Y.
TUD	Comp.Sci.Dept., Techn.Univ.of Denmark, Techn.Rept.
Vienna TR-*XX*	IBM *Vienna* Laboratory, Vienna , Austria; Technical Report No. TR-*XX*

VDL BIBLIOGRAPHY

The following references constitute an alphabetically sorted bibliography on the VDL:

[Bandat 65a] [Beech 73a] [Lauer 68a]
[Lee 69a-72b] [Lucas 68a-71a] [Lucas 81a]
[Moser 70a] [Neuhold 71a] [Ollongren 74a]
[ULD66,68,69] [Wegner 72a] [Zimmerman 69a]

VDL→VDM BIBLIOGRAPHY

The following references constitute an alphabetically sorted bibliography to the Vienna-based literature influencing & preparing for the VDM:

[Allen 72a] [Bekić 70a] [Bekić 73a]
[Henhapl 70a-71a] [Jones 71a-73a] [Lauer 73a]
[Lucas 73a-78a] [Walk 73a]

VDM BIBLIOGRAPHY

The following references constitute an alphabetically sorted bibliography to VDM:

[Bekić 74a] [Bjørner 77a-83*] [Bundgaard 80a]
[Clemmensen 81a-82b] [Dommergaard 80a-b] [Flensholt 81a]
[Folkjär 80a] [Haff 80a] [Hansal 76a]
[Hansen 80a] [Hansen 82a] [Henhapl 75a-78a]
[Izbicki 75a] [Jones 75a-80b,81a] [Lamersdorf 80ab]
[Lindenau 81a] [Løvengreen 80a-b] [Madsen 77a-81ab]
[Neuhold 80a-81a] [Nilsson 76a-81a] [Olnhoff 81a]
[Schmidt 80a] [Weissenböck 75a-b]

A

[Abrial 80*] J.R.Abrial: (1) *The Specification Language Z: Basic Libray,* 30 pgs.; (2) *The Specification Language Z: Syntax and "Semantics",* 29 pgs.; (3) *An Attempt to use Z for Defining the Semantics of an Elementary Programming Language,* 3 pgs.; (4) *A Low Level File Handler Design,* 18 pgs.; (5) *Specification of Some Aspects of a Simple Batch Operating System,* 37 pgs.; Oxford University, Programming Research Group, Internal reports, April-May 1980.

[ACM 66a] ACM: *Conference on:Programming Languages and Pragmatics* -- San Dimas, California, August 1965. Excerpts in: CACM 9, 6, 1966.

[Ada 79ab] *Preliminary Ada Reference Manual* - and - *Rationale for the Design of the Ada Programming Language* SIGPLAN 14, 6, June 1979 (Parts A & B).

[Ada 80a] *Reference Manual for the Ada Programming Language.* Proposed Stnd. Document. Cii Honeywell Bull, 1980.

[Ada 80b] *Requirements for Ada Programming Support Environments, "Stoneman".* U.S. Department of Defense, Research and Engineering, Feb. 1980.

[Ada 80c] V.Donzeau-Gorge, G.Kahn, B.Lang et al.: *Formal Definition of the Ada Programming Language* INRIA 1980.

[Aiello 77a] L.Aiello, G.Attardi & G.Prini: *Towards a more Declarative Programming Style,* in: [Neuhold 77a],

[Allen 72a] C.D. Allen, D.N. Chapman & C.B.Jones: *A Formal Definition of ALGOL 60,* IBM (Hursley, UK), TR12.105, August 1972.

[Andersen 82a] Fl.Andersen & A.V.Olsen: *A Formal Model of* Pascal Plus - *and its Realization,* TUD, M.Sc.Thesis,1982.

[ANSI 66a] ANSI X3.9-1966: *The* FORTRAN *Programming Language,* 1966.

[ANSI 74a] ANSI X3.23-1974: *The* COBOL *Programming Language,* 1974.

[ANSI 76a] ANSI X3.53-1976: *The* PL/I *Programming Language,* 1976.

[ANSI 81a] ANSI/X3/SPARC DBS-SG *Relational Data Base Task Grp* Final Report, SPARC-81-690, (eds.: M.L.Brodie & J. W.Schmidt), Sept. 1981.

[Arsac 79a] J.R.Arsac: *Syntactic Source to Source Transforms and Program Manipulation,* CACM 22, 1, pp.43-54, 1979.

[Ashcroft 71a] E.Ashcroft & Z. Manna: *The Translations of 'GOTO' Programs to 'While' Programs,* Stanford CS-188, 1971.

B

[Bandat 65a] K.Bandat: *Tentative Steps Towards a Formal Definition of the Semantics of PL/I*, Vienna TR25.065, July 1965.

[Bachman 69a] C.Bachman: *Data Structure Diagrams*, 'Data Base', Journal of ACM SIGBDP, 1, 2, Summer 1969.

[Backus 60a] J.W.Backus: *The Syntax and Semantics of the proposed International Algebraic Language of the Zürich ACM-GAMM Conference*, ICIP Proceedings, Paris 1959, Butterworth's, London, pp 125-132, 1960.

[Backus 63a] J.W.Backus,et.al.: *Revised Report on the Algorithmic Language ALGOL 60*, (ed.P. Naur) CACM 6, 1, pp. 1-17,1963.

[Backus 72a] J.W.Backus: *Reduction Languages and Variable-Free Programming*, San Jose RJ-1010, 1972.

[Backus 73a] J.W.Backus: *Programming Language Semantics & Closed Applicative Languages*, San Jose RJ-1245, and: POPL, Boston, pp 71-86, 1973.

[Backus 78a] J.W.Backus: *Can Programming be Liberated from the von Neumann Style? A Functional Style and its Algebra of Programs*, CACM 21, 8, pp. 613-641, Aug. 1978.

[Barron 63a] D.W.Barron, J.N.Buxton, D.F.Hartley, E.Nixon & C. Strachey: *The Main Features of CPL*, Comp.J. 6, pp. 134-143, 1963.

[Barron 68a] D.W.Barron: *Recursive Techniques in Programming*, MacDonald, 1968.

[Bauer 79a] F.L.Bauer & M.Broy (eds.): *Program Construction*, LNCS 69, 1979.

[Beech 73a] D.Beech: *On the Definitional Method of Standard PL/I*, pp 87-94. POPL, Boston, Oct. 1973.

[Bekić 70a] H.Bekić: *On the Formal Definition of Programming Languages*, in: ICS'70, GMD, Bonn, Nov. 1970.

[Bekić 71a] H.Bekić: *Towards a Mathematical Theory of Proccesses*, Vienna TR25.125, Dec.1971.

[Bekić 71b] H.Bekić & K.Walk: *Formalization of Storage Properties*, in: [Engeler 71a], 1971.

[Bekić 73a] H.Bekić: *An Introduction to ALGOL 68*, in: Ann.Rev. 7, 1973.

[Bekić 74a] H.Bekić, D.Bjørner, W.Henhapl,C.B.Jones & P.Lucas: *A Formal Definition of a PL/I Subset*, Vienna TR25. 139, Dec. 1974.

[Berztiss 75a] A.T.Berztiss: *Data Structures Theory and Practice*, Academic Press, 1975.

[Biller 74a] H.Biller & E.J.Neuhold: *Formal View on Schema-Subschema Correspondence*, in: IFIP'74, 1974.

[Biller 75a] H.Biller & G.Glatthaar: *On the Semantics of Data Definition Languages*, GI-5, Jahrestagung, LNCS 34, 1975.

[Biller 76a] H.Biller: *On the Semantics of Data Bases: The Semantics of Data Manipulation Languagesd*, 'Modelling in Data Base Management Systems' (ed. G.M. Nijssen), IFIP TC-2 Working Conf., N-H, 1976.

[Bjørner 77a] D.Bjørner: *Programming Languages: Linguistics & Semantics*, in: [Morlet 77a], pp.: 511-536, 1977.

[Bjørner 77b] D.Bjørner: *Programming Languages: Formal Development of Interpreters & Compilers*, in: [Morlet 77a] pp.1-21, 1977.

[Bjørner 78a] D.Bjørner: *The Systematic Development of a Compiling Algorithm*, in: *Le Point la Compilation* (eds. Amirchahy & Neel), IRIA Publ., Paris, pp. 45-88, 1979.

[Bjørner 78b] D.Bjørner & C.B. Jones (eds.): *The Vienna Development Method: The Meta-Language*, LNCS 61, 1978.

[Bjørner 78c] D.Bjørner: *Programming in the Meta-Language: A Tutorial*, in: [Bjørner 78b] pp. 24-217, 1978.

[Bjørner 78d] D.Bjørner: *Software Abstraction Principles: Tutorial Examples of an Operating System Command Language Specification - and a PL/I-like On-Condition Language Definition*, in [Bjørner 78b], pp.337-374, 1978.

[Bjørner 78e] D.Bjørner: *The Vienna Development Method: Software Abstraction and Program Synthesis*, 'Math. Studies of Information Processing', LNCS 75, 1979.

[Bjørner 80a] D.Bjørner (ed.): *Abstract Software Specifications* LNCS 86, 1980.

[Bjørner 80b] D.Bjørner *Experiments in Block-Structured GOTO-Modelling:Exits vs. Continuations*, in: [Bjørner 80a] pp. 216-247, 1980.

[Bjørner 80c] D.Bjørner *Formalization of Data Base Models*, in: [Bjørner80a], pp 144-215, 1980.

[Bjørner 80d] D.Bjørner: *Formal Description of Programming Concepts: a Software Engineering Viewpoint*, MFCS'80, LNCS 88, pp. 1-21, 1980.

[Bjørner 80e] D.Bjørner: *Application of Formal Models*, in: 'Data Bases', INFOTECH Proceedings, October 1980.

[Bjørner 80f] D.Bjørner & O.Oest (eds.): *Towards a Formal Description of Ada*, LNCS 98, 1980.

[Bjørner 80g] D.Bjørner & O.Oest: *The DDC Ada Compiler Development Project*, in: [Bjørner 80f], pp.1-19, 1980.

[Bjørner 81a] D.Bjørner: *The VDM Principles of Software Specification and Program Design*, in: 'Formalization of Programming Concepts', LNCS 107, pp. 44-74, 1981.

[Bjørner 82a] D.Bjørner (ed.): *Formal Description of Programming Concepts (II)* IFIP TC-2 Work.Conf., Garmisch-Partkirschen, N-H, 1982.

[Bjørner 82b] D.Bjørner & S.Prehn: *Software Engineering Aspects of VDM* Int'l.Seminar: 'Software Factory Experiences 2', Capri, Italy, May 1982 (planned proceedings: N-H 1982).

[Bjørner 82c] D.Bjørner: *Formal Semantics of Data Bases*, 8'th Int'l. Conf. on Very Large Data Base Conf., Mexico City, Sept.8-10, 1982.

[Bjørner 83*] D.Bjørner: *Software Architectures and Programming Systems Design*, approx. 1000 pages lecture notes, TUD, 1983.

[Bobrow 73a] D.G.Bobrow & B.Wegbreit: *A Model and Stack Implementation of Multiple Environments*, CACM 16, 10, 1973.

[Bochmann 76a] G.V.Bochmann: *Semantic Evaluation from Left to Right*, CACM 19, 2, pp 55-62, 1976.

[Boyer 79a] R.Boyer & J.Moore: *A Theorem Prover for Recursive Functions* SRI Technical Rept. CSL-91, June 1979.

[Branquart 71a] P.Branquart, J.Lewi, M.Sintzoff & P.L.Wodon: *The Composition of Semantics in ALGOL 68*, CACM 14, 11, pp 697-708, 1971.

[Branquart 82a] P.Branquart, G.Louis & P.Wodon: *An Analytical Description of CHILL, The CCITT High Level Language* LNCS 128, 1982.

[Bron 76a] C.Bron, M.M. Fokkinga & A.C.M. De Haas: *A Proposal for Dealing with Abnormal Termination of Programs*, T.H. Twente, Memo no. 150, Nov. 1976.

[BSI 82a] British Standards Institution: *Specification for Computer Programming Language Pascal* BS6192, 1982.

[Bundgaard 80a] J.Bundgaard & L.Schultz: *A Denotational (Static) Semantics Method for Defining Ada Context Conditions*, in: [Bjørner 80f], pp 21-212, 1980.

[Burge 72a] W.H. Burge: *Combinatory Programming and Combinatorial Analysis*, IBM Journal of Res. & Devt., 16, 5, pp 450-461, 1972

[Burge 75a] H.Burge: *Recursive Programming Techniques*, 'Systems Programming Series', Addison-Wesley, 1975.

[Burstall 68a] R.M.Burstall: *The Semantics of Assignement* in: MI 3, pp 3-20, 1968.

[Burstall 69a] R.M. Burstall & P.J. Landin: *Programs and their Proofs: An Algebraic Approach*, in: MI-4, pp.17-43, 1969.

[Burstall 69b] R.M.Burstall: *Proving Properties of Programs by Structural Induction*, Comp.J.12,1, pp 41-47, 1969.

[Burstall 74a] R.M.Burstall: *Program Proving as Hand Simulation with a Little Induction*, IFIP'74.

[Burstall 77a] R.M. Burstall & J.A. Goguen: *Putting Theories together to Make Specifications*, (IJCAI) Int'l.Joint Conf. on AI, Boston, Aug. 1977.

[Burstall 80a] R.Burstall & J.Goguen: *The Semantics of CLEAR: A Specification Language*, in: [Bjørner80b], pp. 292-332, 1980.

C

[Cadiou 73a] J.M. Cadiou & J.J. Levy: *Mechanizable Proofs about Parallel Processes*, SWAT 1973.

[Carnap 37a] R.Carnap: *The Logical Syntax of Language*, Harcourt Brace & Co., N.Y., 1937.

[Carnap 42a] R.Carnap: *Introduction to Semantics*, Harvard Univ. Press, Cambridge, Mass. 1942.

[CCITT 80a] *CHILL Language Definition*, CCITT Recommendation Z200, Period 1977-80, Study Grp XI, May 1980.

[Chomsky 59a] N.Chomsky: *On Certain Formal Properties of Grammars*, Information & Control,2,2, pp. 137-167,1959.

[Church 41a] A.Church: *The Calculi of Lambda-Conversion*, Annals of Math. Studies, 6, Princeton Univ. Press, N.J., 1941.

[Church 56a] A.Church: *Introduction to Mathematical Logic*, The Princeton Univ.Press, N.J., 1956.

[Cleaveland 77a] J.C. Cleaveland & R.C. Uzgalis: *Grammars for Programming Languages*, Elsevier Comp. Sci.Lib., Prgr. Lang. Ser. 4, N.Y., 1977.

[Clemmensen 81a] G.B. Clemmensen: *A Formal Model of Distributed Ada Tasking* M.Sc. Thesis, TUD, Sept. 1981.

[Clemmensen 82a] G.B.Clemmensen: *A Formal Model of Distributed Ada Tasking* Ada-TEC Conference, October 1982, SIGPLAN.

[Clint 72a] M.Clint & C.A.R.Hoare: *Program Proving: Jumps and Functions*, Acta 1, pp 214-224, 1972.

[CODASYL 71a] *Data Base Task Group (DBTG), CODASYL 1971 Report* ACM, 1971.

[Comer 79a] D.Comer: *The Ubiquitous B-Tree*, ACM Comp.Surv.,11, 2, pp 121-137, 1979.

[Cooper 68a] D.C.Cooper: *Some Transformations & Standard Forms of Graphs with Applications to Computer Programs*, in: MI-2, pp.21-32, 1968.

[Curry 58a] H.B.Curry & R.Feys: *Combinatory Logic I*, N-H,1958.

[Curry 72a] H.B.Curry, J.R.Hindley & J.Seldin: *Combinatory Logic II*, N-H, 1972.

D

[Dahl 66a] O.-J.Dahl & K.Nygaard: *SIMULA - An ALGOL-based Simulation Language*, CACM 9, 9, pp 671-678, 1966.

[Dahl 72a] O.-J.Dahl, E.W.Dijkstra & C.A.R.Hoare: *Structured Programming*, Academic Press, 1972.

[Dahl 72b] O.-J. Dahl & C.A.R. Hoare: *Hierarchical Program Structures*, in: [Dahl 72a], pp 197-220, 1972.

[Dahl 75a] O.-J.Dahl: *An Approach to Correctness Proofs of Semi-Coroutines*, in: MFCS'75, LNCS 28, pp 157-174, 1975.

[Dahl 78a] O.-J.Dahl: *Can Program Proving be Made Practical* ? Oslo University, Institute of Informatics, Report 33, ISBN 82-90230-26-5, May 1978.

[Darlington 78a] J.Darlington: *A Synthesis of Several Sorting Algorithms*, Acta 11, pp 1-30, 1978.

[DDC] *Danish Datamatics Centre* "Portable Ada Programming System" reports: (1) *Ada Static Semantics - Well-formedness Criteria* [02/1982-03-15],(2) *Ada Static Semantics - AS1 → AS2 Transformation* [02/1982-02-09],(3) *Dynamic Semantics - Description of Sequential Ada* [02/1982-03-18], (4) *Dynamic Semantics - Description of Ada Tasking* [02/1981-11-18],(5) *Dynamic Semantics - Input-Output Model* [02/1981-10-13]. H.Bruun,J.Bundgaard,G.B.Clemmensen,P.Folkjär, P.Gøbel, I.Ø.Hansen, J.Jørgensen, H.H.Løvengreen & J.Storbank Pedersen. 1981-1982.

[de Bakker 68a] J.W.de Bakker: *Axiomatics of Simple Assignment Statements*, MR94, Math.Centrum, Amsterdam, pp 1-37 1968.

[de Bakker 69a] J.de Bakker: *Semantics of Programming Languages*, in: 'Advances in Information Systems Sciences, 2, chap.3, Plenum Press, pp. 173-227, 1969.

[de Bakker 71a] J. de Bakker: *Recursive Procedures*, Math. Centre Tracts, 24, Amsterdam, 1971.

[de Morgan 76a] R.M.de Morgan,I.D.Hill & B.A.Wichman: *Modified Report on the Algorithmic Language ALGOL 60* Comp.J. 19, pp.364-379, Nov. 1976.

[Dennis 75a] J.B.Dennis: *Modularity*, in: 'Software Engineering' LNCS 30, pp. 128-182, 1975.

[de Roever 74a] W.P.de Roever: *Recursion and Parameter-Mechanisms, an Axiomatic Approach*, in: ICALP, LNCS 14, pp. 34-65, 1974.

[Dijkstra 60a] E.W.Dijkstra: *Recursive Programming*, Num.Mathematik, 2, 5, pp. 312-318, 1960.

[Dijkstra 62a] E.W.Dijkstra: *An ALGOL 60 Translator for the X1* Ann. Rev. 3, pp 329-356, 1962.

[Dijkstra 62b] E.W.Dijkstra: *An Attempt to Unify the Constituent Concepts of Serial Program Execution*, in: 'Symbolic Languages in Data Processing', Proceedings ICC Symp., Rome 1962, Gordon & Breach,New York,pp.237-251, 1962.

[Dijkstra 68a] E.W.Dijkstra: *The Structure of THE Multiprogramming System*, CACM 11, 5, pp. 341-346, 1968.

[Dijkstra 68b] E.W.Dijkstra: *Goto Statement Considered Harmful* Letter to the Editor, CACM 11, pp 147-148, 1968.

[Dijkstra 69a] E.W.Dijkstra: *Notes on Structured Programming*, in: [Dahl 72a], pp 1-82, 1972.

[Dijkstra 74a] E.W.Dijkstra: *A Simple Axiomatic Basis for Programming Language Constructs*, Indagationes Mathematicae, 36, pp 1-15, 1974.

[Dijkstra 75a] E.W.Dijkstra: *Guarded Commands, Non-Determinacy & Formal Program Derivation*, CACM 18, 8, pp 453-457, 1975.

[Dijkstra 76a] E.W.Dijkstra: *A Discipline of Programming*, Prentice-Hall, 1976.

[Dommergaard 80a] O.Dommergaard: *The Design of a Virtual Machine for Ada* in: [Bjørner 80a], pp. 435-605, 1980.

[Dommergaard 80b] O.Dommergaard, S.Bodilsen: *A Formal Definition of P-Code*, TUD, 1980.

[Donahue 82a] J.Donahue, R.Cartwright *The Semantics of Lazy (and Industrious) Evaluation* in: Proc., 1982 'LISP and Functional Programming', ACM, Pittsburgh, Aug.1982.

E

[ECMA 74a] European Comp.Mfg.Assoc.: *PL6I BASIS6I* ECMA/TC10 & ANSI X3J1, Basis/1-12, July 1974.

[ECMA 76a] European Comp.Mfg.Assoc.: *PL6I* ECMA/TC10 & ANSI X3.53-1976, July 1976.

[Elgot 64a] C.C.Elgot & A.Robinson: *Random-Access-Stored-Program Machines:an Approach to Programming Languages* JACM 11, 4, pp. 365-399, 1964.

[Engeler 71a] E.Engeler (ed.): *Symposium on Semantics of Algorithmic Languages*, S-V Lecture Notes in Mathematics Vol. 188, 1971.

[Ershov 77a] A.P.Ershov: *On the Partial Computation Principle*, IPL 6, 2, pp. 38-41, April 1977.

[Ershov 77b] A.P.Ershov: *On the Essence of Compilation*, in: [Neuhold 77a], pp 1.1-1.28, Aug.1977.

[Ershov 77c] A.P.Ershov & V.Grushetsky: *An Implementation-Oriented Method for Describing Algorithmic Languages*, IFIP'77, pp 117-122, Aug.1977.

[Ershov 77d] A.P.Ershov & V.E.Itkin: *Correctness of Mixed Computation in ALGOL-like Programs*, MFCS'77, LNCS 53, pp 59-77, Sept. 1977.

[Evans 68b] A.Evans: *PAL -- A Language Designed for Teaching Programming Linguistics*, Proc.ACM Nat'l Conf., pp. 395-403, 1968.

[Evans 72a] A.Evans Jr.: *The Lambda-Calculus and its Relation to Programming Languages*, unpubl. Notes, MIT, 1972

F

[Fielding 80a] E.Fielding: *The Specification of Abstract Mappings and their Implementation as B^+-Trees* PRG-18, 1980.

[Flensholt 81A] J.Flensholt: *Conceptual Graphs: A Denotational Semantics Approach*, M.Sc. Thesis,Dept.of Comp. Sci., Copenhagen Univ., Dec. 1981, 97 pages.

[Floyd67a] R.W. Floyd: *Assigning Meanings to Programs*, in: [Schwartz 67a], pp. 19-32, 1967.

[Fokkinga 77a] M.Fokkinga: *Axiomatization of Declarations and the Formal Treatment of an Escape Construct*, in: [Neuhold 77a], 1977.

[Folkjär 80a] P.Folkjär & D.Bjørner: *A Formal Model of Generalized CSP-like Language*, IFIP'80 (ed. S.H.Lavington), pp. 95-99, 1980.

[Forino 66a] Carraciolo di Forino: *Generalized Markov Algorithms and Automata*, in: 'Automata Theory', (ed. E. R.Caianello) Academic Press, pp.115-130 1966.

[Frege 92a] G.Frege: *Über Sinn und Bedeutung*, Zeitschrift für Philosphie und Philosphisches Kritik,vol. 100, pp. 25-50, 1892.

G

[Gaudel 80a] M.C.Gaudel: *Specification of Compilers as Abstract Data Type Representations*, pp.140-164, in: [Jones 80c], 1980.

[Ganzinger 80] H. Ganzinger: *Transforming Denotational Semantics into Practical Attribute Grammars*, in: [Jones 80c] pp 1-69, 1980.

[Gerhart 78a] S.L.Gerhart: *Program Verification in the 1980's: Problems, Perspectives, and Opportunities*, Univ. of Southern California, Report ISI/RR-78-71, Aug. 1978.

[Gøbel 82a] P. Gøbel, H. Ascanius, H.S. Nonfjall & H. Tümmler: *The Formal Development of an* Edison *Compiler and Run-Time System*, TUD, Term Projects, 1982.

[Goguen 73a] J.A. Goguen: *A Junction between Computer Science and Category Theory*, IBM RC4526, 1973.

[Goguen 75a] J.A.Goguen, J.W.Thatcher, E.G.Wagner & J.B.Wright: *Abstract Data Types as Initial Algebras and Correctness of Data Representations*. ACM Conference on Computer Graphics, pp 89-93, May 1975.

[Goguen 77a] J.A.Goguen, J.W.Thatcher, E.G.Wagner & J.B.Wright: *Initial Algebra Semantics and Continuous Algebras*, JACM, 24, 1, pp 68-95, Jan. 1977.

[Goguen 78a] J.A.Goguen, J.W.Thatcher, E.G.Wagner & J.B.Wright: *An Initial Algebra Approach to the Specification, Correctness & Implementation of Abstract Data Types*, in 'Current Trends in Programming Methodology', ed.R.Yeh, Prentice-Hall, 1978.

[Goguen 78b] J.Goguen: *Some Ideas in Algebraic Semantics*, Naropa Inst., Boulder, Co., UCLA Dept. Comp. Sci., Los Angeles, Calif., USA, 1978.

[Good 78a] D.Good, C.Hoch, L.Hunter & D.Hare: *Report on the Language GYPSY* ICSCA-CMP-10, Sept. 1978.

[Gordon 73a] M.J.Gordon: *Models of Pure LISP*, Ph.D. Thesis, Experimental Prgr. Res. Grp., Rept. no.31, Theory of Comp.Grp., Univ. of Edinburgh, 1973.

[Gordon 78a] M.Gordon: *Operational Reasoning & Denotational Semantics*, Proc.Int.Symp.: 'Proving & Improving Programs, Arc-et-Senans, pp. 83-98, IRIA, 1978.

[Gordon 79a] M.Gordon: *The Denotational Description of Programming Languages, an Introduction*, S-V 1979.

[Gordon 80a] M.Gordon, R.Milner, & C.Wadsworth: *Edinburgh LCF*, LNCS 78, 1980.

[Gries 71a] D.Gries: *Compiler Construction for Digital Computers*, J.Wiley & Sons, N.Y., 1971.

[Gries 76a] D.Gries: *Some Comments on Programming Language Design*, in: 'Programmiersprachen' S-V Informatik-Fachberichte, 1, pp 235-252, 1976.

[Guttag 75a] J.V.Guttag: *The Specification and Application to Programming of Abstract Data Types*, Ph.D. Thesis, Univ. of Toronto, 1975.

[Guttag 77a] J.Guttag: *Abstract Data Types and the Development of Data Structures*, CACM 20, 6, June 1977.

[Guttag 78a] J.V.Guttag, E.Horowitz & D.R.Musser: *Abstract Data Types and Software Validation*, CACM 21,12,pp.1048-1064, Dec. 1978.

H

[Habermann 72a] A.N. Habermann: *Synchronization of Communicating Processes*, CACM 15, 3, pp 171-176, 1972.

[Habermann 73a] A.N. Habermann: *Critical Comments on the Programming Language PASCAL*, Acta 3, pp 47-57, 1973.

[Haff 80a] C.C.I.T.T. Period 1980-1984, Working Party XI/3, Geneva 7.Dec.-17.Dec 1981: *CHILL Formal Definiton*, Vol.I: Parts I-II-II, Vol.II: Part IV,Dec.1981.

[Halaas 75a] A.Halaas: *Event Driven Control Statements*, BIT 15, pp 259-271, 1975.

[Hansal 74a] A.Hansal: *'Software Devices' for Processing Graphs Using* PL/I *Compile Time facilities*, IPL 2, pp 171-179, 1974.

[Hansal 76a] A.Hansal: *A Formal Definition of a Relational Data Base System*, IBM (Peterlee,UK) UKSC0080,June 1976.

[Hansen 70a] P.Brinch Hansen: *The Nucleus of a Multiprogramming System*, CACM 13, 4, pp 238-250, 1970.

[Hansen 71a] P.Brinch Hansen: *Structured Multiprogramming*, ACM Comp. Survey, 15, pp 574-578, 1972.

[Hansen 73a] P.Brinch Hansen: *Operating System Principles*,Prentice-Hall Series in Automatic Computation, 1973.

[Hansen 75a] P.Brinch Hansen: *The Programming Language Concurrent PASCAL*, SE-1, 2, pp 199-207, 1975.

[Hansen 77a] P.Brinch Hansen: *The Architecture of Concurrent Programs*, Prentice-Hall, 1977.

[Hansen 80a] B.S.Hansen & S.U.Palm: *A Formal Model of System R*, TUD, Aug. 1980 (IBM Confidential).

[Hansen 82a] B.S.Hansen & M.R.Hansen: *LUCAS: A Generic Application Programming System*, M.Sc. Thesis, TUD, 1982.

[Hantler 75a] S.L.Hantler & A.C.Chibib: *EFFIGY Reference Manual* IBM RC5225, Jan.1975.

[Hantler 76a] S.L.Hantler & J.C.King: *An Introduction to Proving the Correctness of Programs*, IBM RC5893, 1976.

[Hardgrave 72a] W.T.Hardgrave: *A Retrieval Language for Tree-Structured Data Base Systems* in:'Informations Systems' COINS IV,ed.J.Tou, Plenum Press, pp.137-160, 1972.

[Henderson 75a] D.A.Henderson: *The Binding Model: A Semantic Base for Modular Programming Systems*, MIT TR-145, 1975.

[Henderson 80a] P.Henderson: *Functional Programming: Application & Implementation*, Prentice-Hall Int'l, 1980.

[Henhapl 70a] W.Henhapl & C.B.Jones: *The Block Concept and Some possible Implementations, with Proofs of Equivalence*, Vienna TR25.104, Apr. 1970.

[Henhapl 70b] W. Henhapl & C.B. Jones: *On the Interpretation of GOTO Statements in the VDL*,Vienna LN25.3.065,1970.

[Henhapl 71a] W. Henhapl & C.B. Jones: *A Run-Time Mechanism for Referencing Variables*, IPL 1, 1, pp 14-16, 1971.

[Henhapl 75a] W.Henhapl, H. Izbicki, C.B. Jones & F.Weissenböck: *Some Experiments with using Formal Definitions in Compiler Development*, Vienna LN25.3.107, Dec.1975.

[Henhapl 78a] W.Henhapl & C.B.Jones: *A Formal Definition of ALGOL 60 as described in the 1975 modified Report*, in: [Bjørner 78b], pp: 305-336.

[Hill 72a] I.D.Hill: *Wouldn't it be Nice if We Could Write Computer Programs in Ordinary English-or would it?* Computer Bulletin, 16, 6, pp 306-312, June 1972.

[Hitchcock 72a] P.Hitchcock & D.M.R.Park: *Induction Rules and Termination Proofs* in:ICALP, pp 225-251,M.Nivat (ed.) N-H, 1972.

[Hitchcock 77a] P.Hitchcock & F.Pace: *An Approach to Conceptual Data Analysis*, IBM (Peterlee, UK) Report UKSC0090, 1977.

[Hoare 69a] C.A.R.Hoare: *The Axiomatic Basis of Computer Programming*, CACM 12, 10, pp. 567-583, Oct. 1969.

[Hoare 71a] C.A.R.Hoare: *Procedures and Parameters: An Axiomatic Approach*, in [Engeler 71a],pp.102-116,1971.

[Hoare 71b] C.A.R.Hoare: *Proof of a Program: FIND*, CACM 14,pp. 39-45, 1971.

[Hoare 72a] C.A.R.Hoare: *Notes on Data Structuring*, in: [Dahl 72a], pp 83-174, 1972.

[Hoare 72b] C.A.R.Hoare: *Proof of Correctness of Data Representations*, Acta 1, pp 271-281, 1972.

[Hoare 72b] C.A.R.Hoare: *A Note of the 'FOR' Statement*, BIT, 12, pp 334-341, 1972.

[Hoare 72d] C.A.R.Hoare: *Proof of a Program: 'The Sieve of Eratosthenes'*, Comp.J. 15, 4, pp 321-325, Nov.1972.

[Hoare 72e] C.A.R.Hoare: *Towards a Theory of Parallel Programming*, in: 'Operating Systems Techniques' (eds.C.A. R. Hoare & R.H.Perrot) Academic Press, 1972.

[Hoare 73a] C.A.R.Hoare: *Hints on Programming Language Design*, POPL, Boston, Oct. 1973.

[Hoare 73b] C.A.R.Hoare: *Recursive Data Structures*, IJCIS 4, 2, pp. 105-132, 1975.

[Hoare 73c] C.A.R. Hoare: *A Structured Paging System*, Comp. J. 16, 3, pp 209-215, Aug. 1973.

[Hoare 73d] C.A.R.Hoare & N.Wirth: *An Axiomatic Definition of the Programming Language PASCAL*, Acta 2, pp. 335-355, 1973.

[Hoare 74a] C.A.R.Hoare & P.Lauer: *Consistent and Complementary Formal Theories of the Semantics of Programming Languages*, Acta 3, pp. 135-153, 1974.

[Hoare 76a] C.A.R.Hoare: *Parallel Programming:An Axiomatic Approach*, in: Language Hierarchies & Interfaces,LNCS 46, pp 11-39, 1976.

[Hoare 78a] C.A.R. Hoare: *Communicating Sequential Processes* CACM 21, 8, Aug. 1978.

I

[IBMa] IBM: *OS* PL/I *Checkout and Optimizing Compilers: Language Reference Manual*, IBM GC330009.

[Ichbiah 74a] J.D.Ichbiah & S.P.Morse: *General Concepts of the SIMULA 67 Programming Language*, Ann.Rev.7, pp. 65-93,1974.

[Irons 61a] E.T.Irons: *A Syntax Directed Compiler for ALGOL 60* CACM 4, pp 51-55, 1961.

[Irons 63a] E.T.Irons: *The Structure and use of the Syntax Directed Compiler*, in: Ann.Rev. 3, pp 207-227, 1963.

[Izbicki 75a] H.Izbicki: *On a Consistency Proof of a Chapter of the Formal Definition of a PL/I Subset*, Vienna TR 25.142, Feb. 1975.

J

[Jensen 76] K. Jensen & N. Wirth: *Pascal User Manual & Report*, LNCS 18, 1976.

[Jones 71a] C.B.Jones & P.Lucas: *Proving Correctness of Implementation Techniques*, in [Engeler 71a], pp 178-211 1971.

[Jones 72a] C.B. Jones: *Formal Development of Correct Algorithms: An Example Based on Earley's Recognizer*, SIGPLAN 7, 1, Jan.1972.

[Jones 73a] C.B. Jones: *Formal Development of Programs*, IBM UK (Hursley) TR 12.117, June 1973.

[Jones 75a] C.B.Jones: *Formal Definition in Program Development*, in: 'Programming Methodology', LNCS 23, pp. 387-443, 1975.

[Jones 75b] C.B.Jones: *Yet Another Proof of the Block Concept*, Vienna LN25.3.075, presented at IFIP WG2.2 meeting Boston 1970.

[Jones 76a] C.B.Jones: *Formal Definition in Compiler Development*, Vienna TR25.145, Feb. 1976.

[Jones 76b] C.B.Jones: *Program Development Using Data Abstraction*, IFIP WG2.3 meeting, Grenoble, Dec. 1976.

[Jones 77a] C.B.Jones: *Program Specification and Formal Development*, in: [Morlet 77a], pp 537-554, 1977.

[Jones 77b] C.B.Jones: *Structured Design and Coding: Theory versus Practice*, Informatie, Jaargang 19,6,pp.311-319 June 1977.

[Jones 78a] C.B.Jones: *The Meta-Language: A Reference Manual*, in: [Bjørner 78b], pp 218-277, 1978.

[Jones 78b] C.B.Jones: *Denotational Semantics of GOTO: an Exit Formulation and its Relation to Continuations*, in: [Bjørner 78b], pp 278-304, 1978.

[Jones 78c] C.B.Jones: *The Vienna Development Method: Examples of Compiler Development*, in: 'Le Point sur la Compilation' (ed.Amirchachy & Neel), IRIA Publ.,1979.

[Jones 79a] C.B.Jones: *Constructing a Theory of a Data Structure as an aid to Program Development*, Acta 11, pp. 119-137, 1979.

[Jones 80a] C.B.Jones: *Software Development: A Rigorous Approach*, Prentice-Hall International, London 1980.

[Jones 80b] C.B.Jones: *Models of Programming Language Concepts* in: [Bjørner 80b], 1980.

[Jones 80c] N.Jones (ed.): *Semantics Directed Compiler Generation*, LNCS 94, Aarhus Univ. Workshop, Jan.1980.

[Jones 81a] C.B.Jones: *Development Methods for Computer Program Including a Notion of Interference* D.Phil. Thesis,PRG 25, June 1981.

[Jones 81b] C.B.Jones: *Towards more Formal Specifications* in: 'Software Engineering - Entwurf und Spezifikation' eds.:C.Floyd,H.Kopetz,B.G.Teubner,TH Berlin, 1981.

[Jones 81c] C.B.Jones: *Formal Methods in Software Development* in: INFOTECH State of the Art Review, pp. 107-113, 1981.

K

[Kennedy 74a] K. Kennedy & S.K. Warren: *Automatic Generation of Efficient Evaluators for Attribute Grammars*, ACM Nat'l.Conf., pp 32-49, 1974.

[King 75a] J.C.King: *A New Approach to Program Testing*, 'Programming Methodology', LNCS 23, pp. 278-290, 1975.

[Knuth 68a] D.E.Knuth: *Semantics of Context-Free Languages*, Math. Sys. Theory, 2, pp 127-145, and 5, pp. 95-96 (errata), 1968.

[Knuth 71a] D.E.Knuth: *Examples of Formal Semantics*, in: [Engeler 77a], pp 178-211, 1971.

[Knuth 74a] D.E.Knuth: *Structured Programming with GOTO Statements*, ACM Comp. Surv. 6, 4, pp 261-302, 1974.

L

[Lamersdorf 80ab] W.Lamersdorf & J.W.Schmidt: *Semantic Definition of Pascal R* Reports 73-74, Inst.of Informatics, Univ. of Hamburg, July 1980.

[Landin 64a] P.J. Landin: *The Mechanical Evaluation of Expressions*, Comp.J. 6, 4, pp 308-320, 1964.

[Landin 65a] P.J. Landin: *A Correspondence Between ALGOL 60 and Church's Lambda-Notation*, (in 2 parts) CACM 8,2-3, pp 89-101 & 158-165, Feb.-March 1965.

[Landin 65b] P.J.Landin: *Getting Rid of Labels*,Univac Sys.Prgr. Res. Grp., N.Y., 1965.

[Landin 65c] P.J.Landin: *A Generalization of Jumps and Labels*. Univac Sys. Prgr. Res. Grp., N.Y., 1965.

[Landin 65d] P.J.Landin: *An Analysis of Assignment in Programming Languages*, Univac Sys.Prgr.Res.Grp., N.Y., 1965.

[Landin 66a] P.J.Landin: *The Next 700 Programming Languages*, CACM 9, 3, pp 157-166, 1966.

[Landin 66b] P.J.Landin: *A Lambda Calculus Approach*, in: 'Advances in Programming and Non-Numeric Computations', (ed.L.Fox) Pergamon Press, pp 97-141, 1966.

[Landin 66c] P.J.Landin: *A Formal Description of ALGOL 60*, in: [Steel 66a], pp 266-294, 1966.

[Landin 72a] P.Landin, R.M.Burstall: *Programs and their Proofs: An Algebraic Approach*, in: MI-4, 1972.

[Lauer 68a] P.E.Lauer: *Formal Definition of ALGOL 60*, Vienna TR25.088, Dec.1968.

[Lauer 73a] P.E.Lauer: *Consistent & Complementary Formal Theories of the Semantics of Programming Languages*, Vienna TR25.121, 1971 & TR-44 Univ.of Newcastle upon Tyne, Comp. Lab., 1973.

[Lee 69a] J.A.N.Lee & W.Delmore: *The Vienna Definition Language, A Generalization of Instruction Definitions* SIGPLAN Symp. on Programming Language Definitions, San Francisco, Aug. 1969.

[Lee 72a] J.A.N.Lee: *Computer Semantics*, Van Nostrand Reinhold Co., 1972.

[Lee 72b] J.A.N.Lee: *The Formal Definition of Basic Language* Comp.J. 15, pp 32-41, 1972.

[Lee 81a] S.Lee & S.L.Gerhart (eds.): *AFFIRM Users Guide*, USC/ISI, Feb. 1981.

[Ledgard 71a] H.F.Ledgard: *Ten Mini-Languages:A Study of Topical Issues in Programming Languages*, ACM Comp.Survey,3 3, pp 115-146, 1971.

[Ligler 75a] G.Ligler: *A Mathematical Approach to Language Design*, in: POPL, pp 41-53, 1975.

[Ligler 75a] G.Ligler: *Surface Properties of Programming Language Constructs*, in: Proving & Improving Programs IRIA Publ., pp 299-323, 1975.

[Lindenau 81a] J.Lindenau: *Eine Deskriptive Anfragesprache für das Netzwerk-Datenmodell mit formaler Definition der Semantik in Meta-IV*, M.Sc. Thesis (in German), Kiel Univ., Inst. für Informatik, March 1981, 175 pages.

[Lipschutz 66a] S.Lipschutz: *Finite Mathematics* McGraw-Hill, 1966.

[Liskov 74a] B.H.Liskov & S.N.Zilles: *Programming with Abstract Data Types*, in 'Very HighLevel Languages', SIGPLAN 9, 4, pp 59-59, 1974.

[Liskov 75a] B.H.Liskov & S.N. Zilles: *Specification Techniques for Data Abstractions*, SE-1, 1, pp 7-19, 1975.

[London 69a] R.L.London: *Bibliography on Proving the Correctness of Computer Programs*, in:MI-5,pp.569-580,1969

[London 78a] R.L.London et al.: *Proof Rules for the Programming Language Euclid* Acta, 10, pp.1-26, 1978.

[Lorho 75a] B.Lorho & C.Pair: *Algorithms for Checking Consistency of Attribute Grammars*, in: Proving & Improving Programs, IRIA Publ., 1975.

[Lucas 68a] P.Lucas:*Two Constructive Realizations of the Block Concept and Their Equivalence*,Vienna TR25.085,June 1968.

[Lucas 69a] P.Lucas & K.Walk:*On the Formal Description of* PL/I Ann. Rev. 6, 1971.

[Lucas 70a] P.Lucas: *On the Semantics of Programming Languages and Software Devices*, in [Rustin 72a], 1972.

[Lucas 71a] P.Lucas: *Formal Definition of Programming Languages and Systems*, IFIP'71, 1971.

[Lucas 73a] P.Lucas: *On Program Correctness and the Stepwise Development of Implementations*, in: Proceedings 'Convegno di Informatica Teorica', Univ. of Pisa, Italy, pp.219-251, March 1973.

[Lucas 78a] P.Lucas: *On the Formalization of Programming Languages: Early History and Main Approaches.*, in: [Bjørner 78a].

[Lucas 80a] P.Lucas: *On the Structure of Application Programs.* in: [Bjørner 80b], 1980.

[Lucas 81a] P.Lucas: *Formal Semantics of Programming Languages VDL* IBM Journal of Devt. & Res., 25,5, pp 549-561, 1981.

[Løvengreen 80a] H.H.Løvengreen: *Parallelism in Ada*, in: [Bjørner 80f], pp. 309-432, 1980.

[Løvengreen 80b] H.H.Løvengreen & D.Bjørner: *On a Formal Model of the Tasking Concepts in Ada*, Proc. ACM SIGPLAN Ada Symp., Boston 1980.

M

[Madsen 77a] J.Madsen: *An Experiment in Formal Definition of Operating System Facilities*, IPL 6, 6, pp 187-189, Dec. 1977.

[Madsen 80a] J.Madsen: *Modular Operating System Design*, Ph.D. Thesis, TUD, ID805, 194 pages, Aug.1980.

[Madsen 81ab] J. Madsen: *A Computer System Supporting Data Abstraction*, Pts.1-2, SIGOPS 15, 1-2, pp. 45-72, 38-78, 1981.

[Manna 72a] Z.Manna & J.Vuillemin: *Fixed-Point Approach to the Theory of Computation*, in: SIGPLAN, Jan.1972.

[Marcotty 76a] M.Marcotty, H.F.Ledgard & G.V.Bochmann: *A Sampler of Formal Definitions*, ACM Comp. Surv., 8, 2, pp. 191-276, 1976.

[McCarthy 60a] J.McCarthy: *Recursive Functions of Symbolic Expressions and their Computation by Machines, Pt:I,* CACM 3, 4, pp 184-195, 1960.

[McCarthy 62a] J.McCarthy: *Towards a Mathematical Science of Computation*, IFIP'62 (ed. C.M.Popplewell), pp. 21-28, 1963.

[McCarthy 62b] J.McCarthy et al.: *LISP 1.5, Programmer's Manual*, MIT Press, Cambridge, Mass., 1962.

[McCarthy 63a] J.McCarthy: *A Basis for a Mathematical Theory of Computation*, in: Computer Programming and Formal Systems, N-H, 1963.

[McCarthy 66a] J.McCarthy: *A Formal Description of a Subset of ALGOL*, in: [Steel 66a].

[McCarthy 67a] J.McCarthy & J.Painter: *Correctness of a Compiler for Arithmetic Expressions*, in: [Schwartz 67a],pp. 33-41, 1967.

[Milne 74a] R.Milne: *The Formal Semantics of Computer Languages and their Implementation*, Ph.D.Thesis, PRG 13, 1974.

[Milne 76a] R.Milne & C. Strachey: *A Theory of Programming Language Semantics*, Chapman and Hall, London, Halsted Press/John Wiley, New York, 1976.

[Milner 71a] R.Milner: *Program Simulation: An Extended Formal Notion*, Memos 14 & 17, Univ.of Swansea, Dept.Comp. Sci., 1971.

[Milner 71b] R.Milner: *An Algebraic Definition of Simulation between Programs*, Stanford CS-205, 1971.

[Milner 73a] R.Milner: *An Approach to the Semantics of Parallel Programs*, in: Proceedings 'Convegno di Informatica Teorica', Univ. of Pisa, Italy, March 1973.

[Milner 73b] R.Milner: *Processes: A Mathematical Model for Computing Agents*, Proc. Colloq. in Math. Logic, Univ. Bristol, England, N-H, 1973.

[Milner 80a] R.Milner: *Calculus of Communication Systems* LNCS 94, 1980.

[Morlet 77a] E.Morlet & D.Ribbens: *International Computing Symposium 77*, European ACM, N-H, 1977.

[Morris 38a] C.Morris: *Foundations of the Theory of Signs*, in: 'International Encyclopedia of Unified Science',1, 2, Univ. of Chicago Press, 1938.

[Morris 55a] C.Morris: *Signs, Language and Behaviour*, G.Brazillier, New York, 1955.

[Morris 70a] F.L.Morris: *The next 700 Programming Language Descriptions*, unpubl. ms., Univ. of Essex, Comp.Ctr. 1970.

[Morris 73a] F.L. Morris: *Advice on Structuring Compilers and Proving them Correct*, in:POPL, Boston, pp.144-152, Oct. 1973.

[Morris 68a] J.H.Morris: *Lambda-Calculus Models of Programming Languages*, Ph.D.Thesis, MIT TR-57, 1968.

[Moser 70a] E.Moser: *On a Formal Description of an Indexed Sequential Dataset*, Vienna LR25.1.010, March 1970.

[Moses 70a] J.Moses: *The Function of FUNCTION in LISP*, SIGPLAN pp 13-27, 1970; also: ... - *or why the FUNARG Problem should be called the Environment Problem*, Memo-248, AI-199, MIT, 1970.

[Mosses 74a] P.D.Mosses: *The Mathematical Semantics of ALGOL 60* PRG-12, January 1974.

[Mosses 75a] P.D. Mosses: *Mathematical Semantics and Compiler Generation*, Ph.D. Thesis, PRG, 1975.

[Mosses 75b] P.D. Mosses: *The Semantics of Semantic Equations*, MFCS'75, LNCS 28, pp. 409-422, 1975.

[Mosses 76a] P.D.Mosses: *Compiler Generation using Denotational Semantics*, in: MFCS'76, LNCS 45, pp.436-441, 1976.

[Mosses 77a] P.D.Mosses: *Making Denoational Semantics Less Concrete*, Pres.Bad Honnef, Germany, March 1977.

[Mosses 81a] P.D.Mosses: *Abstract Semantic Algebras* in:[Bjørner 82a], 1982.

[Muchnick 80a] S.Muchnick & N.D.Jones (eds.): *Program Flow Analysis: Theory & Application*, Prentice-Hall, New Jersey, 1980.

N

[Naur 63a] P.Naur (ed.): *Revised Report on the Algorithmic Language ALGOL 60*, CACM 6, 1, pp. 1, 1963.

[Naur 63b] P.Naur: *The Design of the GIER Algol Compiler*. BIT 3, 2, 1963.

[Naur 66a] P.Naur:*Program Translation Viewed as a General Data Processing Problem*, CACM 9, 3, pp 176-179, 1966

[Naur 66b] P.Naur: *Proof of Algorithms by General Snapshots*, BIT 6, pp 310-316, 1966.

[Naur 69a] P.Naur: *Programming by Action Clusters*, BIT 9, pp. 250-258, 1969.

[Naur 72a] P.Naur: *An Experiment on Program Development*, BIT 12, pp 347-365, 1972.

[Nelson 79a] P.A. Nelson: *A Comparison of Pascal Intermediate Languages*. Proceedings of the SIGPLAN Symposium on Compiler Construction, Denver, Colorado, August 6-10, 1979.

[Neel 74a] D.Neel & M.Amirchahy: *Semantic Attributes and Improvement of Generated Code*, ACM Nat. Conf., pp 1-10, 1974.

[Neuhold 71a] E. Neuhold: *The Formal Description of Programming Languages*, IBM Systems Journal, 10, 2, pp. 86-112, 1971.

[Neuhold 77a] E.Neuhold (ed.): *Formal Description of Programming Concepts (I)*, Proc.IFIP TC-2 Work.Conf.,St.Andrews Canada, Aug. 1977, N-H, 1978.

[Neuhold 80a] E. Neuhold & Ths. Olnhoff: *The Vienna Development Method (VDM) and its Use for the Specification of a Relational Data Base System*, IFIP'80 (ed.S.Lavington), 1980.

[Neuhold 81a] E.Neuhold & Th.Olnhoff: *Building Data Base Management Systems Through Formal Specifications*, LNCS 107, pp 169-209, 1981.

[Newey 77a] M.C.Newey: *Proving Properties of assembly Language Programs*, IFIP'77 (ed. B. Gilchrist), 1977.

[Nilsson 76a] J.F.Nilsson: *Relational Data Base Systems: Formalization and Realization*, Ph.D. Thesis, TUD, ID641, Sept.1976.

[Nilsson 81a] J.F.Nilsson: *Specification and Development of a PROLOG System* TUD, ID960, July 1981.

[Nori 76a] K.V. Nori et al.: *The Pascal <P> Compiler Implementation Notes*. Eidgenössische Technische Hochschule, Zurich 1976.

O

[Ollongreen 74a] A.Ollongreen: *Definition of Programming Languages by Interpreting Automata*, Academic Press, 1974.

[Olnhoff 81a] Ths. Olnhoff: *Funktionale Semantikbeschreibung von Anfrageoperationen in einem drei-schictigen relationaler Datenbanksystem*, Ph.D. Thesis, Stuttgart/ Hamburg Univ.,Inst.f.Informatik, May 1981,210 pgs.

[Owlett 77a] J.Owlett: *Deferring and Defining in Databases* in: 'Architecture & Models in DBMS's', Proc.IFIP Work. Conf. on Modelling in DBMS, N-H, 1977.

[Owlett 79a] J.Owlett: *A Theory of Database Schemata:Studies in Conceptual and Relational Schemata* D.Phil. Thesis, PRG, Oxford Univ., 1979

P

[Park 70a] D.M.R.Park: *Fixpoint Induction and Proofs of Program Properties*, in: MI-5, pp 59-78, 1970.

[Park 80a] D.M.R.Park: *On the Semantics of Fair Parallelism*, in: [Bjørner 80a], pp 504-526, 1980.

[Parnas 72a] D.L.Parnas: *A Technique for Software Module Specification with Examples*, CACM 14, 5, May 1972.

[Plotkin 76a] G.D.Plotkin: *A Power Domain Construction*, SIAM J. Comp. 5, pp 452-487, 1976.

[Plotkin 81a] G.D.Plotkin: *A Structured Approach to Operational Semantics* Univ. of Edinburgh, Comp.Sci.Dept.,1981.

[Polak 81a] W.Polak: *Compiler Specification and Verification*, rev. Ph.D. Thesis, Stanford, LNCS 124, 1981.

Q

[Quine 60a] W.V.Quine: *Word and Object*, Technology Press,J.Wiley, MIT, Cambridge, Mass., 1960.

R

[Raskovsky 80a] M.Raskovsky, P.Collier: *From Standard to Implementation Denotational Semantics*, pp. 94-139, in: [Jones 80c]

[Reynolds 70a] J.C.Reynolds: *GEDANKEN -- A Simple Type-less Language based on the Principle of Completeness and the Reference Concept*, CACM 13,5, pp 308-319,1970.

[Reynolds 72a] J.C.Reynolds: *Definitional Interpreters for Higher -Order Programming Languages*, Proc.25th ACM Nat'l. Conf., pp. 717-740, 1972.

[Reynolds 74b] J.C. Reynolds: *Towards a Theory of Type Structure* in: 'Programming' Symposium, LNCS 19, pp. 408-425, 1974.

[Reynolds 78a] J.C. Reynolds: *Syntactic Control of Interference,* POPL, pp 39-46, New York, 1978.

[Reynolds 78b] J.C.Reynolds: *User-defined Types and Procedural Data Structures as Complementary Approaches to Data Abstractions,* in 'Programming Methodology',(ed. D.Gries), S-V, pp 309-317, 1978.

[Richards 69a] M.Richards: *BCPL Reference Manual,* Techn. Memo.No. 69/1, The Univ.Math.Lab., Cambridge, UK, 1969.

[Richards 71a] M.Richards: *The Portability of the BCPL Compiler.* Software Practice and Experience, Vol. 1, 135-146, 1971.

[Richards 72a] M.Richards: *INTCODE - an Interpretive Machine Code for BCPL.* The Computer Laboratory, Corn Exchange Street, Cambridge, December 1972.

[Robinet 74a] B.Robinet (ed.): *Programming Symposium* Paris, April 9-11, 1974, LNCS 19, 1974.

[Rosen 73a] B.K.Rosen: *Tree Manipulating Systems & Church Rosser Theorems,* JACM 20, 1, pp 160-187, 1973.

[Russell 05a] B.Russell: *On Denoting,* Mind 14, pp 479-493, 1905.

[Russell 10a] B.Russell: *The Principles of Mathematics,* Allen & Unwin, London, 1910.

[Rustin 72a] R.Rustin (ed): *Formal Semantics of Programming Languages,* Prentice-Hall, 1972.

S

[Sallé 80a] P.Sallé: *Echappements et Continuations en Semantique Dénotationelle* in: LNCS 83, pp.298-310,1980.

[Sanderson 73a] J.G.Sanderson: *The Lambda Calculus, Lattice Theory and Reflexive Domains,* Math. Inst.Lect. Notes, Oxford Univ., 1973.

[Schmidt 81a] U.Schmidt & U.Völler: *Die Formale Entwicklung der Maschin-Unabhängigen Zwischensprache CAT,*in: GI-11 Jahrestagung, Informatik Fachberichte, S-V, pp 57-64, 1981.

[Schwartz 67a] J.T.Schwartz (ed.): *Mathematical Aspects of Computer Science* Proc.of Symp.in Appl.Math.,Am.Math. Soc., RI, 1967.

[Schwartz 73a] J.T.Schwartz: *The SETL Language & Examples of its Use,* Courant Institute, New York University, 1973.

[Schwartz 75a] J.Schwartz: *A Comment on Correctness Proofs*, SETL Newsletter 159, Courant Inst. of Math., N.Y.Univ., pp. 6-15, 1975.

[Scott 70a] D.S.Scott: *Outline of a Mathematical Theory of Computation*, Proc. 4th. Ann.Princeton Conf.on Inf. Sci.& Sys., pp 169, 1970.

[Scott 71a] D.S. Scott & C. Strachey: *Towards a Mathematical Semantics for Computer Languages*, in: MRI-XXI, 1971.

[Scott 72a] D.Scott: *Mathematical Concepts in Programming Language Semantics*, Proc.AFIPS, Spring Joint Computer Conference, 40, pp 225-234, 1972.

[Scott 73a] D.Scott: *Lattice-Theoretic Models for Various Type Free Calculi*, Proc. 4th Int'l. Congr. for 'Logic, Methodology and the Philosophy of Sci.', Bucharest (ed.P.Suppes) N-H, pp. 157-187, 1973.

[Scott 75a] D.Scott: *λ-Calculus & Comp.Sci.Theory'*,(ed:C.Böhm) Symp.Proc., LNCS 37, 1975.

[Scott 76a] D.Scott: *Data Types as Lattices*, SIAM Journal on Computer Science, 5, 3, pp 522-587, 1976.

[Scott 77a] D.Scott: *Logic and Programming Languages*, CACM 20, 9, 634-41, 1977.

[Scott 81a] D.Scott: *Lectures on a Mathematical Theory of Computation* PRG-19, 1981 - & in: 'Theoretical Foundations of Programming Methodology', (eds. M.Broy & G.Schmidt) D.Reidel, Doordrecht Publ., 1982.

[Sintzoff 80a] M.Sintzoff: *Suggestions for Composing & Specifying Program Design Decisions*, in '4th Int'l Colloq. on "Programming", LNCS 83, April 1980, Paris.

[Smyth 76a] M.B.Smyth: *Powerdomains*, Theory of Computation Report 12, Department of Computer Science, University of Warwick, 1976.

[Steel 66a] T.B.Steel (ed.): *Formal Language Description Languages*, IFIP TC-2 Work.Conf., Baden, N-H, 1966.

[Storbank 80a] J.Storbank Pedersen: *A Formal Semantics Definition of Sequential Ada*, in: [Bjørner 80f], pp 213-308.

[Stoy 72ab] J.E.Stoy & C.Strachey: *OS6 - An Experimental Operating System for a Small Computer*, Part 1: *General Principles and Structure*, and Part 2: *Input-Output and Filing System* Comp. J., 15, 2-3, pp. 117-124, 194-203, 1972.

[Stoy 75a] J.E.Stoy: *The Congruence of Two Programming Language Definitions* Journal of Theoretical Computer Science, 1981.

[Stoy 77a] J.E.Stoy: *Denotational Semantics: The Scott-Strachey Approach to Programming Language Theory,* MIT Press, 1977.

[Stoy 80a] J.E.Stoy:*Foundations of Mathematical Semantics*,in: [Bjørner 80b] pp. 43-99.

[Stoy 81a] J.E.Stoy: *Data Types for State of the Art Program Development* INFOTECH 'Programming, New Directions' London 1981.

[Strachey 66a] C.Strachey: *Towards a Formal Semantics,* in: [Steel 66a], pp 198-220.

[Strachey 67a] C.Strachey:*Fundamental Concepts in Programming* Unpubl. lect. notes, NATO Summer School, Copenhagen, 1967.

[Strachey 70a] C.Strachey & D.Scott: *Mathematical Semantics for Two Simple Languages* Princeton Univ., Aug. 1970.

[Strachey 73a] C.Strachey: *The Varieties of Programming Languages* PRG-10, 1973.

[Strachey 74a] C. Strachey & C.Wadsworth: *Continuations: A Mathematical Semantics which can deal with Full Jumps,* PRG-11, 1974.

[Sufrin 81a] B.Sufrin: *Formal Systems Specifications: Notation and Examples,* in: Tools & Notions for Program Construction, (ed. D.Neel), Cambridge Univ.Press,1982

[SVG 79a] Stanford Verification Group: *Stanford Pascal Verifier User Manual* Stanford CS-79-731, 1979.

T

[Tarski 55a] A.Tarski: *A Lattice-Theoretical Fixpoint Theorem and its Application;* Pacific J.of Math. 5, pg. 285 1955.

[Tennent 73a] R.D.Tennent: *Mathematical Semantics and the Design of Programming Languages*,Ph.D.Thesis,Toronto Univ. 1973.

[Tennent 73b] R.D. Tennent: *The Mathematical Semantics of SNOBOL 4,* in: POPL, Boston, pp 95-107, Oct. 1973.

[Tennent 76a] R.D.Tennent: *The Denotational Semantics of Programming Languages,* CACM 19, 8, Aug. 1976.

[Tennent 77a] R.D.Tennent: *A Note on Files in Pascal,* BIT,17, 3, 362-366, 1977.

[Tennent 77b] R.D.Tennent: *Language Design Methods based on Semantic Principles,* Acta 8, pp 97-112, 1977.

[Tennent 77c] R.D.Tennent: *On a new Approach to Representation--independent Data Classes*, Acta 8, pp 315-324, 1977.

[Tennent 78a] R.D.Tennent: *Another Look at Type Compatibility in Pascal*, Software: Practice & Experience, 8, 1, pp. 85-97, 1978.

[Tennent 80a] R.D.Tennent: *Principles of Progamming Languages*, Prentice-Hall, Int'l, 1981.

[Tennent 82a] R.D.Tennent: *The Semantics of Interference* ICALP, LNCS, July 1982.

[Tsichritzis 82a] D.C.Tsichritzis & F.H.Lochovsky: *Data Models*, Prentice-Hall, N.J., 1982.

U

[ULD66] PL/I Definition Group of the IBM Vienna Lab: *Formmal Definition of* PL/I, ULD Version 1, Vienna TR 25.071, Dec. 1966.

[ULD68] PL/I Definition Group of the IBM Vienna Lab.: (a) M.Fleck & E.Neuhold: *Formal Definition of the* PL/I *Compile-Time Facilities*, TR.25.080; (b) K.Walk, K.Alber, K.Bandat, H.Bekic, G.Chroust, V.Kudielka, P.Oliva, & G. Zeisel, *Abstract Syntax and Interpretation of* PL/I, TR.25.082; (c) P.Lucas, K.Alber, K. Bandat, H. Bekic, P. Oliva, K. Walk & G.Ziesel, *Informal Introduction to the Abstract Syntax and Interpretation of* PL/I, TR. 25.083; (d) K.Alber, P. Oliva, & G. Urschler, *Concrete Syntax of* PL/I, TR.25.084; (e) K.Alber & P.Oliva, *Translation of* PL/I *into Abstract Text*, TR. 25.086; (f) P.Lucas, P.Lauer & H.Stiegleitner, *Method and Notation for the Formal Definition of Programming Languages* -- all reports Version 2, Vienna, 1968.

[ULD69] (a) M.Fleck, *Formal Definition of the* PL/I *Compile-Time Facilities*, TR.25.095; (b) G.Urschler, *Concrete Syntax of* PL/I, TR.25.097; (c) K.Walk, K.Alber, M.Fleck, H.Goldman, P.Lauer, E.Moser, P.Oliva, H.Stiegleitner, & G.Zeisel, *Abstract Syntax & Interpretation of* PL/I, TR.25.098; (d) K.Alber, H.Goldman, P.Lauer, P.Lucas, P.Oliva, H.Stiegleitner, & K. Walk, *Informal Introduction to the Abstract Syntax and Interpretation of* PL/I, TR25.099 -- all Version 3, Vienna, 1969.

V

[van Wijngaarden 62a] A.van Wijngaarden: *Generalized ALGOL*, in: 'Symbolic Languages in Data Processing', Proc. ICC Symp., Rome, Gordon & Breach, N.Y., pp.409-419, 1962.

[van Wijngaarden 63a] A.van Wijngaarden: *Generalized ALGOL*, in: Ann.Rev. 11, pp 17-26, 1963.

[van Wijngaarden 63b] A.van Wijngaarden: *Recursive Definition of Syntax and Semantics*, in [Steel 66a] ref. 31, pp 13-24.

[van Wijngaarden 75a] A.van Wijngaarden et al.: *Report on the Algorithmic Language ALGOL 68*, Acta 5, pp 1-236, 1975.

W

[Wadsworth 71a] C.P. Wadsworth: *Semantics and Pragmatics of the Lambda-Calculus*, Ph.D.Thesis, PRG, 1971.

[Wadsworth 76a] C.P.Wadsworth: *The Relation between Computational and Denotational Properties for Scott's D-Models of the Lambda-Calculus*, SIAM J. Comput., 5, 3, pp. 488-521, 1976.

[Walk 73a] K.Walk: *Modelling of Storage Properties of High-Level Languages*, IJCIS 2, 1, 1973.

[Wand 75a] M.Wand: *On the Recursive Specifications of Data Types*, in: 'Category Theory applied to Computation and Control', LNCS 25, pp 222-225, 1975.

[Wand 80a] M.Wand: *Continuation-based Program Transformation Strategies*, JACM 27, pp 164-180, 1980.

[Wand 80bc] M.Wand: *Deriving Target Code as a Representation of Continuation Semantics* and *Different Advice on Structuring Compilers and Proving them Correct* Indiana State Univ., Bloomington, Dept.of Comp.Sci. Techn.Repts. 94-95, June 1980.

[Wand 82a] M.Wand: *Semantics-Directed Machine Architecture*, POPL, Jan. 1982.

[Wang 71a] A. Wang & O.-J. Dahl: *Coroutine Sequencing in a Block-Structured Environment*, BIT 11, pp. 425-449, 1971.

[Wang 76a] A.Wang: *An Axiomatic Basis for Proving Total Correctness of GOTO Programs*, BIT 16, 1, pp 88-102, 1976.

[Wegner 72a] P.Wegner: *The Vienna Definition Language*, ACM Comp. Survey, 4, 1, pp 5-63, 1972.

[Weizenbaum 68a] J.Weizenbaum: *The FUNARG Problem Explained*, unpubl. note, Proj.MAC, MIT, 1968.

[Weigbreit 71a] B.Wegbreit: *Procedure Closure in EL1*, Comp. J. 17, 1, pp 38-43, 1971.

[Weyhrauch 72a] R.W.Weyhrauch & R.Milner: *Program Correctness in a Mechanized Logic*, Proc.1st USA-JAPAN Computer Conf. pp 384-390, 1972.

[Weissenböck 75a] F. Weissenböck & W. Henhapl: *A Formal Mapping Description*, Vienna TN25.3.105, Feb. 1975.

[Weissenböck 75b] F. Weissenböck: *A Formal Interface Specification*, Vienna TR25.141, Feb. 1975.

[Wilner 72a] W.T.Wilner: *Formal Semantics Definition using Synthesized and Inherited Attributes*, in: [Rustin 72a] 1972.

[Wirth 63a] N.Wirth: *A Generalization of ALGOL*, CACM 6, pp.547-554, 1963.

[Wirth 66a] N.Wirth & C.A.R.Hoare: *A Contribution to the Development of ALGOL*, CACM 9, 6, pp 413-432, 1966.

[Wirth 66b] N. Wirth & H. Weber: *EULER: A Generalization of ALGOL, and its Formal Definition*, CACM 9, 1-2, pp. 13-23 and pp. 89-99, Jan-Feb 1966.

[Wirth 70a] N.Wirth: *Programming and Programming Languages*, ICS 70, GMD, Bonn, 1970.

[Wirth 71a] N.Wirth: *The Programming Language PASCAL*, Acta 1, 1, pp 35-63, 1971.

[Wirth 71b] N.Wirth: *Program Development by Stepwise Refinement*, CACM 14, 4, pp 221-227, 1971.

[Wirth 73a] N.Wirth: *Systematic Programming*, Prentice-Hall, 1973.

[Wirth 76a] N.Wirth: *Algorithms + Data Structures = Programs*, Prentice-Hall, 1976.

[Wise 75a] D.S.Wise, D.P.Friedman, S.C.Shapiro & M.Wand: *Boolean-Valued Loops*, BIT 15, pp 431-451, 1975.

[Wulf 76a] W.A.Wulf, R.L. London and M. Shaw: *An Introduction to the Construction and Verification of Alphard Programs*, SE-2, 4, pp 253-265, Dec. 1976.

Z

[Zahn 74a] C.T.Zahn: *A Control Statement for Natural Top-Down Structured Programming*, in: 'Programming', LNCS 19, pp 170-180, 1974.

[Zemanek 66a] H.Zemanek: *Semiotics and Programming Languages*, in: [ACM 66a], pp 139-143, 1966.

[Zemanek 75a] H.Zemanek: *Formalization -- History, Present and Future*, in: Programming Methodology, LNCS 23, pp. 477-501, 1975.

[Zemanek 80a] H. Zemanek: *Abstract Architectures*, in: [Bjørner 80a], pp 1-42, 1980.

[Zimmerman 69a] K. Zimmerman: *Outline of a Formal Definition of FORTRAN*, Vienna LR25.3.053, June 1969.

[Zimmerman 70a] K.Zimmerman: *Moving Assignments out of a Loop Body* Vienna LN25.3.071, May 1970.

GLOSSARY OF NOTATION

Boolean

Bool	= {*false*, *true*}	37
¬	negation	37
∧	and	37
∨	or	37
⊃	implies	37
≡	equivalent to	37
∀	for all	38
∃	there exists	38
∃!	there exists exactly one	
Δ	unique description: $(\Delta x)(P(x))$: the unique x such that $P(x)$; if non-existing or not unique, then undefined	

Arithmetic

Int	$= \{\ldots, -2, -1, 0, 1, 2, \ldots\}$	39,76
Nat0	$= \{0, 1, 2, \ldots\}$	39,76
Nat	$= \{1, 2, 3, \ldots\}$	39,76

with the usual operators: +, -, *, ×, /, **, <, ≤, =, ≠, ≥, >, etc.; / is integer division, ** exponentiation

Quotation Values

Quot	Set of enumerated specification specific elementary objects, e.g. LABEL, AND, NULL, ...	43,76
=	equal to	
≠	different from	

Token Values

Token	Set of specification specific elementary objects whose representation is not exposed.	43
=	equal to	
≠	different from	

Sets			39,79
-set	Set forming operator; defines all finite subsets of given set.		
$\{a_1,a_2,\ldots,a_n\}$	Explicit enumeration		
$\{a \mid P(a)\}$	Implicit formation		
$\{a\in Set \mid P(a)\}$	Implicit formation		
$\in$	membership		
$\neg\in$	non-membership		
$\cup$	union		
$\cap$	intersection		
$-$	difference	(sometimes: $\backslash$)	
$\subset$	proper inclusion		
$\subseteq$	inclusion		
$=$	equal to		
$\neq$	different from		
card	cardinality		
union	distributed union		
Tuples (Lists)			41,80
* +	Tuple (or list) forming operator; defines all finite tuples whose elements are from the given set, * generates empty tuple, + does not.		
$<a_1,a_2, \ldots a_n>$	Explicit enumeration		
$<f(i) \mid P(i)>$	Implicit formation - where order defined		
hd	head	(sometimes: *h*)	42
tl	tail	(sometimes: *t*)	42
[ ]	index	(rarely: ( ))	
len	length	(sometimes: *l*)	42
inds	index set, indices	(sometimes: *ind*)	41
elems	elements		41
^	concatenation		42
$=$	equal to		
$\neq$	different from		
conc	distributed concatenation		42

Maps		40,80
$\overrightarrow{m}$	Map forming operator; defines all finite maps between given sets, $\overleftrightarrow{m}$ generates only one-to-one maps.	40 40
$\overleftrightarrow{m}$		
$[a_1,a_2, \ldots ,a_n]$	Explicit enumeration	40
$[d \mapsto f(d) \mid P(d)]$	Implicit formation	40
$(\ )$	application	
$\circ$	composition	32
$\cup$	merge	41
$+$	override extend (sometimes: $+$)	41
$\backslash$	remove (with)	41
$\mid$	restrict to	41
dom	domain	
rng	co-domain, range	41
$=$	equal to	
$\neq$	different from	
merge	distributed merge	41

Trees

$::$	Tree forming operator; defines *mk-A(t)* trees,where *A* is the given left operand identifier, and *t* is any object denoted by the right operand domain expression.	44,78
$\times$	Tree forming domain operator; defines cartesian product, un-named trees.	66,67
mk-	Named tree constructor function name prefix. $mk\text{-}A(b_1,\ldots,b_n)$ constructs A named trees; assumes: $A: B_1\times\ldots\times B_n$ with $b_i \in B_i$, $(c_1,\ldots,c_m)$ consructs anonymous trees; implies $(C_1\times\ldots\times C_m)$, with $c_i \in C_i$.	44,78
s-	Selector function name prefixes; $s\text{-}B_j$, $s\text{-}C_k$ selects B_j, respectively C_k objects.	44,78
$=$	equal to	
$\neq$	different from	

<u>Abstract</u> <u>Syntax</u>		42,78
$A = E$	Domain equations; = gives the name A to the set of objects denoted by E,	43,78
$A :: E$	:: gives the name A to the set of tree $mk\text{-}A(e)$ tree objects, where e is any object in domain E.	43,78
-set	-- see under Sets above	39
*, $^+$	-- see under Tuples above	41
$\overrightarrow{m}$, $\overleftrightarrow{m}$	-- see under Maps above	40
$\times$	-- see under Trees above	66,77
$\rightarrow$	(total) functions	28-32,78-9
$\overset{\sim}{\rightarrow}$	partial functions	28-32,78-9
$\underline{\cup}$	Map domain merging	
[ ]	Optional domain forming operator; defines domain of given set union $\{\underline{nil}\}$.	43
|	Non-discriminated union forming domain operator.	43,66,77
is-	Domain membership test predicate name prefix, $is\text{-}A(o)$ corresponds to: $o \in A$.	
<u>Function</u> <u>Definitions</u>		78
$\lambda x.e$	Function from x domain to domain of e values.	29-30
$f(a) \underline{\underline{\Delta}} B(a)$	f: function name, a argument(s), $B(a)$ is any clause: stament or expression (sometimes $\underline{\Delta}$ or just = is used).	28
<u>*type*</u>: $A \rightarrow B$ } f: $A \rightarrow B$ } <u>*type*</u>: f: $A \rightarrow B$ }	three synonymous type expressions	
=>	used only in type expressions; defines state usage: $A \Rightarrow B$ is thus equal to $A \rightarrow (\Sigma \rightarrow (\Sigma \times B))$	114

Applicative Combinators

let *id=e* *in* *b*	Block expression; defines all free occurrences of *id* in *B* as bound to *e*. Non-recursive *lets* correspond to: $(\lambda id.b)(e)$.	
f(a)	Function application	

Imperative Combinators

dcl v:=*e* *type* *D*	declaration of assignable variable: v	
c	contents operator; applied to a variable ('v'), *c* v defines its contents.	113
v := e	assignment	113
;	statement composition	33,92,107
def *id:e; s*	imperative *let* clause	34,94
while *e* *do* *s*	while loop	
for *i=m* *to* *n* *do* *S(i)*	iterative loop; steps in ordered sequence from static lower bound *m* to static upper bound *n*.	
for *all* $e \in Set$ *do* *S(e)*	iterative loop; steps in arbitrary sequence with *e* ranging over static set *Set*.	
return(v)	raises pure value to "imperative value": ($\lambda v.\lambda\sigma.(\sigma,v)$)	34,94

Structured Combinators

if *t* *then* *c* *else* *a*	If-then-else clause	
$b_1 \rightarrow c_1, \ldots b_n \rightarrow c_n$	*n*-way if-then-else clause	

cases e_0: $e_1 \rightarrow c_1, \ldots, e_n \rightarrow c_n$	n-way cases selector clause	

Exit Combinators

trap *id* *with* *E(id)* *in* *B*	Non-recursive exit stopper	
always *E(id)* *in* *B*	Non-recursive exit filter	37,108
tixe [$a \rightarrow b$ | $P(a,b)$] *in* *B*	Recursive exit stopper	36,107
exit	exit causer -- no value passing	36
exit(e)	exit causer -- with value passing	36,107

Overloaded Symbols (for references, see above)

+, +	integer addition	-- map extension
|	domain union	-- map restriction
-	integer subtraction	-- set difference
*	integer multiplication	-- tuple domain former
×	integer multiplication	-- cartesian domain former
∪	set union	-- map merge
→	function domain former	-- conditional clause delimiter
[ ]	map object delimiter	-- optional domain former
[ ]	tuple index operator	-- syntactic argument delimiter
=	equality between any object pair	
≠	in-equality between any object pair	

INDEX